SOVIET NATIONALITY POLICIES AND PRACTICES

SOVIET NATIONALITY POLICIES AND PRACTICES

edited by
Jeremy R. Azrael

PRAEGER PUBLISHERS
Praeger Special Studies

New York • London • Sydney • Toronto

Library of Congress Cataloging in Publication Data

Main entry under title:

Soviet nationality policies and practices.

    Bibliography: p.
    Includes index.
    1. Minorities--Russia--Addresses, essays,
lectures. 2. Nationalism--Russia--Addresses,
essays, lectures. 3. Russia--Politics and govern-
ment--19th century--Addresses, essays, lectures.
4. Russia--Politics and government--20th century--
Addresses, essays, lectures. I. Azrael, Jeremy R.,
1935-
DK33.S669   301.45'0947   77-83478

ISBN 0-03-041476-8

PRAEGER PUBLISHERS
PRAEGER SPECIAL STUDIES
383 Madison Avenue, New York, N.Y. 10017, U.S.A.

Published in the United States of America in 1978
by Praeger Publishers,
A Division of Holt, Rinehart and Winston, CBS, Inc.

89   038   987654321

© 1978 by Praeger Publishers

PREFACE
by Jeremy R. Azrael

The essays in this volume share a common concern with the character, functioning, and development of the USSR as a multinational polity and society. Given the enormity of this subject, the coverage that it receives necessarily is highly selective. What has governed the selection is a consensus among the principal investigators of the project from which this volume stems about the particular importance of research on the following general topics: the changing character of the "national question" as perceived by the Soviet regime and its tsarist predecessor; the role of non-Russian elites as power brokers and participants in the imperial or all-union policy process; the design and implementation of comprehensive plans of ethno-national social engineering; and the dynamics of national identity change and ethnic assimilation.

With these topics in mind, the essays in this volume have been divided into five parts. In the first, "Regime Perspectives," S. Frederick Starr explores the imperial dimension of the tsarist polity; and Hélène Carrère d'Encausse analyzes Bolshevik perceptions of the national question and Soviet decision-making arrangements for dealing with it. In the second part, "Non-Russian Elites," John A. Armstrong considers the role of the Baltic Germans as a mobilized diaspora in the tsarist period; Yaroslav Bilinsky compares the careers of two Ukrainian "national Communists," Mykola Skrypnyk and Petro Shelest; and Charles H. Fairbanks, Jr., investigates the attempt by Lavrenti Beria to use the national cadres as a political base in his drive for power. In the third part, "Ethno-National Policy Making and Planning," Steven L. Burg analyzes Soviet decision making with respect to antisemitism in the period since 1945; Jonathan Pool assesses Soviet attempts at language planning; and Brian D. Silver examines the effect of Soviet educational policies and sociodemographic changes on rates of linguistic russification. In the fourth part, "National Identity: Persistence and Change," Barbara A. Anderson examines the effects of linguistic russification and sociodemographic change on rates of ethnic reidentification of ASSR nationalities in the RSFSR; Alexandre Bennigsen traces the history of the Sufi brotherhoods in the north Caucasus and considers their possible role in future movements among the Muslim peoples of the USSR. S. Enders Wimbush explores the emergence of a new Russian nationalism and its meaning for both the Russians and the Soviet state. Finally, the fifth part consists of my own essay on some emergent nationality problems

v

that will complicate the lives of Brezhnev's successors and could put the viability of the Soviet empire to a fundamental test.

ACKNOWLEDGMENTS

The essays in this volume are outgrowths of a project funded by a grant from the Ford Foundation to the Research and Development Committee of the American Association for the Advancement of Slavic Studies (AAASS). Although the individual authors bear sole responsibility for their contributions, all of them have been stimulated and encouraged in their work by the opportunities that this project has provided for periodic meetings at which they could discuss their ideas and findings with interested and informed colleagues. Accordingly, they are all in the debt of the project sponsors and, more particularly, of Dr. Ivo Lederer and Ms. Felice Gaer of the International Division of the Ford Foundation, Professors George Hoffman and William Zimmerman of the AAASS Research and Development Committee, and Professor Warren Eason, executive secretary of the AAASS. In addition, they are all indebted to Paul Goble of the University of Chicago, whose editorial assistance has been instrumental in the preparation of this entire volume.

CONTENTS

PREFACE
by Jeremy R. Azrael   v

ACKNOWLEDGMENTS   vi

LIST OF TABLES   ix

LIST OF FIGURES   xi

PART I: REGIME PERSPECTIVES

1   TSARIST GOVERNMENT: THE IMPERIAL
    DIMENSION
        by S. Frederick Starr   3

2   DETERMINANTS AND PARAMETERS OF SOVIET
    NATIONALITY POLICY
        by Hélène Carrère d'Encausse   39

PART II: NON-RUSSIAN ELITES

3   MOBILIZED DIASPORA IN TSARIST RUSSIA:
    THE CASE OF THE BALTIC GERMANS
        by John A. Armstrong   63

4   MYKOLA SKRYPNYK AND PETRO SHELEST: AN
    ESSAY ON THE PERSISTENCE AND LIMITS OF
    UKRAINIAN NATIONAL COMMUNISM
        by Yaroslav Bilinsky   105

5   NATIONAL CADRES AS A FORCE IN THE SOVIET
    SYSTEM: THE EVIDENCE OF BERIA'S CAREER,
    1949-53
        by Charles H. Fairbanks, Jr.   144

PART III: ETHNO-NATIONAL POLICY
MAKING AND PLANNING

6   THE CALCULUS OF SOVIET ANTISEMITISM
        by Steven L. Burg   189

7   SOVIET LANGUAGE PLANNING: GOALS,
    RESULTS, OPTIONS
      by Jonathan Pool   223

8   LANGUAGE POLICY AND THE LINGUISTIC
    RUSSIFICATION OF SOVIET NATIONALITIES
      by Brian D. Silver   250

PART IV: NATIONAL IDENTITY:
PERSISTENCE AND CHANGE

9   SOME FACTORS RELATED TO ETHNIC
    REIDENTIFICATION IN THE RUSSIAN REPUBLIC
      by Barbara A. Anderson   309

10   MUSLIM CONSERVATIVE OPPOSITION TO THE
     SOVIET REGIME: THE SUFI BROTHERHOODS
     IN THE NORTH CAUCASUS
       by Alexandre Bennigsen   334

11   THE GREAT RUSSIANS AND THE SOVIET STATE:
     THE DILEMMAS OF ETHNIC DOMINANCE
       by S. Enders Wimbush   349

PART V: EMERGENT PROBLEMS

12   EMERGENT NATIONALITY PROBLEMS IN THE USSR
       by Jeremy R. Azrael   363

ABOUT THE EDITOR AND CONTRIBUTORS   391

LIST OF TABLES

Table

3.1 Mobilization Characteristics of Riga City
Population, 1883 and 1925   68

3.2 Imperial Service Attainments of Dorpat
Matriculants, 1802-70   76

6.1A Distribution of Soviet Scientific Workers, by
Nationality, 1950-73   212

6.2A Rate of Change in Absolute Number of Scientific
Workers, by Nationality, 1950/55-1970/73   213

6.3A National Composition of Scientific and Technical
Cadres, Uzbek Republic, 1960-73   214

6.4A Percentage Rate of Increase in Absolute Number
of Scientific and Technical Cadres, Uzbek
Republic, 1960/61-1971/73   216

6.5A Percentage Distribution of Students in Higher
Educational Institutions, by Nationality,
1960/61-1972/73   217

6.6A Percentage Rate of Change in Absolute Number of
Students in Higher Educational Institutions, by
Nationality, 1960/63-1970/73   218

7.1 Use of Republic Language as Medium of Instruction
in 12 Union Republics, 1967-68   230

8.1 Highest Grade Level at Which Textbooks Were
Reported Printed in Mathematics and Natural
Science, by Language and Year of Printing,
1935-69   258

8.2 Mean Percentages of Non-Russians Linguistically
Russified, by Urban-Rural Residence, 1970   270

8.3 Correlations between Linguistic Russification
and Maximum Available Years of Native-
Language Schooling, 1958 and 1959   290

9.1   Number Surviving per Thousand Population,
      and Socioeconomic Variables, for Selected
      Soviet Ethnic Groups   314

9.2   Pearson Correlations among Survival Ratios
      and Socioeconomic Variables for ASSR-Level
      Nationality Groups   321

12.1 Changing Composition of USSR Population,
      1959-70   366

LIST OF FIGURES

Figure

3.1   Dorpat-Iurev University   78

3.2   Annual Increments to Higher Medical Staff,
      1845-85, and Total Supply at Circa 1845   79

3.3   Baltic Germans and the Empire   95

6.1   Conceptual Ranges of Compliance with Policy   202

6.2   Relationships between the Elements in the
      Calculus of Soviet Antisemitism   202

8.1   The Effect of Contact on Shift to Russian as a
      Native Language among (a) Orthodox and (b)
      Muslim Nationalities   271

8.2   The Effect of Contact on Acquisition of Russian
      as Second Language   272

8.3   The Effect of Contact on Percentage of Orthodox
      and Muslim Nationalities Speaking Russian as
      either Native or Second Language   273

8.4   The Effect of Contact on Acquisition of Russian
      as Second Language among Orthodox and
      Muslim Nationalities   285

9.1   Relationship between Average Survival Ratio and
      Number Citing Russian as Mother Tongue in 1959   323

9.2   Relationship between Average Survival Ratio and
      Number not Living in Their Designated ASSR
      in 1959   324

12.1 Average Annual Population Growth Rates of Major
      "European" and "Non-European" Nationalities,
      1959-1970   364

PART I
REGIME PERSPECTIVES

TSARIST GOVERNMENT: THE IMPERIAL DIMENSION 1

S. Frederick Starr

In the two and one-half centuries before 1917, tsarist Russia became one of the largest and most populous contiguous land empires of the modern world. The numerous subject nations, many with strong, independent cultural and religious traditions, often had centers within the empire from which they exerted considerable influence abroad.

Until the February Revolution this imperial aspect of tsarist Russia grew steadily. Not only did the population outside Great Russia grow faster than that of the historic Russian areas, but its role in the economic life of the empire expanded yearly, as can be seen from the growing size and importance of such cities as Riga, Kiev, Odessa, and Baku.[1] Such changes made the task of imperial rule increasingly difficult, to such an extent that it became a preoccupation of Russian politicians (notwithstanding the deliberate underrepresentation of the non-Russian peoples in the Imperial State Duma after 1907).

How was this complex empire governed? Was there a single, centrally established "imperial policy" that was adapted as necessary to local circumstances, or did Russia rule its empire through a series of ad hoc arrangements arising directly from contact with the diverse localities? What similarities, if any, exist between the techniques of Russian imperial governance and those applied by Great Britain, Austria-Hungary, France, Portugal, or the Ottoman Empire? Finally, what impact did the imperial experience have upon the subject peoples and, conversely, in what ways did the burden of empire affect Russia's own political culture?

SCHOLARLY NEGLECT OF RUSSIAN IMPERIALISM

Although the concept of empire as such was central to Russia's political existence, such questions as those posed above have not been extensively explored by Western scholars.[2] To be sure, a number of monographs consider this an important issue; but except for Georg von Rauch's important analysis, Russland: Staatliche Einheit und nationale Vielfalt,[3] the larger questions remain unanswered and even unposed. This has been reflected in the almost total neglect of tsarist Russia in the ongoing Western debate over the character of imperialism as a whole.[4] In their indifference to the distinctively imperial dimension of Russian policy, Western students have, to a considerable extent, simply followed the Great Russian tradition of scholarship. Despite his Turkic name, the nineteenth-century historian N. M. Karamzin saw no need to devote special attention to the manner in which the non-Russian peoples of the empire were ruled, nor did V. O. Kliuchevskii.[5] During the Soviet period, research on the non-Russian peoples has flourished on a massive scale, but has not been accompanied by a corresponding increase in the study of the methods of Russian rule in their territories.[6]

Why have Russians devoted so little attention to the imperial dimension of their political system? A prime cause for this neglect has been the strong support of the Russian public for imperial expansion. Rarely have Russians so opposed their own government's policies in this area that they have written attacks as scathing as J. A. Hobson's Imperialism, a Study, which grew out of its author's opposition to the Boer War.[7] When they have registered opposition, as in the case of Alexander Herzen's support for the Polish rebellion in 1863, it has, more often than not, met with general opprobium. In this context, it is revealing that Lenin's analogous study, Imperialism: The Highest Stage of Capitalism, was rooted more in opposition to the imperialism of the Western powers than in opposition to Russian imperialism--the reality of which he never doubted. Without a tradition of national self-criticism, Russian scholars were denied an important stimulus to study.[8]

Only during the decade following the Revolution of 1905 did an influential part of the Russian public evince the degree of skepticism about imperial rule that was commonplace in the West. But while a number of studies and tracts called for the partial dismantling of the imperial administration as it then existed, the two most significant works of the period--Studies on Russian State Law (1911), by a Constitutional Democrat, Boris Nolde, and Marxism and the Nationality Question (1912), by a Social Democrat, Iosif Stalin[9]--acknowledge local claims only within the context of the larger, unified political structure.

A second factor that discouraged Russians from studying their government's imperial policies was the nature of those policies. Because Russia ruled its territories through administrative measures, rather than through the application of a body of general law, it was difficult for the public to gain a picture of the policy as a whole, or even to conceive of it as a single phenomenon. This, along with the general lack of publicity given to state policies, rendered the details of imperial policy all but invisible even to the educated public. In this context, nothing is more striking than the lack of discussion of imperial questions during the most dynamic period of imperial innovation in Russia--the years between Catherine II's administrative reforms and Alexander I's acts affecting Finland, Poland, Bessarabia, and Siberia.

INTERPENETRATION OF IMPERIAL, FOREIGN, AND DOMESTIC POLICIES

A third and more fundamental element underlying the lack of attention to Russian imperial politics and administration is the undefined nature of the problem. The term "imperial policy" implies a difference from other types of policy, and such a distinction did not exist under the tsars. The Russian government neither had nor sought to create a centralized agency to devise and implement its colonial policy. The closest it came to integrated agencies in this area were the Moscovite state's territorial departments or prikazy and the interministerial committees that existed in the nineteenth century to oversee policy in such provinces as the Baltic, Siberia, and the Caucasus. But the prikazy never possessed a monopoly on colonial administration; and the interministerial committees did little more than exchange information on policies that were, for the most part, devised elsewhere. Hence, the function of ruling the non-Russian peoples was divided among numerous, often ill-coordinated, agencies.

Russian imperial policy was no more clearly defined than the institutions that created it. No clear distinction existed between the realms of colonial administration and foreign policy, nor between colonial administration and internal Russian policy. Foreign-policy institutions and interests constantly impinged on colonial rule, and vice versa.

Examples of this interrelationship can be found throughout Russian history. For example, in 1563, Ivan IV, in a letter to King Sigismund II of Poland, referred to himself as "Lord of Siberia," although he continued to deal with the local Khan Kuchum through ambassadors, rather than through domestic administrators.[10] For several generations after the capture of Kazan in 1552, its affairs continued to be handled in part through the Posolskii prikaz (Foreign Office). And in 1727 the administration of the Russian-ruled Ukraine was transferred back from the Senate to the College of Foreign

Affairs.[11] In the nineteenth century the powerful Asiatic Department of the Ministry of Foreign Affairs freely involved itself in both imperial and foreign policy. Clearly, functional specialization progressed much further in the administration of the Great Russian territories than it did in the non-Russian areas of the empire.

The confusion of "domestic" and foreign affairs is not unique to Russia; in France it occurred until the fifteenth century. What is distinctive about the Russian case is that it penetrated so many aspects of daily administrative practice as late as the twentieth century. Thus, from the sixteenth to the eighteenth centuries, Russian officials continued to take hostages as a means of assuring local compliance with their edicts in Bashkiria, although the practice is normally associated with relations among warring states.[12] This lack of distinction between foreign and colonial policy was also legitimized by the Traktat of 1654 assuring Russia's presence in the Ukraine. This document has the dual character of a treaty between independent nations and an edict by which the tsar rules his realm.[13]

A prime reason for this interpenetration of imperial and foreign policies lies in the fact that often political and ethnic borders did not coincide. Actions by Lithuanians and Ukrainians outside the imperial borders directly affected Russian Lithuania and Poland. For instance, the first Lithuanian newspaper, Aušra, which figured centrally in the revival of Lithuanian nationalism within the Russian empire, was published in Prussian-ruled Tilsit; the similarly influential Ukrainian paper, Prosvita, appeared in Austrian-ruled Lemberg, but exerted great influence across the Russian borders.

Russia's territorial expansion was based on the desire for power in international affairs; thus it is not surprising that the policies pursued within its territories should have been calculated, in part, in response to international pressures. Such was the case with the late nineteenth-century program of russification in Poland and the Baltic, which countered Otto von Bismarck's cultural policies to the west. Also, it is not surprising that local nationalists should have turned this against Russia, as did the underground Polish leader Jozef Pilsudski in 1904, when he entered into negotiations with Japan during the Russo-Japanese War.

Parallel to the interaction of its colonial and foreign policy was the mixing of Russia's colonial concerns with issues of a purely domestic (Great Russian) nature. This could scarcely have been otherwise when the various regional committees (such as the Siberian Committee) in St. Petersburg were staffed by precisely those officials who, in their other capacities, created Russia's domestic policies. Not infrequently, an agency or institution devised for a colonial mission was extended to Great Russia. The regional administrative post of <u>voevoda</u>, for example, was developed in part as a means of ruling the Kasimov Tatars in the sixteenth century, but was soon extended to the Russian province of Novgorod.[14] Both the office of governor-general and the territorial unit of the military district[15] also spread from the periphery to the center, eventually being established virtually throughout the empire.

Since they were parts of a land empire, both the Russian and the non-Russian regions inevitably felt the impact of developments in each other more directly than might otherwise have been the case. Serfdom did much to stimulate an exodus from Great Russia that had to be controlled, or at least reckoned with, elsewhere in the empire; the conditions of temporary obligation introduced with the emancipation in 1861 only perpetuated this condition, with effects that were felt in Central Asia and Siberia until 1905.[16] The isolation of Great Russia from the major international trade routes forced Russians to conduct foreign trade partly through their colonial peoples; this tended further to link domestic and imperial economic concerns.[17]

SPATIAL AND TEMPORAL PARAMETERS
OF THE PROBLEM

The overlapping of foreign, domestic, and imperial policy is not the sole cause of the apparent imprecision of the notion of "imperial policy" in Russia. Common to practically all analyses of tsarist policy in the empire is a pervasive uncertainty over the spatial and temporal dimensions of the problem. Should one speak of policies that were applied only to specific geographical regions, as opposed to a single mode of rule prevailing throughout the empire? This has been argued effectively for the north versus the south, for the forest regions as opposed to the steppe,[18] and, more commonly, for the treatment of Europeans as opposed to Asians, Christians as opposed to Muslims, and agricultural people as opposed to nomads. But while the diversity of policy necessitated by local conditions cannot be denied, it can be exaggerated. The actions of Russian officials indicate that they readily acknowledged the differences of approach that each region required, yet their career patterns indicate with equal clarity that colonial administration was viewed as a special area of service, in which the skills of a Mikhail Vorontsov or an Ivan Paskevich could be readily transferred from Poland to the Caucasus or to Central Asia.

Similarly, the need for a periodization of Russian colonial administration has been forcefully defended by both Marxist and liberal writers. One may think that this is too obvious to require elaboration since, as Lenin put it, the lumping together of premodern

and modern empires is an "empty banality."[19] But having admitted
the need for periodization, neither Marxist nor liberal scholars have
proposed a scheme for Russian imperial policy and practice that
adequately fits the case. The former, bound by their ideology to
associate imperialism with capitalism, have little with which to account for the character of Russian imperial rule before the rise of
industry and also tend to exaggerate the "capitalist" character of
Russia's late nineteenth-century policies.[20] The latter either reject neat periodization entirely, or propose phases that apply more
accurately to individual subject peoples than to the chronology of the
empire as a whole.[21]

What, then, are the chronological limits of Russian imperial
policy? While many students, both Soviet and Western, have concentrated exclusively on the nineteenth century, others have traced
the origins back to Peter I and beyond.[22] Two Soviet scholars have
argued the case for beginning with the reign of Ivan IV; and several
Western scholars have claimed that the basic patterns of Russian
imperial policy were set well before Ivan's conquest of Kazan: in
the fourteenth- and fifteenth-century "gathering of the Russian lands"
by the Grand Duchy of Moscow, or even in Novgorod's twelfth-century
push into the lands of the Permiaks, Votiaks, and Komi-Zyriane.[23]

While this broad temporal horizon seems fully justified by the
evidence, it can too easily give rise to a conception of Russian imperial policy that denies the dramatic fluctuations that occurred over
time. In fact, Russian imperial administration was in constant flux,
with periods of decreased centralization often followed by phases in
which centralizing forces held sway. Thus, only one generation
after Catherine's campaign to integrate the administration of the non-
Russian territories into the Russian civil administration, Poland,
Bessarabia, and Finland were granted the legal status of autonomous
"states" (gosudarstva) within the empire.[24] If the existence of such
abrupt reversals of policy must be acknowledged, so must the anomalous presence, in the late imperial period, of practices that harken
back several centuries--a case in point being the resemblance of
Russian rule in Bukhara in the 1870s to Muscovite rule in Kazan
three centuries earlier.[25]

THE CONTINUITIES

The governance of the Russian empire evolved through several
distinct phases over the four centuries before 1917. In every phase
anachronisms were preserved intact from earlier epochs, and the
actual style of rule was modified in practice to accord with the social
and economic circumstances of different geographic areas. But what

of the continuities? For all the obvious elements of diversity and change in Russian imperial rule, are there any enduring traits whose influence is felt regardless of time and place, and that would, potentially, provide a basis for comparing Russia's governance of its empire with the other major empires of the early modern and modern eras?

At the risk of oversimplification, one may speak of five such traits: (1) the central importance of the Russian state and its administration in the management, development, and even the settlement of the non-Russian territories; (2) the paramount role of the Russian army as the embodiment of the state's presence, and the consequent militarization of colonial rule; (3) the prominence in colonial administration of powerful individuals--great leaders who, by their energy, could make up for shortcomings in the civil and military administrations; (4) the relatively subordinate role of the Russian Orthodox Church as an instrument of colonial policy; (5) the systematic and, on the whole, successful co-optation of local elites as colonial administrators, combined with an equally systematic refusal by the Russians to recognize the existence of rights against the Russian state (as opposed to privileges within it). Each of these aspects of the Russian colonial system made itself felt over so many centuries and in such diverse settings as to permit its consideration as a fundamental trait of Russian imperial rule.

The Primary Role of the Russian State

Against the background of the British, Dutch, and French charter companies, the absence of analogous institutions in Russia's empire is striking. The great commercial companies embodied the maritime empires of the West until their gradual governmentalization in the nineteenth century. They ruled India, settled America, and as late as the nineteenth century were being founded to consolidate and expand the Western presence in Africa. Typically, they were created through government charter but were expected thereafter to manage their own affairs. Though they often maintained their own armies and navies, these companies produced sufficient revenue to assure their welfare within the mercantile protection systems established by their governments.[26]

The absence of free capital and strong banking institutions in Russia, along with the relatively low return on imperial investments, prevented the development of powerful charter companies. Neither the new banking laws of the 1730s nor the explicit encouragement of trading companies through the promise of state funds by Peter III in 1762 sufficed to enable the few trading companies to flourish.[27] By the time the Russian-American Company was founded in 1799, massive government support could be relied upon in Russia (as it could in the West). But despite a substantial government subvention, this ambitious project was virtually moribund by the 1820s, its "dividends" more often than not being merely the distribution of state subsidies to stockholders.[28] Even before 1828, when the diplomat-playwright A. S. Griboedov proposed the formation of the Russian-Transcaucasian Company, to be modeled after the East India Companies, hope that Russians could develop nonstate trading agencies had died.[29]

Certain of the colonial functions executed by the British and Dutch trading companies were carried out by hereditary Russian freeholders or votchiniki, whose role bears a strong resemblance to that of the concessionaires in the French colonies. In 1572, Ivan IV issued a decree permitting the votchiniki to maintain their own armies, local administration, and courts in the new Ural territories, permission that the Stroganov family rapidly turned to its immense advantage.[30] But for all the glitter of the Stroganovs' wealth, they were an exception and by no means so autonomous from state support and control as has sometimes been claimed.[31] Though concessions were still being developed in the Far East timber market at the end of the nineteenth century, their era had passed long before Catherine II reclaimed some of the manufacturing operations that had been set up by concessionaires in the Urals under Peter I.[32] Since neither charter companies nor concessionaires were able to provide the organizational nexus for Russian colonial rule, the entire task fell to the state, which had to organize the local administration of justice, the collection of taxes, and the defense of the territory. This was easier said than done. The borders of the empire were constantly in flux, necessitating a continual redrawing of administrative boundaries; this resulted in confusion and lack of continuity at every level.

Despite its vast responsibilities, the tsar's imperial administration was, even by its own standards, woefully undermanned-- even more so, in fact, than Great Russia's own civil administration. The situation in the Siberian Office (Sibirskii prikaz) was typical in this respect. Founded in 1636, this agency was charged with the administration of the vast territories and diverse peoples of the easternmost part of Europe and northernmost zone of Asia. But qualified personnel were lacking, and those few who could be found often could not be paid.[33] Hence, local administrators began hiring cossacks, former peasants, and virtually anyone who would consent to sit in an office.[34] Poor pay or payment in useless goods encouraged local officials to preserve in practice the ancient rite of "feeding" (kormlenie) off the local population long after it had been rejected as official policy. This accounted for much of the brutal exploitation experienced by the more backward peoples of the Urals and Siberia.

This picture improved in the nineteenth century, and the records of the Ministry of Internal Affairs give reason to think that there were by then more administrators per capita in the more backward parts of the empire than there were in Great Russia.[35] But since the growth of communications more than kept pace with the increase in personnel, these "improvements" were to prove illusory. The nominally all-powerful colonial administrators constantly encountered bureaucratic impediments that robbed them of effectiveness.

The absence of other forms of an official Russian "presence" in the colonial territories isolated the government's colonial representatives and caused tsarist officials to seek other means of securing their imperial claims. Among these "substitutes" for a strong administrative presence, none was more important than the efforts to foster colonization. The institution of serfdom within Great Russia created a population outflow that the administration sought to check through its colonial policy in the eastern and southern territories. But, realizing that out-migration was inevitable and, if controlled, highly desirable, the government early showed a keen interest in organizing the colonial migration. Indeed, however much scholars may argue over the misleading juxtaposition of "popular" and "governmental" initiatives in the colonization of the empire, the degree of official involvement in the process was substantial.[36] Within a generation after the conquest of Kazan in 1552, the understaffed government had established a network of Orthodox bishoprics and set down what amounts to a plan of colonization of towns within the Tatar region.[37] In numerous pieces of legislation over the following centuries, the government candidly admitted its interest in colonization as a means of increasing the Russian presence in a given territory and of bringing the non-Russian nationalities into closer touch with Russia.[38] At times these objectives were pursued with a crassness that makes the efforts of nineteenth-century transatlantic shipping lines look restrained; so zealous was Catherine to lure Russians to her new southern lands that she paid her agents five rubles for every woman delivered to the colonial area![39]

The gradual incorporation of cossack settlements into the Russian administrative structure and the direct borrowing of military colonization from the Hapsburgs and the Ottomans did much to foster Russian objectives. Though military colonists were never more than a small fraction of the total number of Russians to move into the borderlands, they were of particular importance: first, because they set down a blanket of security that enabled "free" migrants to come in and, second, because the inability of the treasury to pay them in anything but land and labor meant that they helped to spread the institution of serfdom into many non-Russian territories.[40] These efforts culminated in the establishment of a government agency to facilitate the Russian migration and the exploitation of government-sponsored railroad lines in both Siberia and Central Asia to organize and promote settlement. [41]

The Military Character of Russian Colonial Rule

The absence of a strong nongovernmental Russian presence in the subject territories and the relative weakness of the civil administration meant that the military had to assume a far greater share of the responsibility for ruling the empire than would otherwise have been the case. To be sure, the restiveness of the subject population made it extremely unlikely that the military presence would have been anything but strong. But the military role never was confined to pacification and security. In the Baltic and elsewhere, it was the military that first secured Russia's presence; once established in a territory, it quickly arrogated to itself many tasks that might otherwise have been carried out by civilian agencies of government.

If anything, the degree of militarization increased over time. It is true that the territorial voevodas exercised vast civil and military powers in the sixteenth and seventeenth centuries, and that most of them rose to their positions through military careers. [42] But during the early centuries, Moscow's lingering fear of the kind of autonomy once exerted by the appanage princes caused it to watch carefully over these officials. By the time the military governor-generalships were established, these fears had been put aside and the new functionaries were able to be the true masters (khoziaeva) of their regions. Whereas in the seventeenth century the army did little more than build outposts and extract furs from the native populace of the East, [43] by the eighteenth century it had become a cornerstone of Catherine's colonization policy and a prominent force for the development of both agriculture and industry in New Russia. [44]

The army thus became the chief agent for change in the subject societies. By the nineteenth century, military personnel were designing railroads in Central Asia and directly supervising many of the state's "political agents" in the vassal states of Bukhara and Khiva. [45] The army also was a powerful force for assimilation. Many Tatar leaders from Kazan became russified through their service with the army of the Grand Duchy of Moscow and, in the nineteenth century, it was the introduction into the Bukharan army of Russian-style weapons, field manuals, and even music that prepared the way for more complete political integration. [46]

The scale and diversity of the army's presence in the colonial territories gave the administration as a whole a decisively military cast. The Russian scholar S. Prutchenko has aptly characterized

all Siberia in the seventeenth century as a vast military encamp-
ment,[47] and much the same can be said of most other areas.
Georgia remained under exclusively military jurisdiction from the
time of its incorporation into the empire until the arrival of
Vorontsov as governor-general in 1845, and Poland was under a
military dictatorship from 1832 to 1856.[48]

If militarization was at times a tactical step imposed under
threat of rebellion, at others it was a long-term measure enshrined
in law. The statutes by which the Kalmyks and other peoples were
ruled explicitly assigned to the Russian military all control over the
civil and economic life of the area, with no presumption that it would
later revert to civilian authorities.[49] In such circumstances the
Ministry of Internal Affairs and Ministry of Finances had to be content with minor supporting roles. This situation was especially common in the South, where the open steppe created peculiar problems
of communications and defense; but it was by no means unknown
elsewhere.

The army was, in fact, the chief agent of Russian imperial
policy. And like the Warsaw Pact troops today, the tsarist army's
main opponents on a year-to-year basis were "domestic" rather
than foreign enemies. The deployment of troops in the 1860s demonstrates this with some clarity, for their numbers correspond more
to the instability of a given territory than to any danger posed by
forces beyond the frontier. Thus, while all of Siberia could, by the
1860s, be secured with only 18,000 troops, the Ukrainian districts
of Kharkov, Odessa, and Kiev had 72,000, 61,000, and 60,000, respectively; the volatile Caucasus demanded 128,000 men; and Warsaw,
126,000. St. Petersburg, seat of the tsar's own garrison, had 84,000
troops. It might be noted that in all of India the British had but
60,000 troops and 1,000 policemen.[50]

The military cast of Russian imperialism has by no means escaped scholarly notice; but with the exception of Lenin, no one has
attempted to build a theory of Russian imperialism around it. Because Lenin wrote his <u>Imperialism: The Highest Stage of Capitalism</u>
against Western imperialism, and under the strict control of tsarist
censorship, he did not develop in it his notion of Russian imperialism
as a distinct phenomenon. Elsewhere, however, he repeatedly
stressed the "military," "feudal," and "bureaucratic" character of
Russian imperialism, and contrasted this unfavorably with the capitalist imperialism of the West.[51] Lenin saw the military as serving
its own interests and those of "feudal" Russia in the colonial territories, and believed those interests to be a characteristic trait of
Russian imperialism.

The Role of Strong Leaders

The history of Russian imperial rule is the collective biography of several dozen individuals wielding virtually unlimited powers as lieutenants or namestniki, voevody, vice-regents, grand dukes, governors, or military governors-general. Such men as Grigori Potemkin, Mikhail Speranski, Ivan Paskevich, N. N. Muraviev-Amurskii, and A. I. Bariatinskii wielded authority that was in no way less sweeping than that exercised by such governors-general of British India as Warren Hastings. With only a few exceptions, no individuals functioning within Great Russia possessed the ability to influence society so directly and in such diverse spheres as these men. They were less trammeled by bureaucracy than were their colleagues in St. Petersburg, and less subject to infighting from rivals within their immediate offices. In these respects, the crown agents were truly the "bosses" (khoziaeva) of their localities, preserving autocratic principles in the colonies even after their erosion by bureaucratism in the metropolis. [52]

Normally, one would expect the great colonial administrators to dominate the scene during the early post-conquest era when the administrative fabric was still weak and functions had to be exercised from a few strong points, but to disappear thereafter. In the Russian Empire the reverse was true. Fewer great provincial administrators arose during the sixteenth and seventeenth centuries than in the eighteenth and nineteenth centuries, and even the advent of the telegraph did not prevent Generals K. P. Kaufman and A. P. Ermolov from exercising enormous powers in Central Asia.

Why did the role of powerful personalities increase, rather than decrease, over time? First, as has been noted, during the Muscovite phase of the empire, fear of centrifugal tendencies caused the tsars to rein in even their own agents if they exhibited excessive autonomy in the execution of their duties. The Muscovite practice of naming two governors to fulfill the same function is an extreme example, but not otherwise unusual. [53] Second, the growing complexity of the Muscovite state rendered it decreasingly possible for the tsar to become so directly involved in the conquest and pacification of new areas as Ivan IV had been with Kazan. In this respect Peter I was unusual for his military activism in the Baltic. Third, the gradual conversion from duties in kind to taxes in money and the growing need for revenue created by the state's ever-increasing military budget fostered rebelliousness in the conquered territories on a scale that could not be handled except through the concentration of military-civil authority in a single governor-general.

Finally, the introduction of the collegial system in the eighteenth century and, even more, the creation of the ministries in

1803 increased the need for a powerful official at the regional level.
The Muscovite prikazy had integrated a wide range of functions, including control of taxation, mining, defense, and the administration
of justice. [54] As these functions became specialized and divided, it
fell to the governors-general to coordinate and control the bureaucracy on the local level. In this sense the efforts of the great colonial
administrators of the nineteenth century can be seen as an attempt to
re-create under the ministerial system the kind of concentrated, independent authority that Potemkin had possessed under Catherine
II. [55] General Paskevich, who came as close to winning such authority as anyone in his century, set forth the problem with great clarity
in a letter to Nicholas I:

> In so large a state as Russia, it is impossible for a
> government concentrated in the hands of ministers to
> be sufficiently strong and swift in the border regions,
> where circumstances almost daily go beyond the usual
> practices. [The ministerial system] of necessity ties
> one's hands: where one should be acting, only corre-
> spondence takes place. Then disagreements between
> ministers and the local leadership give rise to further
> difficulties and business breaks down entirely. While
> letters are passing back and forth, the time for action
> passes. . . . The ministers simply cannot see to
> everything themselves. . . . [56]

In another memorandum to the tsar, Paskevich indicated that
his own problems in Poland would be solved if that country were integrated into Russia. Short of this, there was no choice, he argued,
but to set up in Poland an "exceptional power, untrammelled by law
and by the administrative forms established by law. "[57]

It is these factors, rather than the mere lust for power, that
explain the degree of independent authority exercised by vice-
regents, generals, and governors-general in the late eighteenth and
nineteenth centuries. It is true that there were dramatic examples
of willful independence by local military leaders, one being Captain
G. I. Nevelskoi's establishment of Fort Nikolaevskii at the mouth of
the Amur in 1849, against the advice of the Minister of Foreign Affairs. [58] But even if local officers and officials lobbied hard for certain courses of action, they certainly were not so independent of
control as has sometimes been claimed. While responding to conditions imposed by distance and by the prevailing system of administration, they in fact maintained reasonably close liaison with St.
Petersburg. [59] In general, one can only be astonished at the degree
to which Russia's top provincial administrators resisted the

temptation to transform themselves into more or less autonomous satraps, as did some French governors before the mid-seventeenth century.

Personal power was a substitute for the concentrated adminis- trative presence that was lacking in the borderlands. As the gov- ernment's expectations of control increased, so did its willingness to entrust its principal local agents with exceptional authority. While the Kakhanov Commission of 1881 blunted this tendency by placing limits on the power of the governors-general, it did not reverse it-- nor was it intended to do so.

The Church Nonmilitant

Several colonial powers, notably Spain and Portugal, depended heavily upon the Roman Catholic Church and its clergy in their efforts to extend control over alien peoples and to transform them into loyal subjects of the crown. While this practice reached its zenith during the Counter-Reformation, it also flourished under Protestant regimes down to the twentieth century. The Russian Orthodox Church played an analogous role under the tsars. Certainly the activities of St. Stephen of Perm in the fourteenth century or of Hilarion of Kazan in the early eighteenth century bear comparison with the proselytizing of such Catholic martyrs as St. Francis Xavier. Nor did such activ- ity cease with the rise of the secular state, as the missionary work of N. I. Ilminskii among Muslim Tatars in the Volga basin in the late nineteenth century attests.

For its part, the Russian state often showed itself to be even more zealous than the church or Christian laymen in promoting the faith among its newly conquered subjects. During the 1660s mass baptisms were administered to whole villages of Mordvinians, Cheremiss, and Votiaks.[60] In 1747 alone, 80,000 Chuvash received baptism, thanks in part to the Office of New Converts established in Kazan during the 1740s.[61] As a stimulus to Russia's non-Christian subjects, the state offered tangible incentives to conversion in the form of a three-year exemption from taxes and military service,[62] a practice that caused the weakening and even dissolution of entire communities until it was revoked.

Conversion was not the sole objective of Russian colonial pol- icy with respect to religion. More narrowly, political and adminis- trative factors figured with equal prominence in the state's church policies. The decision to move the Kiev metropolitan's seat to Moscow in 1685 had little doctrinal significance but was entirely sound as a means of integrating a newly acquired territory more closely into Great Russia.[63] Similarly, the rapid establishment of

monasteries and convents in the Kazan region after 1552 may or may
not have won souls for Orthodoxy; but it certainly provided bastions
of Russian control, since all lands and people controlled by religious
foundations enjoyed immunity from local, non-Russian juridical
authorities. [64] With centuries of such church-state collaboration, it
is quite fitting that the first Russian to pass through the gate of
Tashkent after the conquest should have been an Orthodox priest. [65]

While such actions suggest a close involvement of the Orthodox
Church in Russian imperial policy, the evidence is far from conclusive. Important contrary tendencies must also be taken into account. Over the centuries, Orthodox Christianity has never been a
vigorous proselytizer. There was never a Russian organization comparable with Great Britain's procolonial Society for the Propagation
of the Gospel, and the nineteenth-century Russian Bible Society was
the creation of English Protestants. Unlike the Roman Catholic
clerics of medieval and early modern Europe, the Orthodox clergy
did not hold civil offices in Russia. Moreover, few sons of Russian
priests found their way into colonial administration. [66]

Any full assessment of the role of Orthodox Christianity in
Russia's imperial strategy must acknowledge the numerous measures by which the Russian state restricted its own proselytizing
and that of its Christian subjects throughout the empire. In
seventeenth-century Siberia, for example, clerics were required
to seek the permission of local administrators before baptizing any
native. Even if this rule was often ignored in practice, it was not
without a practical rationale: since Christians were exempt from
paying the traditional tribute or iasak, every conversion meant a
potential loss of revenue to the state. [67]

Catherine II's edict assuring toleration of all faiths marked
the high point of Russia's policy of limiting the tsar's church for the
sake of the tsar's empire. "Would it not be well to assure complete
freedom of belief to foreigners who have been invited to settle in
Russia by the government itself?" asked the Holy Synod's delegate
to the 1767 Legislative Commission. [68] On these practical grounds
the edict of toleration was approved, and in 1785 was extended to
the practice of religion in all cities and towns.

Catherine's gesture toward her non-Orthodox subjects meant
both less and more than it may at first appear. On the one hand,
the law simply codified what was already a fact. However zealous
Orthodox missionaries had been in their efforts to convert tribal
groups in Siberia, they normally had refrained from undertaking
massive campaigns against peoples with more settled and sophisticated cultures. Toward the Muslims of Kazan and, even more, the
Protestants and Roman Catholics of the Baltic, the state had for the
most part pursued a laissez-faire policy.

On the other hand, the guarantee of toleration did not signify that the state had lost interest in the political dimension of the religions of the empire. Quite the contrary. Beginning with Catherine's decree, the imperial government redoubled its efforts to transform the non-Orthodox religions, and particularly Islam, into agents of Russian imperial policy. At the very time that it was boasting abroad about its ambition to return the cross to the dome of Hagia Sofia in Istanbul, Catherine's government was bending its efforts to win the loyalty of its Muslim subjects, not only by building mosques and even Muslim schools for them--a practice that had actually been pioneered much earlier[69]--but also by encouraging loyal Muslims from Kazan to convert Kazakh tribesmen, lest the mullahs from Bukhara reach them first. Far from repressing alien religions, then, the imperial government sought to co-opt them, to build them a sufficiently hospitable environment within the empire to shift their pattern of loyalties toward St. Petersburg, even as the government cut them off from contact with their coreligionists abroad.

Repression doubtless occurred. In several cases in which schismatic religious groups refused utterly to cooperate with the state, they were transferred en masse to the otherwise unguarded borderlands of the realm, much as the Byzantine Empire had dealt with the heretic Bogomils. But in such cases as the closing of 500 parish schools in the Caucasus in 1882, or the transfer of parish schools from the control of the Gregorian Church of Armenia to the Ministry of Enlightenment in 1897,[70] the measures that are so easily interpreted as being directed specifically against national religions were in fact part of a general campaign of secularization that was aimed first against Great Russia's own Orthodox Church. However great the religious persecution in the later nineteenth century, especially of Jews and Roman Catholics, toleration continued to have some influence until the Revolution.

The Co-optation of Local Elites

Russia's ability to acquire new territories was greater than its capacity to rule them. As we have seen, Russian imperial rule was a governmental affair; but the government did not possess the requisite personnel. The army provided a useful surrogate for the local administration that was lacking, but could not do the job alone. To a greater extent than European empires operating in less developed areas, imperial Russia relied upon the subject peoples themselves.

Much has been written of the relative openness of the Russian aristocracy to newcomers from abroad and from the empire. One

will not find among the aristocracy of any other European state so
many great families tracing their ancestry to the subject areas:
Suvorov, Bargration, Loris-Melikov, Charkasskii.[71] To be sure,
the Russians had no choice: they could either co-opt the local elite
or abandon the area. Choosing the former, they opened their aristocracy to the subject peoples, accepting without question the prevailing local definitions of gentility[72] and quibbling not at all about
the ethnic or even religious origins of the newcomers, provided they
were able and willing to carry out on a day-to-day basis the practical
duties of members of the Russian elite. For holders of less than top
positions, they did not even insist upon conversion to Orthodoxy, with
the result that many prominent local agents of the old Kazan Office
(Kazanskii prikaz) were Muslims. [73] There is no parallel for this
even in the relatively open imperial system of Portugal.

Given this dependence upon the conquered peoples for leadership, there was no place for racism, at least in the sense that the
term is generally used today. Though Russia's nineteenth-century
colonial cities in Central Asia were as segregated as any British
settlements in Africa, top members of the local elites were fully integrated into the Russian community by virtue of their having accepted russification. Only late in Russia's imperial history does
one find such baldly racist statements as Aleksandr Gorchakov's in
1864: "It is a peculiarity of Asiatics to respect nothing but visible
and palpable force."[74] For most of their history, Russians were
only too glad to accept any Asian leaders who would rally to their
banner, and quite willing to bribe them handsomely to do so. Estates
were handed to co-opted leaders as a matter of course and, if necessary, the native elites were given direct state subsidies. [75]

In several instances there was no adequate local elite to whom
the Russians could turn. In the case of the Kirghiz of Orenburg,
this problem was solved by creating one. The 1884 Statute on a
School for Kirghiz Children stated:

> The main goal in founding this school, besides dis-
> seminating a knowledge of the Russian language and a
> degree of literacy among the Kirghiz, is the prepara-
> tion of capable people for work with the Border Com-
> mission . . ., and also for other functions to which
> only Kirghiz are named. [76]

The benefits to the Russians of a co-opted elite were considerable. Local leaders were the best means of mobilizing native
troops into the Russian army. More important, they were invaluable
in pacifying their own people. Thanks to the help of Aiuk Khan of the
Bashkirs, Peter I's voevoda, P. Apraksin, was able to put down both

the 1705–06 uprising in Astrakhan and the 1707–08 Bashkir uprising. The co-opted cossack elders or _starshinas_ of the Ukraine figured centrally in the stabilization of Moscow's authority in that region after the Treaty of Pereiaslavl in 1654, though not without resort to major force.[77] This general pattern recurred throughout the empire as starshinas, princes, and other traditional leaders were gradually transformed into _hommes de service._

While the importance of Russia's co-optation of local elites has long been recognized, the precise method by which it was accomplished has not. Normally, one might expect that such co-optation would be accomplished by confirming certain privileges that the local leaders considered important. This was done in many areas, including Estland and Courland, where the mandate of 1710 establishing Russian control specifically recognized the privileges, laws, and customs that had been abrogated under Swedish rule.[78] When Poland, Finland, and Bessarabia were incorporated into the empire, the confirmation of local prerogatives was even more thorough. Yet it would be wrong to conclude that the practice of the Russian government was to disturb the preexisting rights of the local elites as little as possible. First, it must be stressed that the Russian state was extremely loath to recognize rights against itself, as opposed to privileges. Rather than acknowledge rights, the tsar preferred to grant privileges, the assumption being that he could also take them away. Second, with the exception of Congress (of Vienna) Poland and the Grand Duchy of Finland--both dating to the same brief period of Alexander I's "liberal" phase--the privileges in question were granted not to regions, nationalities, or individuals but to estates, classes, corporations, or cities.[79] As such, they were ill-suited to become the focus of national agitation.

One of Russia's greatest achievements in imperial rule was to devise a system of rewards that elicited the loyalty of local elites without recognizing rights in return. Until 1905 it permitted less suffrage in the empire than the 1680 Spanish Laws of the Indies provided to towns in the New World.[80] In this, of course, the government was merely applying its own principles to the non-Russian territories, principles that ultimately derived from the absence in Russia of a strong tradition of feudal autonomy.

Until the early nineteenth century, this mode of co-optation was more or less successful. But in the late eighteenth century it began to break down. Worried over the Baltic nobility, Catherine declared their privileges to be a "phantom" and rescinded many of them in 1783 by extending Russia's internal administrative institutions into the non-Russian areas.[81] Signs of trouble appeared elsewhere as well. The independence shown by local gentry assemblies (_sejmiki_) in Poland caused Alexander I to restrict them in 1802, on the ground that they constituted a "state within a state."[82] For the same reason, the self-government of Bessarabia and Congress Poland was virtually abolished between 1828 and 1832. The apostasy of the formerly loyal Adam Czartoryski during the Polish Revolt of 1830 had its parallel in the rebellion of the Georgian nobility in K'art'lian in the same year.[83]

By midcentury the policy of co-opting local elites was in a shambles. Henceforth, in all regions except Finland, local privileges were perceived as anomalies within the imperial system; and the self-governing institutions with which they were associated were feared as potential threats to Russian rule. By the 1840s the Kirghiz-staffed agencies in Orenburg were defined in law as merely "private administration,"[84] and a generation later Russia's elite-dominated local elective bodies or zemstvos institutions were considered too dangerous to be extended to the newer parts of the empire.

RUSSIA'S IMPACT ON ITS COLONIES

Given the immense effort that Russia expended on ruling its imperial territories, it is worth asking in what ways, if any, it changed them. Scholarly consideration of this question has reverted continually to two dominant images. Either Russia has been viewed as having followed a passive course with regard to the development of local societies and economies, or it has been credited with a more active role only to the extent that it has intervened to thwart change.

One need not look far for documentation of each of these views. The traditional Mongol iasak duties were actually strengthened by Russia's conquest of Kazan;[85] cossack privileges and customs were confirmed by the absorption of the Ukraine into the Grand Duchy of Moscow; and in virtually every other region of the empire the Russian conquerers took great pains to pay their respects to local peculiarities. Consistent with this, imperial agents built their administrations in Siberia and Central Asia on the preexisting ulus or clans, taking them as the basis for their executive territories (volosti) rather than imposing entirely new units.[86] Similarly, the original provincial units in Bashkiria and in the Southeast generally reflected the old territories or dorogas of the khanate period.[87] The fact that the Kasimov "tsars" were perpetuated for a century and a half (until 1681) after the incorporation of their territory into the Grand Duchy of Moscow; that Catherine II's decision to require all Jews to enroll in the traditional communal organization (Kahal) actually strengthened that dying institution; and that the old dynasties of Dagestan were restored after the Russians overthrew Shamil in 1859[88] all suggest that the Russians were quite justified in presenting themselves as the upholders of local tradition.

However, the most characteristic Russian policies toward the colonial possessions were dynamic and actively interventionist. To some extent in the western provinces and Poland, but particularly in the southern, southeastern, and eastern expanses of the empire, where an extensive, European-type infrastructure was lacking, Russia imposed itself on diverse aspects of the subject peoples' lives. However backward many regions of Central Asia and the Caucasus may have appeared in 1917, Russia's imperial presence had already given them a shock that would later speed the Soviet drive for modernization.

The deliberate manipulation of the social structures of non-Russian peoples exemplifies this interventionism. We have touched upon the policy of co-opting local elites through giving them the same benefits and rewards received by the Russian gentry. This could not be done without subjecting the rest of the local population to the same treatment their peers within Great Russia received, as the enserfment of the Ukrainian peasantry clearly demonstrates. In numerous instances the extension of privileges to the elite caused the gradual "feudalization" of the peasantry or tribal groups, a process not dissimilar to the Spanish creation of an Aztec nobility in Mexico.[89] Some groups, such as the cossacks, won assurances from the government that checked the descent of former freemen into bondage; but the degree of "feudalization" imposed was sufficient to make them ready recruits for rebellion.

In this process of intervention, conscious policies of cultural penetration played only a secondary role. After Nicholas I's ringing declaration that henceforth the inhabitants of Poland "would constitute with the Russians a single people (narod) of consenting brothers . . .,"[90] he enacted measures aimed more toward achieving administrative unity than cultural synthesis. Alexander II, too, was not unmoved by the arguments of Pan-Slavs; but in his actual policies he consistently opposed the redefinition of sovereignty in cultural terms, opting instead for the type of administrative integration that had been the hallmark of Russian imperial policy since Peter I. That his government would censure Iurii Samarin for his russification campaign in the Baltic attests to Alexander's commitment on this point.

Mass russification was actively pursued for only a few decades at the end of the nineteenth century, and was never more than a brief phase in the history of Russian imperial policy.[91] However brief, though, it exerted a profound influence on the subject peoples, as the case of Finland demonstrates. Protected by its special position in the empire and by Alexander III's good will--he had a country house or dacha there--Finland never suffered anything more severe than the imposition of a three-year military service requirement on some 5,600 men.[92] The heart of the conflict that eventually exploded in 1905 was not russification but the belief by Finland's Swedish elite that Finland remained a quasi-sovereign state, and hence was fully entitled to an independent tariff policy that would, coincidentally, favor them. In their efforts to pressure the imperial government, this group exploited every action by St. Petersburg and twisted it to appear as part of a sinister Kulturkampf directed against the Finns. That the Finns themselves came to accept these claims, and enshrined them in the subsequent historiography, does not alter the fact of Russia's innocence.[93]

This is not to say that Russia did not take nationality into account in its imperial policy, as has sometimes been contended. The locally based military commissions set up in Bashkiria in the 1730s took nationality as their organizing principle; Catherine II's Legislative Commission of 1767 included representation by "peoples" (55 non-Russian members were included); Russia accepted the notion of nationality that underlay the Congress of Vienna's acts regarding Poland; and Nicholas I readily granted the status of narod to numerous tribes and peoples of the East.[94] Far from being unaware of national loyalties or indifferent to them, Russia exploited them systematically over many centuries, particularly in the Caucasus and Central Asia, playing one people off against another in an effort to situate itself as the arbiter among nations and thereby gain a decisive hand in the affairs of all parties.

It is a truism that the rhetoric of nationalism in much of the colonial world derived from internal debate within the metropolitan countries. There being so much less debate over imperial issues within Russia than in the West, large-scale transfer did not occur in this manner within the tsar's empire at least until the late nineteenth century, when it was initiated by radical parties. Ideological transfer did take place, though, in large measure through the Russians' own policies. The clearest examples of this process are found in the Ukraine and the Baltic. During the 1830s the Russian Ministry of Public Enlightenment actively sought to foster historical and ethnographic research in the Ukraine, despite the fact that such studies were found to stimulate Ukrainians to view themselves as constituting an ethnic and linguistic community. The southwestern branch of the Imperial Geographic Society carried on this work later in the century, and became a hotbed of nationalist agitation. It is no exaggeration, therefore, to say that the Society of Sts. Cyril and Methodius and similar nationalist groups in the Ukraine were the natural offsprings of Russia's own institutions and policies.[95]

The situation was much the same in Latvia, where the emancipation of the serfs in 1817-19 led directly to the establishment of parish schools and, in the 1830s, to the creation of the first normal schools.[96] In Latvia, and later in Estonia,[97] such schools acted as social condensers for localist feeling. In both cases, the fact that Russia's own institutions had successfully communicated their nationalist rhetoric to the subject people was as important as any overt acts of repression in arousing local feeling.

Compared with the persistent Russian drive for bureaucratic standardization, the short-lived campaigns of russification are of secondary importance in terms of their effect at the local level. The drive for standardization had its origins in Russia's need for money. The only way to get it was through the labor-intensive process of taxation. For hundreds of years it relied on the iasak, a form of protection money not dissimilar to the duties a corrupt policeman might levy on merchants on his beat. The iasak required little institutional infrastructure at the local level, nor did it substantially alter the preexisting institutional or social order. The gradual shift to money payments, however, and the acquisition of territory occupied by urban and commercial peoples, invited a more active institutional intervention by Russia. Because the central agencies of the empire were undermanned and lacked the sophisticated procedures necessary to handle diverse and complex arrangements with the localities, there was a natural pressure for standardization that made itself felt from the sixteenth through the nineteenth centuries. The decision by Peter to reorganize the provinces and the decision by Catherine in 1783 to extend Russian local institutions into most of the newly acquired territories were only the most conspicuous manifestations of this tendency.

The standardization of tax collection opened the possibility of standardizing other institutions as well. By 1845 each Baltic province had a Russian-type provincial directorate (pravlenie), treasury office, office of public provisioning, and office of state properties. In 1877 Baltic towns were placed under Russia's 1869 urban statutes,[98] and by 1888 the police of each province had been integrated into the general imperial system. The courts followed the next year. A similar process occurred in White Russia, though earlier; in Siberia with Mikhail Mikhailovich Speranskii's reforms of 1822; and in Poland, which Nicholas I in 1832 defined as a "Russian territory" and transformed its local institutional structure accordingly.[99] In each case the Russian quest for institutional standardization had at least as much impact locally as any deliberate program of cultural intervention.

Because the history of Russian institutional and cultural programs in the empire has so often been viewed from the standpoint of the subject nationalities, it is easily forgotten that some of the most interventionist policies were quite "progressive." The abolition

of slavery in Siberia in 1826 (half a decade before England abolished
slavery in India), the introduction of Russia's reformed judicial institutions into Central Asia in 1884, and the reduction of taxes on
the native population of Turkistan achieved by the introduction of
Russian institutions there in the 1830s all justify the use of the term
"liberal imperialism."[100] Few Pan-Slavs of the late nineteenth century advocated more extensive intervention in local autonomy than
did Col. D. N. Logofet in Central Asia, yet none were more severe
than he in castigating Russian injustices of the past.[101] The existence of this strain in Russian imperial rule calls for some qualification of Lenin's conclusion that Russia set a world record for the
ferocity of its suppression of subject peoples.[102]

Given the "thinness" of its resources, it is all the more surprising that Russia would have impinged so directly on as many aspects of the lives of the subject nationalities as it did. From the
outset the Russian presence was a force for urbanization. The lines
of forts constructed along the western, southeastern, and eastern
flanks of the empire in the seventeenth and eighteenth centuries became centers of attraction or bench marks both for Russian settlement and for those natives seeking commercial gain through contact
with the imperial power. Even if Russian imperialism never exploited the urban unit to the extent that Spain did,[103] the impact in
this area is striking. Russia also stimulated the development of
native agriculture, initially because of the need to provision far-
flung Siberian garrisons but later because it understood that an
agrarian population would be both easier to control and more productive of revenue for the local administration than a nomadic one
would be.

Russian economic policies were, on the whole, actively sup-
portive of non-Russian commercial interests. Armenian, Greek,
Central Asian, and Baltic German traders all thrived under Russian
protection, and came to play a central role in the empire's economic
life—so central a role, in fact, as to elicit indignant protests in the
nineteenth century from the nationalist-minded merchants of Moscow.[104] Catherine II was particularly devoted to the development
of commerce and industry in the colonial territories, not as ends in
themselves but in order to build up the taxable resources of the
state. While Russia's dedication to the development of its imperial
economy continued to increase over time, greater emphasis was always placed on commerce than on manufacturing, thus underscoring
the empire's roots in a mercantile rather than a liberal and industrial order.

ANTI-IMPERIAL VIOLENCE AND ITS COST

Expanding into vacuums left by collapsing empires or into territories that had never been politically organized above the tribal level, Russia enjoyed a relatively free hand in its colonies. Nonetheless, limits to intervention did exist, as was demonstrated repeatedly. Native revolts in Siberia, rebellion after rebellion in Poland, the savage resistance of Caucasian peoples to Russian hegemony all attest to the omnipresent reality of colonial resistance in the Russian empire.

By no means all resistance was violent. When in 1887 the Ministry of Internal Affairs dropped its plan to introduce Russian into the Muslim schools, it did so as much in response to what it thought the Muslim clergy might do as to anything it actually did. But violence or the threat of it was a constant feature of Russian colonial relations. The two greatest peasant revolts in Russian history, the Stenka Razin rebellion of 1670-74 and the Pugachev revolt of 1773-75, both had their origins outside Great Russia and involved numerous minority peoples. The Bolotnikov rebellion of 1606-08, the prolonged campaigns of pacification in the Caucasus in the early nineteenth century, the Polish revolts of 1830 and 1863, the Revolution of 1905, and the 1916 Kirghiz uprising were all quite unintelligible without the element of anti-imperial resistance.

Repeated attempts were made to disarm the potential internal enemy, among them the ban on the sale of firearms, axes, and knives to Siberian tribesmen in the seventeenth century.[105] That violence was anticipated is evident from the number of beds available in military hospitals in the various districts (1874).[106] Thinly populated Turkistan required as many hospital beds as the large and populous Moscow military district, while the fractious western districts of Warsaw and Vilna had more than twice as many. The Caucasus, where guerrilla fighting had persisted for three-quarters of a century, had more than 12 times as many beds in military hospitals as all Siberia had. The fact that per capita expenditures on police during the late nineteenth century were far higher in practically every non-Russian province than in Moscow shows that the price of empire was perpetual fear of violence.[107]

There exists no taxonomy of violence within the Russian empire, so only the barest sketch will have to suffice. Certainly much armed resistance to Russian rule--especially in the earlier centuries--had a distinctly anti-modern character. Peoples who had been organized into local tribes, clans, or estates naturally resisted the imposition of any political structure that subordinated their traditional political and social units to the needs of a bureaucratic state; much the same form of resistance to the rule of Paris

had been raised within France until the early modern period. At
the same time, some of the sharpest clashes in the last half-century
of imperial rule arose from the fact that the Russian state had failed
to adjust adequately to the emergence of a fully modern national consciousness among Poles, Estonians, Latvians, and other peoples,
just as it had failed to reckon with the effects of the social differentia-
tion that its policies had produced.

Much of the early anti-Russian violence took the form of native
resistance to their own leaders who had been co-opted by the Russians. The hanging of co-opted starshinas by cossacks during the
1708 Bulavin uprising is a typical example.[108] Popular hostility to
old elites that had not been successfully co-opted by Russia also occurred, as in the case of the Finnish agitation that led to the 1863
language law putting Finnish on a par with Swedish.[109] A second
source of resistance was popular hostility to those charged with col-
lecting taxes for the Russians.[110] Toward the end of the tsarist
era, a third source of anti-imperial animus made itself felt: opposition to the terms of Russian military service. The revised Army
Bill of 1898 brought forth resistance in Finland, and the full-scale
induction of Central Asians into the imperial army in 1916 led to the
massive strife in Kazakhstan in that year.[111]

In British North America and in New Spain, settlers from the
metropolitan country were the leading figures in anti-colonial violence. The closest parallel to this in the Russian Empire was the
involvement of cossacks in most of the major peasant rebellions in
the Don and Volga basins. Still more common throughout the world
has been the hostility of native peoples to settlers from the imperial
homeland. This was an enduring feature of Russia's imperial relations as well, as the example of Bashkiria indicates. After the
founding of the city of Orenburg in 1735, Russian settlers began
usurping grazing land from the nomadic Bashkirs, with the result
that the latter rebelled in 1735-41, 1755-57, and 1773-75.[112] A
century later the same drama was replayed in Bukhara.

Extant documentation on the human cost of anti-imperial violence in the Russian Empire is impressionistic at best. The few
non-Russian nationalities for whom any preconquest data exist are
the ones who tended to be treated with greatest mildness after the
conquest. Certainly the level of violence was high by any measure.
One authority claims that a third of the Bashkir population was an-
nihilated in the process of conquest by Russia.[113] The analogous
statistic for the Kirghiz in the period 1903-13 is one-tenth, a figure
that was surely matched in the Caucasus during the 1830s by the
Cherkess, against whom a policy of virtual extermination was pursued.[114] That the Siberian Ostyaks would have resorted to mass
suicide in 1627 suggests the depth of hatred upon which such conflicts fed.[115]

The fact that many of the most conspicuous instances of anti-imperial violence involve Muslim or Asiatic peoples might readily be taken as evidence of some special Russian ruthlessness toward people regarded as inferior. Alternatively, it could be viewed as evidence that the greatest resistance to empire arose from peoples unaccustomed to living under governments operating above the tribal or clan level. Lest such interpretations be carried too far, however, it is well to recall that the reciprocal violence involved in the Russian conquest of the Ostyaks or Cherkess probably was no greater than in the Muscovite conquest of Novgorod or Tver.

PROFITABILITY OF RUSSIA'S IMPERIAL POLICY

Surely such casualties would not have been inflicted had the Russians not expected to profit immensely from their colonial possessions. In many instances they did. The priceless furs obtained through the Siberian iasak duty provided up to 10 percent of the entire income of the Muscovite state in the seventeenth century,[116] and the Central Asian cotton industry brought high profit to private entrepreneurs in the late nineteenth century. But there were equally impressive instances of loss. Despite the eighteenth-century debate on the potential profitability of Georgian mineral resources for Russia, Georgia was not self-supporting until the mid-nineteenth century.[117] Nor were the resources of the Urals a significant factor in the Russian economy until the late eighteenth century. Prior to the rise of the iron industry there, the state depended upon the lowly salt tax for much of its "imperial" revenue.[118] After pelts, potentially the most lucrative product of Siberia was lumber. Yet through the grossly inefficient management of this resource by the government, the leasing of vast Siberian tracts brought only deficits until the end of the imperial period.[119] Only with the opening of the Baku oil fields in the late nineteenth century did the revenue from "imperial" resources rise far above the levels it had reached previously through iron.[120]

With little direct gain deriving from the exploitation of the natural resources of its colonial territories, the Russian government might be expected to have fallen back on a rigorous tax system to repay the costs of conquest. This in fact occurred; and the taxes on timber, salt, trade, and on serfs in the non-Russian territories all added to the government's receipts. Yet if the Russians intended to milk the empire through taxation, they did a poor job. As part of the compromise that was struck in the 1650s, Moscow neither invested funds in the Ukraine nor extracted taxes from it until the early eighteenth century.[121] Even in the nineteenth century, the non-Russian territories could scarcely be considered the backbone of the empire's tax base. In 1881, for example, the sum of all taxes paid by these territories (excluding Siberia and the Ukraine) amounted to less than a fifth of total receipts.[122] Granted that the figures upon which this approximation is based are aggregated in such a way as to obscure the non-Russian contribution in several key categories, the purely imperial contribution remains less than overwhelming. In the same year the entire kingdom of Poland paid into the imperial treasury--as opposed to purely local duties--only some 5.5 million rubles, scarcely 11 percent of the amount paid in dues by the former serfs of Great Russia.[123] Turkistan added less than half this sum to the imperial coffers in St. Petersburg, an amount equal to only 1.9 percent of the state's total receipts.[124]

Against these receipts must be reckoned the expenditures that the empire required. While they may not have equaled the British figure of one-sixth of all investment, they were certainly high. Not only were the per capita expenditures on imperial administration higher than for Great Russia, as has been noted, but gross costs were generally far higher as well; for the Polish provinces alone the figures were twice to three times those for Great Russia.[125] The expense of maintaining military installations in the non-Russian areas was also great throughout the imperial era. The initial appropriation required for the trans-Kama line of forts in the 1730s was 46,000 rubles, while the annual yield on all customs collected in Orenburg was only 4,000 rubles.[126] During the nineteenth century, the expenditure on fortifications rose to staggering sums, especially in Poland and the Caucasus, where the internal enemy posed the greatest threat.[127] Next to the construction of St. Petersburg, these fortifications constitute the single largest and most costly construction projects undertaken by the imperial regime until the building of the Trans-Siberian Railroad.

In this discussion it is impossible to enumerate adequately the numerous factors that should be considered when drawing up a complete balance sheet on Russia's imperial holdings. On the one hand, there were certainly substantial private revenues that went unrecorded because they escaped taxation. Nor can the benefits to Russia of its new pool of labor and skills be neglected. On the other hand, the costs of empire, besides the army, included the employment of large bands of officials, diplomats, and others, not to mention the allocation of scarce resources for their maintenance. Finally, these factors should be weighed against the economic situation that would have existed had Russia not been transformed into an empire. While acknowledging that such calculations have not been carried out, it is nonetheless clear from readily available data that until late in the tsarist regime, at least, the benefits of empire were not primarily economic.

What, then, did Russia gain from its imperial territories? In several instances they provided laboratories where innovations could be tested before being applied to Russia. This was Catherine II's hope with her 1787 experiment in self-government for the state peasants of New Russia,[128] just as it was Alexander I's dream to apply aspects of the Polish Constitution to Russia, and Alexander II's intention to use the Nazimov reforms in the western provinces as the basis for a general emancipation. Just as often, however, the existence of the empire placed severe limits upon reforms being conducted within Russia. A typical example is the immense and negative impact of the Polish revolt of 1863 on the reforms being carried out within Russia. Applying a bureaucrat's categorical imperative, Russian administrators rightly perceived that the extensive self-government that reformers envisaged for Great Russia's provinces and cities would bring down the empire if it were applied in Poland.

The benefits that Russia derived from its empire cannot be gauged purely in administrative or financial terms, nor even in domestic terms. Since so much of the empire was acquired in response to international pressures, its maintenance intact was the best possible means of proving to the world that Russia could resist these pressures. Whatever their actual cost to the metropolis, the non-Russian territories could certify Russia's status as a great power. Far from being an irrational factor, as Joseph Schumpeter suggested, imperialism--in Russia, at least--endowed the state with an identity, a name, a place in the consort of nations, and a raison d'être that it would otherwise have lacked. Until the expansion of the empire in the eighteenth century, the Grand Duchy of Moscow was both smaller geographically and less populous than contemporary Japan.[129]

Beyond these considerations, which existed consciously or unconsciously in the minds of all Russia's leaders from Ivan IV to Nicholas II, the non-Russian territories stimulated the development in Russia of a number of traits that, together, defined imperial Russia's existence as a political society. First, the acquisition, pacification, and consolidation of the empire required Russia to maintain the largest army in Europe from the late seventeenth century to 1914. Dominating the government's institutional structure, the army constituted a national school in which the technical and administrative skills necessary to manage large organizations were developed and transmitted. The size of the army, in turn, imposed the need for a large bureaucracy to levy and collect taxes. The diversity of the non-Russian territories, the speed with which they were acquired, and Russia's understaffed and undertrained bureaucracy reinforced the Muscovite tendencies toward administrative standardization and centralization. Without the constant pressure of the empire's administrative needs, it is doubtful that the equation of pluralism with weakness would have been preserved with such vitality in Russia's political life. Nor is it likely that Russia would have had reason to develop to such an extent the instruments of control that enabled it to keep the empire intact.

To maintain the empire was an end in itself, the chief objective of Russian political life. This was far more important than the spread of Russian values, religion, customs, or language within the empire. Through this emphasis, it can be said, imperial Russia, to a greater extent even than the Germany of Otto von Bismarck, was organized around the notion of the primacy of foreign and imperial policy over purely domestic affairs. This idea permeated every aspect of Russian imperial policy, which, especially later, was planned and executed with an eye first to its impact on the other imperial powers and only secondarily to its effect on Russia's domestic well-being.

This concern to maintain the empire permitted the utmost flexibility in the practice of imperial policy. The only absolute requirement was to preserve the imperial order as such. In spite of the Revolution of 1905, this requirement was met until 1917, undoubtedly because seceding regions would have had little chance to practice independence in the context of the existing international order but also due to the policies that Russia had pursued over the centuries. Indeed, with few exceptions, most anti-imperial movements before 1917 sought not full independence but autonomy within a federated Russian state.[130] The Bolsheviks actually established such a state--if only in words--thereby attesting to the strength of this ideal. Their hostility toward granting independence confirms the enduring power of centripetal forces within the Russian polity.

NOTES

1. A. G. Rashin, Naselenie Rossii za sto let (Moscow, 1956), pp. 68, 74, 93.

2. As exceptions, see Marc Raeff, "Patterns of Russian Imperial Policies towards the Nationalities, in Soviet Nationality Problems, ed. Edward Allworth (New York, 1970), pp. 22-42; Dietrich Geyer, "Russland als Problem der vergleichenden Imperialismusforschung," in Das Vergangene und die Geschichte: Festschrift für Reinhard Wittram am 70. Geburtstag (Göttingen, 1973), pp. 337-68. Both this essay and Geyer's Der russische Imperialismus. Studien über den Zusammenhang von innern und auswarter Politik, 1860-1914 (Göttingen, 1977), lay greater stress

on the process of acquiring territory than on the subsequent technique of rule, as does Gladys Scott Thompson, Catherine the Great and the Expansion of Russia (New York, 1950). See also Emanuel Sarkesyanz, "Russian Imperialism Reconsidered," in Russian Imperialism from Ivan the Great to the Revolution, ed. Taras Hunczak (New Brunswick, N.J.: Rutgers University Press, 1974), pp. 45-81.

3. Georg von Rauch, Russland: Staatliche Einheit und nationale Vielfalt, vol. 5 of Veröffentlichungen des Osteuropa-Institutes München (Munich, 1953). George L. Yaney, The Systematization of Russian Government: Social Evolution in the Domestic Administration of Imperial Russia, 1711-1905 (Urbana: University of Illinois Press, 1973), at least acknowledges that he is not treating the imperial question. The best overall treatments of the problem of governance in its various parts by a Western scholar remain George Vernadsky, A History of Russia, 5 vols. (New Haven and London, 1943-69); and Hugh Seton-Watson, The Russian Empire 1801-1917 (Oxford, 1967).

4. See, for example, George H. Nadel and Perry Curtis, Imperialism and Colonialism (New York, 1969); J. Parry, Europe and a Wider World (London, 1966); and George Lichtheim, Imperialism (New York and Washington, 1971), all of which ignore the Russian experience.

5. Soloviev, too, ignored the imperial question as such, although his stress upon governmental institutions, combined with his interest in colonization, enabled him to advance several provocative theses in this area. S. M. Soloviev, Istoriia Rossi s drevneishikh vremen, 6 vols. (Moscow, 1960), esp. vol. 3.

6. A recent exception is A. P. Okladnikov, ed., Voprosy istorii Sibiri dosovetskogo perioda, Bakhrushinskie chteniia (Novosibirsk, 1973).

7. See R. Koebner, "The Emergence of the Concept of Imperialism," The Cambridge Journal 5 (1952): 726-41.

8. See Edward C. Thaden, "Samarin's 'Okrainy Rossii' and Official Policy in the Baltic Provinces," Russian Review, October 1974, pp. 406 ff.

9. Baron B. E. Nolde, Ocherki russkogo gosudarstvennogo prava (St. Petersburg, 1911), continued as La formation de l'empire russe: Études, notes et documents (Paris, 1952); Iosif Stalin, "Marksizm i natsionalnyi vopros," in his Sochineniia (Moscow, 1951), 2: 291 ff.

10. A. A. Vvedenskii, Dom Stroganovykh v XVI-XVII vekakh (Moscow, 1962), p. 76.

11. Nolde, op. cit., p. 300.

12. Alton S. Donnelly, The Russian Conquest of Bashkiria (New Haven, Conn.: Yale University Press, 1968), p. 153.

13. Nolde, op. cit., pp. 291 ff.

14. George V. Lantzeff, Siberia in the Seventeenth Century, a Study of Colonial Administration (Berkeley and Los Angeles: University of California Press, 1943), p. 29.

15. von Rauch, op. cit., pp. 57 ff.; Gen.-Lt. Bogdanovich, comp., Istoricheskii ocherk deiatelnosti voennogo upravleniia v Rossii v pervoe dvadsati-piati-letie blagopoluchnogo tsarstvovaniia gosudaria imperatora Aleksandra Nikolaevicha (6 vols., St. Petersburg, 1879-81), 4: 338 ff.

16. See François Xavier Coquin, La Sibérie, peuplement et immigration paysanne au 19º siècle (Paris, 1969); and Donald Treadgold, The Great Siberian Migration: Government and Peasant Resettlement from Emancipation to the First World War (Princeton, 1957).

17. This point is well developed in Alfred J. Rieber, "Cultural Leaders and Entrepreneurs in the Rise of Great Russian Nationalism," paper presented to Seminar on Multicultural Societies, University of Pennsylvania, February 10, 1976.

18. For the forest versus the steppe, see Donnelly, op. cit., p. 2. For the north versus the south, see A. D. Kolesnikov, "S. V. Bakhrushin o formakh kolonizatsii," in Okladnikov, op. cit., p. 179.

19. Quoted in V. Ia. Laverichev, "K voprosu ob osobennostiakh imperializma v Rossii," Istoriia SSR (1971), no. 1: 80.

20. Although it has been challenged by certain Soviet scholars, Chermenskii's argument on this point is still generally accepted by Soviet scholars: E. D. Chermenskii, Istoriia SSSR, period imperializma (90-e gody XIX v.-mart 1917 g.) (Moscow, 1965), p. 11.

21. Cf. Raeff's phases of "acquisition," "incorporation," and "assimilation," op. cit., pp. 26-27.

22. A. L. Sidorov, "V. I. Lenin o russkom voenno-feodalnom imperializme (o soderzhanii termina voenno-feodalnye imperializm)," Istoriia SSSR (1961), no. 4: 51; P. G. Galuzo, Agrarnye otnosheniia na iuge Kazakhstana v. 1867-1914 gg. (Alma-Ata, 1965), pp. 7, 51.

23. The relevance of the "gathering of the Russian lands" was suggested by Raeff, op. cit., p. 27; and by Henry R. Huttenbach, "The Origins of Russian Imperialism," in Hunczak, op. cit., pp. 18-44; on Novgorod, see Michael Rywkin, "Russian Colonial Expansion before Ivan the Dread: A Survey of Basic Trends," Russian Review, July 1973, pp. 286 ff. See also David M. Goldfrank's argument in favor of the Mongol era, "Tsarist Russia's Dynastic-Imperial System Viewed Historically" (manuscript, Georgetown University, 1977, no. 25).

24. Nolde, op. cit., pp. 432 ff.

25. See especially the terms of the 1867 partial settlement with the emir of Bukhara and of the 1873 Russia-Khiva Treaty in

Seymour Becker, Russia's Protectorates in Central Asia; Bukhara and Khiva, 1865-1924 (Cambridge, 1968), pp. 43-76.

26.	The companies and syndicates that underwrote most Dutch trade in the sixteenth century were independent of the government, just as the British East India Company, after being chartered in 1600, received no direct subvention from the crown. See Parry, op. cit., pp. 89 ff. Also see Nadel and Curtis, op. cit., pp. 30 ff.

27.	S. B. Okun, Rossiisko-Amerikanskaia kompaniia (Moscow, 1939), pp. 9-19.

28.	Ibid., pp. 65 ff.

29.	David Marshall Lang, The Last Years of the Georgian Monarchy, 1658-1832 (New York, 1957), p. 273.

30.	See Vvedenskii, op. cit., p. 80.

31.	Soloviev, op. cit., 3: ch. 7; Vvedenskii, op. cit., pp. 76-85.

32.	Nolde finds the use of concessions to have been an important feature of colonial rule in the sixteenth and seventeenth centuries, but not later. La formation de l'empire russe . . ., pp. 68-69.

33.	L. S. Rafienko, "Politika rossiiskogo absoliutizma po unifikatsii upravleniia Sibiriu vo vtoroi polovine XVIII v.," in Okladnikov, op. cit., p. 231.

34.	V. V. Rabtsevich, "K voprosu ob upravlenii aborigennym naseleniem zapadnoi Sibiri v 80-kh godakh xviii-porvykh desiatiletiiakh XIX stoletiia," in ibid., pp. 310-11.

35.	Ministerstvo vnutrennykh del, "Soderzhanie gubernskikh i oblastnykh pravlenii . . .," in Prilozhenie k smete raskhodov Ministerstva vnutrennikh del na 1875 god (St. Petersburg, 1874), pp. 65-90.

36.	The first scholar to raise this issue was P. A. Slovtsov, Istoricheskoe obozrnie Sibiri (St. Petersburg, 1838). For other contributions to this important debate, see S. V. Bakhrushin, Nauchnye trudy, 5 vols. (Moscow, 1952-59), esp. vol. 4; also D. I. Bagalei, Ocherki po istorii kolonizatsii stepnykh okrain moskovskogo gosudarstva (Moscow, 1887); and the journals Voprosy kolonizatsii and Trudy kolonizatsionnogo instituta.

37.	Nolde, La formation de l'empire russe, p. 77.

38.	See, for example, the particularly candid statement in Polozhenie o voennom poselenii na kavkaze (St. Petersburg, 1837), p. 1.

39.	James A. Duran, Jr., "Catherine II, Potemkin and Colonization Policy in South Russia," Russian Review, January 1969, p. 31.

40.	An early description of these colonists is in August von Haxthausen, Studies on the Interior of Russia, ed. S. Frederick Starr (Chicago, 1972), ch. 7.

41. On the government agency, see L. M. Goriushkin, "Iz istorii zemelnogo-lesnogo khoziaistva kazny v Sibiri kontsa XIX-nachala XX veka," in Iz istorii ekonomicheskoi i obshchestvennoi zhizni Rossii, ed. L. V. Cherepnin (Moscow, 1976), p. 125; on Siberia, see Treadgold, op. cit.; on Central Asia, see George J. Demko, The Russian Colonization of Kazakhstan, 1896-1916 (Bloomington: Indiana University Press, 1969).

42. S. M. Troitskii, "Sibirskaia administratsiia v seredine XVIII v.," in Okladnikov, op. cit., pp. 310 ff.

43. Lantzeff, op. cit., pp. 109 ff.

44. Marc Raeff, "The Style of Russia's Imperial Policy and Prince G. A. Potemkin," in Statesmen and Statecraft of the Modern World; Essays in Honor of Dwight E. Lee and H. Donaldson Jordan, ed. Gerald N. Grob (Barre, 1967), pp. 5 ff.

45. See Becker, op. cit., pp. 125-55.

46. Ibid., p. 116.

47. S. Prutchenko, Sibirskie okrainy, 2 vols. (St. Petersburg, 1899), 1: 2.

48. On Georgia, see Lang, op. cit., pp. 274 ff.; on Poland, see R. F. Leslie, Reform and Insurrection in Russian Poland, 1856-1865 (London, 1963), p. 46.

49. Polozhenie ob upravlenii Kalmykskim narodom (Iurev, 1834), pp. 2-3.

50. Nadel and Curtis, op. cit., p. 32.

51. See V. I. Lenin, Polnoe sobranie sochinenii, 55 vols. (Moscow, 1967-70), 30: 58. For a thorough discussion of Lenin's notion, see A. L. Sidorov, "V. I. Lenin o russkom voenno-feodalnom imperializme (o soderzhanii termina 'voenno-feodalnyi imperializm),'" Istorii SSSR (1961), no. 4, pp. 36 ff.; and Laverichev, op. cit.

52. For a comprehensive view of these offices, see Ivan Andreevskii, O namestnikakh, voevodakh i gubernatorakh (St. Petersburg, 1864).

53. Michael Rywkin, "The Prikaz of the Kazan Court: The First Russian Colonial Office," Canadian Slavonic Papers (1976), no. 3: 296.

54. This need lay behind many of the reform projects of the era of Alexander. See G. Vernadsky, La charte constitutionelle de l'Empire russe de 1820 (Paris, 1933); B. Meissner, "Die Entwicklung der Ministerien in Russland," Europa-Archiv Heft 2-4 (1948); also Yaney, op. cit., ch. 5.

55. Raeff, "The Style of Russia's Imperial Policy . . .," pp. 30 ff.

56. Aleksandr P. Shcherbatov, General Feldmarshal Kniaz Paskevich, ego zhizn i deiatelnost, 5 vols. (St. Petersburg, 1888), 5: app., p. 600.

57. Ibid.

58. Seton-Watson, op. cit., p. 297.

59. P. Morris, "The Russians in Central Asia, 1870-1887," Slavonic and East European Review, October 1975, pp. 521 ff.

60. Nolde, La formation de l'empire russe, p. 121.

61. Ibid.; and Alan W. Fisher, "Enlightened Despotism and Islam under Catherine II," Slavic Review, December 1968, p. 542.

62. Fisher, op. cit., p. 544.

63. A. V. Kartashev, Ocherki istorii russkoi tserkvi, 2 vols. (Paris, 1959), 2: 291-97.

64. Nolde, La formation de l'empire russe, p. 81.

65. Edward Allworth, Central Asia: A Century of Russian Rule (New York, 1967), p. 1.

66. Troitskii, op. cit., pp. 307-11.

67. Lantzeff, op. cit., p. 101.

68. A. V. Kartashev, Ocherki po istorii russkoi tserkvi, 2 vols. (Paris, 1959), 2.

69. Fisher, op. cit., pp. 513 ff.; Donnelly, op. cit., p. 77.

70. Seton-Watson, op. cit., p. 500.

71. This point forms the basis for A. Romanovich-Slavatinskii's Dvorianstvo v Rossii ot nachala XVIII-ogo do otmeny krepostnogo prava (2nd ed.; Kiev, 1912).

72. Raeff, "The Style of Russia's Imperial Policy . . .," pp. 14-15.

73. Rywkin, "The Prikaz of the Kazan Court . . .," pp. 298-99.

74. Becker, op. cit., p. 18.

75. See Donnelly, op. cit., p. 85; Rywkin, "The Prikaz of the Kazan Court . . .," p. 298; Nolde, La formation de l'empire russe, pp. 68-69.

76. Polozhenie o shkole dlia kirgizskikh detei; 14 iunia (June) 1844 (St. Petersburg, 1844), p. 27.

77. A. P. Pronshtein, "Voisko-donskoe nakanune Bulavinskogo vosstaniia," in Voprosy voennoi istorii Rossii. XVIII i pervaia polovina XIX vv., ed. V. I. Shunkov (Moscow, 1969), pp. 321 ff.

78. Ia. Zutis, Ostzeiskii vopros XVIII veke (Riga, 1946), pp. 59 ff.; Nolde, Ocherki russkogo gosudarstvennogo prava, p. 331.

79. This point is rightly made by Marxist scholars. See Zutis, op. cit., chs. 1-2.

80. Nadel and Curtis, op. cit., pp. 42-43.

81. Nolde, Ocherki russkogo gosudarstvennogo prava, pp. 388-90.

82. Ibid., pp. 429-31.

83. Lang, op. cit., p. 260.

84. Polozhenie ob upravlenii orenburgskimi kirgizami (St. Petersburg, 1844), p. 7.

85. Rywkin, "The Prikaz of the Kazan Court . . . ," p. 297.

86. Lantzeff, op. cit., p. 92.

87. Donnelly, op. cit., pp. 143-44.

88. See John D. Klier, "The Ambiguous Legal Status of Russian Jewry in the Russia of Catherine II," Slavic Review, September 1976, pp. 507 ff.; and Sarkesyanz, op. cit., pp. 78-79.

89. Nadel and Curtis, op. cit., pp. 40-41.

90. Quoted in Nolde, Ocherki russkogo gosudarstvennogo prava, p. 448.

91. Even Hans Kohn admits as much, in his Pan Slavism, Its History and Ideology (Notre Dame, Ind., 1933), pp. 170 ff.

92. See Anatole G. Mazour, Finland between East and West (Princeton, 1956), pp. 18 ff.

93. This argument is based on the excellent dissertation submitted to the University of Giessen in 1977 by Robert Schweitzer, "Autokratie und Autonomie: Das gross Furstentum Finland in russischen Reich, 1869-1894."

94. On Bashkiria, see Donnelly, op. cit., p. 145; on the Legislative Commission, see Fisher, op. cit., p. 544.

95. This argument is defended by Orest Pelech, "Towards a Historical Society of the Ukrainian Ideologies in the Russian Empire of the 1830s and 1840s" (Ph.D. diss., Princeton, 1976); the traditional view is presented by P. A. Zaionchkovskii in his Kirillo-Mefodievskoe obshchestvo, 1816-1847 (Moscow, 1959).

96. Alfred Bilmanis, A History of Latvia (Westport, Conn., 1951), pp. 238-39.

97. The entire Estonian movement, and its interaction with Russian policy, is analyzed by Toivo Raunn, "The Revolution of 1905 and the Movement for Estonian National Autonomy" (Ph.D. diss., Princeton, 1969).

98. Nolde, Ocherki russkogo gosudarstvennogo prava, pp. 407-10.

99. See Marc Raeff, Siberia and the Reforms of 1822 (Seattle: University of Washington Press, 1956); and, on Poland, Nolde, Ocherki russkogo gosudarstvennogo prava, p. 448.

100. See D. S. M. Williams, "Fiscal Reform in Turkestan," Slavonic and East European Review, July 1974, p. 391; Lichtheim, op. cit., ch. 3. See also Bernard Semmel, Imperialism and Social Reform (London, 1960).

101. See his Bukharskoe khanstvo pod Russkim protektoratom (St. Petersburg, 1911).

102. Lenin, loc. cit.

103. Nadel and Curtis, op. cit., p. 42.

104. Rieber, op. cit., pp. 8 ff.

105. Lantzeff, op. cit., p. 97.

106. Bogdanovich, op. cit., p. 403.

107. "Soderzhanie gorodskikh, uezdnykh i okruzhnykh politseiskikh upravlenii po guberniiam," in Prilozhenie k smete raskhodov Ministerstva vnutrennikh del na 1875 god (St. Petersburg, 1874), pp. 128 ff.

108. Pronshtein, op. cit., p. 325.

109. This and related aspects of developments in Finland are analyzed in K. G. T. Rein, Iovan Vilgelm Snelman: Istoriko-biograficheskii ocherk (trans. from Swedish), 2 vols. (St. Petersburg, 1905).

110. E. B. Bekmakhanov, Prisoedinenię Kazakhstana k Rossii (Moscow, 1957), pp. 115 ff.; also Becker, op. cit., p. 83.

111. E. Sokol, The Revolt of 1916 in Russian Central Asia (Baltimore, 1954).

112. N. V. Ustiugov, Bashkirskoe vosstanie 1737-1739 gg. (Moscow and Leningrad, 1950); Donnelly, op. cit., p. 130.

113. Donnelly, op. cit., p. 5.

114. Sarkesyanz, op. cit., p. 76; Firuz Kazemzadeh, "Russian Penetration of the Caucasus," in Hunczak, op. cit., p. 253.

115. Lantzeff, op. cit., p. 110.

116. R. H. Fisher, The Russian Fur Trade, 1550-1770 (Berkeley and Los Angeles: University of California Press, 1943), pp. 118 ff., 230 ff.

117. Lang, op. cit., pp. 246, 273 ff.

118. Vvedenskii, op. cit., p. 279.

119. Goriushkin, op. cit., p. 130, table 1.

120. Kazemzadeh, op. cit., p. 254.

121. Nolde, Ocherki russkogo gosudarstvennogo prava, p. 322.

122. Ministerstvo Finansov, Departament Okladnykh Sborov, Otchet gosudarstvennogo kontrolla po ispolneniiu gosudarstvennoi rospisi za smetnyi period 1881 goda (St. Petersburg, 1882), pp. 42-46.

123. Ibid.

124. Ibid., p. 8.

125. Prilozhenie k smete raskhodov Ministerstva vnutrennikh del na 1875 god, pp. 65-90.

126. Donnelly, op. cit., p. 162.

127. Bogdanovich, op. cit., 4: prilozhenie 70.

128. Duran, op. cit., p. 33.

129. Cyril E. Black et al., The Modernization of Japan and Russia (New York, 1975), p. 17.

130. von Rauch, op. cit., ch. 8.

DETERMINANTS AND PARAMETERS OF SOVIET NATIONALITY POLICY 2

Hélène Carrère d'Encausse

For orthodox Marxists the 1917 Bolshevik Revolution was in every respect anomalous. It occurred in a backward society still in the midst of an economic "takeoff." And it carried in its train all the nations of the tsarist empire but did not spread to other, more advanced societies. However, while Marx and his most orthodox followers, such as Rosa Luxemburg, would have regarded this situation as both disconcerting and inconsistent with the original revolutionary plan, Lenin had deliberately created and enthusiastically accepted such a revolution. He had long been skeptical concerning the revolutionary capabilities of the Western proletariat, which he had seen evolve toward reformism, and had already, before 1914, turned his attention and hopes to the "weakest link" of the capitalist system. Lenin thus incorporated into his revolutionary strategy a place for those forces that Marx had more or less ignored: nations and the peasantry.

Lenin's revolutionary strategy, criticized by his own party, was responsible for the Bolshevik success in 1917. However, Lenin and his party then confronted the problem of integrating into the new system those national forces that the Bolsheviks had manipulated in order to come to power. What made the incorporation of these national forces into a socialist state especially problematical was the fact that the Bolsheviks, including Lenin, were still basically guided by two convictions. First, the socialist state should be a unitary state. Second, proletarian internationalism, the basic principle underlying the organization of the socialist state and determining its composition, could allow no room for national differences and aspirations.

Despite these convictions, the situation created by the 1917 Revolution forced the Bolsheviks to establish a federal state that recognized the existence of nations. Furthermore, Bolshevik ideology, which until then had asserted that nations would have no future once the proletarian revolution had taken place, was revised to account for the survival of nations under socialism. These adaptations, in turn, raise a number of important questions. Was there a new Bolshevik vision of the national problem after 1917? Did it constitute a major revision of Lenin's earlier position? Did this vision change over time? Was Bolshevik nationality policy the product of ideology or of circumstance? And did this policy have common elements across time and space? These are some of the questions to which this essay is addressed.

LENIN'S NATIONAL POLICY

It is completely wrong to divide Lenin's nationality policy into two periods, one in which he applied a policy of self-determination and the other in which he tried to recover what he had earlier conceded. An examination of his policy demonstrates that Lenin believed all along that the right of self-determination should be employed to end demands for national independence, and not to satisfy them. When he granted independence to Finland, he was recognizing a reality he could not have changed; but he openly expressed regret that this was so. As early as January 15, 1918, Lenin attempted to use the right of self-determination of Finnish "workers" to reverse that decision and to return Finland to the revolutionary fold.[1] This episode clarifies the Bolshevik position at that time. Self-determination was to be no more than a brief moment of independence, leading rapidly to social revolution and, thence, to the reestablishment of a unitary, revolutionary, workers' state. If one remembers that at this time Soviet juridical conceptions approved the idea of an open state whose borders would expand with the progress of the revolution, one can deduce that the end of this process was to be political unity, which in the Leninist theory of self-determination is the alternative to separation. This restricted interpretation of self-determination corresponded to the Bolsheviks' profound conviction that nations must disappear in the socialist world they were in the process of creating. It was also a response to demands for security and even for survival of the revolution. Those nations that had applied the principle and had separated themselves from Russia were seeking support from foreign powers (Germany, in the case of Finland); this threatened the young Soviet state, still very weak and not able to accept the fact that the emancipated nations were turning into enemy outposts at its very borders.

Policy Before 1920

By 1918, therefore, Lenin realized that self-determination, far from benefiting the Russian proletariat, was exacerbating the threats it had to face. He also recognized that even a socialist state would have to adapt to certain universal political and economic necessities. Consequently, despite his faith in world revolution and in the withering away of the state, Lenin sensed that the Soviet state would continue to exist for a long time and that it would have to be territorially, institutionally, and economically viable. The double necessity of making the Soviet state viable and of maintaining the principle of national self-determination led him to accept the idea of a federation even though he had always rejected this idea in the past. However, as he had done in the case of national self-determination, Lenin attempted to develop this federation in such a way as to deprive it of any real meaning.

Bolshevik treatment of the Ukraine is a clear illustration of Lenin's understanding of the proper limits of federalism. The Ukraine was one of the most important economic bases of the proletarian state and was necessary for its continued survival. Thus Lenin wanted to reassure the Ukrainians as well as to keep them within Russia's orbit. To do this he preserved the right of self-determination for all, defending it against the opposition of Nikolai Bukharin and Iurii Piatakov at the Eighth Congress of the Russian Communist Party (RCP).[2] At the same time, however, he asserted that the right of self-determination must be "corrected through propaganda and organizational unity." To accomplish this, Lenin placed Iosif Stalin in charge of the Ukrainian Communist Party, instructing him to complete the bond between the two parties. In this way Russian control over the Ukrainian Communist organization was ensured. Furthermore, due to certain economic requirements, Lenin increased the number of organizations in the Ukraine that would be dependent on the RSFSR. All these measures quickly reduced Ukrainian independence to nothing.

During the period 1918-20, therefore, while the principle of self-determination was being applied in practice and was resulting in a process of separation, Bolshevik nationality policy sought to check its application wherever possible and to prepare for the ultimate consolidation of the Soviet state. Although the Bolsheviks still believed in world revolution, Lenin devoted his attention to the establishment of institutions and administrative organs that would become the framework of a powerful and centralized Soviet state. He thus was responsible not only for the Bolsheviks' initial national strategy but also for the design of those institutions that were charged with applying it: the state, <u>Narkomnats</u> (the People's Commissariat for Nationality Affairs), and the Communist Party.

As soon as these organizational structures were established, the question of how functions should be distributed among them was raised. At the two extremes were to be the Party, embodying the ideology of unity and serving as an instrument for integrating all the nations into the state, and Narkomnats, representing national interests at the center. Between them was the federal state, which was charged with reconciling the aspiration for unity with the actual diversity of Soviet society. Thus, there existed an institutional balance between the plan for unity and the concessions to Soviet reality. Lenin was able to establish this balance because most of the Bolsheviks were not much interested in the nationality question. But, busy with the enormous number of problems facing the Soviet government, he was not able to control day-to-day decisions. Consequently, those who retained some organizational authority for decision making in this area often applied policies far removed from Lenin's general directives. Only when problems became critical did Lenin attempt to regain control over nationality policy. Decision making, therefore, was characterized by three features. First, Lenin alone defined the general thrust of nationality policy. Second, decisions within the general lines established by Lenin were made by a number of decision-making centers that sometimes cooperated but often were in conflict. And third, there was room for both improvisation and individual initiative even though the system already was quite structured.

Between 1918 and 1920, Lenin followed two different policies. The more viable and familiar of these was to satisfy national demands and to recognize the right to self-determination. The instrument for the execution of this policy was Narkomnats. This commissariat was conceived by Lenin as an instrument for his policy of national self-determination, that is, for the internationalist education of nations. It was supposed to be a national forum whose very existence would show that Bolshevik egalitarianism was not an empty word. This explains why the original Narkomnats statute placed all national groups on an equal footing: the great nations still linked to Russia, others that had separated from Russia (the Poles), nations without any territory (the Jews), and even very small ethnic groups. But this institution never fulfilled Lenin's hopes because the people who ran it had views and adopted policies quite foreign to his directives.

This undoubtedly was due, in part, to Stalin's role as commissar. But Stalin focused most of his attention on his duties as general secretary of the Communist Party and on influencing the

future structure of the Soviet state in the commission then preparing the new constitution. While he certainly influenced the selection
of cadres in Narkomnats, Stalin delegated his basic responsibilities
to his assistants in that organization. Because of the lack of serious
candidates, national commissars frequently were deeply russified
people who advocated the establishment of a centralized state in
which the nationality problem would be regarded as solved. This explains why Narkomnats was generally unable to attract to responsible positions national cadres who retained strong ties to their
original communities; why it had little influence on the nations during this period; and why it played no role in Soviet policy before
1920, not even as a transmission belt.

Policy in the 1920s

After 1920, on the other hand, when there was no longer any
hope for a world revolution and the Bolsheviks had to reinforce
their state to ensure its survival, Narkomnats was reorganized and
strengthened. It was given a specific task: the organization of
cooperation between the center and the periphery. The difficulties
that the Bolsheviks had encountered in the Caucasus and in Central
Asia convinced them that this cooperation could not depend solely
on flexible institutions claiming to lie halfway between the interests
of the state and of its national constituents. Consequently, Narkomnats was to work in two directions at the same time. It was
supposed to be both a coordinating center for information on the
periphery's situation and demands that would be forwarded to the
central authorities, and an intermediary in charge of regulating the
application of central directives in the republics. In this second
capacity Narkomnats went far beyond Lenin's directives. Its envoys
to the republics often behaved like proconsuls and spent their time
trying to restrict in every possible way the competence of national
institutions.[3] In Moscow, meanwhile, the leadership of Narkomnats
was restricting direct relations between republican governments
and the central leadership by requiring the former to direct its
communications to the central authorities through Narkomnats.
Increasingly devoted to central interests, Narkomnats frequently
acted in close collaboration with the Party, which at this time constituted the instrument for the execution of Lenin's other major
policy: to regain control over the dispersed nations and to place
the initiative back in the hands of the Russian proletariat--or, better still, in the hands of its Bolshevik avant-garde. Collaboration
between Narkomnats and the Party, therefore, reinforced the tendency of the latter to become an agent of centralization. As a

result, Narkomnats ended up being little more than-an instrument
of the Communist Party in the latter's drive toward centralized
consolidation.

The Bolsheviks' nationality policy took on new and more precise forms, but it did not change in any fundamental sense. The
end of the world revolution forced the Bolsheviks to shift their attention to the revolutionary base they had established and from
which they had to fashion a durable bastion for socialism. Protecting the Soviet state thus became a task of the highest importance.
This state had to be coherent and able to defend itself. Instead of
open revolutionary borders, it required specific and defensible
ones. This explains the great importance attached to the border
treaties made in the early 1920s. The principle of self-determination
became more limited, given this defensive perspective. It could
no longer operate to reduce the consolidated borders, but only to
extend them. It thus became urgent to provide a definitive statute
on national relations within Soviet Russia, an statute much more
restrictive than the contractual bonds that had been established
until then.

Simultaneous with this realization of their international isolation, the Bolsheviks were disquieted by the discovery of another
consequence of Lenin's national strategy: the development of national Communism. Various events led to this discovery: the revolutionary developments in Central Asia, the Baku Congress, and
the theses of Sultan Guliev, who enjoyed a considerable following
among the Muslim peoples in Russia.[4] From Lenin's call for national emancipation as well as from Marxism, some Communists
and Muslim nationalists created an explosive combination: the idea
that oppressed nations enjoy a special destiny and that revolution
in these nations must follow a special course, conforming to their
individual national traditions and characteristics. Islam and Turk-
ish civilization were incorporated into this ideology, which spread
rapidly throughout the southern periphery of the Soviet state and
was all the more worrisome in that it disguised itself in Marxist
terms (the idea of international solidarity among the oppressed).
The carriers of this idea justified it both by the end of the revolution
in the West and by the growth of revolutionary ferment in the colonial
and semi-colonial worlds. They wished to be the avant-garde of
this movement.

It did not take the Bolsheviks long to see the dangers of national Communism. Its success would preclude forever any possibility for the development of a centralized Soviet state, because it
would place in opposition to Moscow a coalition of Muslim states
demanding special roads of development. The inevitable results of
this process would be the dislocation and "orientalization" of the

Soviet state. Were that to happen, the entire world labor movement, with the Soviet Union at its center, would be threatened by the possibility of fragmentation along national lines, with each nation demanding attention to its specific peculiarities and seeking privileges for itself.

The Bolsheviks could not accept the development of such national Communism, which would mean the destruction of their deepest convictions and the end of the policy they had pursued until then. They could not accept the possibility that the revolution--which for Russia meant both modernization along European lines and the opening of a new historic path that the Western world would follow --might slide toward an "orientalization" of Marxism. Nor could they tolerate the division of Marxism into a European branch represented by Russia and an Asiatic branch that would be reinforced by revolutions that seemed on the verge of exploding in several eastern countries.

There was, moreover, another, more circumstantial reason, linked to the Soviet ideology of the 1920s, that militated against the acceptance of national Communism. From 1918 to 1920 the ideological underpinnings of Soviet actions had been war Communism. This ideology was utopian, radical, and egalitarian. It was predicated on the idea that human nature would change immediately and radically in the homeland where revolution occurred and that a new man, stripped of all the prejudices and faults of the previous world, would emerge from the revolutionary crucible. This egalitarianism undoubtedly was closely related to Russian poverty, but it also stemmed from revolutionary enthusiasm. In 1921, when the New Economic Policy (NEP) replaced war Communism, this initial utopianism gave way to a moderate and gradualist vision of social change. In certain respects, however, the NEP's gradualist ideology continued to be influenced by the radical and egalitarian ideas of war Communism.[5] This was especially the case with regard to the nationality question. The ideas of egalitarianism and the radical cultural revolution survived in Bolshevik nationality policy because they served the Bolsheviks' interests. In the name of equality among nations, the Bolsheviks could shatter the pan-national blocs that existed or threatened to appear. They could then force the creation and consolidation of individual nations that would be less dangerous to the center than were the larger groups from which they were carved.

Whatever its ulterior motives, this stress on egalitarianism, along with Lenin's frequent injunctions about the need for prudence, meant that the Soviet state's policy of consolidation was not simply transformed into a policy of Russian domination. The growth of such domination was slowed by egalitarian policies that allowed the

nations to develop culturally and to assume some political responsibilities, through the rapid promotion of native cadres. Undoubtedly,
this ideological factor was less important than were purely political
considerations. However, the Bolshevik policy of the 1920s should
not be reduced to a mere study of political power. Once consolidated, the Soviet state proudly and publicly associated itself with
Marxism and used the latter in its Leninist variant to justify its increasing domination over the nations. The national doctrine of the
Bolsheviks was already an "ideological ideology," in Karl Mann-
heim's sense. But, at the same time, certain elements of the
original utopia continued to exist until the early 1930s, at least to
the extent that political priorities did not force the Bolsheviks to
discard (entirely) them. If one neglects these ideological elements,
one risks not understanding Soviet nationality policy in all its complexity.

Bolshevik nationality policy in the 1920s was characterized by
two elements: the necessity for organizing the revolutionary base
and the desire to realize a radical sociocultural revolution. As a
result, the NEP had a double significance. From an international
perspective it reflected the Bolshevik recognition that the world
revolution had run its course for the time being. From an internal
perspective it reflected the recognition that the Russian Revolution
did not coincide with the state of Russian society and that social
consciousness lagged behind the institutions established by the
Bolsheviks. The Soviet state's political organization was no more
than a superstructure (nadstroika) by means of which the Bolsheviks
tried to preserve the experience of the revolution. This superstructure, however, was also a compromise on the nationality question.
Lenin had accepted federalism in 1918 as a temporary expedient.
In 1922 he defended it vehemently because he was afraid of aggravat-
ing national oppositions. This evolution from absolute opposition to
federalism before 1917 to uncompromising support of federalism
after 1922[6] bears witness to the dimensions of the nationality problem at that time and to Lenin's acute consciousness of this problem.

Does this change in attitude imply a new vision of the nationality problem? Does it imply a genuine interest in the nations per se?
Certainly not. The unfolding of the constitutional conflict and the
final writings of Lenin both suggest that he separated himself from
Stalin concerning the correct means of solving the nationality problem. Lenin's final goal remained the one he had always pursued:
the elimination of national differences that weaken the unity of the
working class. Federalism, for Lenin, was to be a school of internationalism. What was new in his attitude after 1920 was his recognition that more time would have to be spent on this internationalist
education. He was acutely conscious of the danger of nationalism,

especially since this nationalism was an important factor retarding the development of social consciousness.

This continued refusal to recognize the existence of nationhood explains why Lenin attached such great importance to the second part of his policy, the sociocultural revolution. He believed that by granting rights to nations and by giving them political and cultural autonomy, he could speed the rise of the new socialist man who would be capable of ridding himself of national prejudices. The entire political and cultural part of the NEP--federalism, the cultural development of nations, of their languages, and of their cadres--was thus conceived as one stage in the eventual unification of Soviet society and as a means for attaining this goal, a goal to which Lenin remained faithful until the very end.

STALIN'S NATIONALITY POLICY

When the Stalin era began at the end of the 1920s, a radical change occurred in the perception of the nationality problem. Several factors played a decisive role in this change: Stalin's personality, the new conditions being established in the Soviet state, and, most notably, the absolute power of Stalin, which enabled him to impose his own perception of the nationality problem on the country. Authority to make decisions was concentrated entirely in the Party and, increasingly, in the hands of Stalin alone. As soon as he became the main wielder of power, Stalin attempted to bring all decision making under his control and refused to share even the smallest amount of it with the periphery. He accused the national elites, the majority of whom had arisen under the policy of indigenization or korenizatsiia, [7] of "bourgeois nationalism," and liquidated them. He replaced them with new political elites who were raised according to the new ideology (nonegalitarian, centralizing, and russified) and who were devoted to Stalin because he had selected them. During this period Stalin came to enjoy virtually unlimited decision-making power, which he exercised sometimes alone and sometimes through institutions that were entirely dependent upon him; for example, the Party until 1939, the Soviet state after the war, and the organs of state security throughout. Until 1953 these institutions were reduced to mere executors of Stalin's will.

Unlike Lenin and other Bolsheviks, Stalin regarded the nation as a historical category that was autonomous and permanent. This is most evident in his Marxism and the National Question, which Lenin had ordered him to write so as to counter the influence of Austro-Marxism in Russia. Stalin was careful to place himself within a classical Marxist perspective by defining the nation "as a

product of capitalist development. " However, his actual definition
of the nation stressed those characteristics independent of socioeconomic developments: ethnicity, territory, and culture. Precisely because of his belief in the existence of nationhood, even if it
was never admitted or specifically denied with stereotyped formulas,
Stalin attempted to solve the nationality problem in two new and distinctive ways. First, he placed the most important of the Soviet nations, the Russian nation, in a privileged position and subordinated
the others to it. Second, he considered relations between nations to
be similar to relations between classes, that is, to be determined
by force rather than by education or understanding.

Regarding the nation as a permanent historical fact, Stalin
implicitly concluded that national antagonisms and differences were
permanent and that struggle governs relationships between nations,
just as it does between classes. One can, moreover, deduce from
Stalin's actions that he attached more importance to nations in the
course of history than he did to social classes. Thus he reversed
Lenin's view and treated history as, first and foremost, a continu-
ous series of conflicts between nations. This explains his attitude
in 1922, at the time of the debate over the Soviet Constitution. Be-
lieving at that time that the Russian nation was in the process of
imposing its authority on other nations, Stalin decided to system-
atize this situation by building the Soviet state around the Russian
nation and under its aegis. This is the real meaning of his autonomization plan. Stalin submitted without further discussion when
Lenin forced him to rewrite his constitutional project in terms more
favorable to nationhood and the principle of egalitarianism. This
submission, however, did not mean that he had accepted Lenin's
position. He simply considered that the reality of Russian preeminence would result in the eventual modification of any law that
did not reflect this fact. Until 1953 this Stalinist perception of the
nationality question was at the heart of Soviet policy.

Stalin was able to impose his views in this area because,
apart from Lenin, few Bolsheviks were inclined to devote any attention to the nationality problem. This lack of interest is especially
evident in the case of Leon Trotsky, who, after being ordered by
Lenin to defend the Georgian case against Stalin, remained silent
and allowed Bukharin to fight alone. This indifference to the nationality problem meant that, as of 1922, the Bolsheviks did not
understand what separated them from Stalin, whose hard line toward
the nations seemed, to them, closer to their own analysis than did
Lenin's "national liberalism." Thus, at a time when they still could
have acted against him, the Bolsheviks explicitly or implicitly supported Stalin's policy. Later, when he had consolidated his own
position, Stalin could go even further in his "russification" policies.

A decisive element in Stalin's nationality policy was his conception of the state. He viewed the state not so much as the organized form of power of a particular social class but, first and foremost--and from this stems its permanence--as the framework for a nation's development. Everything in Stalin's work bears witness to this. As soon as he had achieved absolute power, Stalin rejected those conceptions of the state that had prevailed since the Revolution--a transitional state of a new nature having no actual sovereignty, no ties to the former state, and dependent on the working class--and returned to a more traditional understanding. After 1930 the Soviet state began to be defined by its historical dimension and its territory. Stalinist jurists also reintroduced the concept of state sovereignty.[8] These changes were codified in the Constitution of 1936, which legally placed the sovereignty of the state and the sovereignty of the nations that constituted it on an equal footing.

Even more than had the Constitution of 1924, the new Constitution of 1936 established the equality among nations that Lenin had imposed on Stalin in 1922. How can one explain Stalin's apparent adoption of Lenin's views after the latter's death? To what extent did the federal Constitution of 1936 take into account the actual situation with regard to the nations of the USSR? In fact, in 1936 one sees a repetition of what had happened in 1922, the main difference being that Stalin was now the only person making decisions. The state described at the heart of this constitution was a nation-state, and not a new state organized around social classes. But even in 1936 it would have been inappropriate, for reasons of both foreign and domestic policy, openly to grant supremacy to the Russian nation. As a result of the repressive methods by which he had carried out his program of social and political transformation, Stalin was faced with unrest among the peasants and within the army and the Party. Given this situation, he could not afford to add the nations to the list, especially since their capacity for resistance was still very real. The Basmachi revolt, which continued in various forms until the mid-1930s,[9] suggested the persistent danger of national uprisings.

Foreign policy considerations also help to explain Stalin's moderation. Having joined the democratic camp to oppose Adolf Hitler, the Soviet Union wanted to appear as respectable as possible. Were it to move against nationality demands at home in order to benefit the Russian nation, the USSR would be going against the principle of self-determination that formed the basis of the entire interwar European order. Such behavior would appear to justify Hitler's desire to put this order in doubt. Furthermore, the USSR could scarcely represent itself outside Europe as the emancipator of nations if it adopted the form of an imperial power. By main-

taining and preserving the federal principle, Stalin hoped to allay
suspicions and prevent mistrust. During this period, therefore, a
combination of domestic and international reasons led him to preserve the federal framework that Lenin had sought, at least in a
transitional capacity.

Does this imply that Stalin's position had changed? Certainly
not. Even more than in 1922, Stalin could justify his belief that
legal forms did not matter and that Soviet reality would deprive
federalism of any real meaning. Increasingly the Russian center
weighed more and more heavily on the system as a whole. Centralized planning and rapid industrialization, begun in 1928, reinforced the importance of the central organs and the dependence of
the outlying federal republics. In addition, in the early 1930s
Stalin placed the cultural revolution at the service of centralization,
thereby considerably weakening constitutional egalitarianism. In
the 1920s cultural equality had provided a certain compensation to
those nations that had been forcibly incorporated into the USSR.
This equality had guaranteed the further cultural development of
each nation, though this situation was seen as temporary, since all
nations were to progress toward a single international culture after
their own culture had developed. In the 1930s, however, this attitude began to change. National cultures were defined in increasingly
centralized terms and began to be treated as vehicles for a socialist
(Russian) culture. The mass liquidation of national cadres during
this period, and the charge of "bourgeois nationalism" that was
made against any show of sympathy toward national culture, caused
a further weakening of the nationalities vis-à-vis the center.

Any illusion that the nationality problem had been permanently
attenuated by the terror of the late 1930s was dispelled upon the outbreak of the war. The collapse of the USSR in 1941 was not simply
the result of military weakness. If anything, the explosion of the
multinational Soviet state counted even more than did the battle
losses. In the Ukraine, the Caucasus, the Baltic countries--indeed,
everywhere the advance of German armies permitted--the nations
of the USSR demonstrated their tenacity and discontent. What had
happened in 1917 was repeated in 1941. The war opened the way to
centrifugal forces that then tried to find support in the outside world.
Acutely aware of this, Stalin reintroduced concessions to the nations
in order to bring them back into the Soviet fold. After the war,
however, he reverted to his program of the late prewar period, and
carried it even further. Only the Russian nation could now act as
the integrator of other groups. Consequently, Stalin decided that
the Soviet Union thereafter would be a more or less overtly Russian
state. Russia would regain its role of the "elder brother," and its
past and present domination of other nations would be justified by its

historical role and its superior culture.[10] Thus, at the end of
World War II, Soviet nationality policy, after a long series of hesi-
tations, moved clearly in a direction that recalled the prerevolu-
tionary Russian past. The Russian nation was presented both as a
protector and as the bearer of a superior culture to which the other
nations were to adhere.

NATIONALITY POLICY SINCE STALIN

Stalin's successors did not accept either his view of the nationality problem or the practical conclusions that he drew from it.
By 1953, it is true, the authority of the "elder brother" appeared to
have gotten the upper hand over the centrifugal forces and to have
liquidated those national tensions that the war had dramatically revealed. However, Stalin's successors were more sensitive to the
real national tensions revealed by the war than to the seeming national peace that followed it. Aware of the high costs of an attempt
to maintain the Stalinist system, Nikita Khrushchev and his colleagues departed from Stalinism and attempted to strengthen the
Soviet regime by institutionalizing it. The search for greater economic rationality (a preoccupation of all post-Stalin leaders, beginning with Georgii Malenkov) required some deconcentration, if not
decentralization, of decision making. For Stalinist despotism they
wanted to substitute a political system that functioned rationally and
was based on some degree of social consensus. In the realm of
nationality policy, this led them to abandon forced russification in
order to achieve an equilibrium between the dominant Russian political culture and the national cultures. It also led them to accept a
certain degree of political decentralization in order to give some
real meaning to the federal system.

This break with Stalinism was accompanied by another change
that also had an impact on nationality policy. Having denounced
Stalinism, Khrushchev and the others had to give the system a new
basis of legitimacy. They did so by drawing a clear distinction between the accomplishments of Stalinism and the accomplishments of
the Soviet system as a whole. Stalinism had been a deviation,
Khrushchev said; but despite Stalin the Soviet system had remained
dynamic and had accomplished the historical tasks for which it had
been established. It had assured the triumph of socialism and had
started the USSR on the road to Communism. In the field of national
relations, the Soviet system had changed the social consciousness of
the USSR's various national groups. From national consciousness
they had passed on to socialist consciousness and were moving toward
Communist consciousness. As a result, national differences no

longer had a raison d'être, and were mere "survivals of the past."
Khrushchev developed this idea at the Twenty-second Party Congress, where he further suggested that the nations of the USSR,
having already drawn closer to one another (sblizhenie), were advancing toward a point at which they would fuse into a single nation
(sliianie).[11]

One can see the contradiction in which Stalin's successors soon
locked themselves. How could they establish a new legitimacy,
which was to be based on a consensus developed through the recognition of national aspirations, while simultaneously asserting that
the nations of the USSR were moving toward fusion? This contradiction was aggravated by the fact that this assertion had real consequences. Moreover, it was in these consequences that the insoluble
nature of the national problem manifested itself most clearly.

Attempts to institutionalize the Soviet system provided an opportunity for debates at both the center and the periphery on the
difficulties facing the Soviet Union after the death of Stalin. The
emergence of interest groups, even if still weak, was an undeniable
reality. Competition for power led these groups to organize and
regroup--in some instances along functional lines, in others along
national lines. Lavrentii Beria was the first to attempt to use national groups as a force to gain the upper hand over his colleagues.
This competition was kept alive by the maintenance of collective
leadership, which in itself introduced a greater complexity into the
decision-making structure. Now decisions reflected not simply the
wishes of a particular individual but, rather, a balance between
various groups. As a result, with regard to the nationality problem the authority of the Party, the leading group, was sometimes
outweighed by the authority of the army, which was extremely concerned with the security implications of decisions affecting the
nationalities on the periphery of the USSR.

Finally, and this is perhaps the most important point, the
Party itself underwent a profound sociological change. It was no
longer a coherent body with a single voice but, rather a conglomer-
ation of various interests with conflicting views. From its start it
had been a political organ whose members shared a common political education, even if they had some specialized training as well.
Thus, for a long time the Soviet system's rationality was a political
rationality, and found expression in the ideological and decision-
making authority granted to the Party apparatus, which subordinated
other specialists to its own needs. The post-Stalinist apparatus,
however, has changed dramatically because, particularly since the
early 1960s, its recruitment policy has changed. Since then, the
apparatus has recruited its members not only on the basis of political criteria but also on the basis of technical competence. The

consequences of this have been considerable, especially at the periphery. This new technical elite has tended increasingly to hold
that decision making should be a function of reality rather than of
ideology. It has demanded an increasing share of power in decision
making at the highest level, that of the Party, and has refused to
content itself with a subordinate position. At the federal level this
evolution has not yet proved decisive. The political leadership has
retained its supremacy, and the demands of the Party technocrats
are more a source of conflict for the future than a decisive element
determining current policy.

However, in the republics there is evidence that this evolution
has gone further. At this level cooperation has been established
between the Party's political and technocratic components, and this
cooperation often has given priority to rational choices over political ones. In other words, the republic and regional organs have
changed more rapidly than the central apparatus has, and their
evolution has weakened the classical preeminence given to ideology.
The reasons for this difference between the center and the periphery
are clear. At the periphery, national or regional interests have
acted to bring the Party's two components closer together, whereas
at the center, the power struggle has remained a determining factor of attitudes and choices. Increasingly at the periphery, these
shared interests have led to demands that the central apparatus give
up some of its decision-making power. If the technocratic elite in
Moscow could accept such demands because of economic rationality,
the still-dominant political elite could not. As a result, the central
Party elite has attempted to slow the entrance of technocrats into
the decision-making structures.

As long as the Party was coherent and united in its views at
all levels, a partial delegation of power presented few problems.
The present evolution of the Party, however, modifies the situation.
Now even a minor aspect of decision-making power is important to
the extent that problems are approached differently at the center and
at the periphery. As soon as this difference arose, the delegation
of power became a real act of decentralization, entailing the multiplication of decison-making centers. This led to a revival of
those structures and principles that had been sacrificed to centralization in the preceding years: federal institutions and national
capabilities. This new outlook, initiated by Khrushchev, created a
consensus among the Soviet nations. The national elites clearly
understood that the Soviet system was oscillating between federal
stability (which implied a further diffusion of power) and the "construction of Communism" (which pointed to the eventual dissolution
of the federal system). Stalin's successors were unable to choose
between these paths, since they could neither dispense with a national consensus nor renounce their ultimate goal.

This explains why, for five years, the Soviet leadership
placed its hope in "spontaneous" changes that would allow reconciliation of these opposing policy aspects. They were hoping that an
"objective" weakening of national differences would produce a consensus based more on social than on national criteria. Only two
kinds of changes could make this possible: cultural and socioeconomic. Cultural change would emerge from the general use of the
Russian language, which the Soviet leaders believed was already
leading to the disappearance of national languages and cultures. As
for socioeconomic change, Khrushchev and his colleagues believed
that the increased rates of migration and urbanization caused by
development would rapidly create new communities in which ethnic
differences would have no weight.[12] Thus, in the 1960s the Soviet
leadership decided that educational progress and economic development were necessary and sufficient conditions for overcoming national differences.

We may now ask to what extent the post-Stalinist leadership's
perception of the nationality questions represented a radical break
from the Stalinist perception. Clearly, Stalin's successors gave up
the idea of a complete russification of all Soviet nations. Like
Stalin, however, they tried to preserve a basically national and
centralized state. Like Stalin, too, his successors thought that the
Russian nation should play a central role in the organization of the
entire system and that the Russian culture should occupy a pre-
eminent position. What differentiated them from Stalin was their
belief that societal development, per se, would lead to the desired
unity, without any need to resort to force or violence. Embracing
the beliefs of the Second International, the post-Stalinist leadership
hoped that in a developed, industrialized, and urbanized Soviet society, a new social consciousness that would transcend national
aspirations would finally emerge.

The results of the 1970 census[13] dashed all these hopes and
forced the Soviet leaders once again to confront the nationality problem. Without going into detail, it is important to stress the factors
that contributed to this outcome: the demographic stagnation of the
Russians and, indeed, of all Slavic and Baltic groups; the demographic explosion of the "oriental" peoples; the weak migration
(and intermarriage) patterns from the periphery to the center; and
a decline in the use of Russian by some non-Russians, compared
with the 1959 figures. These hard facts negated Khrushchev's
triumphant vision of the drawing together of nations. They removed
any justification for the central integrating role of the Russian nation and for the corresponding system of centralized power. At the
same time, they demonstrated that the fact of nationhood was autonomous of socioeconomic changes and that the future evolution of

the USSR did not imply the future fusion of nations. Finally, these facts emboldened national leaders, who saw the census results as objective reasons and justifications for escalating their demands on the center.

THE NATIONALITY PROBLEM AND FOREIGN POLICY

One final aspect of the Soviet nationality problem is its relation to Soviet foreign policy. This bond between domestic and foreign policy, which has considerable implications for the nationality problem, became particularly evident at the beginning of the 1960s, when Khrushchev responded to his growing domestic difficulties by seeking legitimacy through foreign affairs. Khrushchev's successors have gone even further in this direction, in the belief that peaceful coexistence and cooperation with the other superpower, the United States, is essential for the achievement of their most basic goal: the elimination of Soviet economic difficulties and technological backwardness. However, they have discovered that pursuit of this policy has potentially adverse domestic ramifications. In its dialogue with the capitalist world, the USSR has had to accept some of the other side's rules and, occasionally, to make concessions. By allowing Jews to emigrate in order to satisfy American demands, the Soviet leaders, despite all of their precautions, raised the possibility of emigration for other national groups. Similarly, in signing the Helsinki accord, the Soviet Union agreed to adhere to the humanitarian principles enumerated in the Preamble and Basket Three.

Two of these principles are of particular interest here: the reunion of families and the free movement of people and ideas across state boundaries. In the name of family reunion, Germans who had been detained in the USSR since the war were able to return to their country by the tens of thousands. But their departure from the USSR led to demands for emigration among the Volga Germans, who had resided in Russia for three centuries. Unable to invoke the principle of the reunion of families, they simply invoked national solidarity with those who were leaving and the right of people to emigrate freely. Their example, in turn, prompted other national groups to think about the possibility of joining their compatriots in the West. Emigration apart, moreover, the pursuit of détente with the West has made it riskier for the regime to stifle national dissent by brute force and harder for it to contain the domestic "demonstration effects" of the ongoing and at least partially successful struggle for greater national independence by the Communist countries of Eastern Europe.

Since the early 1970s the Soviet leadership's attitude toward the nationality problem has undergone two modifications. First, the leaders are aware that national difficulties are on the increase; and second, they have come to realize that economic development is going to aggravate these difficulties. Consequently, they have become convinced that the nationality problem must be solved or ameliorated as quickly as possible. Here the phrase "as quickly as possible" does not mean in a generation but, rather, in a few years. The problem has to be solved both before the demographic imbalance, particularly in Central Asia, becomes a threat to the entire system and before militant nationalist sentiments, such as those that have appeared in Georgia and the Baltic republics[14] require massive repression.

The immediate impulse of the current Soviet leadership has been to try to russify the non-Russians by making the ability to speak Russian a virtual requirement for white-collar employment in many of the larger cities of the national republics. Concurrently, the central leadership has sought to russify the national republics by systematically promoting Russians to positions of responsibility there. This russification of political cadres has been quite remarkable, especially in the Armenian Communist Party organization. Nonetheless, the leadership seems aware that such russificatory measures cannot provide a panacea, and has begun an intensified search for alternative possibilities. Among other things, this high-level uncertainty found expression in the creation in 1969 of the Scientific Council, attached to the Academy of Sciences, which is responsible for the investigation of nationality problems under the direction of Academician Evgenyi Zhukov. This council has branches in all the republics. In addition, in 1976 a unionwide conference devoted to nationality problems was organized in Tbilisi by the Soviet Communist Party and by the Georgian Communist organization.[15] And since 1970 more than 200 documentary publications have been issued in the USSR on the same topic. Many of these research efforts have suggested the need for further concessions to national feelings.

This tension between russification and concession to the non-Russians is reflected in the 1977 Constitution. In it, the nations retain the same rights they enjoyed in 1936, with one exception: the right to have national armies has disappeared from the new fundamental law. This, however, had been only a theoretical right, since as of 1938--with the exception of the war years--national armies have been eliminated in favor of individual recruitment (kadrovyi printsip) into corps where nations are mixed and where Russian is the language of command at all levels.[16] In addition, the military law of October 12, 1967, emphasized ethnically mixed units. The

1936 Constitution was thus in opposition to the military laws adopted
after 1936, and the new constitution simply reflects the more recent
laws.

One could have predicted that federalism would be maintained,
given the Soviet leadership's attitude and vocabulary throughout.
The Party continued to repeat that the nations of the USSR have
passed from a state of blossoming (rastsvet) to rapprochement
(sblizhenie), but it did not define the third stage of their evolution
as precisely as it had in the past. For years, national evolution
inevitably ended up in the form of fusion (sliianie), which implies
complete assimilation. More recently, however, a new term has
emerged to indicate this stage: unity (edinstvo), used alone or with
the adjective "complete" (a term first used by Lenin). The difference in meaning between these terms is considerable. Fusion en-
tails not only assimilation but also the eventual dissolution of previously existing elements. Unity, on the other hand, suggests that
the separate elements will continue to exist. The nonassimilation-
ist implications of this concept seem to be a response to criticisms
from the periphery. At the XXV Communist Party Congress held
in February-March 1976, the term "fusion" disappeared from all
speeches; and while Brezhnev referred to the indestructible unity of
the Soviet nations, the delegates of certain republics--including
Moldavia, Georgia, and Estonia--spoke of autonomy.

At the same time, the constitution indicated a hardening at the
center on the issue of centralization, an issue with important national implications. If the constitution preserves the principle of
federalism, it nevertheless defines it very poorly. The republics
have no distinctive legal authority, and Article 73 allows union-
level competence to be extended ad infinitum. Any question need
have only the slightest federal implication for it to pass completely
from republic to central jurisdiction.[17] Although the situation was
not much more favorable for the republics in 1936, at least then
their fields of competence were defined. A second decisive restric-
tion bearing on the republics' sovereignty is related to the leadership role of the Party, now explicitly described in Article 6 of the
new fundamental law, as well as to the introduction of democratic
centralism into the constitution as a fundamental principle of state
organization.* The Party and democratic centralism are institutional arrangements embodying the interests of the working class,
not the interests of the nations. They affirm the supremacy of class
interest over any other kind of interest in the Soviet state.

---

*In 1936 the only mention of the political role played by the
Party was in Article 126, and was very vague.

The 1936 Constitution was much less clear in stressing the importance of these unifying organs, and seemed to affirm the parallel existence of two distinct structures, a federal state and a unified Party. The confusion in the 1977 Constitution suggests that the principle of unity has progressed. Finally, the right to secession has been considerably weakened by the introduction of democratic centralism into the fundamental law. How could this right be exercised when the principle of democratic centralism and the Party stand in opposition to it? Thus the notion of republic competence[18] and the right to secession appear more to be remnants of the past than actual rights that can be exercised. Clearly, the balance of the new constitution has shifted in the direction of increased centralization.

This new balance suggests the current uncertain position of the Soviet leadership, which wants desperately to do something it increasingly realizes it cannot do, and implies that just as had been the case in 1924 and 1936, reality will define the content of the 1977 Constitution--but this time the reality is very different.

NOTES

1. M. Fol. "L'accession de la Finlande à l'indépendance" (Unpublished paper, Paris, 1976).

2. Protokoly VIII. konferentsii RKP (b) (Moscow, 1919), p. 95.

3. N. El'baum, 'Rol' narkomnatsa v nalazhivanii pomoshchi tsentral'nykh raionov strany narodam Srednei Azii," Trudy Institute istorii partii pri TsK KP Turkmenistana (Ashkhabad, TsK KP Turk., 1971), pp. 182 ff.

4. Pervyi s'ezd narodov vostoka (Petrograd, Gosizdat 1920), pp. 31-179. See also A. Bennigsen and C. Quelquejay, Les mouvements nationaux chez les musulmanes de Russie, la sultangalievisme au Tatarstan (Paris, Mouton, 1960).

5. R. Tucker, "Stalinism as Revolution from Above," in his Stalinism, Essays in Historical Interpretation (New York: Norton, 1977), esp. pp. 89-95.

6. V. I. Lenin, Polnoe Sobranie Sochinenii (hereafter PSS) 45: 211-13, 356.

7. H. Carrère d'Encausse, L'Union sovietique de Lenine à Staline (Paris, forthcoming), pp. 421 ff.

8. On this evolution, see Pashukanis, "Mezhdunarodnoe pravo," in Entsiklopediia gosudarstva i prava (Moscow, Gosizdat, 1925) 2: 857 ff.; Pashukanis, Ocherki po mezhdunarodnomu pravu (Moscow, Gosizdat, 1935), pp. 14-15, 20, 78; and N. Kozhevnikov, Sovetskoe gosudarstvo i mezhdunarodnoe pravo, 1917-1947 (Moscow, Gosizdat, 1948), pp. 32 (on the continuity of the state), 180 (on territory).

9. E. Maillart, Des monts célestes aux sables rouges (Paris, n.p., 1934), p. 217, on the Samarkand trial of the Basmachi in 1932; and Observer (pseud. for Jeyoun Bey Hajibeyti), "Soviet Press Comments on the Capture of Ibrahim Bey," Asiatic Review (London) no. 27 (1931): 682-92.

10. For the end of the 1930s, see K. F. Shteppa, Russian Historians and the Soviet State (New Brunswick, N.J.: Rutgers University Press, 1962), pp. 133 ff.; and A. Popov, "Vneshnaia politika samoderzhaviia v XIX veke v krvom zerkale M. N. Pokrovskogo," in Protiv antimarksistskoi Kontesptsii M. N. Pokrovskogo (Moscow, Gosizdat, 1940) 2: 320 ff. For the period after 1945, see "Stalin Honors the Red Army," Pravda, May 25, 1945; and F. Barghoorn, "Stalinism and the Russian Cultural Heritage," Review of Politics 14, no. 2 (April 1952): 178-203.

11. Particularly in XXII. S'ezd Kommunisticheskoi partii Sovetskogo Soiuza. Stenograficheskii otchet (Moscow, 1962), pt. I: 153 ff.

12. Ibid.

13. V. A. Boldyrev, Itogi perepisi naseleniia SSSR (Moscow, Gosstatizdat, 1974); and B. S. Khorev and V. M. Moiseenko, Sdvigi v razmeshchenii naseleniia SSSR (Moscow, Statistika, 1976), pp. 10-14.

14. For example, Zaria vostoka, February 27, 1972, attacks two Georgian workers for "reviving nationalism and supporting sentiments which are foreign to us." Cf. Sovetskaia kul'tura, December 20, 1974. On other "criminal activities" in Georgia, see Zaria vostoka, February 8, 16, and 17, 1977.

15. Zaria vostoka, October 24, 1976, p. 2.

16. On this conference, see Komsomolskaia pravda, October 23, 1976, p. 1; Zaria vostoka, October 23, 1976; and Pravda, October 21, 1976, p. 2.

17. See Paragraph 12 of Article 73, which defines federal competence and reserves to the central government "solution of other questions of federal importance."

18. See Articles 15 and 17 of the 1936 Constitution and Article 19 of the Constitution of the RSFSR.

PART II

NON-RUSSIAN ELITES

MOBILIZED DIASPORA IN TSARIST RUSSIA: THE CASE OF THE BALTIC GERMANS 3

John A. Armstrong

Because of its size and complexity, the Russian polity is an
unusually valuable field for testing general hypotheses concerning
societal interaction over extended periods. In this case study of
the Baltic Germans, I propose to consider six hypotheses concerning the exchange relationship of dominant ethnic elites and mobilized
diasporas. [1] As with all efforts to test theoretical propositions by
using historical evidence, data of uneven value must be utilized.
While much of the analysis here can be based on unusually rich
bodies of quantitative data, [2] documentary evidence on positions of
major individual elite members, expert opinions of historians, and
other, more impressionistic statements must also be used. Presentation of descriptive materials is necessary because the Russian
German diaspora and, especially, its Baltic German core have not
previously been treated in depth in English. Since recourse to varied
types of evidence usually is necessary for scholars studying the
Soviet political system, I hope my approach will suggest some ways
in which a case study of ethnic relations in the contemporary Russian
polity might proceed. The peculiar relationship of the Germans to
the imperial elite was only one link in a chain of mobilized diaspora-
Russian elite interactions that have not yet wholly disappeared. A
detailed examination of this first link can, I believe, provide an indispensable introduction to the contemporary Soviet ethnic complex.

THE BALTS IN THE RUSSIAN GERMAN DIASPORA

The relationship between the Baltic Germans and the entire
German population of the Russian empire as a mobilized diaspora
is fundamental; but it requires examination in some detail, since it
is not derived from my general theoretical framework, nor does it
accord with a superficial observation of the large German population
of nineteenth-century Russia. In sheer numerical terms, by the late

eighteenth century the Balts were an inconsiderable fraction of the total German population of the Russian Empire, which consisted predominantly of agricultural settlements in the southern parts of the empire. These peasant farmers generally were more efficient than their non-German neighbors and, to a limited extent, may have exerted a demonstration effect on them. The large majority of German peasants did not, however, constitute a mobilized diaspora in the way I have defined the term. Nor, with insignificant exceptions, did they provide recruits for the German mobilized diaspora.

This observation does not, however, establish the role of the Balts as the nucleus of the diaspora. It is true that they were a dispersed minority even in "their" provinces. About 8 percent (100,000 among 1,200,000) at the end of the eighteenth century, the Balts slowly declined to 5.5 percent (130,000 among 2,386,000) in 1897. The relatively small area of the provinces permitted the Balts an intensity of social communication often denied to more widely dispersed groups. In numbers and intensity of intercourse they resembled the Athenians or Florentines more than they did most modern ethnic communities. In 1836 Germans in the capital province (St. Petersburg guberniia) were nearly twice as numerous as the Balts (then approximately 110,000). Most of the Petersburgers were urban and had skilled occupations, including a higher proportion of artisans than the Balts. Certainly the Balts even then were not the numerically dominant element in what may be termed a Russian German mobilized diaspora.[3] During the nineteenth and early twentieth centuries, the Balts' relative strength almost surely declined. In fact, they were not even the initial element in the Russian German mobilized diaspora. Some 70 years prior to the incorporation of the Baltic provinces into the Russian Empire,* the "German suburb" (nemetskaia sloboda) of Moscow was officially founded with a population of more than 1,000 (including other West Europeans besides Germans). According to a Balt historian, the sloboda "can be compared to the Jewish quarters, the Ghetto. In principle it was not a new phenomenon in Russia."[4] There were similar ethnic suburbs in Archangel, Nizhnii Novgorod, Voronezh, and Yaroslavl, and in the Urals mining centers. Despite their separate institutions (particularly the Lutheran and Reformed churches), the eighteenth-century Germans tended to assimilate rapidly to the dominant Russian element.[5]

----

*Estonia, Livonia, and the nearby islands were acquired by Russia in 1721; Courland was not acquired until the third partition of Poland (1795), but was associated in many respects with the Russian Empire and its Baltic provinces prior to that date.

The incorporation of the Baltic provinces transformed the situation of the Russian Germans by providing an institutional framework and a high-status reference group as well as a notable numerical reinforcement. While assimilation continued, the permanent presence of a large diaspora of unassimilated Germans in St. Petersburg and Moscow, as well as in the Baltic provinces, was assured for nearly two centuries. Moreover, the same factors (stable institutions and high-status reference group) tended to make this permanent urban diaspora a mobilized diaspora by consolidating its material and cultural advantages compared with the general population of the empire and even with the Russian elite.

The prestige of the Balt nobles (who numbered approximately 2 percent of all Balts) was important in this transformation. Their extremely significant relationship to the imperial dynasty will be treated in detail later. Here one need note only that in this, as in other relationships, both the strength and the weakness of the Balt nobility derived from its sharp contrast with the Russian noble estate. Largely originating in the high Middle Ages, the Baltic nobility was a true nobility of birth, with the traditions and institutions of an autonomous corporative body. Salient among these institutions were the provincial assemblies of the Baltic gubernii, which, despite various imperial measures, maintained until the end of the empire a measure of governmental autonomy second only to that of nearby Finland. The assemblies were estate institutions rather than democratic representative bodies; consequently they were completely dominated by the local nobility.

It is not surprising, therefore, that the nobility was able to assimilate West European noble families (such as the Barclay de Tollys)--or those with successful pretensions to noble status--that acquired estates in the Baltic provinces. Most significant was the way in which the corporate nobility jealously distinguished its status from that of the general nobility of the Russian Empire, which by the eighteenth century was largely a service (chin) nobility. In the imperial service only Germans descended from long-established noble families used the predicative "von." Apparently with official sanction, this style was rigorously denied to the highest Russian officials visiting the Baltic provinces. Only after a period of generations (usually involving intermarriage and the acquisition of local estates) could even Germans who had attained hereditary chin nobility hope for acceptance by the Balt nobility. [6]

It would be wrong, however, to see the "Baltic barons" as the crucial element in consolidating the Russian German diaspora. Baltic urban groups probably were equally strong reference groups for the German diaspora in the Russian cities. Though few of the shopkeepers in the Baltic towns could actually trace their descent from

the Hansa merchants, all benefited from the status of these pioneers
of East European urbanism. The tradition of the free city persisted
in Riga, and to a lesser extent in the smaller cities. Compared with
the new Russian bourgeoisie, virtually severed from its Hansa heritage through the decline of the old centers like Novgorod, the Baltic
burghers retained a pride in mercantile roles and civic participation
to which Germans elsewhere were glad to assimilate. Thus a de-
fender of Balt institutions could make a special point of scorning
Russian urbanism: ". . . and there are no [Russian cities]; there
are residences, ports, villages. Their townsmen are not really
citizens. They have constitutions which stretch their roots in thin
air. Such is the model which was prescribed for the seven-centuries
old Hansa city."[7]

Still more important as a reference group were the Literati.
Occupationally based in the liberal professions--the Lutheran ministry, teaching, law, medicine, and pharmacy--their salient characteristics were their advanced education and cultural attainments.
In this respect they superficially resembled the neighboring Russian
intelligentsia. Other characteristics made the Literati a distinctive
group, however. An intense pride divided them from the merchants
("These good people [who] have a terrible smell of copper coins")
and the "heraldic philistinism" of the Balt nobles, whom the Literati
accused of arrogant, arbitrary manners and protection of their
drunken, loafing offspring.[8] This pride gave more place to devotion
to careers than did the typical Russian intelligent's--or, for that
matter, the Balt noble's. But the principal value held by the Literati
was Bildung as it had emerged in Germany in the early years of the
nineteenth century. The Greek classics constituted the nominal
core of Bildung; but as an intellectual movement, it derived its
prestige from the great literary, philosophical, and scientific writers of the German cultural flowering around 1800. In Germany itself the cultural attainments of the middle classes had led, by the
beginning of the nineteenth century, to a partial accommodation between noble and bourgeois values. It is hardly surprising, therefore, that the Balt nobility found an accommodation with the Balt
bourgeoisie, particularly its Literati, attractive.

As in Germany, the essential elements of this accommodation
were noble acceptance of gymnasium and university education as
formal criteria for admission to public service and polite society.
In return, the professional segment of the bourgeoisie (which a considerable number of nobles eventually joined as scholars and writers,
but not as clergymen) incorporated important elements of the aristocratic life style into the educational system. As in Germany, this
accommodation was compromising, in both senses of the word, for
both the noble and the bourgeois sides. For a long time, however,

within the Russian context it strengthened both elements: the bourgeoisie acquired more of the reflected prestige of the Baltic nobility,
so influential in tsarist court circles; the nobility added valuable
modernizing skills to its semifeudal prestige.

Like other mobilized diasporas, the Balts had high literacy
rates; the relatively high level of women's literacy is especially significant as an indicator of modernization. Not surprisingly, fertility
(or at least the ratio of surviving children) was low, as Table 3.1 indicates. These relationships held for the most significant age groups
even in comparison with the non-German population of Riga, which
had exceptional opportunities in relation to most of the Russian Empire. Elementary education and literacy, while basic to the overall
position of the Balts, played no significant role in the process of
elite accommodation. In this respect, as in Germany, the gymnasium was secondary both as an educational level and as an accommodation mechanism. By 1880 total enrollment in Baltic province
gymnasien (excluding the Russian-language Alexander Gymnasium
in Riga) was about 2,100; it increased by about one-third during the
following decade before significant russification of the secondary
schools occurred. Of this total, three-quarters were Lutheran; and
about 85 percent of the Lutherans were German, resulting in a total
German Baltic secondary enrollment on the order of 1,400 in 1880
and 2,000 ten years later. [9]

As in Germany, the Baltic gymnasium enrolled most of the
sons of the local nobility as well as the various bourgeois strata.
With its emphasis on the classics, its close attachment to the
Lutheran Church, and its Literati teaching staff, the gymnasium
served to assimilate a majority of males of the nineteenth-century
Balt population to the Bildung values inculcated by the Literati.
However (again as in Germany), it was primarily a preparatory
school for the university, in which most of its graduates enrolled.
The university was the principal agency for inculcating noble as well
as bourgeois values. As in some parts of Germany, university education was an established element of the noble and the bourgeois life
styles for centuries before the German cultural revival that, in the
Baltic provinces, culminated in the reestablishment of Dorpat University in 1802. [10] The attention that Balt writers devoted to this
tradition suggests the salience of university education among their
values--and also provides us with quantitative data for unusually remote periods. Naturally data are very fragmentary; but it is clear
that a Dutch institution (Leiden), as well as north German universities, drew sizable numbers of Balts during the sixteenth century.
In 1632 the first Dorpat University opened under Swedish rule. During its 34 years of major activity (Dorpat was intermittently closed
from then on), it matriculated, in the average decade, about 150

TABLE 3.1

Mobilization Characteristics of Riga City Population, 1883 and 1925

Ethnic Group (by language)	Ratio of Children to Women*	Literacy, 1883					School Attendance, 1925 (percent of school-age children)		
		Males 14–30		Females 14–30		Differential (percent)	Male	Female	Difference
		Total	Percent Literate	Total	Percent Literate				
German	.80	10,521	94.2	12,163	89.8	4.4	93.1	92.9	.2
Estonian and Latvian	1.10	6,491	75.7	6,835	52.2	23.5	91.4	91.6	-.2
Russian	.80	5,189	76.6	3,932	43.5	33.1	83.9	84.5	-.6
Jewish	1.14	2,135	65.8	2,691	32.9	32.9	89.3	88.7	.6

*Children aged 0–6, women aged 14–30, in 1883.

Source: Calculations based on statistics in P. Gerstfeldt, "Zur Schulfrage in Riga," Baltische Monatsschrift 32 (1885): 512–14; Jakob Lestschinsky, ed., Schriften für Wirtschaft und Statistik (Berlin: Yiddish Scientific Institute, 1928), p. 246.

young men from the future Baltic provinces and an equal number
from Sweden and Germany. Very incomplete data would suggest
that another 100-200 Balts entered the German universities in each
decade of the seventeenth century. For the eighteenth century the
data, while still incomplete, are much more ample for the Protestant
German universities, which unquestionably attracted an overwhelming majority of Balt university matriculants, some 300 per decade.[11]

Matriculants from the Baltic provinces exhibited a further slow
but steady increase in the decades after Dorpat University was re-
opened. (I have not located figures on Balt enrollments abroad in the
nineteenth century, but the fact that only one-fifteenth of Dorpat
matriculants went on to German universities[12] suggests that those
matriculating abroad would not substantially change the totals in
Table 3.2, nor would the small numbers in Russian elite higher
education.) By West European standards (even if one restricts the
comparable group to urban males) Balt university matriculation was
astonishingly high. The Balt enrollment at Dorpat of about 300 per
100,000 total population in the early 1830s was vastly higher than
the 35 per 100,000 in German Reich universities in the same period,
or even the 1882 Reich figure of 50 per 100,000. In fact, by the
start of the nineteenth century the Balts apparently had attained
levels that France and Germany did not exceed until after World
War II.[13] By the latter part of the nineteenth century it seems safe
to conclude that (1) secondary school graduation and some higher
education--virtual equivalents, since nearly all gymnasium graduates
matriculated--were values so widespread among the Balt population
that they can be considered (as in twentieth-century America) an
achievement norm, even though most boys did not in fact attain the
goal; and (2) Balt educational attainments were so high relative to
the very low standards of the Russian Empire that this factor alone
made the Balts an elite in terms of modernizing capacities.

The significance of Dorpat University education as a universal
achievement standard lies primarily in the latent effects of the actual content of this education upon the bourgeois strata of the Balt
population since, as discussed below, noble accommodation to bourgeois values took place earlier, in the gymnasium. In a purely
formal sense, university education represented a continuation and
intensification of the Bildung values transmitted by the Literati.
The notable contingent of noble professors (contrasted with the virtual absence of nobles among gymnasium teachers) suggests that,
as in Germany, the nobility found the higher institution more congenial. The Dorpat faculty was a major mechanism for transmitting
cultural values from Germany. During its first third of a century,
just under half of the instructors came from Germany, virtually all
of them from the Protestant North. Still, even at that beginning

stage, 46 of 131 faculty members could be recruited from the Baltic provinces themselves; from then on, about half were not only local men but also Dorpat alumni. Hence the faculty tended to become an inbred body with a Herrenvolk attitude that even sympathetic outsiders found irritating. This inbreeding, however, made Dorpat a major factor in amalgamating Balt dialects and customs.[14]

As in Germany, the major institutional mechanism for accommodating noble life styles was the Korporation or student fraternity, the more important at Dorpat because, in contrast with Prussia, it did not have to compete with officer corps loyalties. The first Balt fraternity, Curonia, began in north German universities toward the end of the eighteenth century, although it was not formally organized at Dorpat until 1821. Despite considerable opposition, Estonia, Livonia, and Fraternitas Rigensis were founded shortly afterward. As the names indicate, these fraternities divided the Balts from each province, but tended to unite noble and bourgeois, although the existence of the separate Riga fraternity suggests that the large and prestigious middle-class contingent from the principal urban center preferred--or was compelled--to organize separately.[15] Within each fraternity, peer group loyalties were fostered by ritual beer drinking. A principal effect of these frequent and protracted bouts was to restrict severely the Literati virtues of diligent study while inculcating an aristocratic atmosphere of easygoing scorn for intellectualism. Most important among the mechanisms for assimilating noble values were the duels. Corporate loyalties (extended into postgraduate days by the "old boy" networks) were intensified, since the duels occurred only between members of different fraternities. The whole ritual presupposed the existence of other fraternities of equal status or "honor," which in practice meant membership of Germans drawn from similar social strata.

If one assumes that the German population of the two imperial capitals plus the smaller urban centers in St. Petersburg guberniia was somewhat more than twice the number of the Balts, the numerical impact of Dorpat matriculation was demonstrably much lower on the former. My very approximate estimates indicate that Russian German matriculation from outside the Baltic provinces was about one-eighth of Balt matriculation during 1802-10, rose to one-sixth in the 1830s, and remained at the latter level thereafter. Consequently, scarcely more than 1 percent of the relevant non-Balt Russian German urban males could have matriculated at Dorpat. A number of factors suggests that even this level--low only in comparison with more recent levels in Western Europe and similar areas--had a significant impact on the perceptions and life styles of the Russian Germans. Even those in rural areas (insofar as they were Lutheran) obtained many of their pastors from the Dorpat

theological faculty. Although Lutheranism was not a decisive criterion for membership in the German diaspora, the church organization was a highly important transmission belt for the essential
cultural attitudes. Even when they were only loosely connected with
German communities, the multitude of Dorpat-trained specialists
scattered in important posts throughout the empire enhanced the
prestige of Germans in general; and therefore they became, to some
extent, reference figures.

It remains to be demonstrated how, and to what extent, the
accommodation of noble and bourgeois values through the socializing
experience of Dorpat University extended to other urban Germans of
the Russian Empire. First, one must accept the fact that numerous
highly placed Russian German families (particularly in St. Petersburg, but to some extent among the Balt nobility itself) preferred a
different socializing experience for their sons. The reestablishment of Dorpat University preceded the opening (1811) of the most
important imperial training institution, the Tsarskoe Selo Lycée,
by only nine years. The Imperial School of Jurisprudence, founded
24 years later, was hardly less significant. Both were highly selective, with 25 to 35 as each school's annual matriculation. Admission was formally restricted to boys from families that had already
obtained noble status, most commonly as chin nobles. The most
appropriate preparation for entry (both elite schools were essentially secondary institutions with an additional two or three years of
higher education stressing law) was attendance at upper-class preparatory schools in St. Petersburg and Moscow.

Taken together, the two elite institutions and the preparatory
schools (in St. Petersburg the latter graduated only 100 per year)
provided an extraordinarily favorable route to high posts in the imperial government. No family ambitious for its sons' success could
lightly reject this route in favor of the Baltic educational system,
however attractive the latter might be from the ethnic standpoint.
According to Allen A. Sinel's calculation, graduates of the Tsarskoe
Selo Lycée (renamed the Alexander Lycée in 1843) and the School of
Jurisprudence produced 277 ministers, State Council members, and
senators, between 1812 and 1905,[16] from among graduates totaling
on the order of 3,000 up to 1880, the last year in which graduates
had any likelihood of attaining such high rank by 1905. My own calculation for the first 12 classes of the lycée suggests that about half
attained the high distinction of fourth chin or above.

It is significant, then, that whereas Dorpat University constituted a mechanism for accommodating aristocratic and bourgeois
values within a single ethnic group, the two imperial training institutions (with their homogeneously aristocratic student bodies) constituted mechanisms for accommodating Russian and German ethnic

values. A Lutheran church was constructed in Tsarskoe Selo in
1818, and its pastor officially appointed chaplain for Protestant students. Apparently most of the early instructors at the Lycée were
Russians (often Orthodox seminary graduates), but nearly all had
studied in Germany. When a Roman law course was introduced (as
a preface to Russian law), the teacher, a German-educated Balt
named Egor von Wrangel, spoke Russian poorly--or so the Russian
historian of the school, writing from the vastly altered perspective
of 1911, asserts. [17] In any event Wrangel's courses, at his retirement in 1837, were divided among three Russians. Moreover, Russian history was stressed and the German language assigned merely
a place of parity with French--which, of course, many of the Russian
and some German students spoke habitually.

In fact, the lycée appears to have been a microcosm of St.
Petersburg society, which dismayed both those Russians and those
Germans who were intensely attached to their native cultures. The
bitterly anti-German Slavophile F. F. Vigel described St. Petersburg as a "Babylon" with its mixture of languages and life styles,
although he was confident the "Russian character" would triumph
even over French cuisine. [18] A Balt contemporary echoed Vigel's
scorn without reflecting his optimism: "It [St. Petersburg] has its
own nationality, its own view and customs, even its own speech.
Russian, French, German, and English elements have melted together in it, so that it belongs to none of these nations, which feel
more alien in the Russian government center than in Berlin, Vienna,
Paris, or London."[19] Conversely, the fundamental compatibility of
the elite institutions' socializing process, which ultimately prescribed
the same books, drew on the classical cultural tradition in its West
European version, and inculcated many of the same cosmopolitan
values as the older versions of Bildung, satisfied noble or upwardly
mobile Germans who envisaged the Russian Empire as an ecumenical
institution.

The inescapable tension between easy acceptance of cosmopolitan styles and values, on the one hand, and enhanced devotion to the
culture of their "great society" in Germany, on the other, distinguished the Russian Germans as what I have termed a "situational
mobilized diaspora." In contrast with the "archetypal diaspora,"
which relies primarily on a distinctive religious myth to retain its
identity, the "situational diaspora," which is a fragment of a larger
society, must maintain the conviction that this "great society" has a
superior culture and that the diaspora can maintain its superiority
to the surrounding populations by sharing in this culture. A superficial assessment of the position of the Germans, especially their
Baltic component, would, it is true, give the impression that their
Lutheranism constituted a distinguishing myth. Without in any way

questioning the intense devotion of individual Balts to their church,
I am compelled to conclude that the Lutheran Church did not provide
a permanent focus of identity comparable, say, with Judaism among
the Jewish diaspora or Zoroastrianism for the Parsees.

To a very considerable extent the impression of religious in-
transigence arises from the fierce Balt opposition to Orthodox efforts to convert the peasantry of the Baltic provinces. But these
peasants were Latvians and Estonians, not Germans; and the Balts
rightly saw the missionary activities as an effort to drive a wedge
between them and the lower classes, as a prelude to wholesale
russification of the provinces. This consideration, along with very
natural resentment toward the Orthodox who saw a need to convert
populations that had been Christian for half a millennium, is sufficient to explain the strength of Balt reaction. Naturally, too, many
of the Lutheran clergy, and the small number of Calvinist clerics in
metropolitan areas, all closely associated with the Literati, strove
to maintain the religious identity of their fellow ethnics. One St.
Petersburg pastor remarked, for example, that an admiral of the
Livonian nobility "would not have been a Baltic German of the right
sort if he had not remained as unconditionally loyal to his Protestant
church [as to the German language]."[20]

The most prestigious members of the Balt group perceived no
fundamental religious difference between Lutheranism and Russian
Orthodoxy. One of the grandest of the Balt seigneurs, Count Alexander Keyserling, exemplifies this attitude. Writing to his mother
about his future Orthodox mother-in-law, Countess Kankrin, he commented, "Each evening the dark mother [as the family called the
countess] crosses us and blesses us without fail; still there could
be no more tolerant and sound views concerning the different de-
nominations than this family has."[21] Later he had his own daughter
baptized in the Orthodox faith and, as late as 1874, stressed his belief in the essential religious tolerance of the Russian government.
Even when protesting (in his role as provincial estates officer) official pressure, Keyserling indicated he had no objections to accommodations with Orthodoxy as such: "If free will is to be respected even
in appearance, one readily recognises that one does not compromise
oneself in the least by visiting a strange church. But if the secular
power uses force . . . it is a question of the very heart of the inner
man, of his dignity of conscience."[22]

It would have been hard for a man like Keyserling, on intimate
terms with the Protestant ruling houses of Europe, to take a more
rigorous line toward Orthodoxy, for Protestant princesses regularly
converted when marrying into the Russian imperial dynasty: "For
every daughter of a Protestant prince who agrees to be married off
to Russia 'It [Petersburg] is well worth a Mass.'"[23] To many Balts

the essential point was not a princess's conversion (Grand Duchess Helen Pavlovna, daughter of the duke of Württemberg, gave up not only her religion but also her first name, Friedereke, on marrying Mikhail, younger brother of Nicholas I), but whether she retained close friendships with Balts and "remained in the German world of ideas."[24]

A summary way of viewing the situation of the Russian German mobilized diaspora is to see those involved as objects of two processes of accommodation. One, centering on Balt institutions like Dorpat University, tended to unify and isolate the ethnic group by accommodating its divergent social strata. The other, centering on the imperial elite schools, tended to accommodate the values of very high-status Germans and Russians at the expense of ethnic distinctiveness. Nevertheless, it would be a gross oversimplification to regard these interethnic class accommodations as necessarily incompatible with ethnic persistence, from the standpoint of the interests of individuals actually involved in the patterns of interaction.

In an imperial system with rapidly expanding opportunities, the relatively minor immediate concessions that an upwardly mobile or ambitious person had to make to cosmopolitan values and Orthodox religion did not appear to be incompatible with ethnic values. Even men from Literati families took Russian wives and brought their children up as Orthodox--until, perhaps, a purely personal catastrophe reduced their life chances in the broader society. (For instance, Reinhard Wittram's uncle Theodor had virtually assimilated to the Russian milieu in which he served as an astronomer until his wife, a Reich German, deserted him for a Russian. Theodor had wanted his children to have Russian as their primary language, but after the desertion he took them back to the Baltic provinces for a German education.[25] Ethnic identity in marginal cases is highly susceptible to such accidents.) For the majority of the Russian Germans, and especially the Balts, such reduction in life chances could not proceed from accidents alone, however. In order to understand their ultimate disillusion with their prospects in the empire, and their consequent retreat to more narrowly ethnic values, one has to turn to consideration of the social dynamics of the broader modernizing polity.

THE EXCHANGE RELATIONSHIP BETWEEN DIASPORA AND DOMINANT ELITES

Regarding any pattern of interaction as an exchange relationship requires that there be (1) some equality of bargaining power between the partners to the relation and (2) perception by salient

actors of the reciprocal utilities of the relationship. When the partners are ethnic groups, it is hard to conceive of this relationship as
a conscious one except at the elite level. As far as the Balts or
even all urban Russian Germans were concerned, this qualification
was not troublesome, since, as indicated at various points in this
essay, a large majority of these German groups were "elite" in
terms of their ability to perceive their situation in the Russian polity. For the limited purposes of this study, a Russian "elite" with
similar awareness may be analytically isolated from the Russian
masses. At the same time, as noted earlier, one must always bear
in mind that both elites contained persons from differing social
strata, with correspondingly diverse interests and perceptions.

An initial, but crucial hypothesis concerning the relations between the two elites is that within the multiethnic polity, the mobilized diaspora is temporarily indispensable for the dominant ethnic
elite. This proposition assumes that the Russians (as the dominant
elite) desired economic modernization during the nineteenth century; hence they were eager to secure the requisite skills. It remains to be demonstrated that Russian Germans (notably Balts) in
fact supplied a very high proportion of the strictly limited skills
available. Fortunately, the most significant evidence for this proposition can be summarized rather concisely, for the most part in
quantitative form. There is no doubt that a large portion of the top
elite of the tsarist regime--the high officers of the court, the military, and the civil service--were Germans. The most reasonable
estimates run from 18 percent to more than 33 percent for the late
eighteenth and the nineteenth centuries.[26] My own calculation is
that about 70 of the 214 Tsarskoe Selo Lycée graduates were German,
with a somewhat higher proportion among the half who reached a top
elite position (as indicated by attaining fourth chin). All of these estimates are based on surnames, assisted in a few instances by other
biographical information.

However, a considerable number of men with German names
did not have any contact with the German diaspora as a cultural or
institutional group. Consequently, only after one has identified the
structural features relating a type of official to a German milieu can
one really maintain, even as a statistical generalization, that men
with German names among these officials are apt to constitute part
of the diaspora contribution to the empire's service. Because of the
structural analysis presented earlier, I believe that one can be fairly confident in making such a generalization about graduates of the
Tsarskoe Selo Lycée, its successor, and the Institute of Jurisprudence. Clearly, however, the contribution of Balt institutions like
Dorpat University, with their intensely German socializing experiences, is much more certainly attributable to the German mobilized
diaspora.

As suggested earlier, study at Dorpat University did not provide as certain a path to high office as did the imperial elite institutions. Nevertheless, as indicated in Table 3.2, the relatively few Dorpat matriculants who went on to general civil service (as distinguished from the numerous physicians, scholars, and scientists who, in the Russian system, also attained chin by working in state institutions) and to military service made a very respectable showing in career attainments. In fact, for the period 1802-55, 20 percent of the ethnic German Dorpat graduates in these civil and military careers attained fourth chin (Balts and other Russian Germans made virtually identical showings), compared with 50 percent of the Tsarskoe Selo graduates and a mere 5 percent of all imperial civil servants entering with the advanced standing associated with higher education. In absolute terms (probably somewhat understated because of biographical underreporting), for each of its first 54 years Dorpat supplied the imperial civil service with one civil servant and .75 military officers who attained high rank, whereas the Tsarskoe Selo Lycée German graduates supplied somewhat more than one man per annum in such rank, nearly all in the civil service.

TABLE 3.2

Imperial Service Attainments of Dorpat Matriculants, 1802-70

Period	Civil Servants Attaining		Military Officers Attaining	
	Total	Fourth Chin	Total	Fourth Chin
1802-25 (Alexander I)				
Baltic Germans	46	14	36	20
Other Russian Germans	25	7	23	5
1826-55 (Nicholas I)				
Baltic Germans	131	21	17	6
Other Russian Germans	80	13	7	2
1856-70 (incomplete careers)				
Baltic Germans	38	1	6	0
Other Russian Germans	66	3	6	0

Source: For methods of calculation, see note 2. My estimate of the overall annual rate of attainment of fourth chin is discussed in my The European Administrative Elite (Princeton, N.J.: Princeton University Press, 1973), pp. 341 ff.

Thus Dorpat's overall contribution probably was slightly higher
than Tsarskoe Selo's for this early period, though less than that of
the Germans from both imperial elite training institutions, to say
nothing of those (of less certain ethnic attachments) graduating from
military academies. Together Dorpat and the two elite institutions
may have contributed four men per year around the middle of the
nineteenth century to the top fourth-chin level; my estimate for a
slightly more restricted group (civil servants plus only those of
higher military rank who at some time held civil posts) is 16 per
annum throughout the empire for the same period. The German
diaspora provided, according to this very rough calculation, about
25 percent of the top officers of the tsarist apparatus--an estimate
on the low side compared with those cited above, but undoubtedly a
minimal one because it embraces only men who certainly had socializing experiences attaching them to the diaspora.

The comparisons just discussed demonstrate both the relatively restricted role of Dorpat University in comparison with elite
training institutions, and the high success of the few members of
its student body who chose to embark on imperial civil or military
careers in comparison with those trained in Russia proper. The
main service of Dorpat training for the imperial system as a whole
lay in quite a different direction: the provision of skills desperately
needed in the modernizing polity, particularly in medical fields.
Like many dominant elites in relatively unsophisticated polities, the
Russian rulers and high officials had had to turn to foreigners for
medical skills as early as the sixteenth century. Even in Moscow
the common people regarded medical or anatomical knowledge as
dangerous magic: a German painter whose house caught fire was
almost thrown into the flames by a mob discovering that he possessed
a human skull; two Russian medical students and a foreign physician
were lynched during the Stresltsy uprising of 1682.

After the incorporation of the Baltic provinces, Balts and other
Russian Germans returned from West European studies with highly
appreciated medical skills.[27] Dorpat University began training
physicians and pharmacists immediately after its reestablishment.
It would be easy to calculate the number who completed such training. However, from the standpoint of empire needs, "wastage"
(deaths before careers were really begun, failure to practice medicine, or practice abroad or in the Baltic provinces themselves) was
high and irregularly distributed over time. The net German ethnic
contribution of Dorpat University to the higher medical staff of the
empire (as presented in Figure 3.2) is a far more significant figure.[28] German increments from Dorpat can be calculated for the
entire period 1806-85, but can be related to the total Russian Empire higher medical personnel only after 1845. At that date (as the

FIGURE 3.1

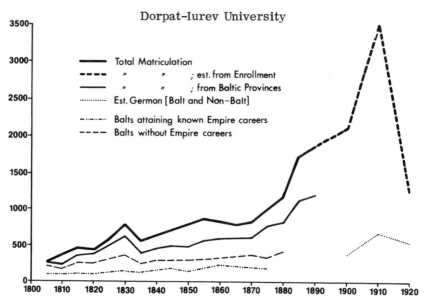

Dorpat-Iurev University

Total Matriculation
    ″   ″   ; est. from Enrollment
    ″   ″   ; from Baltic Provinces
Est. German [Balt and Non-Balt]

Balts attaining known Empire careers
Balts without Empire careers

Source: Author's composition.

figure indicates) the cumulative Dorpat contribution was still relatively small. Although I have not been able to find overall figures
for the following decade, it is evident that the repressive policies
of Nicholas I (for example, the major Polish medical school at Vilna
had been practically closed in 1832) drastically affected the supply
of trained medical personnel. The regime's concern is indicated by
the fact that the 1849 decree limiting university enrollments specifically excepted medicine. During this critical period Dorpat's significantly increased output provided a large share of the domestic
increment, although there was probably a considerable supply of
men trained abroad. Even after a notable influx (which one can estimate fairly accurately) of graduates from Moscow University and
the St. Petersburg Medical-Surgical Academy began in 1857, Dorpat
provided a very substantial proportion of the empire's increments.
Only after 1870, when Kiev, Kharkov, and Warsaw universities began to supply large numbers of higher medical personnel, did
Dorpat's contribution become minor.

    In other words, it was during the most critical quarter-
century (1845-70), or perhaps a few years earlier, when the ground-
work for social modernization (industrial takeoff occurred a generation later) was being laid that the Balts and their university contributed most heavily to the empire's medical needs. As the historian

FIGURE 3.2

Annual Increments to Higher Medical Staff,
1845–85, and Total Supply at circa 1845

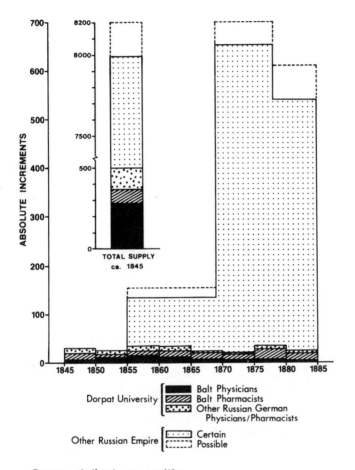

Source: Author's composition.

Roderick E. McGrew puts it: "The physicians were part of an immense cultural revolution which was taking place in Russia and
which, by the middle of the 19th century, utterly changed the character of Russia's internal life." Certainly one cannot assert that
the Balts' contribution was "indispensable" to the imperial polity's
survival, but the rising standards of medical care (compared with
the prevalence of epidemics in the preceding decades)[29] facilitated
the polity's responses to the crisis of the Crimean War and the upheavals accompanying the reforms of the 1860s.

My second hypothesis is that the mobilized diaspora depends for security on the dominant ethnic elite. Under an autocratic regime like that of the tsars, with a high degree of social control (in contrast with polities where conflicting ethnic forces have more leeway to jeopardize a diaspora's position), this proposition may appear to be self-evident. Since the analysis presupposes a conscious exchange relationship between diaspora and dominant ethnic elite, it is important to demonstrate the former's awareness of the situation. This awareness is indirectly demonstrated by the great attention the Balt provincial journals devoted to the affairs of the empire outside their own provinces. This attention (doubtless exceeded by the Petersburg German press) was highest from 1845 to 1865, precisely the years when the Balts were playing their most important role in the social modernization of Russia.

A fairly obvious element of the Russian German diaspora's dependence on the imperial regime was the awareness of the reciprocal relationship between the services that its members performed for the empire and the immense opportunities that the Eurasian polity opened to what might otherwise have been a minor provincial ruling stratum. The theme, which appears in many forms in Balt and other Russian German writings of the nineteenth century, is best conveyed by a few lengthy quotations from contemporaries and from recent historians, such as Reinhard Wittram, who have summarized their attitudes. Wittram writes:

Many factors made movement to Russia attractive [for mid-19th century Balts]: the ease of making a lot of money, the possibility of relatively quickly acquiring an independent position, the breadth of life chances, the aristocratic style of upper-class life (especially for those with higher education), the Russian tolerance for foreign ways. So long as belonging to the nobility was a highly favorable qualification for social position in East Europe, the relatively easy access to the Russian service nobility appeared worth striving for. The Crown service, with its varied opportunities, afforded good compensation and did not require excessive exertion; promotion to high posts was virtually assured to the industrious and honest. . . . A certain risk-taking propensity was required to move into a strange environment. . . . Whoever sought danger could, however, easily find it in Russia by another means: he had only to go farther East, to the neighborhood of the inner Asian nomadic peoples, to the regions of the tundra and icy blizzards. In fact, Germans rapidly became

prominent in the "Asian consular service" as well as
in scientific and technical work in the colonial areas of
the empire.[30]

A lead editorial in the Baltische Monatsschrift (January 1870) says
much the same thing in more deferential terms:

> Up to some fifteen years ago the Baltic provinces were
> in a sense among the most fortunate areas which one
> could see. For a long time they had been under the
> scepter of a powerful Empire, they were spared wars
> and feuds which earlier had made them victims. . . .
> The Russian overlord in fact usually was amicably in-
> clined toward his German subjects. Not that these
> provinces were favored at the cost of the other prov-
> inces of the Empire--they did their share, in fact they
> carried more of the burdens than the others, and they
> could do more because they worked and earned more.
> But they were permitted to work in their own fashion,
> they paid their taxes and no one inquired much as to
> how they did it. . . . We saw everything working in
> favor of our fortunate existence as deriving from our
> German character; every social and political force in
> our area was German, and what was German could be
> sure of attaining power and status in the Empire. . . .
> While we were accustomed to lead at home and to attain
> great success in the Empire, we believed our claim to
> leadership and success to be based on our being Ger-
> man, or rather nobles and bourgeois of Courland,
> Livonia, and Estonia.
>   When we looked to the West we considered our-
> selves uplifted by a vague feeling of belonging to a
> people which strove for high goals and attained great
> successes by struggle and industriousness [but scorned
> the social turmoil then afflicting Germany]. . . . When
> we looked to the East we saw a strong overlord whose
> arm protected us from disorder and preserved for us
> the blessings of peace. Further, we saw a broad field
> in which our sons and younger brothers had always been
> able to make a way and a career for themselves with
> slight effort, where a gracious monarch regarded us
> with great, well-earned trust.[31]

Apart from the stress on career opportunities, two themes stand
out in these passages: the overriding importance of the peace

imposed by the power of the Russian Empire, and the fervent devotion to the imperial dynasty. Both themes implicitly counterpose an
ecumenical polity to narrower bases of political organization. Writing in 1930, Hans Rothfels identified Balt attachment to the ideal of
a supranational empire as aristocratic antipathy toward nationalism.[32]

There is much to support this analysis. The quasi-feudal nature of Balt social organization presupposed a hierarchy of vaguely
delimited powers rather than the sharp partitions of modern sovereignty. The cosmopolitan outlook of many bourgeois as well as
Russian German nobles, dominant in St. Petersburg, though con-
taining a strong German cultural component, was avowedly supranational. The history of the Baltic provinces suggests a further
factor: the nostalgia for a great ecumenical empire. The Balts had
originally conquered their lands as part of the twelfth-century cru-
sading movement; until 1558 they were nominal subjects of the Holy
Roman Empire. Vestigial as the powers of this empire were in such
a remote area, significant symbols of the attachment to the ecumene
of Western Christendom persisted (for example, the highest appeal
court was the Reichskammergericht in Wetzlar).[33] In the mid-
sixteenth century the Reformation turned the dominant Balt elements
against the Roman Catholic Church and the Catholic Hapsburg emperor. Moreover, when the Balts appealed to the latter for aid
against the first Russian invasion under Ivan IV, none was forthcoming, although the Holy Roman Empire agencies did consider the
appeal in their usual ineffectual manner.

The two centuries of warfare and division (Courland went to
Poland, Livonia and Estonia to Sweden) stimulated the nostalgia for
membership in an ecumenical polity; despite the identity of religion,
even Swedish rule was resented as petty tyranny. The strength with
which the Russian Empire returned under Peter I (1721) apparently
led the Balt population to acquiesce with alacrity to Russian rule
even if it did not precisely welcome it.[34] Here was an empire with
most of the symbols of the Holy Roman Empire: supranational
character, Christian legitimization (more compatible with Lutheranism than was Roman Catholicism), and even the Roman eagles.

My third hypothesis is that from the internal standpoint, the
delicate balance of forces maintaining a mobilized diaspora position
within the multiethnic polity is most apt to be upset by a sharp overall rise in social mobility.

As just indicated, the Balts correctly identified the imperial
house as their principal protector. Furthermore, until the late
nineteenth century they enjoyed the protection of nearly all high officials, with whom the Balts had studied in institutions like the Tsarskoe
Selo Lycée and had served as comrades at innumerable far-flung posts.
Occasionally, to be sure, a late eighteenth- or early nineteenth-

century imperial officer would confound a modernizing experiment
among the Balts, derived from their sensitivity to European movements, with subversion. For example, in the 1820s Marquis Filippo
O. Paulucci, governor-general of the Baltic provinces, suspected
the Balt Masonic organizations (Germans constituted about half of the
early Freemasons in St. Petersburg as well) of treasonable tendencies. He also suspected Dorpat University--a more crucial Balt in-
novation--of spreading "utopian" ideas.[35] The conservative nature
of the dominant Baltic elements, and their eagerness to aid the Petersburg regime against its "radical" or nationalist enemies (a common
bugbear was Roman Catholicism, with its local manifestation of Polish
rebelliousness), was so manifest that such friction was merely epi-
sodic.

On the other hand, a significant current of real anti-Germanism
had long been present among nonruling strata (including many old
noble families) in Russia. Revolts against the Westernizing measures
of Peter I had anti-German overtones that persisted strongly during
the next two reigns. Vigorous subordinate officials such as V. N.
Tatishev reacted against the "reign of Germans" (including few Balts)
in the mining industry during the 1730s;[36] and some leaders of the
noble opposition to Catherine II, such as Prince M. M. Shcherbatov,
resented excessive German influence.

Most Balt writers regarded the reigns of Catherine and Alexander I as periods during which strong, wily rulers were able to dim-
inish the force of anti-Germanism.[37] With his tendency to syncretism
between Protestantism and Orthodoxy, Alexander (denounced by some
Russians as "our Russian-German Tsar") was perceived as diminish-
ing the exclusive claims of Orthodoxy, which constituted the real backbone of Russian national distinctiveness.[38] For a long time the Russian Germans tended to see such ethnocentric attitudes as anachronisms that modernization would dissipate. As a leading Balt writer
on the history of the Germans in Russia put it:

> Russia might wish to retain its peculiarity and national
> traits in many respects forever, but it is certain that
> its true entry into world history dates from the time of
> its rapprochement to Western Europe, of the penetra-
> tion and ultimate destruction of the Chinese wall which
> separated Russia from general civilization, from par-
> ticipation in the blessings of general human progress
> in the fields of material, intellectual, and moral devel-
> opment.[39]

From the eighteenth century on, ethnocentric strains in Russian
thought took exactly the opposite position: "German" dress, "Italian"

singing, and "Greek" prayers were resisted while St. Petersburg "early became a symbol of all that was resented and feared as strange, novel, and threatening to established interests and ways of life." A century later Nicholas II adopted, at least ostensibly, the nationalist slogan of "civilizing the Russian people by its own strength, and drawing into it, in creed and language, all subject ethnic groups."[40]

The most percipient Balt historians agreed that this ethnocentric undercurrent emerged as a powerful surface force in Russia precisely in those years (1838-65) when social modernization, with its major Russian German component, was acquiring unprecedented force. This was also the period when more Russians were acquiring higher education, striving to enter professions that contained large proportions of other ethnic elements, and moving generally from the oppressive rigidity of Nicholas I's later years to Alexander II's reform period. Increased social mobility and populist rhetoric went hand in hand: as the "Mamelukes of the Empire," Germans were regarded as a stumbling block for true Russians, "the principal sinners against the Holy Spirit of the Russian people."[41]

Because his career impinged on almost all elements of this complex of changes, Iurii F. Samarin constitutes a kind of paradigm of the new Russian opposition to German influence.[42] His two years in Riga (1846-48) studying the conditions of the peasants constituted a typical "consciousness-raising" experience. Samarin was dismayed by the small Balt minority's subjection of the native Estonians and Latvians, even after a generation of formal emancipation. In his friction with the Balts, he developed an intense resentment toward all Germans and combined this with a new-style Russian nationalism. Later he utilized this experience in his notable role in the Russian emancipation of the 1860s. In between, Samarin's access to imperial court circles and to Slavophile journalism (mainly through his friend Mikhail Katkov) made him a crucial link between the populist nationalism of the intelligentsia and the decision makers who could affect the status of the Russian Germans.

Samarin's relationships with the imperial house are most interesting from the analytic standpoint. In 1849 Tsar Nicholas I saw Samarin's book Pis'ma iz Rigi (Letters from Riga, published the preceding year). He had Samarin imprisoned for a token period, then berated him sternly for his "lies" and slander about the Germans. Samarin had written, "If the Germans do not become Russians, the Russians will become Germans." Nicholas said he should have written, "Russians cannot become Germans; but we must love the Germans and treat them as ourselves." Then Nicholas launched a line of criticism that revealed he was more personally concerned than his paraphrase of the Gospel had suggested: "You directly injure the

Government; you imply that from the time of Emperor Peter I to Me,
We have all been surrounded by Germans and are Ourselves Germans."[43] Here, indeed, was the crux--necessarily obliquely ex-
pressed--of the populist critique. As F. F. Vigel, a more humble
author for Katkov's publishing house, stated the populist nationalist
viewpoint just fifteen years later, "All the great concepts of the
glory of Russia, except those of one woman, arose only in the brains
of native Russians, Godunov, Peter, Potemkin. . . ."[44] The
"woman" was, of course, Nicholas' grandmother, Catherine the
Great; if he had been alive, his resentment of this attack on his an-
cestor would hardly have been mollified by Vigel's tactical concession of praise for Peter the Great.

The next sovereign, Alexander II, was no less critical of
Samarin. While he was still heir apparent, however, he showed an
inclination to reason with Samarin rather than berate him--usually
a hint of future concessions in circumstances like those of the
autocracy. Like his father, Alexander referred to the outstanding
military accomplishments of the Balts (all European monarchies,
with their military origins, necessarily identified with feudal aris-
tocracies). He assured Samarin that he would continue to employ
Balt nobles in the Russian service, and even averred that Catholics
and Lutherans could be as good Christians as Orthodox could.[45]
The obvious and ineradicable weak point in the imperial family's
position arose from the fact that it was German, related by numerous marriages to the German ruling houses, and strongly inclined
to cosmopolitan European, if not specifically German, life styles
and culture.

As a result, the imperial family was threatened by nationalist
populism almost as much as by radical populism. Like numerous
dynasties in similar circumstances, the Romanovs took the line of
least resistance by discarding the supranational, ecumenical character of their rule and trying to become symbols of Russian national
identity. An essential step in this defensive adaptation was to set a
distance between themselves and the unassimilated element with
which the dynasty was in fact most closely associated--the Russian
German mobilized diaspora. Alexander II moved hesitantly along
this path from the mid-1860s on; Alexander III embraced anti-
Germanism eagerly, and perhaps without conscious awareness of the
dynasty's requirements, but nonetheless with curious ambivalences.
The last tsar, Nicholas II, was swept along by the nationalist slogan
"one Tsar, one creed, one law, one language,"[46] without being
strong enough to suppress the glaring inconsistencies that gave his
immediate family the fatal reputation of Germanophiles.

To return briefly to Samarin: he was clever or lucky enough
to set his probe not only on the weak point of the dynasty, but also

on the source of its real dissatisfaction with the Balts. From Peter's time on, the Romanovs had been centralizing absolutists, intent (like most other European rulers) on strengthening their own power and, incidentally, preparing the ground for modernization by dissolving particularistic estate privileges. Most of the high servants of the crown shared this goal, which one may identify as a fundamental operating principle of the imperial bureaucracies. Hence, while the Balt nobility was congenial to imperial governing circles as a cosmopolitan, conservative military aristocracy, as a provincial estate jealous of its autonomy that nobility was at best a minor evil to be tolerated temporarily. Thus I. A. Zinoviev (governor of Livonia 1891-97) argued:

> The cleverest defender of Baltic provincial dogmas will
> lose ground and the population, confused and betrayed
> by these doctrines, will understand that it is better,
> more honorable, and more advantageous to be citizens
> of a fine guberniia [province] of the Great Empire of
> Your Majesty, which the Livonians because of their
> wealth, industry, and love for social activity can
> claim, rather than citizens of an ephemeral, fantastic
> Livonian Duchy. [47]

But the "citizens" at issue, or at least their Balt upper stratum, had too much experience with the central bureaucracy and its operations in the gubernii to be overjoyed by the prospect. Samarin sharply remarked in the Letters that "as long as they keep on reaffirming in Petersburg, and even in Russia, nothing but the loyalty of the Balts, the rule of law in their territory, and the sacred nature of the privileges which the Balts lulled us into conceding," the government could accomplish nothing. [48] Clearly the Slavophiles intended to provide a climate of opinion and a legitimization for measures of administrative centralization and cultural russification that the imperial bureaucrats half-welcomed but would scarcely have initiated in conflict with their German peers.

There is no need in this analysis to discuss the nature of the steps taken in this early period (1838-65), since nearly all directly affected only Baltic provincial institutions, not the career prospects or general situation of the Russian Germans. Some measures, like the efforts to convert Estonian and Latvian peasants, had the strong traditional force of Orthodoxy behind them. Increasingly this force was allied with linguistic russification, which made limited progress in the Baltic elementary school system. Efforts to require use of Russian in the secondary schools and at Dorpat, the institutions most important to Balt identity, were perfunctory. [49] Measures more directly affecting the Balts were, throughout Alexander II's reign, little more than pinpricks. For example, the newly elected marshal of Livonian nobility, Nicholas von Oettingen, was received by Alexander (1870) with the Russian phrases "Chto vy brat' Avgusta?" and "Gde vy vospityvalis'?" (Are you August's brother? and Where were you brought up?). When Oettingen, mistaking the latter question for "Where are you going?" replied "V Rigu" (to Riga), the Tsar sternly rebuked him in German: "Learn Russian from your brother August, and don't forget what I said in Riga" (speech of June 1867, that the Baltic provinces belonged "to the great Russian family"). As is usually the case in a despotic court atmosphere, rumors soon magnified the incident to suggest that Oettingen had deliberately refused to use the "imperial language" when, contrary to custom, the sovereign employed it instead of German or French in an audience with a Balt subject. [50] Obviously Alexander derived symbolic advantage from the affair by identifying with the rising tide of Russian nationalism, and the Balts rightly regarded the incident as a portent of far more serious rebuffs.

THE BALTS BETWEEN TWO LOYALTIES

The very presence of a mobilized diaspora in a multiethnic polity presupposes a high degree of system penetrability, that is, the extension of personal and group ties across polity boundaries, in contrast with the rigid compartmentalization assumed by extreme models of the national state. In fact, absolutist bureaucracies tended to be jealous of the international connections of their subjects (ethnically diverse or not) long before the rise of mass nationalism, just as the bureaucrats disliked particularistic privileges in domestic affairs. The accepted conventions of the prenationalist absolute state did, however, admit a strikingly high degree of personal mobility to high-status individuals. During the Napoleonic Wars, to cite a famous instance, Alexander I urged a prominent Prussian official, Baron Heinrich von Stein, to transfer to his service. Far from taking offense, Stein considered the offer seriously. Seventy years later expectations had altered dramatically. In addition to being a member of the Balt nobility, Count Alexander Keyserling's father was, through circumstances rare even in feudal Europe, a vassal (as count of Rautenburg) of the King of Prussia. According to the older conventions, therefore, it was hardly shocking that Otto von Bismarck offered the son the post of minister of religious affairs; despite Keyserling's immediate rejection of the offer, Tsar Alexander II indignantly commented on the mere possibility, "Ce serait une félonie."[51]

The drastic alteration in the tsarist regime's expectations concerning the international role of the Russian Germans had extremely serious implications, for a major utility of a mobilized diaspora in its exchange relationship with the dominant elite is the superlative ability to act as an intermediary abroad. This may be stated as a fourth hypothesis: In the external relations of the multiethnic polity, the mobilized diaspora is as indispensable (and as transitory) as it is for the internal interests of the dominant ethnic elite. It is striking how long the Russian Germans--especially the Balt nobility--retained an almost dominant position in tsarist diplomacy. Balt observers recognized that the Minindel (Ministry of Foreign Affairs) retained the greatest tolerance for them.

> We did not lack men of high spirit and extraordinary
> talents; but this spirit usually impressed the society of
> St. James and Versailles, these talents shone in the
> Winter Palace and in the May parade. . . . We watched
> the success of Russia's European policy attentively, for
> nearly all our emissaries in all the principal countries
> were diplomats whom we knew on a first-name basis.
> Russia was the first of the Great Powers, and its diplo-
> mats, our cousins, first in the European Concert. Her
> victories were our victories, we hated her enemies with
> a personal hatred. [52]

Evidence of the indispensability of even unassimilated Russian German diplomats is Alexander III's unwonted toleration of evasion of his decree requiring all diplomatic correspondence to be in Russian by emissaries who simply did not know enough Russian to compose dispatches. [53] For slightly more than half of the century between the end of the Napoleonic Wars and the downfall of the regime, German nobles presided over the Minindel: Count Karl von Nesselrode from 1814 to 1856, Nikolai Giers from 1882 to 1895, and Count Vladimir von Lambsdorff from 1900 to 1906. Considering the wide range of importance of the posts involved, a statistical analysis of heads of diplomatic missions and Minindel departments would not be very profitable; but a cursory examination of the nineteenth-century lists suggests that Russian Germans (including some men of Scandinavian descent assimilated to the German ethnic group) carried about half the burden of imperial foreign relations. Equally indicative is the fact that even in 1915 (during the World War I anti-Germanism), 16 of 53 top officials in the Minindel had German names. [54]

A Russian diplomatic critic accused the Balt diplomats of constituting a large portion of the clique ("elite fraternity") that main-

tained control of the personal chancery ("the holy of holies") of the
Minindel by co-opting new members and monopolizing policy decisions. Less plausibly, Alexander P. Izvolsky, the most prominent
non-German minister of foreign affairs, subsequently referred to
"that class of functionaries of German origin, often highly industrious, but who succeeded in rising from a very humble milieu to
the highest ranks of the Russian hierarchy by dint of intrigue and
vile procedures."[55] Skill at bureaucratic politics--an even less
attractive game in the imperial service than elsewhere--undoubtedly
helped the Russian Germans hold their positions. Their exceptional
linguistic abilities, natural in a group with polyglot upbringing, were
directed toward Asia as early as the eighteenth century, when Russian Germans were especially active in learning Armenian and avail-
ing themselves (for missionary work and exploration) of the skilled
Armenian diaspora.[56] Later, during the nineteenth-century imperial expansion, Russian Germans were especially active. Two of
the most prominent directors of the Asian Department of the Minindel,
Giers just prior to his term as minister and Nicholas Hartwig under
Lambsdorff, were of German origin.

To a degree this activity demonstrates that the Russian Germans could excel in diplomacy without recourse to personal connections. Nevertheless, the greatest advantage enjoyed by the Germans
was the network of family connections that provided entrée to nineteenth-century diplomatic circles throughout Europe and trained them
in the social graces and subtle communications skills requisite for
operating in this essentially cosmopolitan, aristocratic milieu. As
an observer put the matter in 1914: "Throughout the entire East, as
far as the colonization sphere of the Teutonic Knights had extended,
connections of interrelated families were present--a world of social
equals which then [early nineteenth century] maintained closer contact
across dividing national frontiers than is possible today."[57]

It was precisely their contribution to the penetrability of the
Russian polity that constituted a major source of Russian nationalist
antipathy toward the Russian Germans. Hence much of the evidence
just presented indirectly supports my fifth hypothesis: Dominant
ethnic elite perceptions of mobilized diaspora disloyalty tend to
negate the value of the diaspora for external relations. The Russian
Germans in the diplomatic service were in an extremely exposed
position because of a peculiar combination of circumstances. Most
were highly conservative but, as Germans, could not often secure
support among the Pan-Slav faction in the Minindel and its vociferous
supporters in the press. Conversely, the Westernizing faction, always strong among the relatively cosmopolitan Russian diplomats,
admired liberal France and England and distrusted men like Lambsdorff, both for their supposed German sympathies and for their real

conservatism.[58] These currents of anti-Germanism tended to combine in the last decade of imperial diplomacy, when Pan-Slav circles
definitely committed themselves to opposition to the Central Powers.
Unstable liberals like Izvolsky (the French ambassador characterized
him as "not German in his heart, but he is from fear [of being forced
out of office in 1907 by German Reich pressure], which is perhaps
worse") disliked Pan-Slavism as much as a German alliance, but
ultimately succumbed to the former.[59]

Although he was far from typical, no diplomat's career better
exemplifies the conflicting pressures on the Balt diplomat than does
that of Alexander von Benckendorff, "the last grand seigneur among
Russian diplomats."[60] A rare Roman Catholic among the Balt Lutherans, Benckendorff was intimately related (through his mother, of
the Austro-Burgundian family of Croyes) to the higher nobility of
both the Austro-Hungarian Empire and the German Reich. Through
his brother Paul, grand marshal of the court, he had ready access
to the imperial family, and had married into a highly placed Russian
family. By conviction Benckendorff was an Anglophile, however;
and his keen sense of aristocratic nuances enabled him to ingratiate
himself with King Edward VII and his ministers both through a carefully cultivated expertise in horses and through an uncompromising
literal veracity rather rare among imperial diplomats.

Benckendorff explicitly based his concept of the ideal polity
the Roman Empire (civis romanus sum as applied to every citizen of
the empire, without regard to ethnic origin).[61] He considered this
ideal compatible with the kind of liberalism he thought was reflected
in the British constitution, yet his personal loyalty was entirely to
the dynasty. To bolster the dynasty, he was willing to embrace Pan-
Slavism, although (as a real Russian remarked) he had no sympathy
for the "little brother Slavs" who constituted the object of Pan-Slav
foreign policy.[62] Benckendorff's abnegation in face of Russian nationalism is suggested by his rejection of Izvolsky's offer of the
Paris embassy: "Religion and old associations would all be against
me. . . . You, on the contrary, are entirely Russian, and will get
along well in Paris. . . ."[63]

The preceding discussion of the crucial role of Russian Germans in tsarist diplomacy could not avoid mention of the role of the
German Reich. My sixth hypothesis specifically points to this factor: The most potent source of the dominant ethnic suspicion of the
mobilized diaspora is the existence of its "homeland" outside the
dominant elite's territorial control. More than the other hypotheses,
however, this proposition requires immediate, careful qualification,
which I quote from my theoretical analysis:

a sharp rise in social mobilization with concomitant
populist pressures is the most important factor jeo-
pardizing a mobilized diaspora. That danger arises,
however, only when a dominant elite's interest in
utilizing a diaspora has eroded and the alternative of
scapegoating affords a short-run advantage. In contrast to this "cynical" calculation, real suspicion that
a diaspora has transferred its loyalty to the occupants
of its homelands pervades the dominant elite itself. [64]

In the Russian situation, the rise of Slavophile populism, associated
with enhanced social mobility, set in motion the events that eroded
the Russian German position. For instance, the measures adopted
by Alexander II in the 1860s contained a large measure of purely symbolic concession to Russian nationalism--a very mild form of scapegoating. The more serious curbs on Russian Germans under Alexander III reflected a real suspicion of the mobilized diaspora's ties
with the powerful German Second Reich.

In demonstrating the accuracy of this analysis, as is usually
the case in longitudinal studies of social interaction, timing is crucial. Earlier I presented some of the more important evidence to
show that the pressures for curbing the Russian Germans arose
strongly in the 20 or 25 years before 1865. Up to 1866 (the Prussian
victory over Austria leading to formation of the North German Confederation), the German "homeland" could not conceivably threaten
the Russian Empire. The leading Protestant state, Prussia, was,
for long periods between 1790 and 1865, virtually a client of the
tsars. Consequently, despite their strong cultural attachment to the
German "great society," Russian Germans tended to take a patroniz-
ing attitude toward its feeble polities in comparison with their own
magnificent opportunities in the powerful Russian ecumenic polity. [65]

The rapid, dramatic rise of Prussia-Germany between 1866
and 1870 from the least to the greatest of the European powers was
almost bound to arouse intense suspicion in St. Petersburg. Naturally extreme nationalists like Samarin regarded this development as
the confirmation of their worst fears: "The identification of all German elements with the new German Empire in the sphere of ideas
and sentiments has taken place before our eyes." [66] As early as
1867, Bismarck tried to avert the Russian nightmare of a Balt-
Prussian conspiracy by telling his friend Keyserling that Prussia
would not take the Baltic provinces as a gift, since they were essential to Russia. [67] A Balt commentator wrote four years later: "The
new German Emperor has neither the pretensions nor the symbols
of the old." [68] But such disclaimers could not dispel the Russian

suspicion that the Balt nostalgia for a powerful ecumenical empire
might combine with their cultural attachment to Germany. I do not
know what led the tsarevich (the future Alexander III) to become, in
contrast with his temporizing father, a convinced exponent of anti-
Germanism. As early as 1880, however, the views he expressed in
private conversation with his cousin, Crown Prince Frederick
William of Prussia, demonstrate the strength of this conviction:

> The German government, in particular Prince Bismarck,
> still intends at the appropriate time to absorb the Baltic
> provinces. But no one in Russia can or will accept that,
> for up until now these have always been the most loyal,
> trustworthy, and civilized provinces of the Empire,
> which have provided the most able and trustworthy
> forces and men. Russia will not give up these prov-
> inces for any price and will fight to the death to keep
> them. [69]

There is little doubt that this attitude, however mistaken, led Alexander III not only to take formal measures such as the russification
of diplomatic correspondence, but also to turn to strongly anti-German
centralizing bureaucrats like Konstantin P. Pobedonostsev, procurator
of the Holy Synod, and Justice Minister N. A. Manasein. By the middle of Alexander's reign (1886), however, strong anti-Balt feeling had
affected persons as influential as the tsarina, Maria Fedorovna, who
denounced a Reich German grand duchess (one of the few who had resisted converting to Orthodoxy on her marriage) to Count Piotr A.
Shuvalov, who demanded the names of any Balts who had "betrayed"
Alexander III. [70]

Under these circumstances, the way in which the Russian Germans reacted to criticism was apt to have a strong influence on the
suspicions of the Russian leaders. The overwhelming tendency of
the Balt nobility and of lesser Russian German officials in St. Petersburg was to stress fealty to the empire and to meet attacks through
confidential interventions at court rather than by polemics: "Like the
howling of wild beasts, Russian attacks call indeed for watchfulness
but not howling in reply." In this vein, a purely defensive proposal
that each speaker at scholarly conventions be permitted to use his
own language, since Russia was a polyglot empire, was reasonable.
So also, no doubt, was restrained public criticism of obviously "subversive" moves of the Slavophiles, such as the Prague Pan-Slav
Congress (1861). [71]

Under these intimate aristocratic tactics did not, however, suit the
style of the Literati. As Wittram writes, "It is an expression of
sociological facts that [Carl] Schirren, the urban pastor's son, could

act as an independent and legitimate spokesman of Livonian estate rights and the increasing consciousness of Livonia as a province-state."[72] Significantly, the strong clerical element among the Literati had far shallower roots (two-thirds of the pastors had immigrated to the Baltic provinces from Germany during the eighteenth century) than the nobility or the urban patricians. Most continued to voice the traditional Lutheran caution that resistance to the established powers was equivalent to "meeting Revolution on its own ground."[73] In fact, Schirren, in his delayed but still illegal reply to Samarin's provocative Letters, stressed attachment to the empire in traditional Balt terms: "Everything is possible as long as the great banner of peace extends its protecting shade over the whole Empire from sea to sea, inviting all subjects of that Empire to come and enjoy equal rights."[74]

But his highly unfavorable comparisons of Russians, as an ethnic group, with Germans, and his attack on the tsar's advisers ("the will of the All-Highest! We seek it in vain, just as vainly as we seek our rights. . . . the ruling race of the year 1867 knows only the arguments of Russian officials.")[75] were inflammatory, particularly since they coincided with the development of Prussia into the German great power. Russians correctly suspected that some Balt Literati were turning to modern ethnic nationalism, or at least contemplating a transfer of loyalties. As early as 1846 one (a gymnasium teacher who had come from Germany) had written to his fiancée (daughter of a Balt pastor) in terms that the most favorably disposed imperial official would have regarded as subversive:

> German blood flows in your veins, too, and a German
> heart beats from you to me. We shall maintain our
> German feeling even if we are separated from that
> beautiful country whose speech and customs are ours
> and which will not let its children fall by the wayside if
> someday--to mention the worst possibility--we have to
> throw ourselves in her arms while fleeing the barbarism
> of the North. [76]

It required nearly half a century (1890) for a cosmopolitan noble like Keyserling to reach this point of contemplating emigration--and then only for his daughter and son-in-law, not himself: "The inherited position of the family in Estonia can never be attained by money, here or elsewhere. All one can do is to obtain other goods in exchange for it: national patriotism, freedom, good government, good schools, religious toleration, which can only be obtained in Germany."[77] In the interval imperial policy had moved from pinpricks to assaults on the key positions of the Balt structure:

severe inroads on provincial autonomy, russification of the secondary schools, attacks on the Dorpat student fraternities, and finally (1893) russification of instruction at the university itself, which, with its town, was given the old, ephemeral Russian name Iur'ev. [78]

Figure 3.1 shows that this official change of status was followed by a steep increase in enrollment; doubtless the new regime facilitated the entrance of large numbers of Russian-speaking students. As the figure also indicates, enrollment had expanded very considerably in the preceding 20 years, no doubt in response to the increasing opportunities in a modernizing polity. The available matriculation data do not permit an accurate assessment of the role of the Balts in this expansion. As Figure 3.1 indicates, however, until 1885 almost all of the increase came from the Baltic provinces and, according to Balt historians, consisted predominantly of Balts, who made up 81 percent of the total enrollment as late as 1880. After 1893 the further increases came very predominantly from outside the Baltic provinces. According to one Balt complaint, the influx was chiefly of inadequately prepared graduates of Orthodox seminaries. [79] In any event it appears clear that about two-thirds of the outside enrollment was Russian, the rest mainly Jewish. The incomplete data for 1900-10 indicate that total Balt enrollments remained fairly uniform in absolute terms.

Figure 3.3, on the other hand, suggests that the proportion of Balt Dorpat matriculants having careers in the empire (outside the Baltic provinces) was beginning to decline by 1885, although the trend was too new to permit definite evaluation. The corresponding trend among Balt matriculants who became physicians was, however, apparent from 1860; the further sharp decrease during the 1880s appears to reflect an established trend. Since matriculants of these periods actually pursued their careers much later, [80] the trend indicates a substantial withdrawal of Balts from empire careers (at least as physicians) following the impact of the russification policies under Alexander III and Nicholas II. This correlation does not, of course, demonstrate a cause-and-effect relation.

But the coincidental decline of the attention that Balt journals devoted to empire affairs, as contrasted with Baltic provincial affairs (Figure 3.3), supports the conclusion that the Balts were withdrawing somewhat from active participation in the multiethnic polity. A brief editorial comment in Baltische Monatsschrift at the start of this period hints at such a development: "When politics are quiet, antiquarianism, entomology, and other harmless sciences flourish. Quiet concern for the history of the fatherland may, in particular, serve as a kind of surrogate for other, passionate kinds of patriotic activity."[81] Such quiet withdrawal may have been the wisest response from the tactical standpoint, as well as the most prudent

FIGURE 3.3

Baltic Germans and the Empire

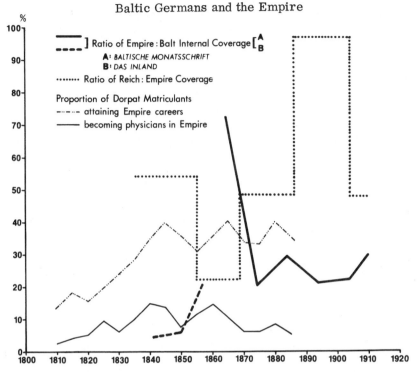

Source: Author's composition.

under the prevailing stringent censorship. But the sharp rise in attention to the German Reich as compared with the Russian Empire, just when the most severe russification measures were introduced, indicates that Balts were, perhaps unconsciously, transferring their psychic, if not their external, loyalties. *

Given these trends, the virtually unanimous Russian German loyalty to the empire when war with Germany began in 1914 may seem surprising. A high military officer who used his advanced age as an

---

*I have no theoretical explanation for the renewed relative interest in empire affairs after 1903. Perhaps it was simply a natural concern with the dramatic events of Russian domestic and foreign policy. Evidently there was a minor and temporary reduction in interethnic tensions as conservative forces tended to see their common interests. After 1910 renewed Balt attention to the Reich might have been too risky. But these are merely suggestions.

excuse to avoid serving against the German army was a rare exception. Even after the collapse of the Russian Empire, Balt and Reich German commentators were virtually unanimous in insisting on the loyalty of Balts in military service until the February Revolution; in at least one instance (the Petersburg Officers' Cavalry School, from which 60 percent of the casualties in September 1917 were German), loyalty persisted down to the October Revolution.[82] The generations of intense Russian German socialization to the supreme value of personal fealty to the sovereign appears to have had enough momentum to keep a considerable number loyal even after the tsar's abdication. Some of those who maintained impeccable formal loyalty to the empire admit, however, that many Balts were at heart sympathetic to the German Reich cause. Enough of such sentiments crept into their correspondence (which was, of course, heavily censored) to raise Russian official distrust, already at a high pitch after the outbreak of war, to fever levels.[83]

Though the estate assemblies were not dissolved, strict martial law was introduced in the Baltic provinces; the Lutheran theological faculty at Dorpat, which for obvious reasons had been permitted to continue using German, closed rather than meet a new order to adopt Russian; the German Association, which had maintained German-language secondary schools as private institutions, was dissolved after the Russian-language paper in Reval, Estonia, denounced it as "traitorous"; and all use of the German language in public was prohibited.[84]

Had a regime more compatible with their middle-class interests survived in Russia, it is possible that Russian Germans would have persisted, though in declining numbers, in major positions after World War I. In fact, the Bolshevik Revolution virtually eliminated the few remaining urban Germans in elite positions. Even if the Russian Germans had maintained attenuated roles as individuals, however, it is extremely unlikely that they could have persisted as a mobilized diaspora after the destruction of the Balt institutional structure. It seems most reasonable, therefore, to regard 1914, and not 1918, as the terminal point of the German mobilized diaspora in the Russian polity.

CONCLUSIONS

Given the limitations of a case study in an extended and relatively remote historical setting, I believe that most of the hypotheses have been confirmed to a small but significant degree. Contrary to predictions of the fifth hypothesis, however, the value of the Russian German mobilized diaspora for imperial external relations was not negated. Whether this exception has general theoretical implications, or whether it derives from historical "accidents" like Izvolsky's unstable personality, is uncertain.

The strong tendency of the nobility and the Literati to diverge in their reaction to Russian pressures suggests that the original conceptual framework requires modification. For situational diaspora of the European type operating in a modernizing context, three points seem pertinent: First, aristocratic elements in the diaspora will tend to retain a semi-feudal allegiance to the multiethnic polity even after the latter's dominant ethnic elite has become overtly hostile. Second, diaspora intellectuals will react much more sharply to the latter development, rapidly transferring their loyalty to an outside polity that they identify as their own. Third, the resultant internal strains in the diaspora tend to preclude full exploitation by the diaspora of the exchange relationship with the dominant ethnic elite; rather, an ascending spiral of mutual hostility rapidly erodes the position of the mobilized diaspora.

NOTES

1. John A. Armstrong, "Mobilized and Proletarian Diasporas," American Political Science Review 70 (1976): 393-400. The last three hypotheses presented in this article are unrelated to the subject of the present case study; examination of the seventh hypothesis has been omitted here.

2. Most of the tables and parts of the figures are based on the unusually large amount (for the Russian Empire) of aggregate statistics presented in Baltic German publications; at some points comparison with general Russian data, notably those recently collected by V. R. Leikina-Svirskaia, Intelligentsiia v Rossii vo vtoroi Polovine XIX veka (Moscow: Mysl, 1971), is feasible. Galina I. Shchetinina, Universitety v Rossii i ustav 1884 goda (Moscow: Nauka, 1976), pp. 205-06, provides some statistics on matriculants' religion. Alexander von Tobien, Die livländische Ritterschaft in ihren Verhältnisse zum Zarismus und russischen Nationalismus (Riga: Löffler, 1925), 1: 340, is especially valuable. A second type of data is obtained by aggregating biographical data in Tartu, Ulikool, Album academicum der kaiserlichen Universität Dorpat, A. Hasselblatt and G. Otto, eds. (Dorpat: C. Mattiesen, 1889). While biographical data are available for semiannual matriculation classes from 1802 through 1889, I collapsed the periods to five-year intervals; consequently all my references to annual rates actually refer to averages for the five-year intervals involved. For the periods through 1879 all students listed as originating in the Baltic provinces are classed as "Balts"

unless they could be identified (by surname or otherwise) as Russians,
Poles, Jews, Latvians, or Estonians. This procedure doubtless includes a few Latvians and Estonians as Balts (Baltic Germans). A
matriculant was classified as having an "outside career" if he occupied any position elsewhere in the Russian Empire for five or more
years (whether or not consecutive); all other Balts (including some
who had no careers but lived in the Baltic provinces, and the few
who lived in foreign countries) were considered as not having "outside careers." Each matriculant with an "outside career" is assigned to one, and only one, occupation. All matriculants who were
active as physicians for five years were considered to be physicians,
regardless of other occupations they may have followed. Pharmacists, government officials, military officers, scholar-teachers,
clergymen, and business, and agricultural occupational classifica-
tions were determined in the same manner, in descending order of
priority. The third type of quantitative data ("indicators of changes
in elite attention") consist of rough, unreplicated content analyses
of the titles in two leading Balt periodicals, Das Inland (1836-58) and
Baltische Monatsschrift (1859-1914). N's for the very long periods
utilized in Figure 3.3 vary from 200 to more than 1,000.

 3. For early statistics see Das Inland, December 17, 1837,
pp. 765-66 (births and deaths in Lutheran communities during 1836),
which suggests about one-tenth as many in St. Petersburg guberniia
as in the Baltic provinces, where Balts were then only 5 or 6 percent of all Lutherans. I have assumed that the higher Estonian-
Latvian birth rates were offset at that early date by lower registra-
tions; see Reinhard Wittram, Baltische Geschichte (Munich: R.
Oldenbourg, 1954), p. 143. For the 1897 census see Frank Lorimer,
The Population of the Soviet Union: History and Prospects (Geneva:
League of Nations, 1946), pp. 8-12, 203 ff.

 4. A. Bruckner, "Die Ausländer in Russland im 17. Jahrhundert," Baltische Monatsschrift 25 (1876): 741 ff.

 5. Ibid., p. 747; A. Brückner, Die Europäisierung Russlands
(Gotha: F. A. Perthes, 1888), p. 263.

 6. Eduard von Behrens, Deutsche Familiennamen in polnischen
und russischen Adelsverzeichnissen des 18. und 19. Jahrhundert
(Poznan: Verlag der Historischen Gesellschaft für Posen, 1938),
p. 11; Reinhard Wittram, Drei Generationen, Deutschland-Livland-
Russland, 1830-1914: Gesinnungen und Lebensformen baltisch-
deutscher Familien (Göttingen: Deuer, 1949), p. 268.

 7. Carl Schirren, Livländische Antwort an Herrn Juri Samarin
(Leipzig: Duncker & Humblot, 1869), p. 53; see also Hans Lemberg,
Die nationale Gedankenwelt der Dekabristen (Cologne: Böhlau, 1963),
p. 84, on some Decembrists' preference for Nizhnii Novgorod as the
future capital because of its "commercial traditions."

8. Wittram, Drei Generationen, pp. 243-44, quoting Wittram's aunt (1868).

9. H. Seesemann, "Die Programme der baltischen Gymnasien im Jahre 1880," Baltische Monatsschrift 28 (1881): 311-29.

10. The Balts had made repeated representations to the imperial authorities during the preceding 80 years of Russian rule, but had always been forbidden to reopen Dorpat. Wittram, Baltische Geschichte, p. 171; W. von Bock, "Die Historie von der Universität zu Dorpat und deren Geschichte," Baltische Monatsschrift 9 (1864): 107-93, 481-512.

11. Eduard Winter, Halle als Ausgangspunkt der deutschen Russlandkunde im 18. Jahrhundert (Berlin: Akademie Verlag, 1953), pp. 288-89; Wilhelm A. Christiani, "Liv- Est- und Kurlander auf der alten Universität Strassburg," Baltische Monatsschrift 64 (1907): 33-55; A. Schiefner, "Einige Bemerkungen zur Matrikel der altesten Universität Dorpat," Das Inland, November 24, 1955, pp. 682-86; Adolf von Harnack, "Baltische Professoren," in Das Baltenbuch, ed. Paul Rohrbach (Dachau: Blumtritt, n.d. [ca. 1918]), p. 49; "Chronik der Universität Dorpat seit dem Jahre 1827," Das Inland, February 12, 1836, pp. 98-110; Tobien, op. cit., 1: 334.

12. Ibid.

13. Comparisons based on data in Raymond Poignant, Education and Development in Western Europe, the United States, and the U.S.S.R.: A Comparative Study (New York: Teachers College Press, 1969), p. 182; and J. Conrad, Das Universitätsstudium in Deutschland während der letzten 50 Jahre: Statistische Untersuchungen unter besonderer Berücksichtigung Preussens (Jena: Gustav Fischer, 1884), p. 106.

14. Harnack, op. cit., p. 51; Tobien, loc. cit.; Walter Mitzka, "Studien zum baltischen Deutsch," Deutsche Dialektgeographie 17 (1923): 5.

15. Alexander Hörschelmann, "Aus der Werdezeit der Universität Dorpat," in Baltische Lebenserinnerungen, ed. Alexander Eggers (Heilbronn: Eugen Salzer, 1925), pp. 31-37; Eberhard Kraus, "Studentische Strömungen in den vierzigten Jahren," Baltische Monatsschrift 35 (1888): 287-92.

16. Allen A. Sinel, "The Socialization of the Russian Bureaucratic Elite, 1811-1917: Life at the Tsarskoe Selo Lyceum and the School of Jurisprudence," Russian History 3 (1976): 2. I am indebted to Professor Sinel for a letter giving me his estimate that Lutherans at the School of Jurisprudence (1835-85) constituted 15 to 20 percent of the student body; this implies a rather larger proportion of Germans, probably not very different from my estimate for the lycée. Data in Shchetinina, loc. cit., indicate that by the late 1880s Lutherans (probably nearly all German) constituted 11 percent

(about 190 among 1,800) of the students at St. Petersburg University, a much less prestigious institution, and far smaller proportions of the enrollments at other universities in the empire.

17. Dmitrii Kobeko, Imperatorskii Tsarskosel'skii Litsei: Nastavniki i potomtsy, 1811–1843 (St. Petersburg: V. F. Kirshbaum, 1911), p. 367; Ivan Ia. Selezhev, Istoricheskii ocherk Imperatorskago byshago Tsarskosel'skago nyne Aleksandrovskago Litseia za pervoe ego piatidesiatiletie, s 1811 po 1861 gode (St. Petersburg: V. Bezobrazov, 1861), p. 128. Most of my information on these schools is derived from these two books. Professor Sinel has written to me that the School of Jurisprudence may have been more popular with Germans, some of whom irritated their Russian classmates by inability to speak Russian.

18. F. F. Vigel, Vospominaniia F. F. Vigelia (Moscow: Universitetskaia Tipografiia Katkov, 1864), 1, pt 2: 29.

19. J. G., "Zur Physiologie russischer Provinzialzustände," Baltische Monatsschrift 3 (1861): 489.

20. Hermann Dalton, Lebenserinnerungen (Berlin: Martin Warneck, 1907), 2: 278.

21. Helene Taube von der Issen, Graf Alexander Keyserling: Ein Lebensbild aus seinen Briefen und Tagebüchern (Berlin: Georg Reimer, 1902), 1: 225. Kankrin's father was a Reich German; the family had become wholly russified. See Freiherr von Nolcken, "Leben und Wirken des russischen Finanzministers Grafen Kankrin," Baltische Monatsschrift 57 (1909): 241–77.

22. Quoted in Tobien, op. cit., 1: 52.

23. W. von Bock, Der deutsch-russische Konflikt an der Ostsee (Leipzig: Duncker & Humblot, 1869), p. 53.

24. Tobien, op. cit., 1: 113.

25. Wittram, Drei Generationen, p. 277.

26. For German estimates see Walter Görlitz, Die Junker: Adel und Bauer im deutschen Osten (Blüchsburg am Ostsee: C. A. Starke, 1957), p. 259; Erik Amburger, Geschichte der Behördenorganisation Russlands von Peter dem Grossen bis 1917 (Leiden: Brill, 1966), p. 517. Alfred Bilmanis, "Grandeur and Decline of the German Balts," Slavonic and East European Review 22 (1944): 68–69, citing a Latvian nationalist source of 1871, suggests even higher proportions of Germans in the top imperial offices. On the other hand, a German Reich occupation officer warned that one should not evaluate the Balts by names alone; some branches of a given family were pro-Reich, others completely russified. Alexis von Engelhardt, Die deutschen Ostsee Provinzen Russlands (Munich: Georg Müller, 1916), p. 174.

27. Brückner, "Ausländer," pp. 689 ff.; and his Die Europäisierung, loc. cit.

28. Annual averages were calculated (see note 2) for the five-year periods in which students who ever had significant medical careers matriculated. In Figure 3.2 and in the text these calculations are reported as annual increments for the following five-year period, since it was during this subsequent period that the matriculant was most likely to have begun his contribution to empire medical needs. Since, after 1879, it is impossible to distinguish the German ethnic component with a high degree of probability, calculations have not been extended beyond the 1876-79 matriculation period; hence increments are reported only through the 1880-85 period. Empire increments (other than from Dorpat) were estimated (approximately, as the open upper ends of the vertical bars are meant to suggest) from data in Leikina-Svirskaia, op. cit., pp. 58, 135, 140, particularly the figure of approximately 8,000 physicians in the empire in 1845 (p. 135). Unfortunately, she presents no data for 1846-55. Apart from its utility in showing the dynamics of medical personnel development, the graphic presentation is more appropriate than a tabular presentation because the former conveys the orders of relative magnitude that the data clearly support without conveying a spurious impression of precision.

29. Roderick E. McGrew, Russia and the Cholera, 1823-1832 (Madison: University of Wisconsin Press, 1965), pp. 25, 156-57.

30. Wittram, Drei Generationen, pp. 254-66.

31. E. B., "Zur Lage," Baltische Monatsschrift 19 (1870): 8-15.

32. Hans Rothfels, Reich, Staat und Nation in deutsch-baltischen Denken (Halle: Niemeyer, 1930).

33. Tobien, op. cit., 1: 3; see also Julius Eckart, "Der livländische Landtag in seiner historischen Entwicklung," Baltische Monatsschrift 3 (1861): 38-78, 116-59; Leonid Arbusow, Grundriss der Geschichte Liv- Est- und Kurlands (2nd ed.; Mitau: E. Behrl, 1890), pp. 100 ff.; Hans von Wedel, Die estländische Ritterschaft: Vornehmlich zwischen 1710 und 1783 (Königsberg: Ost-Europa Verlag, 1935), pp. 11, 117.

34. Wedel, op. cit., p. 117; F. Bienemann, "Zur Geschichte des schwedisch-russischen Krieges, 1788-1790," Russische Revue 5 (1874): 53 ff., 68.

35. "Marquis Paulucci und seine Verfolgung geheimer Gesellschaften in den Ostseeprovinzen," Baltische Monatsschrift 44 (1897): 499-501; see also George V. Vernadsky, Russkoe Masonstvo v Tsarstvovanie Ekateriny II (Petrograd: Dela, 1917), on the St. Petersburg lodges a generation earlier. It is perhaps significant that popular Russian opinion of that earlier period identified the farmazon (like the physician a generation earlier) with the foreign "magician."

36. Roger Portal, L'oural au XVIIIe siècle: Étude d'histoire économique et sociale (Paris: Institut d'Études Slaves, 1950), pp. 61 ff., 99, 105, 138 ff., 378.

37. Reinhard Wittram, Das Nationale als europäisches Problem: Beiträge zur Geschichte des Nationalitätsprinzips vornehmlich im 19. Jahrhundert (Göttingen: Vandenhoeck & Ruprecht, 1954), p. 154; Johannes C. Petri, Neustes Gemählde von Lief- und Esthland unter Katharina II und Alexander I (Leipzig: Dijk, 1809), 2: 5.

38. Lemberg, op. cit., p. 60.

39. Brückner, "Ausländer," p. 765.

40. Tobien, op. cit., 1: 380; Hans Rogger, National Consciousness in Eighteenth-Century Russia (Cambridge, Mass.: Harvard University Press, 1960), pp. 8-9.

41. The Russian journal Den' for June 1862, as quoted by "X," "Wir und die anderen," Baltische Monatsschrift 7 (1863): 457; Tobien, op. cit., 1: 70, refers to 1865 as the onset of intense Slavophile attacks; Wittram, Drei Generationen, p. 65, maintains that russification began with the minister of public instruction, Count Sergei S. Uvarov, in 1838.

42. Most of the following account is drawn from Dmitrii Samarin's introduction to Iurii F. Samarin, Sochineniia, III, Pis'ma iz Rigi i Istoriia Rigi (Moscow: A. I. Mamontov, 1889).

43. Ibid., pp. xci-xcii.

44. Vigel, op. cit., 1, pt. 2: 185.

45. D. Samarin, op. cit., 3: cii.

46. Tobien, op. cit., 1: 81, 136.

47. Ibid., 1: 291.

48. Iu. F. Samarin, op. cit., 3: 160.

49. "Zur Einführung der russischen Sprache in die Geschäftsführung und als akademische Unterrichtsprache der Universität Dorpat (1869-1893)," Baltische Monatsschrift 53 (1902): 152-58.

50. Tobien, op. cit., 1: 58.

51. Hermann Oncken, Historisch-Politische Aufsätze und Reden (Munich: R. Oldenbourg, 1914), p. 109; see also Taube, op. cit., 1: 217.

52. E.B., op. cit., p. 15; see also Tobien, op. cit., 1: 149.

53. M. Shebeko, Souvenirs: Essai historique sur les origines de la guerre de 1914 (Paris: Bibliothèque Diplomatique, 1936), p. 61; Vladimir Korostovets, "Graf Alexander Konstantinovich Benckendorff," Berliner Monatshefte 14 (1936): 887-901.

54. Russia, Ministerstvo Inostrannykh Del, Ezhegodnik: Annuaire diplomatique de l'empire de Russie (St. Petersburg, 1915); see also Amburger, op. cit., pp. 126-32, 442-64.

55. Alexander Izvolsky, The Memoirs of Alexander Isvolsky, Charles L. Seeger, ed. and trans. (London: Hutchinson, n.d.), p. 94; Korostovets, op. cit., pp. 891-92.

56. Winter, op. cit., pp. 295, 298, 336.

57. Oncken, op. cit., p. 97.

58. Izvolsky, op. cit., p. 94; see pp. 98 and 100 on Izvolsky's soi-disant "leftism" and mistrust of "Slavophilism."

59. Maurice Bompard, Mon embassade en Russie, 1903-1908 (Paris: Plon, 1937), pp. 244, 255-56.

60. A. Nekludov, Diplomatic Reminiscences before and during the World War, 1911-1917, Alexandra Paget, trans. (London: John Murray, 1920), p. 130.

61. Ibid., p. 131.

62. Korostovets, op. cit., p. 898.

63. Alexander Izvolsky, Au service de la Russie: Correspondance diplomatique, 1906-1911, Helene Izvolsky, ed. (Paris: Editions Internationales, 1937), pp. 287-89 (Bencenkendorff to Izvolsky, August 2, 1910); in addition to these letters and the memoirs cited above, see Iurii Solov'ev, Dvadtsat' piat let moeie diplomaticheskoi sluzhby (1893-1919) (Moscow: Gosudarstvennoe Izdatel'stvo, 1928), p. 246.

64. Armstrong, op. cit., p. 401.

65. See, for example, Tobien, op. cit., II (Berlin: Walter de Gruyter, 1930), p. 219.

66. Wittram, Baltische Geschichte, p. 195, quoting an 1882 statement by Samarin.

67. Taube, op. cit., 2: 581, quoting Keyserling's diary of March 18, 1890, reflecting on his conversation with Bismarck.

68. A. Bulmerincq, "Kaiser und Reich," Baltische Monatsschrift 20 (1871): 170.

69. Quoted in Tobien, op. cit., 1: 89, note, from the diary of Heinrich von Bock, an official in the Balt noble estates. Use of a secondhand quotation on such a crucial point is unsatisfactory, but it is highly unlikely that the original manuscript could be found. As stated earlier, I make no pretense to exhaustive research on imperial decision making. Doubtless a sharper insight into the motivations and policy making (not to say intrigue) of high court and bureaucratic circles could be attained by archival research in the USSR (if permitted) or by closer scrutiny of published materials. The quotation in Tobien (a biased but scrupulous historian) does, however, fit in with all the material on Alexander III's personal views and proclivities that I have encountered.

70. Tobien, op. cit., 1: 113.

71. The cautionary words are by Keyserling, as quoted by Tobien, ibid., 1: 129; see also Mädler, "Ueber wissenschaftliche Congresse," Baltische Monatsschrift 7 (1863): 381-91; "Die neue Welt des Ostens," Baltische Monatsschrift 4 (1861): 61-67.

72. Wittram, Das Nationale, p. 175.

73. Ibid., pp. 209, 283.

74. Schirren, op. cit., p. 173.

75. Ibid., p. 83.

76. Wittram, Drei Generationen, p. 49.

77. Oncken, op. cit., p. 112; for a contemporary published expression of this attitude, see C. Erdmann, "Das Wesen der Heimat," Baltische Monatsschrift 34 (1887): 197.

78. Tobien, op. cit., 1: 290, 332; 2: 219; Wittram, Drei Generationen, p. 303.

79. Tobien, op. cit., 1: 340; Wittram, Baltische Geschichte, p. 220. Immediately after russification, Lutheran enrollment dropped sharply (from 1,140 in 1889 to 709 in 1894) and apparently never recovered (Shchetinina, loc. cit.).

80. See note 28 (above). A comparison with Figure 3.2 will indicate that the total Balt higher medical personnel increment to the empire supply was sustained only by the increase of pharmacists.

81. "Notizen," Baltische Monatsschrift 24 (1875): 462 ff.

82. F. W. von Oertzen, Baltenland: Eine Geschichte der deutschen Sendung im Baltikum (Munich: F. Bruckmann, 1939), p. 296.

83. Eduard von Dellingshausen, Im Dienste der Heimat: Erinnerungen (Stuttgart: Ausland und Heimat Verlag, 1930), p. 192; Kurt von Braatz, Fürst Anatol Pawlowitsch Lieven im Kampfe gegen den baltischen Separatismus, russischen Bolschewismus und die Awaloff-Bermondt Affäre (Stuttgart: C. Belfer, 1926), p. 22.

84. Tobien, op. cit., 2: 219.

MYKOLA SKRYPNYK AND PETRO SHELEST: AN ESSAY ON THE PERSISTENCE AND LIMITS OF UKRAINIAN NATIONAL COMMUNISM

4

Yaroslav Bilinsky

VSEVOLOD S. HOLUBNYCHY
in memoriam

On August 7, 1963, a month after Petro Shelest had been made First Secretary of the Communist Party of the Ukraine (CPU[CP(B)U before 1952]), volume 13 of the Ukrainian Soviet Encyclopedia was signed for the printer. It contained the most explicit and sympathetic, albeit partial, rehabilitation of the Old Bolshevik revolutionary and founder of the CPU, Mykola Skrypnyk, to be published since his suicide in 1933 and his posthumous denunciation as a Ukrainian nationalist. The encyclopedia article had been written and typeset under Shelest's predecessor, Nikolai Podgorny (Pidhorny in Ukrainian);* but Shelest could still have had it changed.

---

*In view of Podgorny's unceremonious ouster from the CPSU Politburo on May 24, 1977--see Pravda, May 25, 1977, p. 1--the question may be raised whether Podgorny's old ties with the Ukraine and with Shelest in particular were a factor in his dismissal. I believe so, but this is not the place to develop that theme.

I would like to thank for their constructive criticisms all of the participants in the University of Chicago workshop on March 4-5, 1977. I am likewise indebted to Professor John R. Reshetar, Jr., for critically reading the article later. Special gratitude is due to the late Professor Vsevolod S. Holubnychy, who read this essay while it was in draft form and who offered numerous suggestions. It is to his memory that I dedicate this article.

In 1973--40 years after Skrypnyk's suicide--Shelest, too, was accused of having made "nationalist" mistakes in his policies in the Ukraine. He is still alive, but "retired"; he is dead in the political sense. Did Shelest anticipate in 1963 that he would be largely walking in Skrypnyk's footsteps, to a similar end?

This essay constitutes, first, an attempt to investigate the persistence of Ukrainian national Communism, of which the two foremost representatives are Skrypnyk and Shelest. Ukrainian national Communism is defined as an attempt to establish a Ukrainian state, based on Ukrainian national culture but led by the Communist Party and oriented toward the achievement of Communist political, economic, and social goals. Second, this essay probes the exceedingly narrow, not to say drastic, limits of national Communism within the Soviet Union. I will sketch the political and intellectual biographies of the two men; and in the conclusion I will compare their attitudes on specific issues and reflect on the present and future of Ukrainian national Communism.

SKRYPNYK'S LIFE

Skrypnyk was born in 1872, the son of a Ukrainian railroad employee (a telegraph operator, later an assistant stationmaster). His parents had distant acquaintances among members of the Russian revolutionary movements. As a young man Skrypnyk plunged into Marxist literature and politics, and considered himself a member of the Russian Social Democratic Workers Party from 1897. In 1900 he enrolled in the St. Petersburg Institute of Technology. His true vocation, however, was that of a professional revolutionary; and it led him to underground political activity in St. Petersburg, Tsaritsyn (today Volgograd), Saratov, Yekaterinburg (today Sverdlovsk), Perm, Odessa, Kiev, and Riga. Skrypnyk was exiled and jailed several times; once he was even sentenced to death (in absentia). In June 1917 he went to Petrograd, where he later became a member of the Military-Revolutionary Committee headed by Leon Trotsky that was preparing the October Revolution. He took part in the actual fighting.[1]

In his Social Democratic politics Skrypnyk appears to have been a close follower of Lenin, since he had joined the Iskra circle at St. Petersburg in 1901.[2] Being personally well-known and apparently also well-liked by Lenin (his wife served as Lenin's appointments secretary in 1917-18), having worked for the common cause with such Bolshevik greats as Felix Edmundovich Dzerzhinsky and Lev Borisovich Kamenev, and having personally fought in the October Revolution, Skrypnyk was not burdened with an excessive sense of humility vis-à-vis Iosif Stalin.

What was Skrypnyk's attitude toward the Ukrainian question before the Revolution? It is impossible to tell, for his massive bibliography, which encompasses 808 items, does not show that he published anything before 1918.[3] But in his 1921 autobiography, which may have been written under the impact of the Ukrainian renaissance of 1917-20 but probably is factually correct, Skrypnyk says: "The path of my development . . . completely differed from that of the Russian revolutionary intelligentsia."[4] A self-taught man, he had begun his education by studying Ukrainian literature and history. He was strongly influenced by the historical poems of Taras Shevchenko. Tales of his Cossack ancestors, which he heard at home, also left a lasting impression upon the boy.[5] Not having access to detailed biographical information on Skrypnyk's youth, we can only speculate that before 1917 his attitudes toward the Ukraine may have been latent, but that they became fully crystallized shortly after the October Revolution.

Toward the end of December 1917, Lenin personally delegated Skrypnyk to help the Bolsheviks in the Ukraine. That the First All-Ukrainian Soviet Congress in Kharkov had elected Skrypnyk to its Central Executive Committee and made him People's Secretary (Commissar) of Labor appears to have been a convenient pretext (rather than the true reason) for Lenin's dispatching him to the Ukraine despite the voiced misgivings of his wife, who wanted him to stay in Petrograd. When she asked Lenin whether there were no other Ukrainians who could be put to use in the Ukraine, Lenin retorted, with obvious dissatisfaction, "We need not any Ukrainian, but Skrypnyk in particular."[6] This episode shows that the real reason for Skrypnyk's being sent to the Ukraine was that he commanded Lenin's absolute trust.

It is also plausible to assume, as does the late Vsevolod Holubnychy, that Skrypnyk may have convinced Lenin in 1917 that the Ukraine should exist as a separate political entity. With Skrypnyk's departure from Petrograd (apart from two brief but significant interludes), the career of the all-Russian professional revolutionary ended and that of the Soviet Ukrainian statesman began--a career that would lead Skrypnyk in early 1918 to head the Soviet Ukrainian government, then in early 1919 to the post of Ukrainian SSR People's Commissar (PC) of the Workers and Peasants Inspectorate, Ukrainian SSR PC of Interior Affairs (1921), Ukrainian SSR PC of Justice (early 1922-March 1927), Ukrainian SSR PC of Education (March 1927-January 1933), demotion to head of the Ukrainian SSR Gosplan and deputy chairman of the Ukrainian SSR Council of PCs (January 1933) and to his suicide on July 7 of that year.

Early Role in the Ukraine

To judge from Skrypnyk's actions within the first six months after his arrival in the Ukraine (December 1917–June 1918), he developed two master concepts: first, the Ukraine should become a semi-independent republic with a Soviet form of government and federal ties to Soviet Russia; second--and more important--the Ukrainians should establish an independent Communist Party that would cooperate with the Russian Communist Party (RCP) through the soon-to-be-founded Komintern. The Ukraine as a mere provincial extension of the Russian state ("South Russia") and Ukrainian Communists as a mere branch of the RCP did not appeal to Skrypnyk. Lenin, however, would tolerate pro forma independent Ukrainian statehood only so long as the real power continued to rest in Russian Communist hands. He would never countenance the existence of an independent Communist Party of the Ukraine except for the most limited tactical reasons.

The situation was further complicated by the internal weaknesses of the Bolsheviks in the Ukraine. There were relatively few of them,[7] and they were mainly Russians. The Bolsheviks were quarreling bitterly among themselves,[8] and were disunited on the question of autonomous Ukrainian statehood and a separate Communist Party. A majority of the Bolsheviks in the Ukraine were less tolerant of Ukrainian independent or autonomist aspirations than Lenin was. Under the impact of Bolshevik setbacks in the Ukraine in 1918 and 1919, Lenin recognized that new concessions to the quasi-independent Soviet Ukraine had to be made; and he helped Skrypnyk's fellow autonomists to bring the anti-Ukrainian Bolsheviks in the Ukraine into line.

One of Skrypnyk's first important tasks in the Ukraine was to prevent the new Soviet Ukrainian Republic, which had been proclaimed at Kharkov on December 25, 1917, from being immediately dismembered out of existence. The Bolsheviks in the Ukraine were split into several factions. Probably the most powerful was that from the industrialized Donets Basin (Donbas) and Krivoi Rog, led by Artem Sergeev. It wanted to set up an independent Donets Soviet Republic--perhaps with Lenin's secret blessing. The Bolsheviks of Kharkov, the capital of the new Soviet Ukrainian Republic, made common cause with this faction. In vain did Skrypnyk--himself a native of the Donbas--appeal to the delegates of the Donbas-Krivoi Rog Congress of Soviets meeting at Kharkov not to set up an independent republic: he suffered a humiliating defeat.[9] Only after the conclusion of the Treaty of Brest-Litovsk in February 1918, in which the Central Powers rejected any attempts to detach the Donbas-Krivoi Rog region from the rest of the Ukraine; only after the first

Soviet Ukrainian government had been reorganized during its retreat
from Kharkov to Poltava; and only after Skrypnyk had been elected
its new chairman on March 4, 1918, could Skrypnyk proclaim, at
Poltava, on March 7, "the liquidation of all the independent Soviet
republics on Ukrainian territory--i.e., the Donbas-Krivoi Rog,
Odessa and Crimean republics--and their unification with the
Ukraine."[10] Lenin probably supported this action.[11] At the Second
All-Ukrainian Congress of Soviets in Yekaterinoslav in late March
1918, the powerful Donets-Krivoi Rog faction reluctantly recognized
the necessity of setting up a united Ukrainian Soviet Republic.[12]

Nevertheless, while Skrypnyk's government was issuing proc-
lamations, the real authority in the Soviet portions of the Ukraine
still rested with army commander Vladomir Antonov-Ovseenko,
whom Lenin had sent in with troops from Russia at about the same
time he dispatched Skrypnyk. Lenin's relationship with Antonov-
Ovseenko reveals his politically tactful but essentially instrumental
attitude toward Soviet Ukrainian statehood. Lenin had to intervene
to restrain the free-wheeling Antonov-Ovseenko, who sought to appoint his own people to positions of power and to ignore the local men
who had been appointed by the Kharkov Ukrainian Central Executive
Committee, the quasi-representative organ of the Ukrainian Bolsheviks and Skrypnyk's formal superior authority. He wrote to Antonov-
Ovseenko:

> This is _exceedingly important_ [arkhivazhno] in state
> relations. For Goodness's sake, make peace with them
> and recognize any sovereignty of theirs whatsoever
> [vsiacheskii suverenitet]. I strongly [ubeditel'no] re-
> quest that you remove the commissars whom you have
> appointed. We need here the utmost national tact
> [arkhitakt natsional'nyi].[13]

While Lenin was thus playing a double game, insisting on utmost
centralization in the more important Party relations while being very
generous in the subordinate state relations ("recognize any sovereignty of theirs whatsoever"), Stalin would not make even those
verbal legalistic concessions. On April 4, 1918, he told Skrypnyk's
colleague V. Zatonsky: "You have played with a government and a
republic long enough. Enough is enough, it seems; time has come
to stop playing those games."[14]

Skrypnyk was even less successful in Party relations. With
German troops advancing in the Ukraine after the signing of the
Treaty of Brest-Litovsk, and with Skrypnyk having to battle his
fellow Bolsheviks in Yekaterinoslav and Stalin in Moscow, the circumstances could hardly have been less propitious for the consoli-

dation of the scattered Bolshevik groups into a single Communist
Party of Ukraine. This is precisely what Skrypnyk tried to do at the
Party Conference at Taganrog on April 19-20, 1918, though with indifferent success. Kharkov and Donbas were not represented. By a
majority of 35-21 the conference supported Skrypnyk's proposition
to set up the independent CP(B)U, which would be linked with the
(Bolshevik) Russian Communist Party (RCP[B]) only through the
Komintern.[15] By May 18, 1918, the RCP(B) Central Committee approved this proposition "inasmuch as the Ukraine was an independent
country."[16]

Apparently Lenin approved the independence of the CP(B)U
mainly for one tactical reason. By the terms of Brest-Litovsk the
Ukraine had to be surrendered to the Germans. The Ukrainian Bolsheviks vowed to carry on a guerrilla war against the Germans, and
Lenin decided to untie their hands (and his own) by acknowledging
their independence.[17] But a truly successful Bolshevik guerrilla
campaign in the Ukraine did not materialize. At Taganrog the
CP(B)U elected its first organizational bureau with Iurii Piatakov as
its head and Skrypnyk as its secretary. In 1976 the Soviet Ukrainian
historian Iu. Iu. Kondufor confirmed these events almost completely
(unlike Skrypnyk he dates the RCP[B] Central Committee meeting as
May 3, 1918, and mentions that it was attended by Lenin). He tends,
nonetheless, to belittle the significance of the Taganrog Conference
by calling it merely a "consultative meeting" (narada) even though
the official contemporary RCP(B) documents refer to it as a "conference." But Kondufor may be correct in stressing that the decision of May 3, 1918, was a provisional one to be ratified or rejected
by the subsequent CP(B)U "conference" or "congress" originally
scheduled for June 20, 1918.[18] This would be a further partial explanation of the seeming reversal by Lenin's RCP(B) on the question
of the CP(B)U's independence.

At the First Congress of the CP(B)U, which took place at
Moscow on July 2-12, 1918, Skrypnyk did not fare so well; and
Lenin chose not to help him. The Kharkovites, who were lukewarm
toward Ukrainian aspirations, attended this congress. The pro-
Russian Emmanuel Kviring, a Latvian from Yekaterinoslav, proposed that the entire Ukraine should be incorporated into the RSFSR.
He obtained a majority. The resolution that Skrypnyk had introduced
at Taganrog, providing for an independent CP(B)U, was rescinded.
Though Skrypnyk had been the real founder of the CP(B)U at Taganrog
in April 1918, and though he had played an active role in calling for
the congress in July 1918, at Moscow he was not even elected member
of the CP(B)U Central Committee (CC). He was made only a candidate
member, probably as a punishment for having advocated a less centralized Communist Party.[19]

Nor did Skrypnyk have greater success at the Second CP(B)U Congress, convened at Moscow in October 1918. He did not become full member of its CC until two months later. Moreover, for almost six months after the First Congress, apparently with Lenin's approval, he was detached from Party organizational work and sent to the Cheka, where he served immediately under Dzerzhinsky as head of the Section for Struggle with the Counterrevolution.[20] When the Bolsheviks returned to the Ukraine early in 1919, he was given only a second-ranking post, that of PC of the Workers and Peasants Inspectorate. When the Bolsheviks were again pushed out of the Ukraine in June 1919, Skrypnyk was sent to serve as a political commissar in Gomel and then as head of a special section of the southeastern (Caucasian) front, with quasi-political and quasi-internal security responsibilities.[21] Since the CP(B)U, Skrypnyk's child, was still being organized, his mission to the Caucasus probably should be evaluated as an effort to keep him at a distance, a kind of "honorable" political exile.

Skrypnyk's Role in the 1920s

In general, it cannot be overstressed that after the Taganrog Conference of April 1918, Skrypnyk's political power--as opposed to his moral authority--was severely limited. He did not become a candidate member of the CP(B)U Politburo until 1923, or a full member until 1925.[22] He was never allowed into the Secretariat.

In all-Union Party politics Skrypnyk's role also was rather circumscribed. He had been elected candidate member of RCP(B) CC at the Sixth (pre-Revolution) Party Congress of July-August 1917. It was not until the Twelfth Party Congress of April 1923, however, that Skrypnyk regained this position, and not until the Fifteenth Party Congress of December 1927 that he was promoted to full CC member.[23] Surprisingly, his relatively sharp critique of Stalin's nationality policy at the Twelfth Party Congress was not immediately held against him.[24] A few months later, at a meeting of leaders of non-Russian republics on June 9-12, 1923, which had been called to discuss the arrest of Sultan Galiev, Skrypnyk defended Sultan Galiev by saying that excesses of Russian chauvinism had created a fertile ground for nationalist reaction; he also hinted that Sultan Galiev's deviation might have been exaggerated.[25] Skrypnyk was somewhat more noticeable in the Komintern.* But altogether, after April 1918

---

*Skrypnyk was a delegate to the First-Sixth Komintern congresses (1919-28). At the 1928 congress he was elected a member

he did not play a very prominent role either in Ukrainian or in all-Union Party politics, with the possible exception of the increasingly subsidiary Komintern activities. Why?

As an experienced and loyal Bolshevik, Skrypnyk must have understood that he had gone extremely far in trying to set up a truly independent Ukrainian CP(B)U in 1918--even his protector Lenin broke with him on this issue. Above all, in this quest he could not rely on the support of the majority of the Bolsheviks in the Ukraine.

In the 1920s the CP(B)U was not really a Ukrainian party; it consisted predominantly of Russians, and its Ukrainian minority was strongly Russified. According to Holubnychy, at the end of 1920, Ukrainians constituted only 19.0 percent of the Party.[26] In accordance with the detailed figures established by the Party census of April 1, 1922, out of a total of 51,236 CP(B)U members whose nationality could be ascertained, only 11,920 (23.3 percent) were Ukrainians, 27,490 (53.6 percent) were Russians, and 6,981 (13.6 percent) were Jews. (Of the population as a whole, according to the census, 80.1 percent were Ukrainians in December 1926.) But according to the language of usage, only 6,054 (11.3 percent) were Ukrainians, and as many as 42,471 (79.4 percent) were Russified.[27] It was not until January 1927 that Ukrainians formed a majority in the CP(B)U (51.9 percent); at the last CP(B)U Congress attended by Skrypnyk (June 1930), they accounted for 52.6 percent of the members

------

of the Executive Committee. Skrypnyk appears to have invoked the authority of the Komintern to help settle internal CP(B)U disputes. The Komintern also settled the bitter dispute with the CP(B) of the western Ukraine in February 1928.

Skrypnyk's activity in the Komintern also enabled him to acquaint foreign Communists with the problem of the fragmentation of the Ukrainian people and with the desirability of uniting Bessarabia, the Transcarpathian Ukraine, and, above all, the western Ukraine (Polish-held eastern Galicia and western Volhynia) with the eastern Ukraine. In his Statti i promovy, II (Natsional'ne pytannia), pt. 2 (Kharkov: Proletarii, 1931), pp. 404-14, Skrypnyk reprints in full the resolution of the Fifth Komintern Congress (June 17–July 8, 1924) on the nationality question in Central Europe and in the Balkans. Though his authorship of that resolution is not claimed in his massive bibliography, it stands to reason that he had a hand in drafting the document; at the very least, he strongly endorsed it. Part of the resolution is a recommendation that the CP's of Poland, Romania, and Czechoslovakia advance the slogan of the reunification of Ukrainian lands.

as a whole, but only 43 percent of the leading 2,500 workers.[28] As late as June 1953, the First Secretaries of the CP(B)U-CPU were always non-Ukrainians: Iurii Piatakov (March 1919-January 1920), Stanislav Kosior (February-November 1920), Viacheslav Molotov (November 1920-February 1921), Emmanuel Kviring (March 1921- May 1925), Lazar Kaganovich (May 1925-July 1928), Stanislav Kosior (August 1928-December 1937), to name only those under whom Skrypnyk served.

Skrypnyk realized that on the Party front he had been defeated as early as the July 1918 CP(B)U Congress in Moscow. This conviction was reinforced by his transfer to the Cheka in 1918 and to the Caucasian front in 1919-20. Apparently he decided to cut his Party losses and to concentrate on the less constrained state relations. He did participate in the debates on the formation of the Soviet Union, but most of his tremendous energy was devoted to two objectives: unification of all Ukrainians in a single Soviet state, and Ukrainian national development.

What role did Skrypnyk play in the establishment of the USSR? For a man who in 1922-24 was Ukrainian SSR PC of Justice and who served on various constitutional commissions, the only answer can be "A surprisingly small role." One gains the impression that he deliberately kept himself in the background; at the important Twelfth RCP(B) Congress of April 1923, the anti-centralist constitutional arguments were made by the Ukrainian SSR Chairman of the Council of PCs (Prime Minister), Christian Rakovsky, and by the dismissed PC of education, Hryhorii F. Hrynko.[29] Skrypnyk may well have supported the belated Ukrainian SSR draft proposal for the USSR Constitution of May 1923, which had been written in the spirit of Rakovsky; and on June 4, 1923, at a meeting of the Russian Politburo, Rakovsky and Skrypnyk tried, as a last resort, to write into the USSR Constitution provisions for republic commissariats of foreign affairs and foreign trade.[30] After the congress Skrypnyk also advocated changes in the structure and function of the Red Army: the conscripts were to serve in their own republics, and the language of command should be that of the republic.[31] According to Kosior's denunciation of Skrypnyk in November 1933 (a source that is hardly unimpeachable), at the meeting of leaders of non-Russian republics on June 9-12, 1923, Skrypnyk and Rakovsky proposed to eliminate the term "federal state" from the USSR Constitution.[32]

In the constitutional realm Skrypnyk proposed to steer a middle course between a weak confederation and a single and indivisible Russia: a second Chamber of Nationalities should approve all the actions of the central authorities affecting the policies of republican organs. He also advocated that the republics be guaranteed certain revenues, which should be specifically earmarked for them.[33] Still,

I find it somewhat surprising that in 1922-23 Skrypnyk did not take
the lead in arguing the case against a centralized union, especially
since he later employed legal arguments effectively. (According to
Pavel Postyshev's posthumous denunciation of Skrypnyk in November
1933, the latter in 1928 inveighed against the law transferring the
title to all lands from the republics to the USSR--this would reduce
the allegedly sovereign republics to the status of governments without a territory.)[34]

Skrypnyk knew that unlike the CC of the Georgian CP(B), which
in October 1922 resigned as a body, precipitating a serious Party
crisis, the CC CP(B)U was deeply divided on the advisability of resisting centralization: as late as November 17, 1922, the Ukrainian
Communist leader Dmytro Z. Manuilsky went on record in Izvestiia
as advocating the formula of "autonomization" (the non-Russian republics directly joining the RSFSR), though even Stalin had changed
his original advocacy of this formula after Lenin's criticism on September 27, 1922.[35] In the Ukraine the strongest advocate of decentralization, Rakovsky, had become converted only very recently,
perhaps as a result of his sympathies for Trotsky and his antipathy
toward Stalin.[36] That was suspect company: as much as Skrypnyk
disliked Stalin, he may have distrusted Trotsky even more. But the
two most important reasons why Skrypnyk did not resist the constitutional centralizers more strongly may have been his preoccupation
with the gathering of all Ukrainian lands and his conviction that
though the constitutional arrangements might have been objection-
able, the overall policy of korenizatsiia (sinking roots), which was
emphatically reaffirmed at the 1923 RCP(B) Congress, afforded an
excellent opportunity for the disadvantaged Ukrainian people to develop their culture and raise their socioeconomic status. To those
two tasks of a pan-Ukrainian union and Ukrainian national development he gave first priority.[37] Insofar as Lenin in his last years
came to believe in the cultural flourishing of nations as a precondition for an eventual merger, Skrypnyk's policy was Leninist.

Skrypnyk strongly advocated the supply of Ukrainian cultural
services to Ukrainians living outside the boundaries of the Ukrainian
SSR.[38] But he went further: at the Tenth CP(B)U Congress in November 1927, he raised the question of incorporating into the Ukrainian
SSR contiguous territories of the RSFSR with a Ukrainian majority
(such as the Kursk area and western Voronezh oblast).[39] In a conversation that year with the Ukrainian-born French historian Elie
Borschak, Skrypnyk was even more outspoken. When Borschak
asked why he was repeating so often that the Ukraine had not yet
been built, Skrypnyk replied laconically: "We don't have in the
Ukraine either the Kuban region, nor the Crimea, nor something
else. . . ."[40] In the Komintern, Skrypnyk devoted much attention

to the fate of the western Ukraine (then under Poland, Czechoslovakia, and Romania).

Skrypnyk's name has become almost synonymous with Ukrainization (introducing the Ukrainian language into schools, colleges,
offices, and theaters; recruiting Ukrainians into the CP[B]U and into
responsible positions in the state apparatus). Actually, Ukraini zation was the policy of the entire CP(B)U--formally since the Tenth
RCP(B) Congress of 1921 and de facto since the Twelfth RCP(B) Congress of 1923. It was carried out with greater or lesser enthusiasm
by the First Secretaries of the CP(B)U--Kviring, Kaganovich, and
Kosior--and by Skrypnyk's predecessors as PC of Education--
Hrynko (March 1920-fall of 1922), Zatonsky (fall of 1922-1924), and
Oleksander Shumsky (1924-March 1927).[41] From the viewpoint of
the central RCP(B) leadership, Ukraini zation was an effective means
of sinking roots among the masses, especially among the non-
Russified peasants.

As a result of the policy, the number of elementary and secondary schools teaching in Ukrainian increased from about two-
thirds (69.7 percent) of the rural schools and only one-third of the
urban schools (33.7 percent) in 1923-24 to about seven-tenths (69.5
percent of all schools in 1930.[42] Even more tellingly, as Kosior
announced to the Eleventh CP(B)U Congress in June 1930, 2.4 million (83.2 percent of the total) schoolchildren were taught in Ukrainian (the Ukrainian share of the total population being 80 percent), 8.8
percent were taught in Russian (9.7 percent being the Russian share),
3.6 percent were taught in Yiddish (5.4 percent of the population
being Jews), and 1 percent were taught in Polish (Poles being 1.6
percent of the population). In higher schools 33 percent of all courses
were taught in Ukrainian, and Ukrainians constituted 56 percent of
the total student body.[43] (In 1923-24 only 19.5 percent of the higher
schools taught in Ukrainian.)[44] In publishing Ukrainian books constituted less than one-third (31 percent) of all the titles in 1923-24,[45]
more than one-half (54 percent) of all the titles in 1927-28, and four-
fifths of the titles in 1930. Ukrainian newspapers in 1930 made up
almost nine-tenths (89 percent) of all the copies published; as late
as 1928 they had amounted to only 56 percent.[46] All this had been
sanctioned by Moscow and carried out by the Ukrainian Party and
state apparatuses in Kharkov.

Skrypnyk was a particularly energetic advocate of Ukraini zation.[47] He was guided by two considerations: to strengthen Bolshevik power in the Ukraine by winning over the peasantry and to continue to give preferential treatment to Ukrainians (and to any other
disadvantaged peoples in the USSR as well), so as to bring them up
to the educational standards of the other nations (in this particular
instance to that of the Jews and Russians living in the Ukraine). He

wanted genuine korenizatsiia and he wanted to eliminate the inequalities, the "cultural scissors."[48] But it was not to be. Ukrainization gathered momentum in 1925 and 1926. On April 16 and 17, 1926, at a very spirited session of the All-Union Central Executive Committee, Skrypnyk and other Ukrainian Communist leaders defended the Ukrainization program against Russian Communists. Skrypnyk was joined by non-Russian Communists from Georgia, Dagestan, Azerbaidzhan, Belorussia, and Moldavia.[49] Exactly nine days later, on April 26, 1926, Stalin personally intervened against the Ukrainian Communist writer Mykola Khvylovy, who insisted on achieving cultural and psychological independence from Moscow. A month later Kaganovich, with or without Stalin's explicit orders, attacked the Ukrainian SSR PC of Education, Shumsky, whom he accused of abetting "Khvylovism." Evidently the Russian and Russified opponents of korenizatsiia, both within and outside the Ukraine, had managed to catch Stalin's ear.

On the surface, Stalin's letter of April 26 appeared to be the very model of sensible moderation.[50] He both agreed and disagreed with Shumsky, an ardent proponent of rapid Ukrainization; he deplored merely the excesses of the program, such as the forcing of Ukrainian on Russian-speaking proletariat in the cities and Khvylovy's anti-Muscovite stand. Stalin did not question the process of Ukrainization as such, only its tempo--or so it seemed. After his intervention the Ukrainization of elementary, secondary, and higher schools continued to be pursued energetically. (In the eastern Ukraine this process came to a halt by 1938, though during World War II it was resumed on a much smaller scale in the newly occupied western Ukrainian territories; but in the RSFSR, in areas of compact Ukrainian settlement, it was stopped abruptly in the fall of 1932 or, according to an anonymous source, between 1933 and 1937, when Ukrainian-language schools changed to Russian as the language of instruction.)[51] In 1926 the CP(B)U leaders agreed, however, to abandon the Ukrainization of ethnic Russian workers in the Ukraine and to slow the Ukrainization of Ukrainian-born but linguistically Russified workers and of Party personnel.[52] (The Ukrainization of those two groups of the proletariat was stopped by 1938 at the latest; but the enrichment of the cadres of the CP[B]U with ethnic Ukrainians--Ukrainization in the organizational or personnel, as opposed to the cultural, sense--appears to have continued more slowly through World War II and until Stalin's death in 1953.) On the surface little changed when Stalin thundered at Khvylovy's temerity in April 1926.

In reality Stalin's seemingly moderate, common-sense intervention meant that in the cultural-political struggle in the Ukraine, the leaders in Moscow were shifting their support to the opponents of Ukrainization as such, not just to excessively rapid Ukrainization. A struggle was indeed being waged, with excesses committed on both sides. A Ukrainian patriot who met Skrypnyk in the late 1920s confided his uneasiness that an insignificant number of Russian-language papers were published in the Ukraine. "Never mind," retorted Skrypnyk, "they'll get used to it."[53] On the other hand, CP(B)U leader Andreii Khvylia indignantly told the Third Western Ukraine Communist Party Congress (June-August 1928) that there were cases of entire CP(B)U delegations from the cities of the Donets Basin, and even from Kiev, declaring publicly at all-union Party meetings that they represented Russia, not the Ukraine.[54] But the prize for acerbity goes perhaps to Russian writer Fedor Gladkov, who at a meeting in the Ukraine declared:

> Why should we return to the pre-Petrine epoch, why should we galvanize the Ukrainian language which had all been gathering dust? All this hampers socialist construction. . . . The Ukrainian writers aspire to compete with Russian writers, but at the bottom of things this is only an imitation by monkeys.[55]

In this tense atmosphere, Stalin's strong condemnation of Khvylovy for rejecting Moscow was bound to be--correctly--interpreted by all the Gladkovs as a green light to attack Ukrainization from stem to stern. It was suggested at the University of Chicago Workshop that Stalin's idea was that the implementation of Ukrainization should not be entrusted to Ukrainians, but only to non-Ukrainians. The former were liable to engage in militantly nationalistic excesses. I think that this idea goes back to the pre-World War I writings of Lenin and, like many of his earlier ideas, is a counsel of theoretical perfection not supported by facts. Of the non-Ukrainians in charge of the CP(B)U, only Kaganovich (between May 1925 and May 1926) appears to have made an honest effort to further Ukrainization in all its aspects. His predecessors, notably Kviring, either dragged their feet or sabotaged it. Stalin's new anti-Ukrainian policy can essentially be traced to one independent variable: in 1926 the regime was stable enough to begin to retract some of the concessions that had been granted to the non-Russians in the early years of the New Economic Policy and to make fuller use of Russians.

Where did Skrypnyk stand on cultural policy? A historian of the CP(B)U characterizes his attitude as follows:

> The position taken by Khvylyovy and Shumsky split the Ukrainian Communists. The majority, led by Skrypnyk, Chubar, Khvylya, and Hirchak, opposed the position

taken by Khvylyovy and Shumsky, which they feared
would lead to the separation of the Ukrainian SSR from
the USSR. They believed that a separate Ukraine, once
out of the Soviet Union, would not have sufficient
strength to resist its environment, would be unable to
develop economically, and under these circumstances
would undergo a restoration of capitalism. They believed that in spite of some temporary difficulties, the
USSR would eventually become an ideal union of nations
with equal rights and that within such a union the
Ukraine would be guaranteed an opportunity for general
development. They were convinced that the resolutions
of the Twelfth Congress of the CPSU on the nationalities
question would never be violated, that the Party would
combat not only Ukrainian but Russian nationalism as
well, that Ukrainization would be continued and that the
Russification of the Ukraine was an impossibility.[56]

In evaluating Skrypnyk's position it should perhaps be considered
that Stalin had not yet irrevocably turned against the non-Russians
(he would flirt with non-Russian nationalism at the Sixteenth CP[B]SU
Congress in June 1930), and that, above all, for close to a generation Skrypnyk had believed in, had agitated, fought, and killed for
the essentially internationalist idea of Communism. It would take a
major jolt to make him lose his belief: much more than the sniping
of Russian critics within and outside the Ukraine, more than the
necessity to conduct Ukrainization while battling both Ukrainian and
Russian nationalists, more than false accusations and show trials
directed against the Ukrainian intelligentsia.[57]

    Just as Skrypnyk was fighting what he considered to be the ex-
cesses of Shumsky in the cultural field, he turned against the excesses of some Ukrainian economists. An interesting and little-
known aspect of the late 1920s is the protests of Ukrainian economists
against the increasing integration and exploitation of the Ukrainian
economy through the five-year plans. M. Volobuev, who wrote a
scathing denunciation of economic centralism--and whom Skrypnyk
criticized in due course[58]--was an extremely vociferous spokesman
for a group of serious Ukrainian economists who somewhat more
discreetly criticized Stalin's decision to develop a second metallurgical center in the Urals and in western Siberia. (This decision was
publicized at the Sixteenth All-Union Party Congress in June 1930.)[59]
At the immediately preceding Eleventh CP(B)U Congress, in early
June 1930, Kosior bade the assembled Ukrainian Communists to accept the decision, to look at economic tasks "not from a localist
perspective"--how familiar that injunction sounds to students of the

Khrushchev and Brezhnev periods!--and not to show any feelings of
jealousy--an indication that the opposition must have been rather
widespread among the Party leaders. [60] It is plausible to assume
that the Ukrainization of language and personnel may have encouraged this economic nationalism.

Cultural Ukrainization was fatally undermined in 1933, in connection with Stalin's war on the Ukrainian peasant. It was the jolt
that unbalanced Skrypnyk and ultimately led to his suicide on July 7,
1933. His cultural policies had been attacked with increasing vehe-
mence since the end of 1931. [61] But when Skrypnyk joined his fellow
CP(B)U leaders in arguing against the harsh grain delivery quotas,
Stalin's emissary, Postyshev, who may have been a personal enemy
of Skrypnyk's, attacked him mercilessly at the June 1933 CP(B)U
CC plenum for conducting a wrong Ukrainization policy and for shel-
tering all kinds of Ukrainian counterrevolutionaries. It is certain
that Postyshev had instructions from Stalin both to squeeze grain
out of the Ukrainian peasants and to put an end to the rapid Ukrainian
national development. [62]

SHELEST

The years from 1933 until Stalin's death in 1953 were bleak
for the supporters of Ukrainization. Thousands of Ukrainian patriots
were killed in the Great Purge, not counting the millions of peasants
who perished during the collectivization. Millions of Ukrainians
were killed in World War II. For good measure, Kaganovich was
preparing another purge of Ukrainian intellectuals, when (fortunately) he was recalled to Moscow; Nikita Khrushchev took his place in
the Ukraine in December 1947 and put a stop to his preparations.
After Stalin's death, for about five years (1953-58) Khrushchev relied
heavily on the Ukrainian Party apparatus in his quest for power, and
Ukrainian Communists were temporarily favored.

When Shelest was appointed First Secretary of the CPU in mid-
1963, certain conditions had changed for the better. There was no
longer to be any preferential treatment for non-Russians; and the
Party Program adopted at the Twenty-Second CPSU Congress in late
1961 forecast the decreasing importance of republic boundaries and
prophesied the eventual merger ("complete unity") of nations--im-
plicitly under Russian auspices. But all those brave words could
not take away two major and one minor achievements, from the
Ukrainian national Communist point of view: half of Skrypnyk's pan-
Ukrainian dream had been realized by 1954; and his initiative in
setting up an independent CP(B)U in 1918 had been partly vindicated,
in that the CPU had grown into a major semi-autonomous organization.

Third, since 1945 the republic has been a member of the United Nations.

During World War II, Stalin incorporated most of the Ukrainian irredenta held by Romania, Poland, and Czechoslovakia; and in 1954 the RSFSR ceded the Crimea to the Ukrainian SSR. These moves probably were undertaken not out of any sympathies for Ukrainian aspirations, but to bring all the Ukrainians under his direct control-- his Ukrainophobia has been attested to by such diverse sources as Nikita Khrushchev and Academician Andrei Sakharov.[63] Whatever the reason, some of the more politically experienced and nationally conscious Galician Ukrainians entered the mainstream of Soviet Ukrainian cultural, scientific, and economic activity and reinforced the position of eastern Ukrainian autonomists.[64] The problem of extending Ukrainian cultural services to Ukrainians living in the other Soviet republics, notably in the RSFSR, remained, however. In February 1963, before Shelest had taken office, a large five-day conference on the state of the Ukrainian language, sponsored jointly by the Shevchenko University of Kiev and the Potebnia Institute of Linguistics of the Academy of Sciences of the Ukrainian SSR, was held at Kiev. At it the demand was made again that public education in Ukrainian be introduced outside the Ukrainian SSR. But not only was this demand rejected; any mention of it was forbidden in Soviet Ukrainian literature.[65] Shelest did not openly press the issue, as Skrypnyk did; but at least in 1964 and 1965 the Soviet Ukrainian press and Radio Kiev were allowed to air cautious complaints about Ukrainians in the RSFSR not receiving Ukrainian books and not being able to attend Ukrainian plays.[66]

Equally important in the long run is that while Khrushchev was battling for supreme power in 1953-58, the membership of the CPU was significantly expanded and the Party itself--the rank and file and the leaders--was relatively Ukrainized. As of September 1, 1952, the CP(B)U had 777,830 full and candidate members.[67] By September 1, 1961, that number had more than doubled: there were 1,580,171 such members, an increase of 103.2 percent.[68] The national composition of the CPU also had changed. In May 1940 Ukrainians had made up 63.1 percent of the CP(B)U membership, Russians 19.1 percent, and others 17.8 percent.[69] By 1958 the Ukrainian share in the CPU had dropped to 60.3 percent (compared with 76.8 percent Ukrainians in the total population in 1959), while the proportion of Russians had risen to 28.2 percent (16.9 percent in population). "Others" accounted for 11.5 percent of Party membership (6.3 percent in the population).[70] By 1968 (four and a half years after Shelest's assumption of power) the share of Ukrainians in the CPU had risen to 65.1 percent (compared with 74.9 percent of the population in 1970), the Russian share had declined slightly to 26.6 percent

(19.4 percent of the population), and the share of "others" had
dropped to 8.3 percent (5.7 percent of the population).[71]

Above all, from June 1953 until January 1976 both the First
and Second (or personnel) Secretaries of the CPU were Ukrainians,
an unheard-of change. The Ukrainian nationality of the Second Secretary (for personnel) may be more unusual and more important,
provided that he is a Ukrainian not only in name but also in conviction.[72] Unfortunately, pertinent information on Second Secretaries
is more difficult to obtain than that on the more visible First Secretaries. An exception to the rule is Nikolai V. Podgorny (Mykola V.
Pidhorny), the recently deposed titular president of the USSR, who
may be a Ukrainian patriot but who also is much more discreet than
his successor Shelest.* I would agree with Jeremy Azrael that the
development of the CPU may have been strongly helped by the influx
of Ukrainian Party and state officials into Moscow. (A. Kirichenko,
for instance, was Second CPSU Secretary [that is, Khrushchev's
deputy] from December 1957 to January 1960; Podgorny was one of
the CPSU CC Secretaries from June 1963 until Khrushchev's overthrow and, briefly, Leonid Brezhnev's deputy until December 1965.)

---

*From June 1953 until December 1957, Podgorny served as
Second Secretary of the CPU under A. Kirichenko. Prior to that he
had been deputy PC for food industry of the Ukrainian SSR (1939-40),
deputy PC for food industry of the USSR (1940-41), deputy PC for
food industry of the Ukrainian SSR again and simultaneously chief
commissioner of the Ukrainian SSR for the repatriation of the Ukrainian population on Polish territory to the fatherland (1944-46), permanent representative of the Ukrainian Council of Ministers to the
USSR government in Moscow (1946-50), and First Kharkov obkom
Secretary (1950-53). In 1957 Podgorny succeeded Kirichenko as
First CPU Secretary. In 1960 he accompanied Khrushchev to New
York, where he attended the general session of the United Nations
and gave a speech in Ukrainian. Someone who approached Podgorny
in New York with a personal petition was impressed with his willingness to help a fellow Ukrainian: in a dignified way Podgorny rejected
the allegation that he was unable to do anything without prior permission from the Russians. A recent Moscow émigré told the author
that there are reasons to assume that Podgorny is among those high
Party leaders who unsuccessfully lobbied for the removal of the
nationality designation from the Soviet internal passports: the issue
had become too inflammatory. The Ukrainian cultural renaissance
of the 1960s started under Podgorny; it apparently was he who named
Shelest to his first important post in the Ukraine.

Conversely, the "de-Ukrainization" of the Kremlin after 1965 (symbolized by the demotion of both V. Titov and Podgorny from the CPSU Secretariat) may indicate the decline of the CPU.[73] The Ukrainians who have remained in high positions in Moscow (such as Ivan Kazanets, the USSR Minister of Ferrous Metallurgy) have to watch their step lest they be accused of favoring their political home base too blatantly.

Like Skrypnyk, Shelest, a peasant's son born in 1908, did not receive a regular education. In 1935 he finally obtained his engineering degree at the age of 27, studying part-time at the Mariupol Evening Metallurgical Institute while working his way up from shift engineer to shop chief. He became chief engineer of the Sickle and Hammer plant in Kharkov in the late 1930s. A Party member since 1928, in 1940--most likely with Khrushchev's personal approval-- he was appointed secretary of the Kharkov City Committee in Charge of Defense Industry. That was his great opportunity and he made the most of it, rising to Chief of the Defense Industry Department of the Cheliabinsk Party Committee in the Urals, where he had been evacuated from Kharkov; to Instructor of the CP(B)SU CC; deputy secretary of the Defense Industry of the Saratov obkom (Party Province Committee); director of a factory in Leningrad; and in 1954, while Podgorny was Second (personnel) Secretary of the CPU, to Second Secretary of the Kiev City Party Committee. In late 1962 Shelest became the Chairman of the CPU CC Bureau for Industry and Construction; and on July 2, 1963, Khrushchev--most probably on Podgorny's advice--made him Podgorny's successor as First Secretary of the CPU, over the heads of the current second secretary, Kazanets, and the Ukrainian SSR Prime Minister, Volodymyr Shcherbytsky (the latter a Brezhnev protégé).[74]

In Party affairs Shelest continued the policy of his immediate predecessors: Ukrainizing the CPU while expanding its membership. Mostly under Shelest the total membership (full members and candidates) of the CPU grew from 1,580,171 in September 1961 to 2,534,561 in 1971. Interestingly, between 1966 and 1971, a period of unionwide retrenchment, the CPU grew faster than the parent CPSU. As a result, whereas in 1961 Party membership had been 36.4 per 1,000 total population in the Ukrainian SSR, compared with an all-Union average of 44.4 per 1,000, by 1971 the difference was reduced to 53.4 versus 58.9 per 1,000 population.[75]

More difficult to document, but plausible, is the hypothesis that Shelest was among those Party leaders who urged Brezhnev to proceed slowly with the exchange of Party cards that had been decided upon in the spring of 1971 and implemented in 1973-75: heading a Party that had expanded very rapidly, he might stand to lose most from even a relatively mild purge.[76] Better evidence exists

to show that Shelest twice managed to delay temporarily the dismissal of first obkom secretaries: Oleksander Muzhitsky of
Poltava [77] and Kutsevol of Lviv. Reportedly, in November 1971
Kutsevol had incurred the displeasure of none other than Mikhail
Suslov for not being energetic enough in combating Ukrainian nationalism. [78] Credence should, therefore, be given to the veiled accusations that Shelest was deficient in his "cadre policy"--that is, that
he resisted central efforts to appoint high-level Party and state officials against his will; included in cadre policy was the interchange
of cadres (sending Ukrainian officials out of the Ukraine and bringing in non-Ukrainian replacements). [79] In general, as Grey Hodnett
has brought out, Shelest always affirmed the unity of the CPSU. At
the same time he would vigorously assert the autonomy of the CPU
within it. Shelest would stress that Ukrainian Social Democratic
organizations had played a key role in the creation of the Bolshevik
Party. The Ukraine was thus "a charter member of the organization, not simply a passive recipient of party political status." [80]

     As an economic administrator Shelest was fairly open in de-
fending what he considered to be Ukrainian economic interests.
Under him a group of Ukrainian economists was allowed to argue
against the development of Siberia at the expense of capital investments in the fuel industry in the Ukraine. [81] It was under Shelest
that some Soviet Ukrainian administrators privately insisted, in a
conversation with an anonymous central official, that the Ukraine
was being economically exploited: if they had not had to contribute
so much to the Union budget, the Ukrainians would have, for example, solved the housing shortage a long time ago. [82] In 1966, at
the Twenty-Third CPSU Congress, V. V. Shcherbitsky, then Ukrainian SSR Prime Minister, openly pleaded for capital for more power
stations and more transmission lines in the Ukraine, for more funds
for the coal mines of the Donbas. Shelest remained diplomatically
silent. But when, at the 1971 CPSU Congress, Shcherbitsky praised
Brezhnev and his policy of "the most rational allocation of productive
forces" in Siberia rather than in the Ukraine, Shelest bluntly told
the assembled delegates that it was "incorrect" to divert capital investment from the Donbas coal industry in favor of the oil and
natural gas industries. He also demanded from Moscow more and
better-formulated animal feeds and more farm machinery. [83]

     An American student of Shelest has come to the conclusion
"that Shelest's economic performance in the Ukraine was no worse
than Brezhnev's in Moscow." But he also points out that Shelest
and his Ukrainian economists were disappointed, in that Brezhnev
and Aleksei Kosygin did little to widen the increasingly tighter energy bottleneck in the Ukraine: specifically, too little capital was
being invested to expand the Ukrainian coal supply. In 1971 Kosygin

did promise to undertake a broad program of atomic power station
development and to accelerate the technical reequipping of the coal-
mining industry in the European part of the USSR, but no specific
promise was made to modernize the Ukrainian Donbas coal mines.
It would take a number of years for the newly built atomic power
plants in the Ukrainian SSR to overcome the predicted energy shortage resulting from the neglect of coal mining in the Donbas. [84] In
addition, Shelest demanded and obtained unprecedented administrative autonomy. He appears to have been successful in establishing
(March 1969) the only republic ministry of sovkhozes (state farms)
in the entire Soviet Union. After his dismissal the ministry was
converted to a more centralized Union-Republic one in February
1973. [85]

Shelest's relationship to Ukrainian culture is more ambiguous.
On the one hand, he either would not or--more plausibly--could not
prevent the mass arrests and trials of Ukrainian intellectuals in
1965 and, particularly, in 1972. In a recent joint letter to the
London Times the released Russian dissident Vladimir Bukovsky
and others wrote that "the Ukrainian patriotic movement sustained
in 1972 the heaviest single KGB assault since 1953 of any dissenting
group in the Soviet Union." [86] The years 1965 and 1972 were black
years for dissidents throughout the USSR, not only in the Ukraine.
It is interesting, nonetheless, that one of the foremost Ukrainian
dissidents, Ivan Dzyuba, the author of Internationalism or Russification? (1965), has been treated relatively gently. Semi-public and
public denunciations notwithstanding, it was not until March 2, 1972--
two and a half months before Shelest's dismissal as First Secretary
of the CPU--that Dzyuba was expelled from the Writers' Union of
the Ukraine, and not until April 18, 1972--a month before Shelest's
fall--that he was arrested. [87] This would lend credence to supposi-
tions circulating among Ukrainians in the West that Dzyuba's treatise
had been written "with tacit encouragement from higher authorities," [88] and that those authorities--possibly Shelest himself--pro-
tected Dzyuba as long as it was feasible.

Shelest also was not able to forestall the Russification of elementary and secondary schools in the Ukraine. Whereas in 1955-
56, 72.2 percent of all schoolchildren were taught in Ukrainian and
25.9 percent in Russian, [89] by about 1964 the proportions were 70
percent and 30 percent; and by 1974 they had changed to "around 60
percent" taught in Ukrainian and "almost 40 percent" in Russian.
Furthermore, instruction in Russian was said to be spreading, particularly in the cities. [90]

On the other hand, Shelest manfully tried, through a circular
signed in August 1965 by the Ukrainian SSR Minister of Higher Education, Yurii Dadenkov, to Ukrainize the instruction in colleges that

were under the jurisdiction of the Ukrainian SSR ministry (by no means all of the colleges in the republic). He failed, however. [91] Shelest would not give up. In a speech of September 3, 1968, he explicitly called for publication of college textbooks in Ukrainian. [92]

Under Shelest some monumental works of Ukrainian culture were either written or published. Foremost among them was the Entsyklopediia kibernetyky (Encyclopedia of Cybernetics) in Ukrainian. The first such work in the Soviet Union, it appeared in two volumes in 1973, after his fall.[93] Another was the projected multivolume Great History of the Ukrainian SSR, which was published in somewhat different form as Istoriia mist i sil Ukräins'koi RSR v dvatsiaty-shesty tomakh (History of cities and villages of the Ukrainian SSR, 26 volumes [1967-74] again in Ukrainian).[94] The American historian Jaroslaw Pelenski is right in pointing out that it probably was Shelest or someone in his entourage who quietly sanctioned the official attempt to rehabilitate the leading member of the Ukrainian national historical school, Michael Hrushevsky, and who tacitly approved the officially unpublished treatise by historian Mykhailo Iu. Braichevsky, Pryiednannia chy vozz'iednannia? (Annexation or reunification). Braichevsky's treatise sheds considerable doubt on the official 1954 Party theses concerning the "reunification" of the Ukraine with Russia in the Treaty of Pereyaslav (1654).[95] Pelenski says further:

> It can also be argued that positive predisposition on the part of Shelest and his group toward Ukrainian historico-cultural problems made possible the publication of literary works such as O. Honchar's novel Sobor (The Cathedral) (1968), R. Ivanchuk's novel Mal'vy (The Mallows) (1969), and many other works which later came under strong criticism. [96]

Summing up Shelest's contribution in the field of culture and in politics, Pelenski characterizes his period as "a revival of controlled Ukrainian autonomism."[97]

Shelest's position in international relations could perhaps be characterized as "preventive hawkishness." His reputation for hawkishness rests on a well-documented analysis of his active role in the intervention in Czechoslovakia, his voiced reservations against détente in general and Brezhnev's West German policy in particular (he felt that it was at East Germany's expense), and persistent rumors that he opposed the summit meeting with President Richard Nixon in May 1972 after the United States mined the harbor of Haiphong, North Vietnam. [98] Several scholars, however, believe that the last rumors are unfounded, and perhaps may constitute a deliberate piece of

misinformation put out by the KGB.[99]   I would, nevertheless, be
inclined not to reject those rumors out of hand: the timing of
Shelest's dismissal from the First Secretaryship in the Ukraine, on
the eve of the Nixon visit in late May 1972, is very difficult to understand except by reference to international affairs, for there does not
seem to have been any domestic crisis that would have necessitated
such a reshuffling at such a delicate moment. Assuming that Shelest
did involve himself in foreign policy, why did he follow the hawkish
line? Essentially to prevent being accused of a rightist, pronational-
ist deviation in both domestic and foreign policy: it was "preventive
hawkishness." On the other hand, in my judgment Shelest's involvement in foreign policy was the proverbial last straw rather than the
true reason for his fall. In this connection, it should be mentioned
that between 1967 and 1972 a number of articles on the legal position
of the Ukrainian SSR were published in that republic. Some of them
stressed the Ukraine's active participation in international relations
through membership in the United Nations, signing treaties, and
hosting consulates of other countries.[100] This boasting of the international role of the Ukraine could only raise many eyebrows in Moscow and further contribute to Shelest's fall.

A much more likely, albeit intangible, reason for Shelest's
dismissal from his CPU post was the feeling shown in his book O Our
Soviet Ukraine.[101] However, if it was the only cause, it is hard to
explain why Brezhnev waited more than a year after the book's publication in December 1970 before letting Shelest go, and more than
two years before allowing an anonymous author to savagely attack
Shelest in print.[102] The title of the book is as sentimentally patriotic as had been Volodymyr Sosiura's World War II poem "Love
the Ukraine"; and it must have rubbed intolerant assimilators the
wrong way precisely as the earlier poem had done.[103] But, unlike
the poem, the book has not been translated into Russian. Its very
title would have been difficult to translate, for the Russian language
has no vocative.

Although space limitations do not permit a full analysis of the
book, Shelest's work shows pride in Ukrainian statehood and in the
economic and cultural achievements of the Ukraine. The first two
pages establish the key themes:

> The Ukraine is a constituent, inseparable part of
> the great Soviet Union. In the family of Soviet republics
> she has become so mighty and so highly developed.
>
>   .   .   .
>
> Thanks to the victory of the Great October [Revo-
> lution], thanks to the Leninist nationality policy of the

Party the Ukrainian people for the first time in its history has created a <u>national state</u>--the Ukrainian Soviet
Socialist Republic, which has already passed its 50th
anniversary.

Today Soviet Ukraine is a mighty industrial
<u>state</u> with a highly developed agriculture, with first-
ranking [<u>peredovoiu</u>] science and culture. [104]

Shelest, like Karl Marx, admires the Zaporozhe Cossack Host,
its democratic constitution, and its education. [105] Somewhat pointed-
ly he reminds his readers that before the establishment of Moscow
University in 1755, the Mohyla Academy, founded at Kiev in 1632,
had served as the cultural and educational center not only for the
Ukraine but also for Russia, Belorussia, and the southern Slavs. [106]
Without using the term "Ukrainization," Shelest praises "important
successes obtained in the preparation of national cadres in the fields
of science, technology, literature, and arts" from 1928 to 1933.
Lest anyone come to wrong conclusions, he immediately lauds the
increased publication of books and newspapers in Ukrainian. [107]
Shelest's book is important also for what it does not say: nowhere
is there a reference to the eventual merger of nations.

Last, but not least, there are signs that Shelest wanted to advance the rehabilitation of Mykola Skrypnyk, which had been begun
under his predecessor, Podgorny. The 1963 <u>Ukrainian Soviet Ency-
clopedia</u> article, authorized by Shelest, is very sympathetic in tone.
Its only criticism is contained in one sentence: "Heading the People's
Commissariat of Education of the Ukrainian SSR, Skrypnyk committed errors in the field of national cultural development." [108] Seven
years later, in <u>O Our Soviet Ukraine</u>, Shelest returned to Skrypnyk,
mentioning him favorably but more cautiously. Skrypnyk is not cited
by name in the context of the late 1920s and early 1930s, when he was
Ukraine's PC of education; but the Party policy with which he was
identified--the struggle against both (Russian) chauvinists and (Ukrainian) national-deviationists--is. [109] Shelest, however, does not completely conceal his admiration for Skrypnyk. He describes him as
the chairman of the first government of the Ukrainian Soviet Republic, which is historically inaccurate, and as one of the leaders of
the Bolshevik caucus at the Second Ukrainian Congress of Soviets
(March 1918), which is true. In the most unlikely, barely noticeable, place, however, the travelogue-style description of the Donets
area, Shelest's admiration for Skrypnyk breaks through: "In the
Donets region there [was] born: the Old Bolshevik and the outstanding Party and State official M. O. Skrypnyk. . . ."[110]

Shelest's opposition in Party affairs and in economic and administrative matters, his sympathy for Ukrainian history and culture,

and his occasional meddling in foreign policy could not be tolerated: he was abruptly dismissed from the First Secretaryship of the CPU on May 19, 1972, at a CC CPSU plenum in Moscow; at the April 1973 CC CPSU plenum in Moscow, after publication of the review of his book, he was "retired" from his full seat on the CPSU Politburo.[111]

SKRYPNYK AND SHELEST

What do Skrypnyk and Shelest have in common, and what separates them in terms of concrete issues? Skrypnyk, the professional all-Russian revolutionary turned architect of the Soviet Ukraine, dreamed of setting up an independent Communist Party of the Ukraine that would be joined with the RCP only through the Komintern. Shelest, the graduate of Stalin's Great Purge and of the postwar Russian reaction, could not indulge in such dreams; to him the CPU appears as an integral part of the CPSU, but he insists that it is not a part wholly subordinate to the--informal--Russian section of the CPSU. The relationship he sees is on the order of fellow charter members, or perhaps that of a junior to a senior partner, not that of a subordinate to a superior. Apart from the formal difference (Skrypnyk's insistence on Party independence under the Komintern), the attitudes of the two men are similar. I have not been able to find any concrete pronouncements by either Skrypnyk or Shelest on Party cadres policy (influx of ethnic Russian officials, as opposed to the advancement of ethnic Ukrainian Party officials). It appears that in the 1960s and early 1970s, as in the 1920s and 1930s, the issue was exceedingly sensitive. Furthermore, Skrypnyk had no official responsibility for Party cadres policy. If anyone broke the silence on such issues, it was Kosior; and even Kosior, an ethnic Pole, was not brash enough to stress that the CP(B)U was really not an ethnic Ukrainian party. Shelest quietly expanded and progressively "Ukrainized" the CPU, continuing the work of Kirichenko and of Podgorny. It is probable that on Party cadre questions Skrypnyk worked with pro-Ukrainian autonomist elements within the CP(B)U; but if he did, it was behind the scenes.

On the question of Ukrainian statehood, Skrypnyk was more outspoken than Shelest: he insisted on republic rather than All-Union People's Commissariats of Foreign Affairs and of Foreign Trade. With the establishment of Union-Republic (mixed) People's Commissariats of Foreign Affairs in February 1944 and the Ukraine's admission to the United Nations a year later, a reasonable step toward the reestablishment of the international personality of the Ukrainian SSR was made (the Soviet Ukraine had played a brief role in international relations prior to 1922). Shelest wisely did not make an issue of the limited nature of Ukrainian representation in international affairs, but used it to buttress his more general assertions of Ukrainian statehood. In foreign policy both Skrypnyk and Shelest appeared to be "hard-liners": they believed in the cause of a Communist world revolution. Unlike Skrypnyk, Shelest did not deal with the centralized character of the Soviet armed forces. Neither did he insist on the unification of all Ukrainian lands and the provision of Ukrainian cultural services to Ukrainians in non-Ukrainian republics. But the conviction that the Ukraine is a state and not a province, an autonomous, or even semi-sovereign state runs like a red thread through both Skrypnyk's and Shelest's writings.

Skrypnyk appears inadequate on economic issues, which are Shelest's strong suit. But the two join forces on the issue of Ukrainian-language education and culture. Skrypnyk was able to continue the Ukrainization of elementary and secondary schools and of a small part of the higher educational establishments, of the press, the theaters, and book publishing. Shelest was less successful in all those aspects, but not for want of trying. A deeper study would also have shown that Skrypnyk continued to battle the old Ukrainian intelligentsia centered in the All-Ukrainian Academy of Sciences. Shelest, on the other hand, seems to have had a harmonious working relationship with the contemporary academicians who wrote the Encyclopedia of Cybernetics and the multivolume History of Cities and Villages in the Ukraine for him. Shelest went even farther: he protected poets, writers, and literary critics, and may have tacitly sanctioned such classics of dissent as Dzyuba's and Braichevsky's treatises. A scholar is tempted to say that Skrypnyk was building the base for the pyramid of Ukrainian cultural development but felt uncomfortable at its top, while Shelest left behind monuments of highest cultural achievements but had to witness the deliberate dismantling of the Ukrainian-language educational base.

Aside from these specific issues, however, what role have Skrypnyk and Shelest played in Ukrainian national development? What causes the persistence of Ukrainian national Communism, and what are its limitations? What will its future be? Both Skrypnyk and Shelest started from a centrist position on the Ukrainian question. On the right both have battled the advocates of Ukrainian independence (Skrypnyk directly in 1917-20; Shelest was promoted to his first responsible Party position in 1940, under Stalin, when there was an open season on genuine Ukrainian nationalists--his later denunciations of Ukrainian "bourgeois nationalists" ring true). Both struggled on the left with aggressive Russian and Russified denationalizers (the Luxemburgists, national nihilists, great power chauvinists, and the like). Both started with the sincere belief that the Ukraine should be a national Communist state--not just a geographic or even an ethnographic expression--with equal rights in the Soviet Union and the even larger future Communist Commonwealth. The difference between them would seem to be that after 1918 Skrypnyk remained on the fringes of political power, whereas Shelest rose to First Secretary of the 2.5 million-strong CPU, the autonomous head of the 48 million citizens of the Ukrainian SSR, and full member of the CPSU Politburo between November 1964 and April 1973. Yet the difference is more apparent than real: on May 19, 1972, Shelest had to surrender his authority over the Ukraine in Moscow, not in Kiev; for in 1972, as in 1918, it was Moscow that held the real power.

Skrypnyk's and Shelest's influence was strongest when the non-Communist or even anti-Communist Ukrainians were relatively powerful and the center in Moscow was not yet fully consolidated (during the Civil War and the New Economic Policy, during the decade of Khrushchev's experiments and the first years of Brezhnev's regime). As the center acquired more power vis-à-vis the Ukrainian villages, towns, and cities, when it felt strong enough to assume that it was no longer necessary to make political concessions to the advocates of Ukrainian autonomy (or, rather, once the conviction had gained ground in Moscow that the integration of the Ukraine was essentially a problem for the military and the police), Skrypnyk and Shelest saw their influence drastically reduced. They were no longer valued intermediaries between Moscow and the Ukrainian masses, but had become unnecessary obstacles to direct rule. Both had underestimated the force of Communist discipline grafted onto the "most profound centralizing inertia" (glubochaishaia tsentralizatorskaia inertsiia) that the Party had inherited from the tsars. [112]

But if we view the political developments in the Ukraine from a wider historical perspective and, above all, if we consider that under Stalin, Ukrainian autonomists had been decimated by the hundreds of thousands, if not by the millions, it appears quite remarkable that a second, "little" Ukrainization could be attempted in the decade 1956-65, or perhaps even in the two decades 1953-72. There are several reasons for this remarkable persistence of Ukrainian national Communism.

Among the interior reasons the foremost is the change in the socioeconomic character of the Ukrainians: from a people of many peasants, few workers, and a sprinkling of nationally conscious intelligentsia, they have advanced to a nation of fewer peasants, more workers, and a numerically significant, highly educated elite. In comparison with the other major nationalities in the USSR--in terms of overall development--they may still rank somewhere in the middle, behind the Russians, behind the Georgians and Armenians, and behind all the Balts;[113] but they are no longer the quasi-ethnographic mass

they were two or three generations ago. Robert G. Kaiser, of the
Washington Post, was not exaggerating too much when he wrote in
1976: "Ukrainians of all kinds, from the humblest peasant to the
most educated professor, share a sense of Ukrainian nationality
which, if aggravated, can manifest itself in dissident behavior."[114]
In his letter to me of March 12, 1977, Vsevolod Holubnychy summed
up the progress of the Ukrainian nation as follows:

> . . . The Ukraine of Shelest differs completely from the
> Ukraine of Skrypnyk, and this--in a positive sense, and
> this--to a large extent thanks to Skrypnyk. In all re-
> spects she is today more powerful, mightier than she
> had been before Skrypnyk and during his time. Recent
> [Soviet] emigrés--Jews and even Russians with whom I
> have talked--unanimously state that the Ukraine can be-
> come an independent state today, "can" in the sense
> that she is so powerful and so developed. Under the
> Tsars and during Skrypnyk's time even the Ukrainians
> themselves did not share this certainty.

In a way, Skrypnyk and Shelest are simultaneously the contributors
to, and the beneficiaries of, the process of building a modern Ukrainian nation, which, at the latest, started at the turn of the century
and may not yet have run its full course.

Among the exterior reasons for the persistence of Ukrainian
national Communism are, in my judgment (in descending order of
importance): the growth of Russian nationalism; fluctuations in
Soviet nationality policy; the upsurge of nationalism in socialist
Eastern Europe (notably in Yugoslavia, Poland, Hungary, Romania,
and Czechoslovakia); the movement for independence in the Third
World (Ukrainians have served on UN organs and on Soviet foreign
aid missions); and--more recently--disagreements among European
Communist parties (Euro-Communism).

Paradoxically, despite its proven persistence, the autonomist
Ukrainian national Communism may be doomed in the long run.
Twice in 50 years controlled Ukrainian national development ("Ukrainization") has been begun, apparently in good faith, only to be terminated
and partially reversed a decade or two later. In pursuing their goal of
political integration, the central authorities appear to have been un-
able--or unwilling--to accept a substantial amount of Ukrainian cultural autonomy, lest this lead to genuine political autonomy, and from
that perhaps proceed to national self-determination under appropriate
international conditions.

In this the central authorities may have been influenced--possibly even misled--by the substantial number of Russians, * Russified Ukrainians, and other Russified nationals who, to a large degree, are still in control of the cities in the Ukraine: Moscow has ultimately sided with the Kvirings instead of the Skrypnyks, the Melnikovs[†] instead of the Shelests. The cause of Ukrainian autonomy also has not been helped by the personal rivalry between Brezhnev's Ukrainian protégé Shcherbitsky and the more independent-minded Shelest; it appears now that Shcherbitsky's victory was achieved at the price of accepting a strongly pro-Russian policy. Since 1972 the main spokesmen for the Ukraine's cultural and political rights are no longer within the Communist Party, but outside--even in the underground--among the increasingly more radical dissidents.

The ferocity with which Ukrainian dissidents have been persecuted since 1972, [115] though some of them may not have gone far beyond Shelest, does not augur well for a moderate, compromise solution in the future. In the eyes of centralist Moscow and in those of dissident Kiev, autonomist national Communism may rapidly become a halfway house that is either too big or too small. With Russian and Ukrainian nationalisms increasingly moving onto a collision course and the central government increasingly siding with the former, the end result could be a tragedy for Russia as well as the Ukraine. For all I know, Shelest could prove to be the last of the Ukrainian national Communists, the last of the autonomists; and the story of Skrypnyk and Shelest may one day be recognized as a sad account of opportunities lost and a classic case study in how not to pursue the goals of political integration.

---

*For certain personal reasons I would be the very last to deny that some Russians who have lived in the Ukraine are proud defenders of the Ukraine and of its territorial interests. In my judgment they constitute a minority.

†Leonid G. Melnikov, an ethnic Russian and a Malenkov protégé, was Stalin's last First Secretary of the CP(B)U (1949-53). In a power play that probably was initiated by Lavrenti Beria and was secretly connived at by Khrushchev, Melnikov was dismissed in June 1953 for having committed mistakes in nationality policy, such as Russifying colleges in the western Ukraine. For more details, see Bilinsky, The Second Soviet Republic, pp. 18, 238 ff.

NOTES

1. M. Skrypnyk, "Moia avtobiohrafiia," in his Statti i promovy, (Kharkov: State Publishers of the Ukraine, 1930), 1: 5-17; reprinted in Ivan Koshelivets' (Iwan Koszeliwec), Mykola Skrypnyk (Munich: Suchasnist, 1972), pp. 261-72.

2. See Koshelivets', op. cit., pp. 268, 270; N. N. Popov, Ocherk istorii Kommunisticheskoi partii (bol'shevikov) Ukrainy (2nd ed.; Kharkov: Proletarii, 1929), p. 55; Mariia Skrypnik, Vospominaniia ob Il'iche (1917-1918) (3rd rev. ed.; Moscow: Publishers of Political Literature, 1965), p. 9.

3. A. Iaremenko, comp., Materialy do bibliohrafii M. O. Skrypnyka (Kharkov-Kiev: Rukh, 1932), the first part of which (materials by Skrypnyk) was reprinted in Koshelivets', op. cit., pp. 278-335. This is an official bibliography prepared for the celebration of Skrypnyk's sixtieth birthday, in the summer of 1932, one year before his suicide.

4. Skrypnyk, op. cit., in Koshelivets', op. cit., p. 262.

5. Ibid., p. 261.

6. Mariia Skrypnik, op. cit., p. 68; Iu. Babko and I. Bilokobyl's'ky, Mykola Oleksiiovych Skrypnyk (Kiev: Publishers of Political Literature of Ukraine, 1967), pp. 118 ff.

7. V. Zatonsky, a Ukrainian Bolshevik leader, wrote in December 1917: "For the time being there is no split among the Ukrainians [Ukrainian nationalist parties] and no such split can be foreseen. For that reason we have to fight the Ukrainian people, and there is only a small bunch (nebol'shaia kuchka) of Bolsheviks." See Popov, op. cit., p. 144, quoting Zatonsky.

8. Wrote Georg Lapchynsky, the General Secretary (Prime Minister) of the first Soviet government in the Ukraine, who had come to Kharkov from Kiev: "[As] is known, the Kharkov Soviet offered us to stay in the jail near the railroad station and gave us several cells. But it was so cold and damp there, and [the cells] smelled so much of disinfectant that we fled after our first night." See his "Pershyi period radians'koi vlady na Ukraini, TsVKU ta narodnii sekretariat (Spohady)," Letopis' revoliutsii (1928), no. 1: 160.

On the early years of the CP(B)U see also John S. Reshetar, Jr., "The Communist Party of the Ukraine and Its Role in the Ukrainian Revolution," in The Ukraine, 1917-1921: A Study in Revolution, ed. Taras Hunczak (Cambridge, Mass.: Harvard University Press for the Harvard Ukrainian Research Institute, 1977), pp. 159-85; Jurij Borys, "Political Parties in the Ukraine," ibid., pp. 145-48; and Y. Bilinsky, "The Communist Take-over of the Ukraine," ibid., pp. 104-27.

9. According to Popov, op. cit., pp. 144-45, he did not get
any support from the Bolshevik delegates and had to withdraw his
resolution (declaring that an autonomous Donetsk republic should remain a part of the Ukrainian Soviet Republic), lest his resolution run
counter to the resolution of the Bolshevik caucus at the congress.

10. Vsevolod Holubnychy, "Outline History of the Communist
Party of the Ukraine," Ukrainian Review (Munich) (1958), no. 6: 71.
Despite its relative conciseness (57 pp.) this remains the best scholarly history of the CPU. See also "Mykola Skrypnyk," Ukraïns'ka
radians'ka entsyklopediia (1963), 13: 228a.

11. It appears to have been in Lenin's interest to have an independent, united Soviet Ukraine carry on war against the Germans
after Brest-Litovsk; see Holubnychy, op. cit., p. 72. The intercon-
nection between the separation of the Ukraine from Bolshevik Russia
after Brest-Litovsk and Lenin's support for the establishment of an
independent Soviet Ukrainian government and CP(B)U is broadly confirmed by the Communist Polish historian Janusz Radziejowski,
"Kwestia narodowa w partii komunistycznej na Ukraine radzieckiej
(1920-1927)," Przeglad historyczny 62, no. 3 (1971): 479.

12. Popov, op. cit., pp. 158-59.

13. As cited in ibid., p. 159, n. Emphasis in original.

14. As cited in Institut Istorii Partii, Kiev, Ocherki istorii
Kommunisticheskoi partii Ukrainy (Kiev: Politizdat Ukrainy, 1964),
p. 243.

15. Ibid., pp. 249-50, and even Popov, op. cit., pp. 161-62,
are somewhat vague on what occurred at Taganrog. The best source
is Holubnychy, op. cit., p. 72. See, however, Iu. Iu. Kondufor,
"Stvorennia KP(b)U--skladovoï i nevid'iemnoi chastyny partiï Komu-
nistiv," Ukraïns'kyi istorychnyi zhurnal (April 1976), no. 4: 45 ff.
The short-lived independence might explain why the CP(B)U central
organ was called a politburo, a courtesy designation it still retains.
All the other republican CPs are headed by bureaus.

16. Skrypnyk, "Vid postanov do dila u natsional'nii politytsi"
(his speech at the Eleventh RCP[B]U Congress, 1922), in his Statti
i promovy z natsional'noho pytannia, Ivan Koshelivets', comp.
(Munich: Suchasnist, 1974), p. 21. Henceforth cited as Skrypnyk
(Koshelivets', comp.), Statti . . .

17. See note 11.

18. Kondufor, op. cit.

19. Skrypnyk, "Moia avtobiohrafiia," in Koshelivets', Mykola
Skrypnyk, p. 271. Confirmed by "Mykola Skrypnyk," Ukraïns'ka
radians'ka entsyklopediia (1963), 13: 228-29. Popov, op. cit., p.
180, says that Skrypnyk was elected a candidate member only at the
Second Congress. This is probably an error, but a significant one.

20. Skrypnyk, "Moia autobiohrafiia," in Koshelivets', Mykola Skrypnyk, p. 271. Babko and Bilokobyl's'ky, op. cit., pp. 138-44, give an imperfectly romanticized picture of that activity.

21. Skrypnyk, "Moia autobiohrafiia," in Koshelivets', Mykola Skrypnyk, p. 272. So far, I have not been able to find out against whom Skrypnyk was fighting.

22. "Mykola Skrypnyk," Ukrains'ka radians'ka entsyklopediia (1963), 13: 228.

23. Ibid.

24. Skrypnyk accused Stalin of not coming out squarely on the side of the non-Russians, of always balancing his critique of Russian chauvinism by references to the militant nationalism of non-Russians. Stalin was practicing a "double bookkeeping on the nationality question," said Skrypnyk. See Dvenadtsatyi s"ezd RKP(b) 17-25 aprelia 1923 goda (Moscow: Izdatel'stvo Politicheskoi Literatury, 1968), pp. 569-73, see 572.

25. Skrypnyk, "Pro spravu Sultan-Galiieva," in Skrypnyk (Koshelivets', comp.), Statti . . ., pp. 29-33. See also the excellent coverage of that conference in Alexandre Bennigsen and Chantal Quelquejay, Les mouvements nationaux chez les musulmans de Russie: Le "Sultangalievisme" au Tatarstan (Paris and The Hague: Mouton, 1960), pp. 165-71, 239-48.

26. Holubnychy, op. cit., p. 124.

27. The total in the linguistic breakdown is somewhat higher: 53,495. Nationality in this case apparently has been established by ethnic descent; there is a note that the first nationality breakdown does not include 2,259 Party members who did not show to what nationality their parents belonged. See Kommunisticheskaia Partiia (b) Ukrainy (Komunistychna Partiia [b] Ukraïny), Vserossiiskaia perepis' 1922 goda chlenov RKP: Itogi partperepisi 1922 goda na Ukraine (Kharkov: Izdanie TsKKP[b]U, 1922), p. xii.

28. S. Kosior, Politychnyi zvit TsK KP(b)U XI z"izdovi KP(b)U (Kharkov: DVU, 1930), p. 72. Holubnychy, loc. cit., has slightly different figures for the summer and for January of 1930—52.9 percent.

29. See Dvenadtsatyi s"ezd RKP(b) . . ., pp. 502-05 (Hrynko's speech), 569-73 (Skrypnyk's), and 576-82 (Rakovsky's). For the history of the rather strange conversion of Rakovsky to the Ukrainian national cause, see F. Conte, "Christian Rakovskij. Commissaire aux affaires étrangères de l'Ukraine," Cahiers du monde russe et soviétique (Paris) 12, no. 4 (October-December 1971): 439-66; and V. Holubnychy, "Kh. Rakovsky," Entsyklopediia ukraïnoznavstva, pt. 2, VII (Paris, 1973), 2465-66.

30. Robert S. Sullivant, Soviet Politics and the Ukraine 1917-1957 (New York: Columbia University Press, 1962), pp. 73-75.

31. Radziejowski, op. cit., p. 484, citing Skrypnyk, "Natsional'ne pytannia i Chervona Armiia, " in his Statti i promovy, II, pt. 1 (Kharkov: State Publishers of the Ukraine, 1929), p. 44. See Skrypnyk (Koshelivets', comp.), Statti . . ., pp. 43-44.

32. S. Kosior and S. and P. Postyschew (Postyshev), Der bolschewistische Sieg in der Ukraine (Reden auf dem vereinigten Plenum des ZK und der ZKK der kommunistischen Partei der Ukraine [Bolschewiki] im November 1933) (Moscow-Leningrad: Verlagsgenossenschaft Ausländischer Arbeiter in der UdSSR, 1934), p. 60. See also Radziejowski, loc. cit.

33. Skrypnyk (Koshelivets', comp.), Statti . . ., pp. 36-37.

34. Kosior and Postyshev, op. cit., p. 138. The law was adopted in December 1928--see Sullivant, op. cit., p. 150.

35. V. V. Pentkovskaia, "Rol' V. I. Lenina v obrazovanii SSSR, " Voprosy istorii (1956), no. 3: 18-19.

36. Richard Pipes, The Formation of the Soviet Union: Communism and Nationalism 1917-1923 (Cambridge, Mass. : Harvard University Press, 1954), p. 278. See also Sullivant, op. cit., pp. 69-70.

37. Holubnychy, op. cit., p. 82.

38. See, for instance, his speech at the Twelfth RCP(B) Congress, Dvenadtsatyi s"zed . . ., pp. 569-73; "Vpered Leninovym shliakhom" (welcoming a Ukrainian newspaper in the Kuban region), in Skrypnyk, Statti i promovy, II (Natsional'ne pytannia), pt. 2 (Kharkhov: State Publishers of the Ukraine, 1931), pp. 69-70; "Vidrodzhenyi narid" and "Proletars'kym shliakhom" (Ukrainians in lower Volga and Kazakhstan) in Skrypnyk (Koshelivets', comp.), Statti . . ., pp. 153-62, 192-200; also "Postanova kolegii NKO, " in Koshelivets', Mykola Skrypnyk, pp. 273-77.

39. M. Skrypnyk, Zavdannia kul'turnoho budivnytstva na Ukraïni: Dopovid' na X z"izdi KP(b)U (Kharkov: State Publishers of the Ukraine, 1928), p. 14; also see his "Pro kordony USRR, " in Skrypnyk (Koshelivets', comp.), Statti . . ., pp. 101-17.

40. Koshelivets', Mykola Skrypnyk, p. 228.

41. The complex process of Ukrainization is analyzed at length by Sullivant, op. cit., pp. 84-148. Radziejowski, op. cit., pp. 484-97, is more concise. Radziejowski dates the beginning of an "intensive campaign of Ukrainization" at April 1925 (p. 485).

42. Y. Bilinsky, The Second Soviet Republic: The Ukraine after World War II (New Brunswick, N.J.: Rutgers University Press, 1964), Table V-4, p. 162.

43. Kosior, op. cit., pp. 64 ff.

44. Bilinsky, op. cit., Table V-7, p. 170.

45. Ibid., Table V-8, p. 175.

46. Kosior, op. cit., pp. 67 ff.

47. For instance, in 1921-23 the CP(B)U dragged its feet on Ukrainization. It appears plausible that it was Skrypnyk, together with Hrynko and Rakovsky, who persuaded Stalin at the Sultan Galiev conference (June 1923) to put some pressure on the pro-Russian Kviring to accelerate Ukrainization. The first measure on spreading the Ukrainian language in the Ukraine was adopted August 1, 1923. Popov, op. cit., pp. 228, 293; Holubnychy, op. cit., pp. 83-84; Sullivant, op. cit., p. 109.

48. See, for instance, Skrypnyk's speech at the Seventh Congress of Education Officials, in A. V. Lunacharskii and N. A. Skrypnik (Skrypnyk), Narodnoe obrazovanie v SSSR v sviazi s rekonstruktsiei narodnogo khozaistva (Moscow: Rabotnik Prosvechcheniia, 1929), pp. 39-40.

49. See John S. Reshetar, Jr., "National Deviation in the Soviet Union," American Slavic and East European Review 12 (April 1953): 166.

50. The letter itself is translated in full in J. V. Stalin, Works, VII (Moscow: Foreign Languages Publishing House, 1954), pp. 157-63. For an analysis, see Sullivant, op. cit., pp. 127 ff.

51. The earlier date is given by I. Bakalo in Volodymyr Kubijovyč, ed., Ukraine: A Concise Encyclopedia (Toronto: University of Toronto Press, 1971), 2: 352a. The later date refers to the closing of all 746 Ukrainian primary schools in the Kuban region; see the unsigned "Ethnocide of Ukrainians in the U.S.S.R." in The Ukrainian Herald iss. 7-8, "Ethnocide of Ukrainians in the USSR" (Spring 1974): 111.

52. Sullivant, op. cit., p. 137.

53. Author's interview with Mr. K. T. in New York, December 29, 1976.

54. Radziejowski, op. cit., p. 486, citing the unpublished protocols of the congress, without specifying the exact dates.

55. Kosior, op. cit., pp. 64 ff., citing Kultura (1929): no. 2-6: 22.

56. Holubnychy, op. cit., p. 86; cited with the author's permission.

57. Skrypnyk, "Za Leninizm v natsional'nomu pytanni," in his Statti . . ., II, pt. 2, pp. 71-79; Skrypnyk's preface to E. F. Hirchak, Na dva fronta v bor'be s natsionalizmom (Moscow and Leningrad: State Publishers, 1930), pp. 5-8; Skrypnyk, "Spilka Vyzvolennia Ukraïny," Bil'shovyk Ukraïny (1930), no. 8: 11-24, which concerns the trial of 45 Ukrainian intellectuals, the leaders of the Union for the Liberation of the Ukraine (SVU), in the spring of 1930.

58. See Skrypnyk, "Z pryvodu ekonomichnoï pliatformy natsionalizmu," Bil'shovyk Ukraïny (1928), no. 6--as cited by Koshelivets', Mykola Skrypnyk, p. 174.

59. One of the economists was Y. Dimanshtein, the author of
Problema raionirovaniia metallopromyshlennosti v sviazi s usloviiami
promyshlennogo razvitiia Ukrainy i Soiuza (Kharkov, 1927)--conver-
sation with V. Holubnychy, November 7, 1976. See also I. S.
Koropeckyj, Location Problems in Soviet Industry before World War
II: The Case of the Ukraine (Chapel Hill: University of North Caro-
lina Press, 1971), passim, esp. Appendix B (pp. 193-99).

60. Kosior, op. cit., p. 10.

61. Sullivant, op. cit., p. 195.

62. Holubnychy, op. cit., pp. 94-97. Most likely those in-
structions were contained in the resolution of the CC of the All-Union
CP(B) of January 24, 1933. It has frequently been referred to by
Postychev and others, but its contents have not been divulged to date.

63. Nikita S. Khrushchev, "Special Report ['Secret Speech'] to
the 20th Congress of the Communist Party of the Soviet Union," February 24-25, 1956, in Boris I. Nikolaevsky, annotator, The Crimes
of the Stalin Era, New Leader pamphlet (1956), S 44-S 45; Andrei D.
Sakharov, "Progress, Coexistence, and Intellectual Freedom" (1968),
in A. D. Sakharov, Sakharov Speaks (New York: Knopf, 1974), p.
82.

64. I have dealt with this problem in my Second Soviet Republic, pp. 84-140, and in my "The Incorporation of Western Ukraine and
Its Impact on Politics and Society in Soviet Ukraine," in The Influence
of East Europe and the Soviet West on the USSR, ed. Roman Szporluk
(New York: Praeger, 1976), pp. 180-228.

65. For further details and documentation, see Bilinsky, The
Second Soviet Republic, pp. 33-34.

66. For detailed documentation, see Y. Bilinsky, "Assimilation and Ethnic Assertiveness among Ukrainians of the Soviet Union,"
in Ethnic Minorities in the Soviet Union, ed. Erich Goldhagen (New
York: Praeger, 1968), p. 156. There is a cryptic reference in the
Ukrainian samizdat (underground press) to Shelest's efforts to open
(or reopen) Ukrainian-language schools in Moldavia, where 0.5 million Ukrainians live: "Although during Shelest's administration the
CPU conducted talks with Moldavian leaders about the possibility of
establishing Ukrainian schools, nothing, as we well know, came out
of this." See "Ethnocide of the Ukrainians in the U.S.S.R.," p. 119.
During the discussion in the University of Chicago workshop it was
mentioned, however, that there might still be some Ukrainian-
language schools left in Moldavia from the time when certain areas
of the republic had been a part of the Ukrainian SSR. Brian Silver
has found that in 1957-58 (before Shelest) there were 38 Ukrainian-
language elementary and secondary schools in Moldavia, with 5,300
pupils. By 1964-65 only 7 Ukrainian-language schools with 1,900
pupils remained. See Narodnoe khozaistvo Moldavskoi SSR v 1964 g.:

Statisticheskii sbornik (Kishinev: Ts.S.U. Moldavskoi SSR, 1965),
pp. 360-61. No such schools existed in the capital Kishinev (from
his letter of May 10, 1977).

    67. Holubnychy, op. cit., p. 124.

    68. See Y. Bilinsky, "The Communist Party of Ukraine after
1966," in Ukraine in the Seventies, ed. Peter J. Potichnyj (Oakville,
Ont.: Mosaic Press, 1975), Table I, p. 258. In the same time
period the parent Party--the CP(B)SU/CPSU--grew more slowly--
from 6,882,145 full members and candidates on October 1, 1952, to
9,716,005 such members on October 1, 1961 (41.2 percent). See
Merle Fainsod, How Russia Is Ruled (2nd ed.; Cambridge, Mass.:
Harvard University Press, 1963), Table 2, p. 249.

    69. Holubnychy, op. cit., p. 124.

    70. Bilinsky, The Second Soviet Republic, Table VIII-2, p. 231.

    71. Bilinsky, "The Communist Party of Ukraine after 1966,"
p. 243.

    72. I owe this apt observation to Dr. Hélène Carrère d'Encausse,
who raised it in the workshop discussion.

    73. Observation made in the workshop discussion.

    74. Based on Grey Hodnett, "Pyotr Efimovich Shelest," in
Soviet Leaders, ed. George W. Simmonds (New York: Crowell,
1967), pp. 95-103.

    75. Bilinsky, "The Communist Party of Ukraine after 1966,"
pp. 241-44, 258.

    76. Ibid., p. 242. Writing in Moscow's Kommunist in August
1971, Shelest pleaded: "Much remains to be done to prepare well for
this important organizational-political measure." Incidentally, his
fears were well-founded; see Y. Bilinsky, "Politics, Purge, and Dissent in the Ukraine Since the Fall of Shelest," in Nationalism and
Human Rights: Processes of Modernization in the USSR, ed. Ihor
Kamenetsky (Littleton, Colo.: Libraries Unlimited, 1977), pp. 173 ff.

    77. Bilinsky, "The Communist Party . . . 1966," p. 253.

    78. "Ethnocide of Ukrainians . . .," pp. 129-30. In late
November 1973 (see Radians'ka Ukraïna, November 29, 1973, p. 3)
he was replaced by Victor Dobryk, whom the underground author
terms a "zealous Russifier" (see "Ethnocide of Ukrainians . . .,"
p. 130).

    79. See "Ethnocide of Ukrainians . . .," p. 130, for the accu-
sation made at a December 1973 meeting of the Bureau of the Lviv
obkom by Dobryk. That Shelest dragged his feet on the interchange
of cadres was hinted by his successor Shcherbytsky in a public speech
on April 17, 1973. See V. V. Shcherbytsky, "Pro zavdannia partiinykh
orhanizatsii respubliky po dal'shomu polipshenniu roboty z kadramy u
svitli rishen' XXIV z''izdu KPRS," Radians'ka Ukraïna, April 20, 1973,
p. 1, or Digest of the Soviet Ukrainian Press 17, no. 6 (June 1973): 15.
See also Bilinsky, "The Communist Party . . . 1966," p. 251.

80. The words are Grey Hodnett's, from his "Ukrainian Politics and the Purge of Shelest," paper delivered at the annual meeting of the Midwest Slavic Conference, Ann Arbor, Mich., May 5-7, 1977, p. 46; cited with permission. He refers to Pravda Ukraïny, April 18, 1970.

81. See, for instance, the technical literature on the location of power plants in the Ukraine cited by Vsevolod Holubnychy, "Some Economic Aspects of Relations among the Soviet Republics," in Goldhagen, op. cit., pp. 87-88, 117-18. See also Akademiia Nauk Ukraïns'koï RSR, Instytut Ekonomiki, Natsional'nyi dokhod Ukraïns'koï RSR v period rozhornutoho budivnytstva komunizmu, ed. O. O. Nesterenko (Kiev: Academy of Sciences of the Ukrainian SSR, 1963), passim.

82. Politicheskii dnevnik (June 1965), no. 9 (Arkhiv samizdata no. 1002). See Radio Liberty, Arkhiv Samizdata, Sobranie dokumentov samizdata, vol. 20, no. AS 1002, p. 33.

83. For detailed documentation see Bilinsky, "The Communist Party . . . 1966," p. 249. See also Jaroslaw Pelenski, "Shelest and His Period in Soviet Ukraine (1963-1972): A Revival of Controlled Ukrainian Autonomism," in Potichnyj, op. cit., pp. 290-92.

84. Hodnett, "Ukrainian Politics . . .," pp. 9-13, quotation on p. 10. Cited with permission.

85. See Radio Liberty, "Ukrainian State Farms Subordinated to Moscow," RL 61/73 (March 5, 1973).

86. See Times (London), January 14, 1977, p. 17; full text reproduced in Svoboda: Ukrainian Weekly Edition, February 6, 1977, p. 2.

87. See M. I. Holubenko, preface to Ivan Dzyuba, Internationalism or Russification? (New York: Monad Press, 1974), pp. xvii ff., esp. p. xxi.

88. See Pelenski, "Shelest and His Period . . .," p. 289.

89. Bilinsky, The Second Soviet Republic, Table V-4, p. 163.

90. From a summary of a speech by the Ukrainian SSR Minister of Education, A. Marinich, in Editorial, "Sovershenstvovat' prepodavanie russkogo iazyka vo vsekh natsional'nykh shkolakh strany," Narodnoe obrazovanie (1974), no. 3: 9. Reference courtesy of Stephen Rapawy, U.S. Department of Commerce.

91. See Bilinsky, "The Communist Party . . . 1966," p. 246; Pelenski, "Shelest and His Period . . .," p. 287.

92. Pelenski, "Shelest and His Period . . .," pp. 287-88.

93. Ibid., p. 292.

94. Ibid., p. 288.

95. Ibid., p. 289. See also Bilinsky, The Second Soviet Republic, pp. 210-21.

96. Pelenski, "Shelest and His Period . . .," p. 289.

97. Ibid., p. 297.

98. On Czechoslovakia, see Grey Hodnett and Peter J.
Potichnyj, The Ukraine and the Czechoslovak Crisis (Canberra:
Department of Political Science, Research School of Social Sciences,
Australian National University, 1970); Richard Lowenthal, "The
Sparrow in the Cage," Problems of Communism 17, no. 6 (November-
December 1968): 10, 14 ff. Some interesting scraps of information
have surfaced more recently. According to Josef Smyrkovsky's
memoirs, Shelest almost wrecked the meeting at Cierna-nad-Tisou
(July 31, 1968) by telling the Czechoslovak delegation that leaflets
printed in Czechoslovakia were being circulated in "Ruthenia" (the
Transcarpathian oblast of the Ukrainian SSR) asking the population
to secede from the USSR and join Czechoslovakia. See Jan F. Triska,
"Messages from Czechoslovakia," Problems of Communism 24, no.
6 (November-December 1975): 28. Dobryk reportedly told a Party
meeting in Lviv that if Shelest had not been removed in time, a
Czechoslovak situation would have arisen in the Ukraine in several
years (this was said in December 1973; see "Ethnocide of Ukrainians . . .," p. 130).

Best on détente and the West German policy is Hodnett, "Ukrainian Politics . . .," pp. 47-55. Somewhat overdramatized and under-
documented, but still suggestive, is John Dornberg, Brezhnev: The
Masks of Power (New York: Basic Books, 1974), pp. 264-65.

On the summit meeting, see Christian Duevel, "Shelest Ousted
from Ukrainian CP Leadership," RL CRD 128-72 (May 30, 1972),
and his "An Unprecedented Plenum of the CPSU Central Committee,"
RL 145/73 (May 3, 1973); and Robert G. Kaiser, Washington Post,
May 26, 1972, p. A-17 and June 11, 1972 (column on "Creative Art
of Kremlinology"). See also Hedrick Smith, The Russians (New York:
Quadrangle, 1976), p. 349; and Marvin Kalb and Bernard Kalb,
Kissinger (Boston: Little, Brown, 1974), pp. 306, 327.

99. Most notably Leonard Schapiro, "Totalitarianism in Foreign Policy," in The Soviet Impact on World Politics, ed. Kurt
London (New York: Hawthorn, 1974), p. 5 (dismissal of "hard-
liner" Shelest would make the remaining leaders look like genuine
friends of détente). See also Pelenski, "Shelest and His Period . . .,"
pp. 283-84. In a conversation, Holubnychy expressed his skepticism
about Shelest's meddling in foreign policy; he mentioned, however,
that the CP(B)U-CPU has always been very orthodox, very leftist in
foreign policy matters.

100. Pelenski, "Shelest and His Period . . .," p. 297.

101. Petro Shelest, Ukraïno Nasha Radians'ka (Kiev: Pub-
lisher of Political Literature of Ukraine, 1970). Henceforth cited
Ukraïno . . . .

102.　Editorial, "Pro seriozni nedoliky ta pomylky odniieï knyhy," Komunist Ukraïny (April 1973), no. 4: 77-82.

103.　See Bilinsky, The Second Soviet Republic, pp. 15-16.

104.　Shelest, Ukraïno . . ., pp. 5-6.　Emphasis added.

105.　Ibid., p. 19.

106.　Ibid., p. 24.

107.　Ibid., p. 60.

108.　Ukraïns'ka radians'ka entsyklopediia (1963), 13: 228-29 (quotation on p. 229), translated in Borys Levytsky, comp., The Stalinist Terror: Documentation from the Soviet Press (Stanford, Calif.: Hoover Institution Press, 1974), pp. 374-76.　Skrypnyk was first partially rehabilitated in January 1962; see Iu. V. Babko, "Zhyttievyi shliakh bil'shovyka (do 90-richchia z dnia narodzhennia M. O. Skrypnyka)," Ukraïns'kyi istorychnyi zhurnal (Kiev) 6, no. 1 (January-February 1962): 148-49.　The article is very laudatory on Skrypnyk's career prior to 1918, glosses over his Ukrainian period, and does not mention his suicide.　Under Brezhnev, Babko wrote a somewhat less friendly encyclopedia article, the third- and second-but-last sentences of which read: "S. did much to implement Leninist nationality policy.　But in this complex work he also committed several [okremi] errors which the Party subjected to just criticism." See Radians'ka entsyklopediia istorii Ukraïny, IV (1972), 111-12. His suicide was not mentioned.　He is described as "State and Party official of the Ukr.SSR" (compared with "eminent [vydatnyi] official of the Communist Party and the Soviet state" in 1962).　Even less enlightening (suicide not mentioned, Ukrainian career slighted)--in fact, almost perfunctory--is the unsigned article in Bol'shaia sovetskaia entsyklopediia, 3rd ed., XXIII (1976), 530: "Soviet State and Party official."

109.　Shelest, Ukraïno . . ., p. 58.

110.　Ibid., pp. 49, 52, 157.　See note 108 for contrast with 1972 and 1976 wordings.

111.　There are several unusual aspects to Shelest's dismissal--see Bilinsky, "The Communist Party . . . 1966," p. 250. See also "Ethnocide of Ukrainians . . .," pp. 114-15.

112.　The expression was used by Hrynko at the Twelfth RCP(B) Congress in 1923; see Dvenadtsatyi s'ezd . . ., p. 503.　In his speech the link with the tsars is implicit.

113.　See Zev Katz and Frederic T. Harned, "Appendix: Comparative Tables for Major Soviet Nationalities," in Handbook of Major Soviet Nationalities, ed. Zev Katz (New York: Free Press, 1975), Table A-28, p. 465.　See also Roman Szporluk, "The Ukraine and the Ukrainians," ibid., pp. 21-48 passim.

114.　Robert G. Kaiser, Russia: The People and the Power (New York: Pocket Books, 1976), p. 445.

115. For instance, Andrii Hryhorenko (Grigorenko)--a persecuted and now expelled Soviet Ukrainian and Soviet Russian dissident in his own right (his father is a Ukrainian, his mother a Russian), and the son of the famous Maj. Gen. Petro Hryhorenko (Piotr Grigorenko)--has recently estimated that Ukrainians make up a "good half" of all the political prisoners in the USSR. See the full text of his speech at a meeting in New York, February 6, 1977, in Svoboda, February 9, 1977, p. 3. Vladimir Bukovsky, the expelled Soviet Russian dissident, has complained in a letter to Aleksei Kosygin that "Russia is now a prison house of nations to a greater extent than she had been 60 years before." He also complains of compulsory russification of Ukrainians, Armenians, Lithuanians, and others. As cited in Svoboda, February 17, 1977, p. 1.

NATIONAL CADRES AS A FORCE IN THE SOVIET SYSTEM: THE EVIDENCE OF BERIA'S CAREER, 1949-53

5

Charles H. Fairbanks, Jr.

This study investigates the political relations between dominant and subordinate nationalities as they were determined by the Stalin regime and as they changed with Joseph Stalin's death. As a key to the role of non-Russian nationalities, I will follow Lavrenti P. Beria's conduct on nationality issues from 1949 to June 1953. In all of Soviet history, Beria was the politician for whom the nationalities issue was most important. Since he was the only man who tried to use this policy issue as his principal weapon in an attempt to become ruler of the USSR, the career of Beria is a kind of test of the maximum weight the national minorities can assume.

NATIONALITY POLICY AT THE NINETEENTH PARTY CONGRESS AND BERIA'S DISSENT

Beria most fully elaborated his position on nationality policy in a speech to the Nineteenth Party Congress (October 5-14, 1952), so it is with this speech that we will begin our analysis. But in order to appreciate the divergence of his speech from the attitudes of the times, we must first consider the other speakers' views on nationalities policy. Stalin did not deliver the authoritative Central Committee report, nor did he discuss nationalities policy in the very short speech he did make. But we can gain a sense of the tone of the congress by noting the patterns of usage of various orthodox slogans referring to the national deviations, the status of various ethnic groups, and the rights of the union republics. At least 23 speakers condemn bourgeois nationalism, the national deviation of the non-Russians; but not one refers to the analogous deviation of the Russians, Great Russian chauvinism. *

---

*Eighty-six speeches were delivered at the congress, of which the 29 given by representatives of the union republics and of the

144

Beria alone uses the somewhat weaker terms "national oppression" and "great power chauvinism." All but four of the speakers choose invariably to refer to the Soviet ethnic groups as "peoples" rather than "nations," although almost all of these groups met the conditions of Stalin's own definition of a nation.[1] In accord with the tendency of the congress speakers to pass over the nominal rights of the union republics, they are called "independent" only once, by Beria,[2] although the Party Program would seem to imply their right to this designation.[3] The "sovereignty" attributed to the republics by the Stalin constitution (Article 15) is omitted entirely. Finally, it goes almost without saying that only the Russian people is entitled to the epithet "great," and only the Russian culture is called "advanced." It is not said of the Russian culture, as it is of the others, that it ought to be "Socialist in content, national in form"--a phrase which seems to restrict the individuality of the national cultures to relatively unimportant externals.

This brief survey reveals a large area of agreement on terms acknowledging Russian predominance and restricting even the outward symbols of minority autonomy. What is the reason for this general agreement? The congress proceedings as a whole give one an impression that the general nationalities line derives from Stalin himself to a greater extent than do other policy lines. It is very unusual for local Party officials to say that their specific actions follow the directives of Stalin himself, but they do say this about nationalities policy.[4] Some speeches even assert that, in some cases, Stalin, who by 1952 presented himself to the public in godlike isolation from the specifics of administration, personally intervened to establish correct nationalities policy. In Georgia the resolutions condemning officials excessively lenient toward "hostile nationalist elements in our republic" were "based . . . on Comrade Stalin's personal instructions."[5]

The evidence suggests that the nationalities issue may have been unusually important for Stalin at this point, although he does not discuss it in public. More recent evidence strengthens this impression. Khrushchev recalls that it was before the Nineteenth Congress that Stalin first circulated the accusations against the Jewish doctors who later were accused of poisoning Soviet leaders in a Zionist plot.[6] This makes it appear likely that Stalin had already planned the later campaign against the Jews and against bourgeois nationalism to culminate in the Doctors' Plot and a blood purge along

---

autonomous republics of the RSFSR, as well as those of important figures in the central leadership, have been examined for the present study.

the lines of those of the 1930s. It establishes that he was, behind the scenes, taking the same direction in nationalities policy as that attributed to him at the congress.

Seen against the background of a consistent congress line on nationalities policy apparently emanating from Stalin, Beria's speech is truly remarkable. Five-sixths of this speech deals with the nationalities question, which Beria discusses in language entirely different from that of the other speakers. To begin with, Beria refers most often to the minority nationalities as "nations" (11 times). Only three other speakers refer to nations at all, and each of them a single time. Beria goes even further. He says that "in the conditions of the Soviet system, all the peoples of our country found and developed their own statehood [gosudarstvennost']"; they have become "genuinely independent [samostoyatel'nie] states."[7] Unless I am mistaken, Beria is the only speaker who calls the nations of the USSR independent; and he is the only one who calls them states.

Beria mentions bourgeois nationalism, the bugbear of the congress, only once: "In the struggle against the enemies of Leninism the Party defended the Leninist-Stalinist national policy and ensured the complete and final overthrow of great-power chauvinism, bourgeois nationalism, and bourgeois cosmopolitanism."[8]

This passage is quite remarkable. The three national deviations are given equal billing, something unique in the congress proceedings. And if the "final overthrow" of bourgeois nationalism and bourgeois cosmopolitanism (Jewish particularism) has been achieved, there is no need for the vigorous attack on these deviations waged since the end of the war. In fact, the harm done by bourgeois nationalism is described nowhere else in the speech, while a whole paragraph is devoted to the evils Great Russian chauvinism wrought under the tsars: "Tsarism was the oppressor and executioner of peoples in Russia. The numerous non-Russian nations were denied all rights . . . the work in all institutions was conducted in Russian, which was not understood by the local nationalities."[9] Whatever may be the balance between the evils of Russian and of local nationalism in Beria's speech, the fact that Beria is the only speaker to mention "great-power chauvinism" and "national oppression" shows how directly he was clashing with current norms.

The treatment of the Russian people in Beria's speech needs deeper consideration. Beria does not use the standard phrase "Great Russian people." In the same way he denies to the Russian people and to its culture the epithet "advanced" (peredovoi); instead, he insists that all the nations of the USSR are now "advanced socialist nations."

Beria does devote four paragraphs[11] to praising the "Russian nation . . . the most outstanding of all the nations comprising the

Soviet Union." But on closer examination his praise of Russia, in
any case less florid than that of most other speakers, proves to be
somewhat complicated. Unlike most writers on the nationalities in
this period, Beria does not allude to the "progressive significance"
of the outlying minorities' annexation to Russia.[12] Neither does he
discuss the importance of the Russian language as a means of communication among the peoples of the USSR,[13] the advanced character
of Russian culture, or its specific connection with Communism. A
short quotation will illustrate how Beria treats Russian culture and
the allegedly distinctive characteristics of the Russian people:

> As a result of consistent application in life of the Lenin-
> Stalin national policy in our country, the real inequality,
> inherited from Tsarism, in social and cultural develop-
> ment between the peoples of central Russia, who had
> moved forward, and the peoples of the outlying regions,
> who had lagged behind them in the past, was eliminated.[14]

Here Beria substitutes for the constantly recurring phrase
"Great Russian people" the strange locution "peoples of central Russia." The effect is to suggest that the former superiority of the
Russian people in economic and cultural development was not due to
the distinctive characteristics of the Russian people as such, to
Russian culture, but to advantageous geographical position, a position shared by other, smaller "peoples of central Russia."

Let us consider the content of the cultures of the non-Russian
minorities, which was being furiously debated during this period.
Numerous works in the non-Russian literatures, ranging from contemporary novels to national epics, had been either suppressed or
expurgated immediately before the congress because of "idealization
of the past," "bourgeois nationalism," "pan-Islamism," and so
forth.[15] But Beria does not discuss how the cultures of the various
nations of the USSR must conform to a socialist standard valid for
the whole union. He gives a list of the five features characteristic
of "advanced socialist nations" such as the nations of the USSR have
now become.[16] None of the five items in the list refers to characteristics that the culture of a nation must have for it to be an "advanced socialist nation." Perhaps this implicitly departs from the
formula devised by Stalin to describe the character that the cultures
of the peoples of the USSR must have: "socialist in content, national
in form." In fact, Beria never cites this formula.

Beria's specific policy proposals also indicate how he wished
to portray himself to the minority cadres as their friend. He emphasizes the need for teaching and using the native languages.[17]
Even more prominent is his concern for the creation and advancement

of cadres of the local nationalities: the third characteristic of an
"advanced socialist nation" is a "highly developed system of higher
education to ensure the training of national cadres of specialists for
all spheres of the economy and culture."[18]

Beria's presentation of a correct nationalities policy openly
contradicts some of the other speakers at the congress, and the situation actually in existence at the time. He criticizes the oppressive
nationalities policy of tsarism, under which "the work in all institutions was conducted in Russian."[19] But after the death of Stalin it
was revealed that the teaching in the universities of the Western
Ukraine was in Russian at this very time.[20] One of the most striking contradictions between speakers at the congress is that between
Beria and A. N. Poskrebyshev, the long-time head of Stalin's personal secretariat, on the legislative powers of the union republics.
Poskrebyshev, who was given exceptional prominence at the congress,* ridicules in his speech[21] the fact that the criminal codes of
the union republics differ in such matters as the number of years'
imprisonment by which accepting bribes is punished; he demands
that the codes be made absolutely uniform. There are other unspecified "branches of legislation [which] have not been properly coor-
dinated." The measure suggested by Poskrebyshev seems to contra-
vene the 1936 Constitution, which reserves to the state all authority
of the union republics except the "determination of fundamental principles" in the sphere of legislation. Beria, on the other hand, states
that "under Soviet rule, the outlying national regions of Tsarist
Russia have been transformed into . . . Soviet republics with their
own legislation."[22] Such obvious public disagreement appeared only
rarely under the Stalin regime.

It comes as a great surprise that Beria takes the side of the
minority nationalities against the other congress speakers. The
difficulty is particularly great because his speech seems to run
counter not only to the specific policies that were in force at the
time but also to the tradition of nationalities policy associated with

---

*This can be seen from the fact that the editors of Pravda
awarded to Poskrebyshev more applause ("Stormy applause, all
rise") than was given to anyone except Stalin, Molotov, Malenkov,
Khrushchev, Beria, Voroshilov, Mikoyan, Kaganovich, and Bulganin;
that is, Poskrebyshev received more applause than two members
and one candidate member of the outgoing Politburo (Andreyev,
Kosygin, Shvernik) and more than most of the members of the new
Presidium, including two of the members of its Bureau (Pervukhin
and Saburov).

Stalin. We can say that the core of the new policy adopted at the urging of Stalin during the 1930s is a change in the relative weight of the two ideological distortions: that the bourgeois-nationalist distortion is much more dangerous than Great Russian chauvinism.[23] By the omission of the expressions that celebrate this Stalinist doctrine, Beria casts doubt on his fidelity to it. The marked divergence between his speech--which seems to be the "nationalities speech" of the congress--and the authoritative Central Committee report must surely have confused the signals to lower-level officials regarding nationalities policy.

The real problem can be posed most sharply in the following way: if we adopt the assumption initially most plausible, we would consider that the congress speeches' very strict attitude toward bourgeois nationalism had been approved by Stalin. It seems reasonable to assume that he would not allow a policy position to be wrongly attributed to him--as the attack on bourgeois nationalism was--on such an authoritative occasion as his last Party Congress, held to lay down his heritage. If these assumptions are correct, a difficulty appears that is important for our understanding of Soviet politics. It is entirely contrary to our preconceptions of the Stalinist system that any leadership figure at a Party Congress could take an opposing position on a policy question that had been decided by Stalin. Such disagreement would appear to the outsider as opposition to Stalin himself. This seems to be one thing the Stalin regime did not allow. Nor would it have been prudent from Beria's point of view.

All of these considerations make it hard to explain why Beria took his unusual stand on nationalities policy at the Nineteenth Congress. To understand his action better, we need to determine the precise circumstances conditioning it and to establish whether his views were chosen for the particular occasion or whether they represented a prior orientation.

BERIA'S POLITICAL SITUATION

Beria's political power probably was greatest during World War II and in the period following the death of Zhdanov in June 1948, when Stalin allowed Malenkov and Beria to destroy Zhdanov's organization (in the "Leningrad case" and other purges), and thereby to increase their own power. But at the end of 1951 Stalin seems to have undertaken a three-pronged attack on the sources of Beria's power. First he lessened Beria's control over the police by replacing his close associate Abakumov with S. D. Ignatov as minister of state security. In addition, several security officials from the Ukraine who had been very closely connected with Khrushchev (I. A. Serov,

A. A. Yepishev, N. Mironov) were given directing positions in the organs of state security in 1951.[24] These appointments suggest an attempt to weaken Beria's control over the organs of state security by establishing within them a competing network of officials responsive to the will of a rival politician, Khrushchev. Moreover, it is clear from Khrushchev's secret speech of 1956 that some of the new subordinate officials in the Ministry of State Security took their orders directly from Stalin, and not from the minister.[25]

At the same time several hundred of Beria's supporters in Georgia were purged "upon comrade Stalin's personal instructions."[26] The effect of this purge was to destroy Beria's ability to dictate policy directly to the leadership of the Georgian Party. Among the formal charges made against the men purged in Georgia was their participation in the now-decried system of shefstvo, domination of territorial units by one patron who decided all local appointments. This could very easily have served as the prelude to bringing the same charge against Beria, whose special relationship with the Transcaucasus was the foremost example of a semi-feudal territorial lordship existing at that time. The secret charges identifying Beria's followers as members of a treasonous "Mingrelian nationalist organization" were even more threatening. Khrushchev went on to say in his secret speech that "resolutions by the Central Committee . . . concerning this case . . . were made without prior discussion with the Political Bureau. Stalin had personally dictated them."[27] Khrushchev does not mention that there seem to have been no plenary sessions of the CC at these times, so that Stalin himself was responsible at every stage for the concoction of the conspiracy charges threatening Beria. In this case, then, we find the attack on bourgeois nationalism used as the principal means of getting at Beria's close associates (and thus at his power), and that Beria knew this when he spoke at the Nineteenth Congress.

In Azerbaidzhan, M. D. Bagirov, the first secretary and perhaps Beria's most important political follower, was in extremely serious trouble at the time of the Nineteenth Party Congress. This is shown by the fact that at the meeting of the Baku party aktiv held to discuss the results of the congress, Bagirov did not give the report, as the republic secretary would, but merely "spoke at the meeting."[28] (The only other first secretary who did not deliver the report at his aktiv meeting was, unless I am mistaken, Kalnberzins (Latvian SSR), who had admitted serious deficiencies in the work of the Latvian CC in his congress speech.)

The third prong of Stalin's attack on Beria perhaps appeared in the still-murky Czech purges of 1951-52, which decimated the local cadres that had worked with Beria and laid the foundation for criminal charges against him. In November 1951, Stalin suddenly resolved

the long Politburo debate over the fate of Slansky and Geminder with
a decision to bring criminal charges against them.[29] These men had
been associated with Beria and may have acted on his instructions in
Eastern Europe.[30] It will suffice to mention this part of the political
campaign here, since its meaning will be analyzed in greater detail
when the period of the Slansky trial in November 1952 is discussed.
Finally, the charges against the Jewish doctors, not yet made public,
constituted a fourth danger to Beria.

What we have established has increased the problem of explain-
ing Beria's speech. Beria must have taken his position on nationalities policy at the Nineteenth Party Congress in full knowledge that
Stalin was bent on limiting his power in a drastic and hitherto unprecedented way. And he must have known that the campaign against him
was being carried out in the name of the correction of bourgeois-
nationalist distortions. In this situation it took the utmost daring to
express the view of nationalities policy that he did.

BERIA'S EARLIER NATIONALITIES POLICY

Our next task is to see whether Beria's position on nationalities
policy at the Nineteenth Congress was developed for this occasion or
was a long-standing orientation. It is not possible here to give as
precise an answer for the earlier period as we can, on the basis of
a careful analysis of all the relevant texts, for the period September
1952-July 1953. But we can get a general notion of Beria's orientation in the period after the death of Zhdanov in 1948 from three public speeches and from what happened in his transcaucasian fiefdom.
The most visible event in nationalities policy in the year after
Zhdanov's death was the anti-Semitic campaign. While a great deal
has been written about this, no one seems to have addressed the question of its relation to factional politics, which is all-important for
understanding the role of the nationalities issue in the Stalin regime.
There clearly was some relation between anti-Semitism and factional
politics. Khrushchev makes these remarks about the period when
Lazar Kaganovich, the ally of Zhdanov, was sent to the Ukraine in
1947: ". . . my own relations with Kaganovich went from bad to
worse. He developed his intensive activities in two directions:
against so-called Ukrainian nationalists and against the Jews. . . .
His anti-Semitism was directed mainly against the Jews who happened to be on friendly terms with me."[31]

The campaign against rootless cosmopolitanism--that is,
against the Jews--was begun by Zhdanov, in the context of the struggle of his faction against that of Malenkov and Beria. The inference
that nationalities policy was an issue between the two sides is con-

firmed by Khrushchev's recollections of the "Leningrad case," in which Zhdanov's followers were purged by Beria and Malenkov: "I never saw the indictments in the Leningrad case, but I assume--also on the basis of conversations I overheard between Malenkov and Beria--that the charges against Kuznetsov's group [the Zhdanovites] were Russian nationalism and opposition to the Central Committee."[32] If this report is correct, Beria and Malenkov returned to power in 1948-49 under the banner of resistance to Great Russian chauvinism. Before this, Zhdanov's campaign against the Jews had certainly been the most overt manifestation of his Russian nationalist orientation. But the anti-Semitic campaign continued during and after the "Leningrad case"; indeed, it grew more intense, reaching its highest pitch in February and March 1949. This is the second great mystery of postwar nationalities politics.

We cannot solve this mystery here, but we can get an indication of Beria's attitude toward the anti-Semitic campaign by comparing its salience in the Moscow press and in Zaria vostoka,* the newspaper of Beria's Georgian fiefdom, during February and March 1949. Attacks on Jewish cosmopolitans appear in Pravda almost every day; but in the issues of Zaria vostoka available in the West, more feeble attacks on cosmopolitanism appear on only seven occasions, and never as front-page editorials.[33] A quick glance at the Azerbaidzhan newspaper Bakinshii rabochii shows the same lack of interest in the anti-cosmopolitan campaign. In the resolution on Bagirov's CC report of the Seventeenth Congress of the Azerbaidzhan CP, the passage dealing with the actualization of the Zhdanov cultural decrees is notably vague and chilly.[34]

This evidence suggests that Beria was not responsible for the intensification of the anti-Semitic campaign in 1949. Furthermore, Ilya Ehrenburg's memoirs depict Beria's client, V. G. Grigoryan, as enthusiastically facilitating the publication of an article that signaled a relaxation in the anti-Semitic campaign in the spring of 1949;[35] it is not unlikely that this reflects Beria's wish to end the campaign. He may have had personal as well as policy reasons for opposing the anti-cosmopolitan campaign. Several bits of information indicate that Beria may have been specifically associated with the Jews and may have defended their welfare. The dismissals after his fall showed that Jews had not been purged from high positions in the

---

*The accuracy of this comparison was limited by the incompleteness of the Library of Congress file of Zaria vostoka read for this study and by the newspaper's illegibility, but the general result is quite clear.

police, as they were from other Soviet organizations in the late 1940s.
Earlier, Beria had played a dominant role in the organization and
sponsorship of the wartime Jewish Anti-Fascist Committee and also,
through Slansky and Geminder, in aiding in the creation of the state
of Israel.[36] When he was in Georgia, he protected the Georgian Jews
and established a museum of international Jewish culture that was
still open in 1952. There were even persistent rumors that Beria
was a Jew.[37] His connection with the Jews was so widely acknowledged in Moscow that Harrison Salisbury speaks of his "known par-
tiality and friendliness to Jews."[38]

Since Beria's connection with the Jews was certainly being exploited against him in 1952-53, it is by no means impossible that
this was one of the purposes of the anti-cosmopolitanism campaign,
or at least that he worked against the campaign because he feared its
implications for his own fate. Only further research could establish
whether this is so. In any case, it is quite clear that during the
height of the anti-cosmopolitan campaign in 1949, Beria already
diverged from the main trend of national policy on the minorities.

This becomes clearer when we analyze the speeches given by
Beria, Malenkov, Molotov, and Khrushchev to celebrate Stalin's
birthday on December 21, 1949, and two later speeches by Beria.
All the birthday speeches take a gentler attitude toward bourgeois
nationalism than predominated at the Nineteenth Congress three
years later. Beria's speech is demonstrably more favorable to the
minority nationalities than are those of Malenkov and Molotov, but
less favorable than Khrushchev's.[39] Five paragraphs are devoted
to praise of the Russian people in the language of Stalin's 1945 victory toast, but the achievements named belong to the Revolution or
the period following it. The "Great Russian people" are not mentioned, and Beria speaks of "equal peoples" and often of "nations."
The most interesting passage is the following:

> Established by Stalin . . . on the basis of economic,
> political, and military mutual aid within the frame-
> work of a single allied state, the fraternal coopera-
> tion basically altered the peoples [emphasis added].

Here and in general Beria very strongly emphasizes the federal character of the USSR. And he never stresses, as Molotov, for example,
does, that "all the peoples of the U.S.S.R., with all the differences
in their historical past . . . are moving along one general Socialist
path of development."[40]

In his electoral speech at Tbilisi, Beria concentrates on purely
Georgian problems.[41] He conspicuously fails to discuss the leading
role of the Russian people, which he never calls "great." He speaks

of "friendship sealed with the blood of the four fraternal peoples [Russians, Georgians, Armenians, and Azerbaidzhanis]," while Mikoyan in his election speech speaks of "[the fraternal peoples of the Transcaucasus] headed by the first among equals, the Russian people."[42] A particularly interesting feature of Beria's speech is a quotation from Sun Yat-sen: "You [the Executive Committee of the USSR] head a union of free republics." The effect of this is to emphasize Soviet federalism abnormally, since the word "free" is applied in Soviet rhetoric of this period only to independent states, never to the "nations" of the USSR. (Thus, a typical title of a newspaper editorial on relations with the East European countries would be "Friendship of Free Peoples," while an article on internal nationalities policy might be titled "Indestructible Union of Fraternal Peoples.")

Beria's speech on the anniversary of the Revolution in 1951, which is devoted almost entirely to the economy and to foreign policy, touches on nationalities policy only in two brief passages.[43] While his failure to emphasize the nationalities issue is surprising, the content of his speech is not. According to Beria, "Every day . . . produces strong new manifestations of patriotism, of the moral and political unity of the Soviet community and of the friendship of <u>nations</u> of the U.S.S.R." [emphasis added]. In other words, there is no nationalities problem, and relations between the nationalities are as they should be. There are no criticisms of bourgeois nationalism or cosmopolitanism anywhere in Beria's speech. In the section on art and literature, where one might expect some criticism along the lines of the Zhdanov decrees, we hear only of a "flowering" of culture that is "educating the masses in the spirit of Soviet patriotism and <u>internationalism</u>" [emphasis added].

There are other indications that Beria's position on the nationalities question was expressed not only in policy statements but also in practice. In the Georgian purges of 1951-52, his appointees were charged with lenience toward Georgian nationalism, and such charges usually are expanded from some real fact. In the organs of state security, where Beria had overseen the appointment of personnel for many years, non-Russians (particularly Transcaucasians and Jews) were represented to a degree unmatched in the other branches of the state and Party.[44]

The evidence we have been considering contains several ambiguities, but it is possible to draw two conclusions with some assurance. First, on repeated occasions Beria either had acted as a spokesman for the leadership in nationalities matters or he had independently chosen to emphasize this above other policy issues. Second, the nationalities policy alternative Beria represented at the Nineteenth Party Congress was not an isolated stand, but a continuation of a long-held position.

This finding is one of the greatest importance for our inquiry. It is not only Beria's speech at the Nineteenth Congress, but also this continuity of policy, that needs to be understood. Beria apparently maintained the same basic orientation toward the nationalities issue under completely different conditions: the personal dictatorship of Stalin, and the oligarchy that followed his death; when he prospered politically (as in 1949-50) and when he faced imminent ruin (1952-53); when the general nationalities policy was relatively close to his own and when it was violently opposed. Beria's political career thus contradicts our expectation that Soviet leaders at the Politburo level will shift freely among opposed policy positions as political expediency dictates. The case that comes most immediately to mind is Khrushchev's reversal on the issue of Stalin at the time of the Twentieth Congress (1956). Khrushchev's own positions on nationalities policy were very flexible. He went from a strongly pro-minority position in December 1949 to cooperation with Stalin's campaign against bourgeois nationalism and the Jews in the fall of 1952; in 1953 he apparently joined Beria's action for minority rights at the beginning of June, attacked Beria in the name of Russian primacy in July, and then himself sponsored a campaign for recognition of Ukrainian national sentiments in 1954-55.

It is not difficult to think of reasons why Beria would be more likely than most of his fellow Politburo members to consistently favor the minorities. We cannot say anything about the role that personal conviction may have played in his nationalities policy, but we can guess how he would have appeared to participants in Soviet politics. Beria, very much a Georgian in comparison with Stalin, was the least russified of the non-Russian members of the Politburo; Khrushchev, for example, remembers him as the only member of Stalin's inner circle who ate native rather than Russian food.[45] Beria was also much more provincial in his political background than any other member of the Politburo; he did not move from the Caucasus to Moscow until he was 39.

A concrete reason for Beria's favoring the non-Russian nationalities more than other leaders did is his territorial fiefdom in the Transcaucasus. By 1952, at least, there was no other Soviet leader in Moscow who had a provincial political base that was remotely comparable. It is possible that the status of the Transcaucasus as a "fiefdom" under his control led Beria to support the rights of the union republics. As the patron of the Transcaucasus, he was able to arrange some things differently than they were in other union republics. But Beria's freedom to use his power as he wished in the Transcaucasus may still have depended somewhat on the general autonomy granted to the union republics. The autonomy he could obtain for Transcaucasia, or that he at least fought for, may have affected his support from local officials.

It is more obvious that the chances of Beria's promoting the officials of his fiefdom and his non-Russian followers in the organs of state security to positions elsewhere would vary inversely with the intensity of discrimination against non-Russians. Thus his hold on the Transcaucasus would impel him to seek changes in nationalities policy favoring the minorities in general. Whatever the reasons, a general process was at work: it was probably Khrushchev's desire to retain his partial fiefdom in the Ukraine that led him to take a pro-minority position in his own speech for Stalin's seventieth birthday in 1949.

Beria's Transcaucasian bastion also provided him with a good opportunity to appeal for the support of the other national minorities. His control over the Transcaucasian republics apparently enabled them to escape the degree of Russian supervision (such as Russian second secretaries) that was normal in the other union republics and procured for Georgia, at least, special consideration in the allotment of scarce goods. What had been achieved in the Transcaucasus in the realm of nationalities policy, under the supervision of Beria, probably was an attractive example for members of the national cadres elsewhere. His powerful non-Russian clients must have been envied by other minority officials chafing under Russian tutelage. In the case of M. D. Bagirov, perhaps the most important Muslim politician of the Soviet period, there is actual evidence of the drawing power of Beria's followers. In his speech at the Nineteenth Party Congress,[46] B. G. Gafurov, the Tadzhik first secretary, praises Bagirov by name for his assertion that the union republics' errors in evaluating the progressive significance of annexation to Russia were not their own fault, but that of the Union of Soviet Writers. Such praise of one union republic leader by another is unique in the congress proceedings. Shayakhmetov, the Kazakh secretary, praises the same position without mentioning Bagirov. It is possible that Beria was able to appeal to Communists of the Muslim nationalities through Bagirov.

These considerations help in understanding why we might expect Beria, in ordinary circumstances, to be generally more favorable to the non-Russian nationalities than most of his fellow Politburo members were. But our investigation of his political situation limits what we can explain in this way. The kinds of political advantages conceived to flow from Beria's nationalities policy in ordinary circumstances would weigh very little in the desperate situation into which he was moving in September 1952. To explain the consistency of Beria's position on nationalities policy even in the circumstances that made it most dangerous requires examining a more complicated series of hypotheses. Since these hypotheses deal more with the structure of the Stalin regime than with the nationalities question,

I have made them the subject of another study. All the conceivable hypotheses can be grouped under two main headings: those resting on the supposition that Stalin was participating normally in the Soviet government and had chosen a specific course in nationalities policy, as we had supposed earlier, and those assuming that Stalin had not effectively decided. We will turn first to the latter group of hypotheses.

If Stalin had not taken an effective position, it would sweep away many of our difficulties. Beria's speech would no longer have the character of dissent, but would continue to be most easily interpreted as a way of maintaining or gaining the support of his non-Russian clients or of other national cadres. In support of this alternative one could note that not all of Stalin's postwar signals on nationalities policy unambiguously resembled the line of the Nineteenth Congress. His treatise Marxism and the Problems of Linguistics, published in 1950, after the extirpation of the Russian nationalist Zhdanovites, implies that the peoples of the USSR will not merge prior to the victory of socialism on a world scale. It is thus entirely possible that Beria's earlier speeches on nationalities policy were made in an atmosphere of enigmatic reticence or even approval from Stalin. If future research shows this to be true, one would obviously have to interpret the history of nationalities policy in postwar Russia quite differently than has usually been done. But as we approach the Nineteenth Congress, it becomes much more difficult to reconcile Stalin's neutrality and the many references to his personal participation in nationalities policy making. It is barely conceivable that other elite members were unaware of a decision by Stalin on nationalities policy, but Beria himself was in the best position to know that the three-pronged attack on him was carefully orchestrated by Stalin himself and that he was being sentenced precisely on the grounds of bourgeois nationalism. This type of explanation thus appears highly unlikely.

The other category of explanations--those assuming that Stalin had actively embraced a nationalities policy opposed to Beria's-- would imply that Beria took a great risk in making his speech. The only reasonable aim of such a gamble would be to win the support of national cadres, particularly those that did not already favor him. The rewards would have to be enormous to make such a risk worthwhile: that is, the help Beria expected from the nationalities would have to be enormous. If any hypotheses of this type are correct, we would have to revise our estimates of the effects of the national cadres' intervention in Soviet politics far upward. We cannot resolve this question here; for our purposes it is sufficient to note that every plausible explanation of Beria's speech at the Nineteenth Congress implies that the nationalities had great political power either at that moment or in the situation expected to arise immediately after Stalin's death.

AFTER THE NINETEENTH PARTY CONGRESS

In the period between the Nineteenth Congress and his death, Stalin was preparing a purge of his lieutenants and a mass terror on the scale of the 1930s. As part of this political project, intense campaigns were launched under the slogan of "vigilance" (bditel'nost) against two closely related national deviations: "bourgeois nationalism" and "Zionism." Among Stalin's lieutenants it was Beria who was most clearly marked for destruction. But, unless Khrushchev is distorting his recollections in his own interest, Beria continued, until Stalin's death, to be a member of the "inner circle of five" (Stalin, Malenkov, Beria, Khrushchev, Bulganin) who met nearly every night, until the day before Stalin's death, to conduct the day-to-day administration of the USSR. [47] It is characteristic of the strangeness of the Stalin regime that a man marked for death (as Beria was after January 13, at the latest) could sit every night with his executioner, calmly discussing winter wheat or canal building. Beria's continued membership in the inner administrative group shows that Stalin did not intend his fall because of dissatisfaction with him as an administrator, nor because of purely personal dislike, but for grander political reasons.

Whatever Beria intended at the Nineteenth Congress, he did not change central nationalities policy in the direction he favored. Press attacks on bourgeois nationalism increased in number and intensity, turning by mid-November into a distinct campaign against violations of correct nationalities policy. Such a campaign must have been decided upon at the highest level, in all probability by Stalin himself. With the new campaign went a distinctive usage of formulas. For example, between the Nineteenth Party Congress and the death of Stalin, Great Russian chauvinism is not mentioned once in the press materials I have read. Similarly, the union republics seem never to be called "independent" by the central press during this period. [48] The campaign against bourgeois nationalism continued, with generally increasing intensity, until Stalin's death. The effect of the vigilance campaign against bourgeois nationalism on the careers of non-Russian officials is known from a later Presidium resolution criticizing Stalin's nationalities policy in Latvia: "Many Party, Soviet and economic leaders, using the pretext of a sham vigilance, expressed a groundless distrust towards local cadres and promoted to directing work mainly non-Latvians" [emphasis added]. As a result, less than half of the raikom and gorkom secretaries were Latvians, and there remained not a single Latvian among the department heads of the Riga gorkom. [49]

The only thematic statement on nationalities policy delivered in this period by a member of the central leadership was made by

A. N. Poskrebyshev, whose speech at the Nineteenth Party Congress had been so menacing to the autonomy of the union republics. He was selected to write the article commemorating the thirtieth anniversary of the creation of the USSR.[50] He was, before his dismissal in early 1953, perhaps personally closer to Stalin than any other Soviet politician of the time.[51] If the correct nationalities policy for this anniversary had to be expressed by Stalin's personal agent, it seems likely that Stalin regarded nationalities policy as crucially important and was intervening in it behind the scenes.

Poskrebyshev's article holds to the triumphant and optimistic tone considered appropriate for anniversaries, but it presents the same fierce insistence on Russian dominance that the other central press materials of this time do. The reader can see this easily by comparing Poskrebyshev's article with Beria's speech at the Nineteenth Party Congress. It is sufficient here to note a few points of contrast. Poskrebyshev never mentions "great power chauvinism" or the "independence" of the union republics, as Beria does. He emphasizes that the Russian people is the "first among the equal Soviet peoples"; unlike Beria, he always calls it the "great Russian people." The special position of the Russian people is especially evident in the extended praise Poskrebyshev gives to the Russian language. Here he and Beria are in complete opposition. Beria speaks of the need for work to be done in the native languages of the minorities, and says nothing about the Russian language.[52] Poskrebyshev virtually ignores the other languages, and speaks of Russian in the following terms:

> An immense role is played by the rich and mighty Russian language in maintaining and developing constant communication among the numerous nations and peoples who inhabit the Soviet Union. . . . The great Russian language, by providing means of communication for all the peoples of the U.S.S.R., has enriched the national culture of the peoples and their national languages.[53]

The strongest and politically most significant feature of the campaign against bourgeois nationalism was the attack on "Zionism"--that is, on the Jews--beginning at the end of October. The new anti-Semitic campaign, unlike that of Zhdanov at one point, is linked with the campaign against bourgeois nationalism in general. Many articles on nationalities policy include attacks on both Zionism and the bourgeois nationalism of another people, pointing out that these deviations are basically the same.[54]

The most massive evidence of the anti-Semitic campaign is the glut of articles in the press describing the activities of corrupt

officials, confidence men, speculators, parasites, and other scoundrels, all with Jewish names.* In many cases a Jewish name is
added in parentheses after an adopted Russian name, as in Zhdanov's
time, so that the reader will not miss the point of the article. By
the middle of November hardly a day passes without a feuilleton or
court report of this type. These articles about Jewish criminals and
the Russians who are tricked by them belong to the general campaign
for vigilance that had already been called for at the Nineteenth Party
Congress. The typical plot of these anti-Semitic articles is the story
of a Jewish criminal who can continue his anti-state activities due to
the lack of vigilance and the gullibility (rotoveystvo) of some Russian;
these key words are repeated again and again. This conveys the message that Russians should be suspicious of Jews. The articles must
have evoked strong memories of the purge of 1937-38, in which
"vigilance" was also the dominant slogan.

These articles form the first stage of the anti-Semitic campaign. The second phase was initiated by two nearly simultaneous
events in Czechoslovakia and in the Ukraine. In Czechoslovakia,
Slansky, Geminder, and others arrested earlier were brought to public trial.[55] They were charged with collaborating with Tito and with
attempting to use the security agencies to seize power. As noted
earlier, Slansky and Geminder may have been personally associated
with Beria. It is also known that during the period of Slansky's
"crimes," the security police of the satellite countries were directly
controlled by the organs of state security of the USSR.[56] The
charges against Slansky, Geminder, Svab, and their accomplices for
criminal use of the security agencies thus cut very close to Beria
himself; he was responsible for the supervision of the Czech security
agencies and thus could have been criminally implicated.

The most striking feature of the trial was its "openly anti-
Semitic character."[57] Both Slansky and Geminder were called Zionists and accused of plotting with other Zionists against Czechoslovakia. The Communist movement has always been opposed to Zionism, but this is the first occurrence of the word "Zionism" that I
have seen in reading the Soviet press since September 1952.[58] While

---

*In a number of articles of this type the criminals are members
of the Muslim nationalities of the USSR (see Izvestiia, November 25,
1952, p. 4; Pravda, December 10, 1952, p. 2). It is quite possible
that Muslims were a subsidiary target in this campaign. Since, however, there was always a small fraction of these articles involving
Russians only, it would take a detailed count to determine whether
the role of Muslims was indeed disproportionate.

the proceedings of the Nineteenth Congress mention "homeless cosmopolitanism" a few times, they do not mention Zionism even once.
Zionism becomes the word that characterizes the anti-Semitic campaign from this point on; by the beginning of 1953 it appears in every
issue of the press. This seems to show that the Slansky trial is
linked with the subsequent development of the anti-Semitic campaign
in the USSR.

At almost the same time a parallel event took place in Kiev.
On November 29, 1952, Pravda Ukraini announced the sentencing of
several Jews to death for "counterrevolutionary wrecking in the provinces of trade and goods turnover," thus equating larceny with trea-
son. This link had earlier been recalled by Poskrebyshev in his
speech at the Nineteenth Party Congress. The Kiev trial was, in
this period, the first time that Jews were publicly sentenced to death,
and the first case brought before a military tribunal.

On January 13, 1953, the pattern of the blood purge moved to
Moscow with the anti-Semitic accusations known as the Doctors'
Plot. While the charges against the doctors apparently were con-
cocted before the Nineteenth Congress, it has been shown by Robert
Conquest that the beginning of November is the likeliest date for their
arrest. [59] The arrest of the doctors thus coincided with the beginning
of the press campaign against bourgeois nationalists and Jews, indicating again how closely the political events of this period fit to-
gether--the result of careful management by Stalin. It is generally
acknowledged that the Doctors' Plot not only heralded a mass terror not unlike that of 1937-39, but also threatened Beria personally.
In fact, Beria could actually have been brought to trial on charges
already hinted at in the accusation against the doctors. [60]

The Doctors' Plot was aimed directly against Beria, and it had
a violently anti-Semitic tone; the Slansky trial resembled it in both
respects. Why are these features linked? In answering this question we will be able to discern Stalin's reasons for designing his
final terror as he did. Because of Beria's close association with the
Jews and the wide diffusion of anti-Semitic attitudes in the USSR, an
anti-Semitic campaign offered a good public justification for the removal of Beria and his followers. On the other hand, the widespread
fear and hatred felt for Beria and his police subordinates would give
the anti-Semitic campaign still greater legitimacy.

More generally, Stalin clearly chose the opposition between
Russian nationalist feelings and the minorities, especially the Jews,
as the issue through which he would arrange his succession, thereby
showing very clearly the intensity and transforming potential of Russian nationalist feelings. In a way the nationalities issue was perfect
for arranging succession. It could create the upheaval that would
renew the ruling elite, but for an essentially conservative aim, the

maintenance of Russian dominance. Thus the process of terror, with all of its accompanying dynamism, ideological purity, and "leftism," would not interfere with its goal--the retention, unchanged, of a political order established by Stalin. The planned slaughter of many of Stalin's older lieutenants likewise served this goal, since figures with long-established authority in the country would be more likely to innovate than those who were largely unknown. The post-Khrushchev leadership perhaps resembles what Stalin wished to create: its relative immobility both in policy and in personnel is a powerful argument for the intelligence of Stalin's succession plan. *

AFTER THE DEATH OF STALIN:
BERIA'S POLITICAL POSITION

Stalin's death in March 1953 prevented him from implementing his plans. Beria was saved politically and personally, and he moved to retain those strongholds he had lost. Working in temporary alliance with Malenkov, Beria restored his authority over the police and reversed the purge of his followers in the Transcaucasus. Khrushchev tells us that he had concluded before the official meeting of the leaders that "Malenkov had already talked things over with Beria and everything had been decided for some time."[61]

Before we can consider Beria's policy response to the situation created by the death of Stalin, we must understand what his political needs and resources were. On the basis of his subsequent actions, we may legitimately assume that he aimed at becoming dictator, if

---

*Since Stalin's plan to execute many of his old companions in arms was perfectly sensible politically, there is no need to attribute it to paranoia. The test of paranoia ought to be not whether a person says unreasonably suspicious things, but whether he does unreasonably suspicious things. By this test Stalin was not suspicious enough-- perhaps not suspicious enough of Hitler in 1941, certainly not suspicious enough of Malenkov and Khrushchev in 1952-53. The bizarre accusations that Stalin did make should perhaps be attributed to his sense of humor or, to put it differently, to his desire to feel his own power by asserting what is preposterous but cannot be contradicted by anyone. Of course, it should always be remembered that a man in Stalin's position has more cause than the average bourgeois to be suspicious of those around him.

only because his police power was so dangerous to the other leaders that he had to increase it or be destroyed. How could Beria hope to achieve this aim? To begin with, he now had formal authority over the whole police apparatus, in addition to the strong patron-client relationships he evidently retained there.

The strength of Beria's patron-client connections is shown by the ease with which he recovered control of the police from those formally in charge of it at the time of Stalin's death. His control of the police ministry gave him considerable influence over politics at the union republic and local levels, since it was the ordinary practice for the police minister of a union republic to sit on the Bureau of the local Party Committee. The police ministry was in charge of important bodies of troops, including the border guards and the Moscow garrisons. [62] In addition, Beria apparently supervised important sectors of the economy, including those dependent on forced labor. [63] Much of the Soviet nuclear program remained within the province of the MVD. Finally, the organs of state security and Beria's own clients had long participated in the agencies carrying out foreign policy.

In one area, the Transcaucasus, Beria possessed a far broader political base. Even after Stalin's purge, many of his followers must have remained at lower levels there. At any rate, in April 1953, Beria carried out a counterpurge in Georgia which ousted nearly all of Stalin's appointees and restored people dependent upon Beria. Only one of the twelve members and candidate members of the Bureau of the Georgian Central Committee, as reconstructed by Beria in April 1953, survived his fall.* This suggests strongly that Party and government appointments in the Transcaucasus were now simply made by Beria and approved as a matter of course by the bodies nominally responsible. A similar situation existed in the other Transcaucasian republics. In essence, from April 1953 until late in June, the Transcaucasus formed a "fiefdom" controlled entirely by Beria, throwing whatever weight it had in all-union affairs on his side. One can see how much political importance Beria attributed to his fiefdom by the role he chose for one of his most eminent followers, Dekanozov, the former ambassador to Germany: rooting out anti-Beria elements in Georgia as local MVD minister.

Thus Beria could count on a regional political machine and, what is more important, on the support of a complex of agencies of state power centered in the organs of state security. This complex

---

*This was Dzhavakhishvili, a holdover from the Bureau created by Stalin during the purges of 1951-52.

wielded enormous coercive power. But the organs of state security
have always lacked legitimate authority in comparison with most
other Soviet political structures, and above all in comparison with
the Party organizations. Consequently we can describe Beria as
politically weak in spite of his control of the police. One index of
this is the political allegiance of Central Committee members, which
can be established by studying career patterns. Of the 120 members
and 103 candidates active in mid-March 1953, only five members and
seven candidates can be clearly identified as followers of Beria. In
comparison, a minimum of 24 full members and 14 candidates were
visible adherents of Malenkov. [64]

Within the Party--traditionally the institution with the greatest
authority--the provincial Party secretaries hold key positions. But
a look at incomplete data on the members of the 1952 Central Committee does not show any regional Party secretaries outside the
Transcaucasian republics whose career patterns link them with
Beria. * Nor did Beria have any identifiable adherents in the Moscow

---

*Among Party secretaries on the Central Committee with un-
explained demotions after 1952, only the following show any possible
links with Beria. P. F. Cheplakov, first secretary in the Sakhalin
oblast, was demoted to candidate member in 1956; he had served as
second secretary in Azerbaidzhan under Bagirov from 1938. See
Deputati verkhovnogo soveta (Moscow, 1959), p. 432. Another official with a police background from the Beria period was V. I.
Nedosekin, first secretary in the Tula oblast, dismissed in November 1953. In neither of these cases is a current (1952-53) personal
relationship with Beria certain. A case has been made that V. M.
Andrianov, first secretary of the Leningrad oblast Party organization, was "a Beria man" (Nicolaevsky, Power and the Soviet Elite,
p. 258). This is argued on the basis of Andrianov's installation during the "Leningrad case" and his dismissal in October (?) 1953.
But Andrianov's earlier career in Malenkovite strongholds and his
excellent standing at the time of the Nineteenth Congress (he was a
member of the Presidium of the congress and of Stalin's large
Presidium of the Central Committee) make it more likely that he
was a follower of Malenkov. Andrianov was charged in 1954 with
having failed to implement the decisions of the July (1953) Plenum
of the CC (Conquest, Power and Policy, p. 233), which might suggest that he had switched his allegiance from Malenkov to Beria
during the spring of 1953. For Andrianov's career, see Boris
Meissner, "Umschau: Innenpolitische Entwicklung," Osteuropa 4
(1954): 45-46.

apparatus of the Central Committee. The tentative conclusion is that in March 1953, Beria was completely isolated from the Party sources of power, except in the Transcaucasus. This was very different from the situation of his chief rivals, Malenkov and Khrushchev. Of the 38 Party first secretaries of the Russian provinces (krai and oblasti) of the RSFSR in the Central Committee, ten were closely associated with Malenkov. As for the state apparatus, Beria may have supervised much of the work of the economic ministries, but none of their CC members were later dismissed as his clients. Subsequent dismissals showed that Malenkov, on the other hand, was the patron of at least a dozen CC members from the government side. The end of Stalin's control over appointments did not solve Beria's problem of lack of a clientele in the Party organizations outside Transcaucasia. He was not in a good position to develop new patron-client ties, since Malenkov controlled (after March 14, through his client Shatalin) the vital Party Organs Department of the Central Committee, which had the greatest authority in filling the several thousand positions in the Central Committee nomenklatura (appointments list).[65] Beria was indeed politically weak; he needed to take a policy initiative to overcome this problem.

THE FUNERAL SPEECHES: DEFINING NATIONALITIES POLICY FOR THE POST-STALIN ERA

Now that we have a rough understanding of Beria's political situation, we can examine how he responded to it in terms of policy. Fortunately, at Stalin's funeral the members of the new triumvirate--Malenkov, Beria, and Molotov--gave speeches sketching the policies they favored and assessing the dead leader. Stalin had won acknowledgment as one of the giants of history and as a second founder of the Soviet regime, but the funeral speeches are relatively restrained in their praise of him. Stalin's son complained at the time that his father had not been respectfully interred.[66] All the funeral speeches share a comparatively damp assessment of Stalin's greatness. Beria, however, is truly disrespectful, as the openings of the three speeches show (emphasis added):

Malenkov	Molotov	Beria
[we] have suffered a most grievous, irreparable loss. . . . Our leader and teacher, the greatest	. . . we are living through a heavy sorrow--the demise of Iosif Vissarionovich Stalin, the loss of a	It is hard to express in words [our] . . . great grief . . . Stalin, the great comrade-in-arms

Malenkov	Molotov	Beria
genius of mankind, Iosif Vissarionovich Stalin, has come to the end of his glorious life-path. . . . Boundless are the grandeur and significance of comrade Stalin's activities. . . . Stalin's cause will live forever.	great leader and at the same time a close, beloved, infinitely dear person. And we, his old and close friends . . . say goodbye today to comrade Stalin . . . who will always live in our hearts. . . .	and inspired continuer of Lenin's work, is no more. We have lost a man who is the nearest and dearest to all Soviet people. . . . The whole life and work of the great Stalin are an inspired example of loyalty to Leninism. . . .

Beria's omission of Stalin's Christian name and patronymic, which are honorific signs in Soviet rhetoric, is clearly disrespectful. The same message is conveyed when he, and he alone, never calls Stalin "comrade." What is most obvious, however, is that Beria diminishes Stalin by presenting him simply as a continuer of the great work of Lenin, and not as a great man in his own right. While there are no significant differences in the number of times the different speakers refer to Stalin himself (Malenkov, 28 times; Molotov, 21; Beria, 22), the case is very different with Lenin. Malenkov and Molotov mention him nine and seven times, respectively; but Beria refers to Lenin no fewer than 19 times.

By his treatment of the greatest symbol of Stalinism--Stalin himself--Beria gives the impression that he wants to demolish important parts of the Stalinist political tradition and that he favors in some way a return to Lenin. Such a revival of a past way, whether symbolic or real, is at home in the Soviet regime, which is characterized by a stronger sense of history than are many Western constitutional regimes. Beria hints in his speech at startling policy departures from Stalinism that do not figure in the other speeches. He mentions, for the first time in years, the rights guaranteed by the Soviet Constitution, and praises the conduct of the CC and government "in the fire of the Civil War and intervention, during the difficult years of struggle against devastation and famine"--that is, the years of the New Economic Policy ended by Stalin.

Malenkov and Molotov give particular emphasis to Stalin's greatness as a theoretician of the nationalities question. Malenkov asserts that "with the name of comrade Stalin is connected the solution of one of the most complex questions in the history of society-- the national question . . . comrade Stalin, the great theoretician of the national question, saw to elimination of the age-old national strife." Molotov is even stronger:

> . . . above all in the matter of developing new, friend-
> ly relations among the peoples of our country, com-
> rade Stalin played a special and exceptionally lofty
> role. In this, Stalin . . . illuminated theoretically the
> most important contemporary problems of the national
> and colonial question, promoting there also the develop-
> ment of the scientific foundations of Marxism-Leninism.

On the other hand, it is perhaps the most striking feature of Beria's
speech that he does not say that Stalin had achieved anything in the
field of nationalities policy. Since Stalin had always been famous as
a specialist on the nationalities question, Beria's silence about this
is quite meaningful. It implies disapproval of the distinctive Stalin
nationalities policy as a whole, and not merely of the way that policy
was being implemented in the last months of Stalin's life.

From the beginning of his speech it is noticeable that Beria defines his audience in a way different from the other two speakers.
Malenkov consistently uses the phrase "Soviet people," while Beria
prefers to speak of the Soviet peoples, in the plural; he begins the
speech by speaking of the grief of "our party and the peoples of our
country." Beria evidently wishes to emphasize that the country he
speaks to is not a monolithic national state but a federation of
peoples. In accord with this intention, Beria uses the formula "multinational state" three times as often as either of his rivals, and he
is the only leader to speak of the "Soviet national republics." He
considers the friendship of peoples and the "firm union of all the
Soviet national republics" to be so important that he ranks them
second only to the alliance between the working class and the peasantry among the foundations of "our internal policy." This emphasis on
Soviet federalism is without parallel in the other funeral speeches.
Molotov, for instance, talks about the "brotherly cooperation and
unification [ob'edinenie] of big and small peoples [which is] growing
before our eyes" and, in the thematic section on the nationalities,
about the "advance in the culture [singular] of the peoples" (emphasis
added).

We can now summarize what we have learned from the funeral
speeches. None of the speakers attacks bourgeois nationalism or
Zionism. This signals the precipitate abandonment of Stalin's nationalities campaign. The decision was not a gradual one, upon
analysis, but one taken in the most authoritative possible way and at
the earliest possible moment. It is clear that the new triumvirate
perceived relations between the nationalities as one of the most pressing problems to be dealt with in governing the Soviet Union. Because
all three members of the triumvirate agree on abandoning Stalin's
campaign against bourgeois nationalism, it is a reasonable supposition

that the regime had had to pay a heavy price in minority dissatisfaction for this policy. It is a strange fact that in the darkest hour for the minorities, the fall and winter of 1952-53, they had an advocate, Beria; but when the tide began to turn immediately after Stalin's death, there was no spokesman for "Great Russian chauvinism."

Even though Malenkov, Beria, and Molotov united in rejecting Stalin's nationalities campaign, they did not cooperate in setting up a common nationalities line to replace it. They must have seen the nationalities question not only as a serious national problem with no single obvious answer, but also as an issue that could profitably be exploited for partisan advantage. *

Beria's funeral speech confirms the charges made by Soviet newspapers in connection with his dismissal and trial, and by subsequent Soviet histories and writings on nationalities policy: that he "undertook . . . to undermine the friendship of the peoples of the U.S.S.R. with the great Russian people," to "activate bourgeois nationalist elements in the Union republics," and more specifically that he made "discriminations between cadres in accordance with their nationality . . . placing cadres of different nationalities in opposition to one another."[67] The credit for the drastic changes in nationalities policy that took place in the spring must have gone to Beria, since he was the only leader who had previously expressed himself as favoring such a radical change.

What did Beria do in the Presidium to put his nationalities policy into practice? Khrushchev's evidence on this point is now available:

---

*It should be noted in passing that the position expressed by Beria is not simply a consequence of the generally "rightist" reaction to Stalin's political tradition that is visible in his funeral speech. In the first place, Beria appears to diverge more from previous rhetorical practice in nationalities policy than in any other area, with the possible exception of constitutional rights. Moreover, the general attitudes of the speakers toward Stalinism do not necessarily predetermine their position on specific policy issues. Although Beria is the speaker most opposed to Stalin in general, he does not seem to diverge as much from Stalin's foreign policy in the direction of conciliation with the West as Malenkov does. Beria must have had quite specific reasons for adopting the funeral speech's nationalities policy. Indeed, he arranges the rhetoric of his entire speech to convey his alternative in nationalities policy. For example, he is careful to say "Soviet peoples" in the plural even when he is not discussing nationalities policy.

The Presidium began to discuss a memorandum by
Beria about the ethnic composition of governing bodies
in the Ukraine. Beria's idea was that local officials
should be kept in positions of leadership in their own
Republics and shouldn't be promoted to the central organization in Moscow. . . . Then a memorandum appeared concerning the Baltic states, followed by another concerning Belorussia. Both stressed the principle of drawing the Republic leadership from the local
population. We passed a decision that the post of First
Secretary in every Republic had to be held by a local
person and not by a Russian sent from Moscow. [68]

The actual text of the (probably typical) Presidium decision on
Latvia, which has become available through samizdat, makes it
clear that in this case Khrushchev harmonized his memory with the
kind of nationalities policy that was respectable later. The actual
decree goes much further, with the Presidium ordering the Latvian
leadership specifically

2) To organize the training, preparation and extensive
   promotion to directing work of people of the local
   nationality; to change the practice of appointing
   cadres not of the local nationality; to recall the
   nomenklatura workers ignorant of the local
   language and place them at the disposal of the
   CC, CPSU.
3) To carry on official correspondence in the national
   republics in the native, local language. [69]

Although this decree, like many Soviet documents, is vague in
important respects, its implications are revolutionary. Since a
large fraction of the important offices in the union republics were
occupied by Russians, decrees of this sort, if followed strictly,
would bring thousands of personnel changes in each republic. In
cases where Russians remained, the rule about knowledge of the
local language would assure that they were Russians who had long
resided in the locality and perhaps had become part of the local
political organization, rather than Russians sent from the center to
do a tour of duty. Thus a powerful tool used by the central government in curbing local autonomy would be wrenched away. We will
see shortly the kind of important personnel changes Beria produced
by pressing these decrees through the Presidium.

From all the evidence surveyed, it is clearly correct to say
that Beria mounted an appeal to minority cadres to cure his political

weakness. But the precise political aim of his appeal to national
cadres has not hitherto been explained in detail. It enabled him,
first, to appeal to the long-revered principle that each people in the
USSR should develop its own Communist leadership. This principle
offered Beria a way of recruiting a following within the Party elite
without controlling the Party Organs Department--of cracking open
the nomenklatura of that department from outside. He had chosen
a general, impersonal principle that would generate appointees who
knew they were indebted to him for their posts without his having
personally chosen them. The general principle would also function
in such a way as to cut out Malenkov, Beria's greatest rival, and
Khrushchev (except in the Ukraine). Malenkov's khvost was largely
Russian, Khrushchev's Ukrainian and Russian. Even if they did dominate the machinery of appointment in the Secretariat, they would
thus be unable to place their own supporters in 14 of the 16 union republics, while any of their Russian or Ukrainian clients already
serving there would be forced out. *

After this has been said, one can still ask how Beria hoped to
prevail by appealing to a minority coalition in a country where the
majority has strongly nationalist traditions and where its predominance had been accepted as a basis for political life since the 1920s.
This question is difficult to answer. The mere fact that it has to be
raised teaches us an important lesson about Soviet political reality:
that in the judgment of an extremely intelligent Soviet politician, the
national cadres could have a greater role in determining the outcomes
of crucial political conflicts than we are used to thinking.

Beyond this, Beria's gamble on the national cadres is easier
to understand if we take into account three features of the Soviet
political system. First, Beria was seeking political support not
only from Khrushchev, but primarily from officials below the Presidium level. We know from the ascents of Khrushchev and Leonid
Brezhnev how powerful such support can be. The difficulty is in
seeing how useful it could be as long as it remained minority support.
The second point, however, is that what Beria needed was not predominant political support, but only a certain level of political support. At many of the decisive moments in Soviet politics (March

---

*It is also possible that appointments under the national cadres
principle would generate some appointees with earlier links to the
police or to Beria, in the light of the biographies of many Central
Asian politicians (such as Zh. Shayakhmetov; see also the biographies
of Tadzhik officials recorded by Teresa Rakowska-Harmstone in
Russia and Nationalism in Central Asia (Baltimore: Johns Hopkins,
1970).

1953, June 1953, 1957, 1964) the outcome probably has been condi-
tioned by the availability of force to the winning side; that is, by a
kind of coup d'état, often against the "legally constituted" authorities.
Beria already had available instruments of coercion in the police and
the MVD troops, especially the Moscow garrison. But the winning
side has never been willing to throw its weapons onto the scales unless it possessed a high level of wider political support. In this
delicate mixture of spontaneous choice, personal bonds, and force
which gives the study of Soviet politics its extraordinary charm,
what Beria lacked was the element of support within the Party organizations. He could gain substantial support by appealing to the
minority cadres; he may have felt that it would not matter, when it
came to the crisis, whether he had more political support than his
enemies.

One could still ask whether Beria sought his political support
from the right group. In the conclusion to this chapter we will see
some reasons why he may have expected the national cadres to be
politically strong. As for his appeal in the spring of 1953, however,
it is enough for now to say that he based his turn to the source of
political support he could most easily mobilize in a short time on
his known policy preferences--that is, to the most dissatisfied large
group of party officials, the national cadres.

Finally, it might help in understanding Beria's strategy to
mention a third characteristic of Soviet political life. As we will
see, Beria's approach to minority cadres promised great rewards,
but also was a very risky course. This is one of the things that
makes it hard for us to understand why Beria acted as he did. That
he took such a risk is characteristic--he took a great chance in making his speech at the Nineteenth Party Congress--but it is not merely the reflection of a personal idiosyncrasy. In the Soviet system,
high performance, from the factory manager level up, requires
bending or breaking regulations; it is thus a system that selects out
and encourages individuals willing to take risks. If this is true of
present-day Soviet society, it applies still more to the Stalin regime,
in which, during periods of terror, the best course was to take the
initiative in denouncing one's fellow officials, with all the risks that
could entail. Beria, formed by this system, was willing to take an
immense chance for great gains.

BERIA'S NATIONALITIES CAMPAIGN

The attitude of the press toward the nationalities changed immediately after Stalin's death, in conformity with the new position
expressed in the funeral speeches. The specific signs of Stalin's

campaign against the Jews disappeared very quickly. A somewhat
sporadic reading of nationalities articles up to the Twentieth Party
Congress (1956) does not disclose any further mention of Zionism or
"Joint," which were keywords of that campaign. The crime reports
accusing Jews decreased markedly, and disappeared entirely by the
end of March. About the middle of March, articles calling for a
more relaxed attitude toward the minorities began to appear. This
soon became a definite press campaign, accompanied by public meetings to propagandize the friendship of peoples and attack the "national
antagonism" exemplified by the Doctors' Plot. The growing campaign for the new nationalities policy brought back into use many
phrases and slogans rarely or never seen in the press since Beria's
speech at the Nineteenth Party Congress. The "statehood" of the
union republics had not been referred to since then, nor had they
been called "independent." [70]

What must have impressed the national cadres most of all was
the return to awareness of the harm done by excessive Russian nationalism. On April 21 Literaturnaya gazeta went so far as to speak
of "Great Russian nationalism," an even stronger expression than
the "great-power chauvinism" which, before Stalin's death, only
Beria and his client Bagirov had dared to mention. [71] This article
says that "national deviation" is "all the same, whether it is a deviation toward Great Russian nationalism or a deviation toward local
nationalism. . . ." This was a return to the dominant nationalities
line of a much earlier period, which also was found (if much less
openly) in Beria's speech at the Nineteenth Party Congress.

The course of the pro-minority campaign in nationalities policy
was by no means even. It seemed to increase progressively in intensity from the middle of March until the end of April. Then came
a halt, perhaps initiated by the publication of two contradictory articles on nationalities policy for May Day. [72] This suggests that the
nationalities campaign was the object of intense disagreement among
the members of the collective leadership. The press discussion of
the nationalities question died down until early June, when another
extremely vigorous campaign against great-power chauvinism built
up. This campaign intensified rapidly and was at its highest pitch
at the time of Beria's fall, the end of June. During this period the
thing most strongly emphasized in the press campaign was Beria's
theme, the great concern of the party for ". . . the raising and dis-
position in directing work of cadres of the native nationality, which
has not been given as much attention as it should have been . . . in
some republics." [73]

It was in June that Beria showed he could go beyond appealing
to sentiment and deliver concrete advantages in return for support.
On June 13 Pravda announced that L. G. Melnikov--apparently a

Russian--had been dismissed as first secretary of the Ukraine and replaced by A. I. Kirichenko, a Ukrainian. At the same time the writer A. Ye. Korneichuk was appointed vice-chairman of the Ukrainian Council of Ministers and added to the Bureau of the Ukrainian CC; Khrushchev remarks that "Beria also proposed" this appointment.[74] Melnikov and the Bureau in general (mainly followers, unlike Melnikov, of Khrushchev) were charged with "distortions of the Lenin-Stalin national policy of our party," including "converting teaching in Western Ukraine higher educational institutions to the Russian language."

On June 27, Yershov, the Russian second secretary of the Latvian CC, was dismissed on the ground that he had violated "the Lenin-Stalin policy of selecting, training and advancing Latvian cadres to leading work. . . ."[75] He was replaced by a Latvian, Vilis Kruminsh, who subsequently was dismissed for opposing Russian dominance. Earlier the Lithuanian CC had performed similar self-criticism.[76] A program of cadre nativization obviously was being extended to the union republics one by one, although it did not strike the most "colonial" area--Central Asia--before Beria's fall.

Beria's nationalities policy clearly provided inducements for lower-level cadres to join him. It is harder to assemble and analyze the evidence necessary to show whether his plan did in fact attract minority officials who were not previously connected with him. From a large number of likely cases, we will discuss only two that have been confirmed by subsequent evidence. Khrushchev recollects the effect of the promotion of Korneichuk, who had hitherto been one of Khrushchev's followers:

> Korneichuk didn't realize he had been promoted in order to further Beria's anti-Party aims, so he said all sorts of favorable things about Beria and Beria's memorandum [on nationalities policy] during the course of the [Ukrainian CC] Plenum.[77]

An even more prominent recruit of Beria's was M. V. Zimyanin, second secretary in Belorussia under the Russian N. S. Patolichev. Only in 1962 did it become known that Zimyanin had, in June 1953, been promoted to first secretary under the terms of Beria's memorandum. But Beria fell before Zimyanin's appointment could be announced.[78] Zimyanin was immediately dismissed, Patolichev restored, and Zimyanin punished by being sent to the much lower position of department head for South-East Europe in the relatively apolitical Foreign Ministry. He would not have been punished in this way if he had not taken Beria's side following his new appointment. In these two important cases we are able to observe how Beria's strategy worked precisely as he wished.

There was a sudden and sharp change in the rhetoric of nationalities policy at the time of Beria's fall, which probably occurred on
June 26. By June 30 all traces of the former nationalities campaign
had disappeared from the press. This reversal is the best piece of
evidence that Beria was primarily responsible for the nationalities
policy of the spring. At once there began a new nationalities campaign that represented a partial return to the language used in
Stalin's last months. It is not accidental that the editorial denouncing
Beria and his nationalities policy mentions the Nineteenth Party Congress and calls Stalin "great."[79] As we would expect, the new nationalities policy was indicated by the oblivion of formerly respectable slogans and the revival of some that were common under Stalin.
References to "great-power chauvinism" or "the ideology of equality"
and the "independence" of the national republics dropped from sight
until the end of the year. On the other hand, "vigilance" and the concern for "strengthening the Soviet state" returned.[80]

Along with this went a vast expansion in the use of formulas
celebrating the dominance of Russia, beginning with the now ubiqui-
tous "great Russian people." Izvestiia went exceptionally far in em-
phasizing the role of the Russian people:

> . . . a decisive role [in the history of the USSR] be-
> longs to the great Russian people. The Russian people
> rightfully merited general recognition as the most out-
> standing, the directing [rukovodyashchaya] nation of
> the U.S.S.R.[81]

There was even the beginning of a trickle of reports about obviously
Jewish swindlers and scoundrels, of the type that clogged the newspapers during the last months of Stalin's life.[82] This new nationalities line showed that Russian nationalist sentiment, to which the
leadership now appealed, had remained strong while being denied
official expression.

What can be concluded about the success of Beria's nationalities policy from his fall? Most obviously, the policy was ultimately
unsuccessful with Beria's colleagues on the Presidium. It had earlier been the vehicle of Beria's alliance with Khrushchev, but it was
now one of the main factors in creating the alliance against him.
The extent to which Beria's appeal to the nationalities frightened the
other leaders, including Khrushchev, is suggested by the prominence
of this subject in the charges against him. It is the first policy
charge mentioned in the formal accusation, and the only one in which
Beria is said to have undertaken "criminal" actions.[83]

Since Khrushchev had benefited from this policy and had repeatedly espoused a relatively pro-minority view, one might have

expected him to have had this aspect of the policy attack on Beria muted unless he were convinced it was very dangerous. If Beria's nationalities policy was unsuccessful with the other Presidium members, this does not imply that it was simply a mistake. A majority in the Presidium in opposition to a rising Soviet politician is not necessarily fatal, as Khrushchev showed in overcoming the Anti-Party Group in 1957. Beria's destruction was probably due most of all to the East German rebellion and to details of palace conspiracy; it does not show that the attempt to mobilize national cadres was a fundamentally mistaken strategy. In fact, the failure of Beria's policy with his fellow Presidium members is a measure of its success with the minority cadres; otherwise it would not have been so frightening to his colleagues.

For comparison it may be useful to indicate what happened in nationalities policy after the denunciation of Beria and his policy had died down. In the fall of 1953 there was a marked loss of interest in nationalities policy in the central press. But at the end of the year a new nationalities campaign began in connection with the forthcoming celebration of the three-hundredth anniversary of the year (somewhat arbitrarily chosen) of the reunion of the Ukraine with Russia. The article that set the tone for this campaign was less centralizing in its tone than any press comment since the Beria period.[84] The difference was that there was now an attempt to give the Ukraine, rather than all the non-Russian nationalities, an equal place with the Russians. For the first time the word "great" was applied to a Soviet people other than the Russians: "two great Slavic peoples," "two great fraternal peoples." The historical account attempts to bond together the Ukrainian and Russian peoples by appealing to a common heritage.

Who was the beneficiary of this new campaign? Obviously Khrushchev, who had a heavily Ukrainian clientele. He tried to use nationalities policy as a factional weapon, as Beria had done. Like Beria, he took the pro-minority side, but with a new twist: Slavic solidarity. Khrushchev was the inventor of this since-successful alternative in Soviet nationalities policy. What is surprising is that a stance favorable to the minorities was not delegitimized by its connection with a repudiated leader and past policies now considered unpatriotic, as Communism, the anti-Dreyfusard cause, and McCarthyism were delegitimized in Western countries. This shows how the Soviet sphere of policy is affected by the absence of public opinion in the Western sense and of the "tyranny of the majority"; it is remarkable how an apparently decided policy issue bubbles up again in a few months. Most of all, Khrushchev's renewed turn to the minorities shows the importance of the minority cadres as a resource for ambitious politicians.

CONCLUSION

The conclusion that has emerged with the greatest certitude from this study is that the nationalities question was a pivotal issue in Soviet politics not only after the death of Stalin but before. This was the issue upon which Stalin centered his attempt to arrange his succession and the issue on which Beria, one of the four most powerful men in the Soviet Union, chose to concentrate in most of his postwar speeches. Beria consistently saw an appeal to the non-Russian nationalities as a way of advancing his political fortunes; after Stalin's death he saw it as the most important of the several means he used. This strategy was successful enough to make many Soviets and East Europeans anticipate, in June 1953, that Beria would soon be dictator.

Stalin's use of the nationalities issue can be understood on the basis of the customary view of the nationalities' role in his regime, but Beria's cannot. Beria's appeal to the nationalities is testimony that they were a very important political force, whether at the moment or in the situation anticipated immediately after Stalin's death. This is a second conclusion that has emerged with certainty from these investigations. I will close this study by exploring some tentative explanations of how national cadres could be politically powerful in spite of Stalin's restoration of Russian nationalism.

We must begin with the fact that the Soviet Union is a multinational state, that it had a formal federal system inherited from the period before Stalin established his absolute rule, and that Marxist doctrine originally provided one of the worst possible climates for Russian nationalism. It is my impression that this last factor was no longer a powerful one in the postwar period. If one were reconstructing the factions of the Stalin era as a sort of thought-experiment, one would expect to find Russian nationalist sentiments voiced by the Malenkov-Beria group, with its pragmatic yielding to what "life itself" calls for. Instead, it is in Zhdanov's camp that one finds Russian nationalism combined with ideological purity and "leftism." This bizarre combination indicates a far-reaching decomposition of Marxism by 1946.

Next we should consider Stalin's own reasons not to concede unlimited authority to the Russians and their nationalism. While Stalin found Russian nationalism very useful in generating support for the regime, it has also, up to today's dissidence, been a banner to which opponents of the regime rallied. Stalin, as a Georgian, must have been well aware of this danger. Moreover, he used the nominal federal structure of the USSR in balancing the power of his lieutenants so that none of them could threaten his authority. If Russian nationalism ever became the sole source of legitimate guidance in nationalities policy, the lieutenant or lieutenants dominant in the Russian Republic would completely overshadow those administering the other union republics, thereby destroying the balance Stalin wished to maintain. The kind of threat to the dictator that might develop is shown by the alleged attempt of the Russian nationalist Zhdanovites to transfer the capital of the Russian Republic from Moscow to Leningrad. [85] This would remove the RSFSR government from the close central control that has generally prevented it from being as important a factional center as the other union republics, create the conditions in which the RSFSR would for the first time have its own Party Committee and Bureau, and perhaps bring all of this machinery under the domination of the Leningrad Party organization. Such a change would have been in line with Russian nationalism, but dangerous to Stalin.

Finally, we should turn from considering Stalin's personal intentions to considering his indirect impact through the political structure he set up. If Beria could consider the nationalities as so powerful, we must question whether the Stalin regime was centralized in the way that we have generally understood it to be. In order to understand the extent and character of centralization in Stalin's Russia, we must pay more attention to the institution of the regional "fiefdom," in which a member of Stalin's inner circle was responsible for almost everything in a given locality, administering it through a network of clients personally linked to him. In this way Zhdanov ran the Leningrad area for 14 years, Beria the three Transcaucasian republics for 19 years. Such "fiefdoms" were a distinctive feature of Stalin's regime as opposed to other autocratic states, where the ruler most often prefers to divide authority both in time and within institutions. [86] It is also uncommon in autocratic states for the local administration to have great power at the center, in the way that the Ukrainian administration was represented by Khrushchev in Moscow, and the Transcaucasus by Beria.

At this point the retort is inevitable: Is it not absurd to speak of Khrushchev or Beria "representing" certain national areas in Moscow? After all, these men were not chosen by the Ukraine or Transcaucasia, but imposed by Stalin from the outside, and in both cases partly to suppress spontaneous local feelings. This is certainly true. But Khrushchev, Beria, and Zhdanov were not only the supervisors of their areas, but also the heads of patron-client networks there. A patron-client network consists of the mutual exchange of favors: clients support a patron and carry out his orders efficiently in return for protection and advancement--that is, for serving their interests. Thus a patron-client relationship is inseparable from representation of a certain kind. While it is surely wrong to say Beria represented Transcaucasia, it is right to say he repre-

sented--in the manner native to this kind of regime--the ruling class
of Transcaucasia. Since one of the kinds of protection clients most
want from their patron is protection against unwanted interference
from Moscow, the patron-client system is potentially a powerful
source of autonomy for the national republics.

Admittedly, this structure does not in itself imply anything
about nationalities policy, and does not necessarily help to explain
Beria's conduct. If there is an absolute ruler such as Stalin at the
center who prefers a policy of harsh assault on bourgeois nationalism, does not this policy then become the "interest" of the clients
that they wish their patrons to pursue? In this event one would have
decentralization of administration, but unanimity of policy; the "representation" of the localities would be rather illusory. It is thus
necessary to think out whether having a patronage relationship to a
non-Russian area has any particular implications for the kind of nationalities policy that one of Stalin's lieutenants will speak for at the
center.

We can begin by assuming that in a national area, a large percentage of the population will be non-Russian and that a large number
of the patron's clients will be non-Russian. In the abstract, there is
some likelihood that officials at the lowest level will incline more
toward a gentle treatment of local nationalism than will the central
leadership in Moscow, since they are in closer contact with the practical difficulties of imposing an unpopular policy. To this must be
added non-Russian officials' personal sentiments of solidarity with
their people and resentment of Russian intervention. For these reasons, in the tacit bargaining that constitutes a patron-client interaction, there will be a tendency for clients to seek their patrons' intervention on the minority side in nationalities policy debates that may
arise within the Politburo. It is important that both patron and
clients have strong motives to exclude outsiders from local politics
and to create opportunities for movement of members of their own
group into national leadership positions; this benefits both clients
and patron. Both aims can be served by a nationalities policy that
calls for use of indigenous cadres in the national republics and restricts demands for Russian predominance in national politics.
These are only tendencies, which can easily be reversed in many
specific cases; but it seems inherent in the very institution of patron-
client relationships in minority areas that the resulting bodies are
more likely to drift toward one side of the nationalities policy debate
than the other.

If the patron of a minority fiefdom does succeed in instituting
a more moderate nationalities policy in his own domain than exists
elsewhere, he is in a position to make an appeal to the interest of
minority cadres who are not his clients. He may develop the minori-

ties into a national "constituency," as Beria may have done. In deciding how to respond to a developing relationship between one of his lieutenants and such a "constituency," a dictator needs to balance his desire for a uniform and unambiguous policy bearing his stamp against the need to maintain healthy competition among his lieutenants. He has to be sure that no matter how firmly established a favorite or a policy may be, he still has the deciding voice. There may, therefore, be inherent in the system itself reasons--if much less conclusive ones--for a dictator not to prohibit all efforts to mobilize the nationalities as a constituency.

Since the provinces of the RSFSR have smaller populations than many union republics, the most important Party organizations within which one could conceivably create a unified clientele are the Russian Moscow and Leningrad provinces and the large union republics: the Ukraine, Belorussia, Kazakhstan, Uzbekistan. To these the three Transcaucasian republics should be added for the Stalin period, since they were treated as a unit. The Moscow Party organization has consistently suffered, as a factional base, from the presence of the national administration, which makes possible its constant interference, so we are left with one Russian and five non-Russian areas. The very size of these non-Russian organizations may give them, if properly used by a politician already influential at the center, a disproportionate weight in Soviet politics. This weight is more likely to be felt on the side of policy decisions favorable to the non-Russian nationalities.

These consequences drawn from the Stalinist institution of the fiefdom are based on abstract reasoning. What does the historical evidence of the postwar period tell us about the political weight of such fiefdoms? The questions to ask are how much importance Stalin's lieutenants attributed to such bases, and how independent Stalin felt them to be. As we have seen, Stalin probably considered Beria's clienteles, including the Transcaucasian "fiefdom," as potentially independent of his own control in some circumstances, since he purged them so slowly. Beria must have considered his "fiefdom" powerful, since he moved to restore its fealty at once and devoted some of his most valuable personnel to this task. Further significant evidence on the importance of territorial fiefdoms emerges from Stalin's attempt to arrange his succession from 1948 on. According to Myron Rush, Stalin designated Malenkov as heir and Khrushchev as counterheir; this interpretation has since been supported by Khrushchev's recollections about the period after his transfer to Moscow in 1949: "I even began to suspect that one of the reasons Stalin had called me back to Moscow was to influence the balance of power in the collective and to put a check on Beria and Malenkov."[87]

In transferring Khrushchev to Moscow, Stalin took away the
Ukrainian first secretaryship and gave it to L. G. Melnikov, who had
no connection with Khrushchev. Stalin must have believed that
Khrushchev's mastery of the Moscow Party organization alone would
not threaten Malenkov's succession, but that if the Ukraine were
added, Khrushchev might be too strong for Malenkov. This is a
powerful testimony to the strength of the Ukraine. Khrushchev
seems to have agreed: after taking up his new duties in Moscow, he
decoted his December 1949 speech to an appeal to minority sentiment on the nationalities issue, referring frequently to the Ukraine.
He apparently believed that at this point his most urgent task was to
retain the influence he still had in the Ukraine through the CC and
oblast secretaries who were his clients.

We have seen how patron-client relationships can decentralize
an autocratic political order and render national cadres powerful.
But this can take place only if patron-client relationships are organized by regions, which they need not be--Beria's police clientele
and Malenkov's clientele in the economic ministries were not. Yet
the Stalin regime did display strong tendencies to organize government regionally. Two examples will suffice. Zhdanov was, before
World War II, charged with general supervision over the Soviet navy.
Why? Simply because the navy was centered at Kronstadt. After
the war Khrushchev was the lord not only of the Ukraine but also of
Moldavia, a separate union republic, through his clients Brezhnev
and Z. T. Serdyuk. Why? Because Moldavia is next to the Ukraine
and had formed an ASSR within it before 1940. In these cases geog-
raphy functions as a principle of organization to a degree unparalleled
in Western countries.

Other autocratic states have also shown this tendency for official activities originally organized on a different basis to redistribute
themselves regionally.* Albert Speer gives a striking example from
Nazi Germany, a regime that had begun by doing away with the
earlier federal system:

> Leipzig was the headquarters of the Reich's Central
> Agency for the Fur Trade. One day the local Gauleiter,
> Mutschmann, informed the director of the agency that
> he had appointed one of his friends as the director's

---

*For example, in the Ottoman Empire at the end of the nine-
teenth century, few provincial governors served for more than a few
months; and even major governorships were regarded as appropriate
posts of exile for politicians who had lost favor at court.

successor. The Minister of Economics protested vigorously, since the director of a central agency could be
appointed only by Berlin. The Gauleiter summarily ordered the director to vacate his post within a few days.
In the face of this power clash, the Minister of Economics resorted to an absurd solution: The night before
the post was to be handed over to the Gauleiter's friend,
trucks from Berlin drove up to the doors and transferred the entire fur trade agency, including its files
and its director, to Berlin. [88]

Perhaps the reason for this pattern is to be found in the "shapelessness," that is, the disruption of normal lines of bureaucratic command and responsibility, characteristic of dictatorial regimes. The
resulting fluidity tends to do away with the administrative structures
"rationally" organized by function, so characteristic of the modern
West, and to substitute as the active political entities organizations
determined by the dictator's convenience in solving a specific prob-
lem--which often will be regionally organized--or bodies constituted
by personal ties among officials ("family circles" or patron-client
networks). The latter also are relatively likely to take a regional
form, rather than being nationally diffused in a "functional" organization, because the personal interactions from which they arise are
easier to carry on in one locality. Regionally organized clienteles
are not only more likely to arise, but are--as Soviet history shows--
also likely to be stronger than those organized only on a functional
basis. Within a region where there is a clientele, shapelessness
tends to permit its total supremacy over nominally independent organizations and its total control over the region: the "fiefdom" per-
fected. At the end of his life Stalin was keenly aware of this phenomenon and in 1951 fought it by organizing oblasti (provinces) in
several republics that had none. [89] This served to break up the unity
of these republics' political machines. Thus the importance of the
national minorities, even under Stalin, may result not only from the
multiethnic character of Soviet society but also from the structure
of the regime. While it is certainly true that autocracy creates centralization with one hand, we may find that it takes it away again
with the other.

NOTES

1. Joseph Stalin, Marxism and the National Question (New
York: International Publishers, n.d.), pp. 9-12.
2. Pravda, October 9, 1952, p. 2.

3. "Programma RKP (b), priniataya na VIII s'ezde partii,"
in Krestomatiya po istorii KPSS, ed. I. Kulikova and V. Shal'neva
(Moscow: Izdatel'stvo Politicheskoi Literaturi, 1965), p. 20.

4. See L. G. Melnikov in Pravda Ukraini, September 25,
1952; M. D. Bagirov, Pravda, October 7, 1952, p. 4.

5. Mgeladze's report to the Georgian Party Congress, Zaria
vostoka, September 16, 1952; see also Arutinov's speech, Pravda,
October 9, 1952, p. 5. Emphasis added.

6. N. S. Khrushchev, Khrushchev Remembers, Strobe
Talbott, trans. and ed. (Boston: Little, Brown, 1970), p. 286.

7. Pravda, op. cit.

8. Ibid., p. 3, col. 1. Emphasis added.

9. Ibid., p. 2, col. 3.

10. Ibid.

11. Ibid., p. 2, col. 6, and p. 3, col. 1.

12. See the congress speeches of Bagirov (Pravda, October 7,
1952, pp. 4-5) and Korneichuk (October 11, 1952, p. 2); see also
Kommunist (1953), no. 1: 104-05.

13. See Mgeladze's Georgian Party Congress report, Zaria
vostoka, September 17, 1952; Bagirov, Bakinskii rabochii, September 1952; A. N. Poskrebyshev, Pravda, December 30, 1952, p. 2.

14. Pravda, October 9, 1952, p. 2, col. 3. Emphasis added.

15. See Mgeladze's Georgian Party Congress report and the
speeches at the Nineteenth Party Congress of Korneichuk, Pidtychenko,
and Arutinov. See also Pravda, July 10, 1951, p. 2; August 2, 1951,
p. 1; September 24, 1952, p. 2.

16. Pravda, October 9, 1952, p. 2, col. 3.

17. Ibid., p. 2, col. 5.

18. Ibid., p. 2, col. 3; see also col. 5.

19. Ibid., p. 2, col. 3.

20. Ibid., June 13, 1953, p. 3. See also Konstantin I. Nefedov
and M. Tyurin, "The Friendship of Peoples of the U.S.S.R., Source
of the Strength of the Soviet State," Izvestiia, June 19, 1953, p. 3.

21. Pravda, October 13, 1952, pp. 9-10.

22. Ibid., October 9, 1952, p. 2, col. 3.

23. For this change, see Robert Conquest, ed., Soviet Nationalities Policy in Practice (New York: Praeger, 1967), pp. 93-94.

24. Myron Rush, Political Succession in the U.S.S.R. (2nd
ed.; New York: Columbia University Press, 1968), pp. 53-54.

25. See the text in Boris Nicolaevsky, ed., The Crimes of
the Stalin Era: Special Report to the 20th Congress of the CPSU by
N. S. Khrushchev (New York: New Leader, 1962), p. S 49.

26. Mgeladze, op. cit., pp. 2-6; Nicolaevsky, op. cit., p.
S 47.

27. Nicolaevsky, op. cit., pp. S 46-S 47. The nationalism
charges are hinted at in Mgeladze's Republican Congress report.

28. Pravda, November 1, 1952, p. 2.

29. Jiri Pelikan, ed., The Czechoslovak Political Trials 1950-1954: The Suppressed Report of the Dubcek Government's Commission of Inquiry, 1968 (Stanford, Calif.: Stanford University Press, 1971), p. 106 (see also pp. 103, 105).

30. Boris Nicolaevsky, Power and the Soviet Elite (New York: Praeger, 1965), p. 170; Robert Conquest, Power and Policy in the U.S.S.R. (New York: Harper Torchbooks, 1967), p. 173. These assertions are supported by the fact that the first set (1949-July 1951) of Soviet security advisers, who presumably were carrying out orders from Beria, obstructed attempts to involve Slansky in criminal charges (Pelikan, op. cit., p. 102). These advisers were dismissed, and replaced in November 1951 (ibid., p. 104). Another indication of Slansky's connection with Beria can perhaps be found in the release of his family from prison in the second half of April 1953, in the first period of Beria's rapid advance. See Jozefa Slanska, Report on My Husband (London: Hutchinson, 1969), p. 175; Eugen Loebl, Stalinism in Prague (New York: Grove Press, 1969), p. 73.

31. Khrushchev, op. cit., p. 263.

32. Ibid., p. 256.

33. See Zaria vostoka, February 3, 1949, p. 3; February 17, 1949, p. 3; February 23, 1949, p. 3 (two articles); February 27, 1949, p. 1; March 12, 1949, p. 3; March 26, 1949, p. 3. The smaller number of Pravda anti-cosmopolitan articles cited in Benjamin Pinkus, "Soviet Campaigns against 'Jewish Nationalism' and 'Cosmopolitanism,' 1946-1953," Soviet Jewish Affairs 2 (1974): 56, table I, must be based on a quite restricted definition of an anti-cosmopolitan article.

34. Bakinskii rabochii, February 19, 1949, p. 1, col. 2.

35. Ilya Ehrenburg, "Lyudi, godi, zhizn'," in Sobraniye sochinenii (Moscow: Izdatel'stvo Khudozhestvennaya Literatura, 1967), 9: 574-75.

36. Nicolaevsky, Power and the Soviet Elite, p. 170.

37. Harrison Salisbury, Moscow Journal: The End of Stalin (Chicago: University of Chicago Press, 1961), pp. 201, 372.

38. Ibid., p. 372.

39. Pravda, December 21, 1949. Beria's speech also seems less severe toward bourgeois nationalism than most anonymous articles in the contemporary press. See, for example, "The Triumph of the Lenin-Stalin Party's National Policy," Pravda, December 16, 1949, p. 2.

40. Pravda, December 21, 1949.

41. Ibid., March 10, 1950, p. 4.

42. Ibid., March 11, 1953.

43. Ibid., November 7, 1951, pp. 2-4.

44. Frederick Barghoorn, Soviet Russian Nationalism (New York: Oxford University Press, 1956), p. 286, n. 6; Harrison Salisbury, To Moscow and Beyond (New York: Harper and Row, 1960), p. 71.

45. Khrushchev, op. cit., p. 300.

46. Pravda, October 9, 1952.

47. Khrushchev, op. cit., p. 281.

48. The Latvian SSR is called "independent" in the Latvian-language newspaper Cina. See Current Digest of the Soviet Press 5, no. 2 (1953): 16-17 (reporting Cina of November 20, 1952, and January 6, 1953).

49. Kalnberzin's report to the Latvian CC on the Presidium decree of June 12, 1953, quoted or paraphrased in Radio Liberty, ed., Sobranie dokumentov samizdata (New York: Radio Liberty Committee, 1972), 21, no. 1042: 3.

50. Pravda, December 30, 1952, pp. 2-3. Poskrebyshev's speech at the Nineteenth Party Congress also was concerned with nationalities policy to a great degree. It is possible that Poskrebyshev was being groomed to replace Beria as the party's main spokesman on nationalities policy. He had no known qualifications for such a role, though he apparently was born in the Bashkir ASSR and represented a district there in the Supreme Soviet.

51. Boris Nicolaevsky interpreted Poskrebyshev as a more or less independent political actor (roughly comparable with Beria or Malenkov) in the period 1949-53; see his Power and the Soviet Elite, pp. 105-17, 257. Nicolaevsky presents little evidence for this interpretation, which is rendered plausible chiefly by not considering the possibility of Khrushchev's role in bringing about political moves that cannot be traced to Beria or Malenkov. The preparations for a new terror continued after Poskrebyshev's fall in early 1953.

52. Pravda, October 9, 1952, p. 2, col. 3.

53. Ibid., December 30, 1952, p. 3. "Enrichment" of the native languages is a semi-technical term that refers to the adoption of Russian technical, political, and other words by the native languages, as opposed to the coining of new words on native roots. See Hélène Carrère d'Encausse, "Linguistic Russification and Nationalist Opposition in Kazakhstan," East Turkic Review 1, no. 1 (1960): 98.

54. For instance, Pravda, January 13, 1953, p. 1; January 31, 1953, p. 2.

55. Ibid., November 22, 1952, pp. 2, 4; November 25, 1952, p. 4.

56. Pelikan, op. cit., p. 80; Loebl, op. cit., pp. 23-28, 45-50, 55. For the charges see also the transcript of the trial in Loebl, op. cit., pp. 125-26, 134, 150, 250.

57. Zbigniew Brzezinski, The Soviet Bloc (rev. ed.; New York: Praeger, 1960), pp. 94-95. See also the trial transcript in Loebl, op. cit., pp. 92, 121, 159, 171-73, 175, 184, 239, and passim.

58. Pravda, November 22, 1953, p. 4.

59. Conquest, Power and Policy, pp. 165-67.

60. A chain of "evidence" was being developed linking Beria with American intelligence through the doctors and the Jewish Anti-Fascist Committee. For the links see Nicolaevsky, Power and the Soviet Elite, pp. 113-14; Yehoshua A. Gilboa, The Black Years of Soviet Jewry (Boston: Little, Brown, 1971), p. 299; Stanislaw Kot, Conversations with the Kremlin and Dispatches from Russia, trans. H. C. Stevens (London: Oxford University Press, 1963), p. 60; E. J. Rozak, Allied Wartime Diplomacy (New York: Wiley, 1958), p. 100; Ehrenburg, op. cit., 9: 565. For evidence on the danger to Beria personally, see Svetlana Alliluyeva, Dvadtsat' pisem k drugu (New York: Harper Colophon Books, 1968), pp. 22, 118-23, 192n.

61. Khrushchev, op. cit., p. 323. Since the period after the death of Stalin has been well understood by Leonhard (see note 65), Conquest, and others, it will suffice to sketch events only in the briefest outline.

62. Conquest, Power and Policy, p. 223.

63. For this, see Teresa Rakowska-Harmstone, Russia and Nationalism in Central Asia: The Case of Tadzhikistan (Baltimore: Johns Hopkins Press, 1970), pp. 119-20; Nicolaevsky, Power and the Soviet Elite, p. 138 (also p. 160); Seweryn Bialer, Stalin and His Generals (New York: Pegasus, 1969), p. 563, n. 36; Khrushchev, op. cit., p. 251; N. S. Khrushchev, Khrushchev Remembers: The Last Testament (Boston: Little, Brown, 1974, p. 96; Sidney Ploss, Conflict and Decision Making in Soviet Russia (Princeton, N.J.: Princeton University Press, 1965), p. 63.

64. The computation is based partly on the data in Conquest, Power and Policy, pp. 425-26, and partly on independent reconstruction.

65. For Shatalin's duties on the Secretariat, see Conquest, Power and Policy, pp. 210-11; Wolfgang Leonhard, The Kremlin Since Stalin (New York: Praeger, 1962), pp. 61, 94.

66. Alliluyeva, op. cit., p. 198.

67. Pravda, December 24, 1953; Izvestiia, July 12, 1953, p. 1; G. O. Zimanas, "Druzhba narodov SSSR: Preodolenie perezhitkov burzhuaznogo natsionalizma," Voprosi filosofii (1958), no. 1: 33. See also Institut Istorii Partii TsK KP Azerbaidzhana, ed., Ocherki istorii Kommunisticheskoi partii Azerbaidzhana (n.p.: Azerbaidzhanskoye Gosudarstvennoye Izdatel'stvo, 1963), p. 653; and Institut Istorii Partii pri TsK KP Gruzii, ed., Ocherki istorii

Kommunisticheskoi partii Gruzii, II (Tbilisi: Izdatel'stvo TsK KP Gruzii, 1963), p. 248.

68. Khrushchev, op. cit., p. 330.

69. Radio Liberty, op. cit.

70. Izvestiia, March 3, 1953, p. 1; June 19, 1953, pp. 2-3.

71. N. Matyushkin, "Great Principles of Internationalism," Literaturnaiia gazeta, April 21, 1953, pp. 2-3; Beria, at the Nineteenth Congress (see above); Bagirov, Pravda, February 10, 1953, p. 2.

72. Pravda, April 30, 1953, pp. 1, 2.

73. K. Nefedov and M. Tyurin, "The Friendship of Peoples of the U.S.S.R. --Source of the Strength of the Soviet State," Izvestiia, June 19, 1953, p. 3.

74. Khrushchev, op. cit.

75. See Pravda, June 28, 1953, p. 2; Boris Meissner, "Umschau," Osteuropa 3 (1953): 290; Radio Liberty, op. cit., p. 9.

76. Pravda, June 18, 1953, p. 2.

77. Khrushchev, op. cit.

78. See Zimyanin's biography in Entsiklopedicheskii yezhegodnik for 1962. I owe this reference to Michel Tatu, Power in the Kremlin, trans. Helen Kafel (New York: Viking Compass Books, 1970), p. 465, n. 1.

79. Izvestiia, August 10, 1953, p. 1.

80. Ibid., July 10, 1953, p. 1; July 11, 1953, p. 1.

81. Ibid., July 12, 1953, p. 1. Emphasis added.

82. Ibid., July 22, 1953, p. 3.

83. Pravda, December 24, 1953.

84. Ibid., December 9, 1953.

85. Conquest, Power and Policy, p. 103, n.

86. Rush, op. cit., pp. 48-49; Khrushchev, op. cit., pp. 246, 250.

87. Bialer, op. cit., p. 567, n. 52.

88. Albert Speer, Inside the Third Reich, trans. Richard and Clara Winston (New York: Avon, 1971), p. 687, n. 6.

89. "Umschau: Verwaltung," Osteuropa 2 (1952): 213-15.

PART III

**ETHNO-NATIONAL POLICY MAKING
AND PLANNING**

THE CALCULUS OF
SOVIET ANTISEMITISM

6

Steven L. Burg

Western scholars frequently employ models of rational decision making to aid in the understanding of Soviet policy outcomes. They rarely do so, however, for Soviet official antisemitism, a policy outcome for which we have the kind of information that makes such analysis possible. Up to now, most Western scholars have explained Soviet antisemitism by pointing to the antisemitic proclivities of Soviet leaders, to power-political conflicts among them, and to changes in the membership of or the power ranking within the Soviet elite. Such factors are not unimportant for the understanding of Soviet official antisemitism. Indeed, they tell us much about Soviet politics. However, explanations based on these factors alone fail to account for the starts and stops of Soviet official antisemitism or for its distinctly differing content and the variety of its applications at different times since the end of World War II.

The historical record suggests that official antisemitism in the Soviet Union is neither an end in itself nor simply an expression of the personal prejudices of the Soviet leaders, and that it may be useful to view official antisemitism as a means by which the Soviet leadership seeks to achieve its substantive policy goals. Viewing official antisemitism in this way suggests, in turn, that the Soviet leadership's use of antisemitism may be determined by its calculation of the utility of such a policy for the achievement of its goals. In this paper I examine Soviet official antisemitism as the outcome of a rational decision-making process by which the Soviet leadership as a group determines its utility.

The author would like to thank his colleague Paul A. Goble for his helpful comments and criticisms during the preparation of this paper.

The use of a rational decision-making approach to the study of official antisemitism in the Soviet Union does not preclude the effects on the policy process of irrational factors such as personal anti-semitic proclivities. In fact, the model of Soviet decision making concerning antisemitism presented in the second section incorporates these factors; but it emphasizes that such prejudices affect the policy-making process primarily by affecting the leadership's perceptions of the effects of antisemitism. The determinant of policy remains the Soviet leadership's estimate of the utility of antisemitism for the achievement of its goals. This model is not only more parsimonious than existing ones but also has greater explanatory power with respect to changes over time in Soviet official antisemitism.

In the first section of the paper, I examine Soviet official antisemitism in the period 1945-65. I do not intend this section to be a historical account either of the period in general or of the content of Soviet official antisemitism in particular. I attempt to identify those Soviet policy goals the achievement of which was most likely to have been affected in some way--either positive or negative--by the use of official antisemitism. I then try to specify those conditions which increased the costs or benefits to the Soviet regime of using official antisemitism and those conditions which increased the costs or bene-fits of not using it or of moving against antisemitism in Soviet society. I search for the factors--other than the personal proclivities of the members of the leadership or power-political conflicts among them--most likely to have affected the Soviet leadership's calculations of the utility of antisemitism, and suggest how such factors could have led the Soviet leadership to decide on the particular policy outcomes of the period. Of course, other factors may have affected the Soviet leadership's calculations, but those identified here cover the range of types.

In the second section of the paper I use these sets of policy goals, conditions, and outcomes as the basis for developing a model of the Soviet leadership's decision-making process with respect to the use of official antisemitism during the period 1945-65. For this I employ some of the language and symbols of mathematics. I do so in order to make possible precise statements about the relationships among the elements in the calculus of the Soviet leadership concerning the utility of antisemitism and Soviet policy outcomes, and in order to direct attention away from specific events and toward categories of functionally equivalent events. This has the additional advantages of directing attention to factors that are often neglected in other studies of Soviet antisemitism and of being able to accommodate any other factors that may have been neglected here.

I have chosen to develop the model on the basis of the period
ending in September 1965 because the post-Khrushchev leadership
appears to have undertaken at that time a complete recalculation of
the utility of antisemitism and to have adopted a new policy concerning its use. This policy therefore represents a base line against
which later policy outcomes may be compared. By dividing the analysis at this point, one can investigate the operation of the calculus
over a different period which also is characterized by frequent and
dramatic changes in policy outcomes, and thus to test the validity of
the model.

In the third section of the paper I use this analytical framework
to examine Soviet policy outcomes concerning the use of antisemitism
in the period since the ouster of Nikita Khrushchev. This leads one
to consider factors not included in other analyses of official antisemitism in the Soviet Union and to identify those conditions and concerns likely to emerge in the future which will be functionally equivalent to factors identified in the past. This allows one to anticipate
the future course of Soviet policy concerning the use of official antisemitism.

OFFICIAL ANTISEMITISM, 1945-65

At the end of World War II, the Soviet leadership adopted three
major policy goals, the achievement of each of which was likely to
be affected by its decisions concerning the use of antisemitism.
First, it sought to reestablish the authority of the regime in those
areas that had been subject to German occupation and intense Nazi
propaganda. Second, it sought to mobilize the entire Soviet population in order to carry out its programs of postwar reconstruction
and development, a task which it felt necessitated closure of the
Soviet system to foreign influences. And third, it sought to establish a client state in the Middle East. In each of these cases, the
leadership manipulated its policies toward the Soviet Jewish minority
in ways that contributed to the achievement of its goal.

In reestablishing the authority of the regime in the formerly
occupied territories, the leadership was confronted by anti-Soviet
local nationalism and by anti-Soviet antisemitism.[1] These two sentiments were mutually reinforcing. If the leadership was to defeat
them, it had to split them and deflect the hostility they generated
away from the regime. In each case the leadership perceived that
its policy toward the Jews was critical; it had to divorce itself from
the Jews in order to negate the Nazi-inspired image of "Judeo-
Bolshevism," and it had to allow the open expression of antisemitism

in order to defuse the emotional force of local nationalism. This could be done in the western borderlands because Soviet evacuation and Nazi exterminations had largely eliminated Jews from critical roles in these areas,[2] and the Soviet leadership had only to avoid bringing Jews back with it. This calculation is reflected in Khrushchev's remark "It is not in our interest that the Ukrainians should associate the return of Soviet power with the return of the Jews." Thus, the Soviet leadership adopted a policy of eliminating Jews from, or hiding Jewish participation in, the Party and governmental apparatuses in the Ukraine, and condoned popular antisemitic sentiments and actions among Ukrainians.[3] In this way the regime provided an outlet for the release of hostilities which otherwise might have been expressed in the form of anti-Soviet actions.

In order to mobilize all resources and concentrate them on the tasks of postwar reconstruction and development, the Soviet leadership sought to discredit values and attachments which arose during the war and which were antithetical to its plans. It attacked individualism, national particularism, and non-Soviet attachments among Soviet citizens, all of which tended to divert energies and detract attention from the collective tasks and were subsumed under the label "cosmopolitanism."[4] Concomitantly, the leadership sought to isolate, differentiate, and stress the superiority of Soviet society and its values. In order to lend authenticity to these efforts, the leadership could have been expected to move against that group in Soviet society which during the war had both established the strongest foreign attachments and experienced an intense revival of national consciousness not sponsored by the regime: the Jews.[5]

This probably would have been the case were it not for the fact that a large proportion of Soviet Jews possessed skills crucial to the fulfillment of the leadership's goals of reconstruction and development,[6] and that the Soviet leadership simultaneously was pursuing a foreign policy goal that made the use of antisemitism on a union-wide scale counterproductive. This goal was the establishment of a client state in the Middle East, a region then dominated by the British. Soviet Jewish contacts with Jewish organizations in the West were an important asset in this Soviet foreign policy offensive.[7] The potential importance to the Soviet leadership of gaining influence in the Middle East precluded the suppression of Soviet Jewish organizations. Although it had adopted antisemitic policies for use at the republic level in the Ukraine, the Soviet leadership moved against central Soviet Jewish organizations and added antisemitic elements to the ongoing unionwide anti-cosmopolitan campaign only when its hopes for influence over the newly created Jewish state were dashed and the domestic costs of pursuing that influence became clear.[8]

This careful attempt to compartmentalize policy toward the
Jews during the postwar period suggests that Soviet decision making
in this area was extremely sophisticated and included the consideration of a number of policy-relevant factors. The weights assigned to
the factors varied over time and among the individual members of the
Soviet leadership. Clearly, for Stalin the benefits to be derived
from isolating Soviet society from foreign influence and protecting
the regime from domestic anti-Soviet sentiments outweighed the potential costs of losing the services of critical Jewish scientific and
technical cadres. Consequently, after the failure in 1948 of Soviet
foreign policy in the Middle East, he moved rapidly to use antisemitism for these purposes. For other members of the Soviet leadership who were to become Stalin's successors, on the other hand,
the weighting was different. In his outspoken position on nationality
problems, Lavrentii Beria, for example, reflects their unwillingness
to pay this price at a time when the mobilization of resources for development was of such crucial importance. Thus, although Stalin was
prepared to eliminate the Jews entirely, as evidenced by the Doctors'
Plot, his lieutenants were not; and, upon his death, they immediately
changed course.

The new leadership calculated that changes in the structure of
the Soviet economy required it not only to remove artificial restrictions on a group of potentially highly successful contributors to the
goal of rapid development, but also to mobilize that group. Indeed,
in the decade following the death of Stalin the Soviet leadership did
mobilize increasing numbers of Jews into the ranks of the scientific
and technical elite. *

This calculation resulted in a significant diminution of anti-
Jewish actions and antisemitic propaganda. They were not completely eliminated, however, for three concerns pushed the results of
Soviet calculations in the opposite direction. First, in order once
more to attempt to gain influence in the Middle East, the Soviet leadership in the period after the 1956 war turned from supporting the
Jewish state of Israel to providing material and political support for
the anti-Zionist Arab countries. Second, in order to ensure socialist

---

*As can be seen from Table 6.2A, the rate of change in the ab-
solute number of Jewish scientific and technical cadres in the USSR
during the decade 1955-65 was a dramatic reversal of the trend for
1950-55. In fact, during 1960-65, the rate of increase in the number
of Jewish cadres is on the same order of magnitude as several of the
union republic-level groups.

norms of behavior in the economy and society, it launched campaigns against "economic crimes" and religious "survivals." And third, in order to increase the rate of development, the Soviet leadership mobilized the native populations of the previously underdeveloped regions of the USSR. As a result it now increasingly came to be confronted by problems arising from competition between native and nonnative cadres for positions in scientific and technical institutions in the union republics. In each case the leadership perceived that the use of antisemitism as official policy would directly affect its ability to achieve its goal.

Despite the failure of its earlier attempt to gain influence in the Middle East by supporting the creation of a Jewish state, the Soviet leadership remained interested in penetrating the region. The 1956 war provided it with another opportunity. In response to the dramatic Israeli victory, which had been supported by the Western powers, the Soviet leadership moved to gain influence in the Arab countries by replacing their material war losses and by providing economic and military assistance. This shift in policy meant that the Soviet leadership no longer had to be as attentive to the reactions of the Israeli political leadership to Soviet domestic events. Consequently, policy goals in the Middle East no longer constituted a negative factor in the leadership's calculation of the utility of antisemitism. By itself, however, the removal of this negative factor did not create additional incentives for the use of antisemitism. Thus, in the three-year period immediately following the leadership's shift in Middle Eastern policy, we do not find a unionwide campaign incorporating antisemitism that can be directly attributed to Soviet policy goals there. This suggests that the campaigns that developed at the end of this period were motivated primarily by domestic considerations.

The campaigns against "economic crimes" and against religious "survivals" were motivated by the leadership's desire to eliminate values and behavior inconsistent with the complete mobilization of all resources for its developmental goals. The first of these campaigns was designed to ensure adherence by managerial elements to socialist norms of economic behavior. [9] Confronted by significant diversion of scarce economic resources to private use, the Soviet leadership was compelled to move against this substitution of individualistic values for socialist ones. In devising its policy, however, the leadership was constrained both by its 1956 decision to use persuasion rather than coercion to ensure compliance, and by its recognition of the costs involved in replacing established cadres with new and inexperienced ones.

In addition, the leadership could anticipate that such a campaign would be met by indifference or even resistance from the very

elements at which it would be aimed. Consequently, it had to devise
some means to discredit individualistic economic behavior among
Soviet managers. Knowing that antisemitism remained strong and
that the popular image of Jewish behavior included the very characteristics it sought to discredit, * the Soviet leadership perceived that
antisemitic propaganda and anti-Jewish actions would be useful in
generating hostility to and contempt for individualistic economic behavior among Soviet managers. Such a campaign could be expected
to deflect the resentment of Soviet managers away from the regime
and direct it onto the Jews, for the behavior of Jews could be made
to appear to be its cause. Thus, the leadership embarked on a vigorous unionwide campaign against "economic crimes" that not only
incorporated antisemitic elements but also led, in a number of cases,
to the well-publicized executions of Jews.[10] Such actions conveyed
two critical messages to Soviet managers: first, that even under the
relaxed conditions of the post-1956 period the most extreme measures
of coercion could, and would, be applied on occasion; and second,
that it was correct to perceive "economic crimes" as Jewish behavior.

At about the same time, the leadership moved against religious
"survivals" in Soviet society because it viewed religion as a potential
source of values incompatible with socialist norms.[11] It attacked
both the values themselves and the institutions which preserved them.
The Russian Orthodox Church, which had enjoyed relative immunity
during the late Stalinist period, was vigorously attacked along with
those churches which had not enjoyed even limited immunity in the
past. Compelled by the same logic which produced its immediate

---

*An analysis of information obtained by the Harvard University
Project on the Soviet Social System revealed that Soviet citizens who
had left the USSR during World War II spoke of the Jews as being
clannish, money-minded, aggressive, pushy, sly, calculating, de-
ceitful, unprincipled, impudent, and cowardly as soldiers. Of those
who mentioned the Jews, 60 percent expressed negative views, while
10 percent were markedly hostile. Many who registered no hostility
to Jews "spoke freely of the wide-spread existence of anti-Semitic
prejudice in the U.S.S.R." There is little reason to believe that the
sentiments of Soviet citizens had changed much by the early 1960s;
and certainly the Soviet leadership had not yet made any effort to effect such a change. "Popular Anti-Semitism in the U.S.S.R.,"
Survey (B'nai B'rith International Council, Washington, D.C.)
November 23, 1960, pp. 2 ff. See also Konstantin Paustovsky, as
cited in Jeremy R. Azrael, Managerial Power and Soviet Politics
(Cambridge, Mass.: Harvard University Press, 1966), pp. 115-16.

postwar policy in the western borderlands, the leadership initiated
even more vigorous attacks on Judaism. In regions where the language of practicing Jews was not the same as that of the majority
population, a large proportion of the anti-Judaism propaganda of this
campaign was published not in the language of the Jews, but in the
languages of the majority: Moldavian, Belorussian, and Ukrainian.[12]
This suggests that these attacks were aimed not so much at practicing Jews as at the adherents of other religions then under attack.
The reason for directing anti-Jewish propaganda at non-Jewish populations probably was to make it clear to these groups that the regime
was not treating the Jews more leniently.

Attacks on Judaism were predicated on a distinction between
Judaism as a religion and the Jewish nationality. This was a difficult
distinction to maintain because the line between religion and nationality was least clear in the case of the Jews. While attacks on other
religions generally were not interpreted by the Soviet masses as attacks on the nationalities which historically practiced them, this was
not the case with attacks on Judaism. Indeed, even in official propaganda the distinction between anti-Judaism and antisemitism was
difficult to maintain.

A particularly blatant example of a failure to maintain this distinction was T. K. Kichko's Judaism without Embellishment. This
book attracted Western attention to the antisemitic elements in both
the anti-religious campaign and the campaign against "economic
crimes." Strong criticism of Soviet policies toward the Jews came
not only from "bourgeois" elements, but from foreign Communist
parties as well. Concerned that this issue might weaken its ability
to control the actions of Communist parties in the West, the Soviet
leadership moved to criticize the book for having crossed the line
from anti-religious propaganda to antisemitism. When this failed to
satisfy Western Communist critics, the leadership withdrew the
Kichko volume from circulation.[13] Soviet policies toward Judaism
as a religion and toward the Jews as a nationality group, however,
remained essentially unchanged.

Given its continuing commitment to rapid economic expansion,
the regime needed an ever-increasing number of skilled cadres. By
the same logic that had compelled the immediate post-Stalin collective leadership group to remove Stalinist restrictions on the Jews,
the Khrushchev leadership was now led to develop potential manpower
resources among other non-Russian, and especially non-Slavic,
groups.* The resultant entry of increased numbers of non-European

---

*As can be seen from Table 6.3A, the rates of increase in the
number of scientific workers among Central Asian nationalities was

cadres into the scientific and technical sectors of the Soviet economy
and their concentration in their native republics* created a new and
potentially more dangerous form of interethnic conflict: that between
the most highly mobilized, and hence nationally conscious, elements
in different national groups. Under Khrushchev the region in which
the highest rates of mobilization of such cadres occurred and in which
this competition became most intense was Central Asia.

European Jews in Central Asia were caught in this conflict between the newly mobilized native cadres and the dominant--largely
Russian--European ruling elite.[†] As Khrushchev noted in 1956,

---

particularly great for the period 1955-60, and remained high through
1970.

*The proportion of the total number of scientific and technical
cadres of each Central Asian nationality that is concentrated in its
native republic has remained very high since the end of World War II.
Since 1960 the proportion of Uzbek, Kazakh, Kirghiz, and Turkmen
cadres found in their respective republics has remained at 90 percent
or above. The proportion of Tadzhik cadres has remained at about
85 percent. These figures can be calculated on the basis of data presented in TsSU, Strana sovetov za 50 let (Moscow: Statistika, 1967),
p. 284; TsSU, Vysshee obrazovanie v SSSR (Moscow: Gosstatizdat,
1961), p. 215; TsSUUzSSR, Narodnoe khoziaistvo Sredneii Azii v
1963 g. (Tashkent: Uzbekistan, 1964), pp. 331-33; TsSUTaSSR,
Narodnoe khoziaistvo (N.K.) Tadzhikskoi SSR v 1965 g. (Dushanbe:
Statistika, 1966), p. 234; TsSUUzSSR, N.K. Uzbekskoi SSR za 50 let
(Tashkent: Uzbekistan, 1967), p. 225; TsSUKaSSR, N.K. Kazakhstana
(Alma Ata: Kazakhstan, 1968), pp. 344-45; TsSUKiSSR, Kirghizstan
za 50 let Sovetskoi vlasti (Frunze: Kirghizstan, 1967), p. 213; and
Vestnik statistiki (1974), no. 4, p. 93.

[†]In Central Asia in 1960, Russians constituted 38-57 percent
of all scientific and technical cadres in each republic, while the native or titular nationality constituted 22-34 percent of the total.
Jews accounted for about 5-8 percent of these cadres. In 1947 the
proportion of native cadres had ranged from 6 to 17 percent. The
proportions of both Russians and Jews, therefore, can safely be assumed to have been higher. In the Uzbek Republic in 1960, Europeans
constituted 53.9 percent of all candidates of science, and 57.2 percent of all doctors of science. Jews constituted 11.3 and 14.4 percent of these cadres, respectively. See TsSU, Vysshee obrazovanie
v SSSR (Moscow: Gosstatizdat, 1961), p. 215 for data on native cadres
in the union republics in 1947 and 1960. For data on the national composition of these cadres in Central Asia see TsSUUzSSR, N.K. Sredneii
Azii v 1963 g. (Tashkent: Uzbekistan, 1964), pp. 331-33; TsSUKaSSR,
N.K. Kazakhstana (Alma Ata: Kazakhstan, 1968), pp. 344-45; and
TsSUUzSSR, N.K. Uzbekskoi SSR v 1967 (Tashkent: Uzbekistan, 1968),
p. 277.

native nationalities in these areas "now have their engineers and professionals"; and native cadres would take it "amiss" if Jews were to "occupy the foremost positions in our republics."[14] Such feelings undoubtedly intensified during the following decade, during which the numbers of native cadres dramatically increased while the rate of expansion of positions in the scientific and technical elite of Central Asia slowly decreased.* Such feelings among native cadres need not have originated and probably did not originate in personal antisemitic sentiments.† Rather, native cadres probably attacked Jewish elite cadres because unionwide antisemitic campaigns against "economic crimes" and religious "survivals" suggested to them that Jews could be attacked with impunity. Russian cadres in Central Asia probably were affected in the same way by these campaigns, and thus were unprepared to defend Jewish cadres against native attack. Indeed, they probably were willing to sacrifice the Jews in order to maintain their own positions.

The extent to which this conflict grew during the Khrushchev years clearly was a matter of concern for his successors. This concern was mirrored in a September 5, 1965, lead article in Pravda, which emphasized that the task of economic development required the exchange of cadres among the various republics and that national exclusiveness in cadres policy would not be tolerated.[15] To reinforce this warning, the article cited Lenin's injunction against nationalism in any form and his specific condemnation of antisemitism. This

---

*The increase in native cadres in the Central Asian republics is reflected in the data for Uzbekistan, shown in Tables 6.3A and 6.4A. On the basis of the data shown in Table 6.3A, the native proportion of the increase in cadres for 1963-66 was calculated to have been 60.7 percent. Since 1969 this proportion has been even larger.

†The long existence of intact, practicing Jewish communities in Central Asia argues against the notion that the nationalities of this region have a natural tendency toward antisemitism. As elsewhere in the Muslim world, the position of the Jewish minority community was transformed with the penetration of the region by large numbers of Europeans. The evacuations and deportations of World War II may have had a particularly strong impact on the native populations of Central Asia and may have contributed to the rise of antisemitic sentiments among them. See, for example, Rachel Erlich, "Summary Report on Eighteen Intensive Interviews with Jewish DPs from Poland and the Soviet Union," and Jerzy Gliksman, "Jewish Exiles in Soviet Russia," as cited in Solomon Schwarz, The Jews in the Soviet Union (Syracuse, N.Y.: Syracuse University Press, 1951), pp. 344-45.

suggests that the central leadership was particularly concerned to protect Jewish cadres from attacks arising from the spillover effect of antisemitic campaigns adopted on other occasions and directed at other objects. Clearly, this article was intended as a warning to both Russians and natives in Central Asia not to attack Jewish cadres.

THE CALCULUS OF OFFICIAL ANTISEMITISM

The use of official antisemitism in the period 1945-65 suggests that it was employed by the Soviet leadership primarily as a means to increase compliance with other policies. This reinforces the view that decisions concerning the use of antisemitism were made on the basis of a specific calculus of utility rather than solely on the basis of the antisemitic proclivities of the leadership. This calculus determines only the utility of antisemitism as a means to achieve policy goals. The goals themselves are determined and assigned relative weight by a decision-making process which is independent of this calculus. The weights assigned to policy goals, however, play an important part in determining the outcome of the calculus. In this section a formalization of the calculus is presented.

This calculus of the utility of antisemitism may be analyzed into a set of axioms, each of which relates the likelihood of the Soviet leadership's using antisemitism as a policy tool to a specific condition. It can be summarized in a single general axiom:

(1.0) When the Soviet leadership perceives that the total benefits to be derived from the use of antisemitism exceed its costs, the leadership will use it.

The converse of this axiom is also true. When the Soviet leadership has decided not to use antisemitism, but perceives that its own goals are threatened by antisemitism in Soviet society arising from the spontaneous prejudice of the masses, from the use of antisemitism by local Soviet officials, from the unintended consequences of its own use of antisemitism in the past, or from other factors, it will move against antisemitism.

It is important to remember that here, and in all axioms that follow, "antisemitism" means the use of antisemitic propaganda, the taking of anti-Jewish actions, or both. When, on the basis of this calculus, the leadership decides to use antisemitism, it may use it in either of two modes. Soviet antisemitism may be either essentially accommodationist in nature, wherein the leadership permits the expression of antisemitic sentiments among, and the taking of anti-Jewish actions by, lower-level officials or the masses; or it may be interventionist, in which case the central leadership not only permits the expression of antisemitism by others, but itself employs antisemitic propaganda and/or takes anti-Jewish actions. The particular variety of antisemitism adopted by the Soviet leadership and the mode of its use are determined in each case by its utility. When, on the other hand, it decides to move against antisemitism, the leadership may do so in a variety of ways and with differing intensity. Its actions in these cases may be divided into those that are essentially based on persuasion, and those that are essentially based on coercion.

The utility of antisemitism (U), which may be either positive or negative, is determined by the leadership at any point in time by its summation of three elements: the sum of the estimated utilities of antisemitism for regime authority (ΣA), the sum of the estimated utilities of antisemitism for the achievement of substantive policy goals--regime efficacy--(ΣP), and the sum of the personal proclivities of the members of the leadership (ΣL). * When the value of U is positive, the leadership will use antisemitism; when it is negative, the leadership will not, and may even move against it. This cost-benefit calculation may be represented by the following formula:

$$U = \Sigma A + \Sigma P + \Sigma L$$

The value of U is determined by ΣL, the sum of the personal proclivities of the members of the leadership, when and only when the sum of $\Sigma A + \Sigma P$ approaches zero.† It is important to keep in mind that the sum of these personal proclivities may push Soviet decisions in the direction of either the use or the rejection of antisemitism. Because antisemitism in Soviet society may arise from sources other than the actions of the central leadership, when ΣL determines the value of U the central leadership may decide to

---

*It is important to remember that the Soviet leadership is treated here as a single decision-making unit, rather than as a number of individual decision makers who aggregate their views. This does not affect the validity of the calculus presented here, nor does it exclude the effects of conflict and political struggle among the members of the leadership over decisions and policies with respect to the use of antisemitism. In fact, these effects are included, by definition, in the elements of the calculus.

†This can occur when the utility of antisemitism for one element is canceled out by its disutility for the other, or when both ΣP and ΣA approach zero.

sponsor, encourage, tolerate, or suppress such antisemitism, depending on the nature of the personal proclivities. This has been, however, an empirically rare situation in Soviet political history. The more frequent and more important role of these personal proclivities has been their effect on the leadership's estimates of the other two elements in the formula. Consequently, the estimates of the Soviet leadership concerning the utility of antisemitism for regime authority (ΣA) and for regime efficacy (ΣP) are defined to include the effects of personal proclivities (ΣL).

In estimating the utility of antisemitism for regime authority (ΣA) or regime efficacy (ΣP), the Soviet leadership must assess its effect on domestic Soviet elite groups, domestic Soviet mass groups, * and foreign elite groups. Each of these categories of course contains numerous groups, not all of them relevant in every policy calculation. For each group perceived as relevant to a particular policy, the leadership must estimate the importance of the compliance of that group with that particular policy and the effect of the use of antisemitism on the level of compliance of that group. The effect of the use of antisemitism, in turn, is estimated in terms of the intensity and direction of the group's response to its use. Levels of compliance range from perfect, voluntary fulfillment of policy to absolute resistance, at which point the regime has lost control. The Soviet leadership may estimate antisemitism to be useful when compliance falls within either the range of levels at which it perceives that only the efficacy of the regime is in question or the range of levels at which it perceives that the authority of the regime is in question. It may judge any single response to a policy as falling within either or both of these ranges, or outside them. This may be represented schematically as shown below. In those cases where the leadership perceives compliance of a particular group as falling outside these ranges, the estimated utility of the use of antisemitism with respect to that group approaches zero.

The estimated utility of antisemitism for all policy responses perceived by the Soviet leadership as affecting regime authority will be aggregated by it to form the summary estimate of the utility of antisemitism for regime authority (ΣA). The same will be done for all policy responses perceived as affecting regime efficacy (ΣP). The leadership's estimates of the utility of antisemitism for policy

---

*The domestic mass groups most relevant to this calculation are nationality groups. This is because individuals at the mass level tend to respond to ethnic issues on the basis of their own ethnic identity.

responses which fall in the authority range, and its estimates for responses which fall in the efficacy range, are governed by different sets of axioms.

The location in the calculus of the constituent elements is shown schematically below.

FIGURE 6.1

Conceptual Ranges of Compliance with Policy

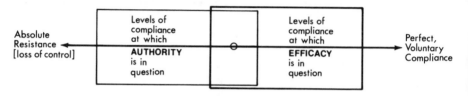

Source: Author's composition.

FIGURE 6.2

Relationships between the Elements in the Calculus
of Soviet Antisemitism

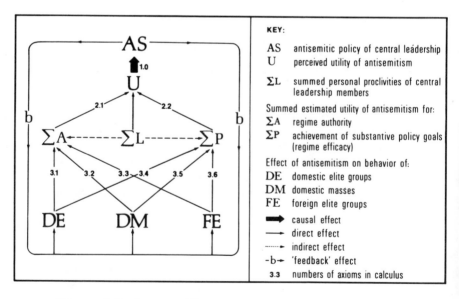

Source: Author's composition.

The specific axioms associated with the second and third levels of the calculus are grouped here into those governing Soviet calculations when the leadership perceives that regime authority is in question and those governing Soviet calculations when the leadership perceives that regime efficacy is in question. Those dealing with regime authority are the following:

(2.1a) When the Soviet leadership perceives that the use of antisemitism will decrease resistance to regime authority, it is more likely to use it.

(2.1b) When the Soviet leadership perceives that the use of antisemitism will increase resistance to regime authority, it is less likely to use it.

(3.1a) When the Soviet leadership perceives that the use of antisemitism will decrease resistance to regime authority among subordinate elite groups, it is more likely to use it.

(3.1b) When the Soviet leadership perceives that the use of antisemitism will increase resistance to regime authority among subordinate elite groups, it is less likely to use it.

(3.2a) When the Soviet leadership perceives that the use of antisemitism will reduce the threat to regime authority posed by mass challenges based on primordial ties, it is more likely to use it.

(3.2b) When the Soviet leadership perceives that the use of antisemitism will increase the threat to regime authority posed by mass challenges based on primordial ties, it is less likely to use it.

(3.3a) When the Soviet leadership perceives that the use of antisemitism will decrease resistance to regime authority among critical foreign elite groups, it is more likely to use it.

(3.3b) When the Soviet leadership perceives that the use of antisemitism will increase resistance to regime authority among critical foreign elite groups, it is less likely to use it.

Axioms dealing with regime efficacy are listed below.

(2.2a) When the Soviet leadership perceives that the use of antisemitism will decrease regime efficacy, it is less likely to use it.

(2.2b) When the Soviet leadership perceives that the use of antisemitism will increase regime efficacy, it is more likely to use it.

(3.4a) When the Soviet leadership perceives that the use of antisemitism will negatively affect the performance of critical domestic elite groups, it is less likely to use it.

(3.4b) When the Soviet leadership perceives that the use of antisemitism will positively affect the performance of critical domestic elite groups, it is more likely to use it.

(3.5a) When the Soviet leadership perceives that the use of antisemitism will decrease the levels of compliance of domestic mass groups, it is less likely to use it.

(3.5b) When the Soviet leadership perceives that the use of antisemitism will increase the levels of compliance of domestic mass groups, it is more likely to use it.

(3.6a) When the Soviet leadership perceives that the use of antisemitism will cause critical foreign elite groups to respond in ways that reduce regime efficacy, it is less likely to use it.

(3.6b) When the Soviet leadership perceives that the use of antisemitism will cause critical foreign elite groups to respond in ways that increase regime efficacy, it is more likely to use it.

Thus far, the Soviet calculus of the utility of antisemitism has been presented in its static form. The calculations of the Soviet leadership, however, are a dynamic process which occurs continually. Repetition of the entire calculus occurs only rarely, and usually is associated with a major change in the summed personal proclivities of the leadership (ΣL). This typically follows major changes in the composition or the ranking of the members of the Soviet leadership. In the absence of such major changes, the leadership adjusts its estimate of the utility of antisemitism (U) when it perceives changes in the utility of antisemitism for questions of regime authority ($\Delta\Sigma A$) or regime efficacy ($\Delta\Sigma P$). Changes in the perceived utility of antisemitism (ΔU) are determined by the sum of changes in the summed estimate of its utility for regime authority ($\Delta\Sigma A$), changes in the summed estimate for regime efficacy ($\Delta\Sigma P$), and changes in the sum of the personal proclivities of the members of the leadership which are the result of learning ($\Delta\Sigma L$), a process which occurs as the result of the feedback mechanism rather than of changes in composition or ranking. This yields the following dynamic expression of the calculus:

$$\Delta U = \Delta\Sigma A + \Delta\Sigma P + \Delta\Sigma L$$

Because I have defined ΣA and ΣP, and hence $\Delta\Sigma A$ and $\Delta\Sigma P$, as including the effects of ΣL ($\Delta\Sigma L$), I will not examine the independent effect of $\Delta\Sigma L$ in what follows.

OFFICIAL ANTISEMITISM SINCE KHRUSHCHEV

Following the ouster of Khrushchev in October 1964, his successors undertook a complete recalculation of the utility of antisemitism, the results of which were reflected in a September 1965

lead article in Pravda. This article warned against national exclusiveness in cadres policy and cited Lenin's specific condemnation of
antisemitism. Clearly, for the new leadership, which was strongly
committed to economic development, the most important element in
the calculus was the negative effect of antisemitism on the performance of Jewish scientific and technical cadres. The weight assigned
by the leadership to the performance of these Jewish cadres resulted
in a high negative value for ΣP. In the absence at that time of high
positive values for ΣA or ΣL, this meant that the perceived utility
of antisemitism (U) was negative. That this led the Soviet leadership
to move against antisemitism indicates how great this negative value
was.

The Soviet leadership's perception of the utility of antisemitism
did not change sufficiently to affect policy until June 1967, when its
estimation of the value of U shifted from negative to positive. This
shift (ΔU) can be attributed to both changes in the estimated utility
of antisemitism for regime authority ($\Delta \Sigma A$) and changes in its estimated utility for regime efficacy ($\Delta \Sigma P$). Changes in the estimated
utility of antisemitism for regime authority resulted from the Soviet
leadership's perception of the emergence of a threat in the Ukraine,
against which it felt compelled to move.[16] As we have seen, in the
past antisemitism had been extremely useful for deflecting Ukrainian
national hostilities away from the Soviet regime.

The central Soviet leadership must have perceived official antisemitism as particularly useful at this point in time because Ukrainian
national dissent in 1966 included liberal elements which focused their
attention not, as so often had been the case in the past, on the Jews,
but on the exploitation of the Ukraine and on the russification of
Ukrainians by Great Russians.[17] Such attention among domestic
elites in itself constituted a threat to the authority of the central
Soviet leadership. Changes in the estimated utility of antisemitism
for regime efficacy resulted from the Soviet leadership's assessment
that it would have to offer Arab political elites, after their defeat by
Israel, more than the continuation of material aid in order to maintain Soviet influence in the Middle East. Thus, the Soviet leadership
came to perceive that antisemitism could be used to prevent the
spread of anti-Russian sentiments from dissident Ukrainian elites to
the Ukrainian masses, and to provide psychic compensation to Arab
political elites for the failure of Soviet matériel to provide military
victory over Israel.

Thus, by June 1967 the Soviet leadership's perception of the
utility of antisemitism had changed. By this time $\Delta \Sigma A$ was strongly
positive as a result of the leadership's assessment of the effects of
the use of antisemitism on Ukrainian nationalism. The estimated
utility of antisemitism for regime authority (ΣA), which had been

minimal in recent years, had become positive. $\Delta\Sigma P$ also was strongly positive as a result of the leadership's assessment of the effects of the use of antisemitism on Arab political elites. Therefore ΣP, which had been strongly negative because of the leadership's assessment of the effects of antisemitism on Jewish scientific and technical cadres, was now reduced in value or even changed in sign. The summed effect of these two changes was a strongly positive value for ΔU, which was sufficient to change the value of U from negative to positive. These changes did not, however, affect the leadership's assessment of the effect of antisemitism on Jewish cadres. Consequently, the Soviet leadership sought to devise an antisemitic campaign which it thought would maximize benefits in terms of regime authority and the responses of foreign elites, and at the same time minimize the costs in terms of the performance of Jewish cadres. It did this by adopting an antisemitic campaign in the form of anti-Zionism propaganda.

The Soviet leadership probably estimated that antisemitism in the form of anti-Zionism would minimize the domestic costs of using antisemitism. It was making its calculation, however, on the basis of its past assessments of the reactions of Jewish cadres, assessments which had been invalidated by the impact of the Middle East war on the Soviet Jewish minority. The war generated an increased sense of national identity and group solidarity among Soviet Jews, including those in the scientific and technical elite. As a result, Jews became more sensitive to attacks on any aspect of Jewish identity--be it religion, culture, or attachment to Israel--and more assertive in the defense of their national rights. Therefore, Jewish scientific and technical cadres were no longer able to dissociate themselves from the targets of antisemitic propaganda or anti-Jewish actions. They perceived the use of antisemitism in the form of anti-Zionism as an attack on themselves.

Between June 1967 and the end of 1969, the Soviet leadership's perception of the utility of antisemitism underwent another change. During this period $\Delta\Sigma A$ was negative. At the beginning the Soviet leadership had moved against and crushed the Ukrainian dissidents,[18] thus eliminating them as a major element in its calculations. During this period, too, dissidents in other areas of the USSR became more active and increasingly focused their attention on human rights issues. These liberal dissidents opposed the use of antisemitism by the central Soviet leadership, viewing such practice as a reversion to Stalinism.[19] Its use, therefore, promised to generate increased activity among these dissidents, activity which threatened to provide a model for other groups with other concerns.[20] Even the possibility of such activity was likely to have raised for the Soviet leadership the specter of a threat to its authority. Hence, the responses of liberal dissidents to the use of antisemitism added a negative value to $\Delta\Sigma A$ for this period. ΣA therefore became less positive by the end of this period and may even have changed sign. In any case its value, and thus its effect on the calculation of utility, was small.

During this period $\Delta\Sigma P$ was strongly negative. Although anti-semitism was still useful with respect to Arab political elites, these foreign elites had become less important to the Soviet leadership as the result of both the stalemated situation in the Middle East and the emergence of a serious threat to Soviet hegemony in Eastern Europe. As the antisemitic nature of the Soviet anti-Zionism campaign be-came clear in the West, and evidence of Soviet Jewish reactions to that campaign became available, Western Jewish organizations launched a campaign of their own to exert pressure on the Soviet leadership and to extend support to dissident Soviet Jews. * The direct effect of this campaign, however, was limited. The summed effect of changes in the intensity, direction, and importance of the responses of foreign elite groups on the value of $\Delta\Sigma P$, therefore, was negative for this period but not strongly so. A more powerful negative value was added to $\Delta\Sigma P$ by changes in the responses of domestic elite groups. Foremost among these, of course, was the changed response of the nationally conscious Soviet Jewish minority. The anti-Zionism campaign exacerbated the disaffection of Soviet Jews from the Soviet regime; this disaffection led to the emergence of a powerful Zionist movement that penetrated even into the ranks of Jewish scientific and technical cadres and led to demands for im-mediate emigration to Israel.[21] The intensity, direction, and impor-tance of this response contributed strongly to the negative value of $\Delta\Sigma P$. Disaffection and demands for emigration among Jewish scien-tific and technical cadres threatened the ability of both the Soviet military and managers of high-technology enterprises in the Soviet economy to maintain and advance the production, research, and de-velopment capacities of their respective sectors.[22] The negative re-sponses of these important domestic elite groups to the disaffection of Jewish cadres undoubtedly were communicated directly to the Soviet leadership, and added a still stronger negative value to $\Delta\Sigma P$ during this period. Thus, by late 1969 ΣP had become strongly negative.

---

*Organized Jewish efforts in support of Soviet Jewry during 1967-69 can be followed in the pages of Jewish journals such as Jews in Eastern Europe (usually documented in a section entitled "Inter-ventions") and of the American and British press.

The summed effect of $\Delta\Sigma A$ and $\Delta\Sigma P$ now yielded a strongly negative ΔU. Consequently, over this period U became less positive and at its end changed in sign. This led the Soviet leadership to abandon antisemitism as a tool of policy late in 1969. Just as it had sought to construct a campaign that would maximize benefits and minimize costs when it had adopted antisemitism in 1967, so now the Soviet leadership sought to do the same after having decided to abandon it. It continued to use anti-Zionism propaganda to pursue its foreign policy goals in the Middle East, but by early 1970 dramatically changed the content of this propaganda. It did so in response to, and in an attempt to reduce, the disaffection of domestic Jewish scientific and technical cadres.[23]

This new content, which may be characterized as "rational" anti-Zionism, consisted of attempts to convince Soviet Jews to remain in the USSR by contrasting the positive aspects of life there for Jews with the hardships of life for émigrés in Israel.[24] At the same time, the Soviet leadership made it clear that some Jewish emigration would be permitted.[25] It did this in order to make it possible for the most disaffected to leave, in the hope that disaffection would thereby be prevented from spreading to others. In marked contrast to earlier antisemitic, anti-Zionism propaganda, the tone of most of these messages was calm and reasoned. This appeal to essentially material interests, however, failed to discourage Soviet Jews from demanding emigration, and may even have led more of them to demand it. The Soviet leadership's attempts to hold on to its Jews in the face of increasing demands to leave prompted Jewish groups in the West to take more vigorous action.* This action by Western Jewish organizations was to have important consequences for Soviet calculations over the next five years.

In the period between 1970 and early 1975, the Soviet leadership's perception of the utility of antisemitism became strongly negative. In its calculations during this period $\Delta\Sigma A$ approached zero. Consequently, ΔU was determined by the strongly and increasingly negative value of $\Delta\Sigma P$. This negative value, in turn, was determined by changes in the intensity of, and the importance assigned to, the reactions of foreign elite groups (U.S. political and economic elites and Arab political elites) and of domestic elite groups (Jewish scientific and technical cadres, the military, and managers of high-

---

*The most dramatic sign of this increased activity came with the convening of a world conference at Brussels in 1970 to discuss the fate of Soviet Jewry, a conference that focused Western attention on the issue and was attacked bitterly in the Soviet press.

technology enterprises) to the use of antisemitism by the Soviet leadership.

The political and economic elites of the United States were the most important foreign elite groups in the calculations of the Soviet leadership during this period. Their reactions became increasingly important because the Soviet leadership was turning to them for agreements limiting strategic arms, granting trade concessions, and providing capital and technological assistance in order that it would have the resources necessary for the achievement of its ambitious developmental goals.* The reactions of these U.S. elites to the use of antisemitism by the Soviet leadership became increasingly negative as Jewish organizations in the United States brought pressure to bear on them. The Soviet leadership's perceptions of the utility of antisemitism for its dealings with Arab political elites continued to be positive. However, the relative importance in the calculations of the reactions of these elites declined. As a result, the negative value added to $\Delta\Sigma P$ by the negative reactions of U.S. elites was significantly greater than the positive value added by the perceived utility of antisemitism for dealing with Arab political elites, even in the months following the 1973 Middle East war.

Among domestic elite groups, the reactions of Jewish scientific and technical cadres continued to be assigned the greatest importance in the calculations of the Soviet leadership. Their growing disaffection,† which was manifested in increased dissident activity and increased demands for emigration, had important negative consequences for the ability of the Soviet leadership to achieve its policy goals. This was especially true because during the early 1970s the Soviet leadership was deeply concerned about the shortage of scientific manpower.[26] These negative consequences were felt most strongly by the military and by managers of high-technology enterprises in the economy.[27] These two domestic elite groups, therefore, undoubtedly continued to add strong negative values to $\Delta\Sigma P$ during this period.

----

*The turn to the West was part of the general onset of "détente" and the opening of a period of "cooperation" between the United States and the USSR.

†The increasing disaffection of Soviet Jewish cadres led to an appeal to the "unquestioned loyalty" of the vast majority of the Soviet Jewish minority in an attempt to stem the tide of demands for emigration, but to no avail. Thus, the Soviet government found it necessary in 1972 to take measures to check an anticipated request for permission to emigrate to Israel by several key members of the strategic missile program. See New York Post, April 12, 1972.

Thus, $\Delta\Sigma P$ for the period 1970 to early 1975 was strongly negative; and therefore, by the end of this period, ΣP had become strongly negative as well. Consequently, ΔU was strongly negative. This increased the negative value of U still further. As a result, the Soviet leadership not only did not use antisemitism as a tool of policy, but even moved to accommodate Jewish demands for emigration--at first in an attempt to quell Jewish disaffection and dissent, and later in an effort to use the emigration of Jews to win important concessions from the political and economic elites of the United States.[28] Both these attempts failed, but the willingness of the Soviet leadership to negotiate a possible exchange of Soviet Jews for Western capital and technology is a clear demonstration of the fundamentally instrumental character of Soviet decision making concerning policy toward the Jews.

CONCLUSION

As can be seen, decisions concerning antisemitism conform to the general pattern of Soviet leadership decision making. The calculus by which the Soviet leadership determines the utility of anti-semitism directs research attention to the wide variety of factors the Soviet leadership considers when it makes its decisions. And--given sufficient information--by using the calculus we may anticipate the direction of future decisions by identifying the most likely set of conditions that will confront the Soviet leadership.

Since early 1975, evidence concerning the outcomes and even the elements of the Soviet leadership's calculations of the utility of antisemitism have been unclear and contradictory. In order to trace the operation of the calculus, one needs a great deal of information about at least some of its elements. If available information concerns outcomes, the calculus may be used to discover additional information about the Soviet leadership's perceptions of groups relevant to policy. If, on the other hand, available information concerns the reactions of groups, it may be used to simulate the Soviet leadership's calculation, and thereby to anticipate policy outcomes. For the period since 1975 there is not enough information for any of the elements of the calculus to permit its use in either of these ways. In the absence of such information, this conceptual framework nevertheless remains a useful guide to the kinds of developments to which one should be most attentive.

Since 1965 the Soviet leadership's calculations of the utility of antisemitism have become increasingly complex. As we have seen, this has largely been the result of two important changes in elements of the calculus: First, still-critical Jewish scientific and technical cadres have become disaffected from the Soviet regime; and second, the number of domestic elite groups and foreign elite groups relevant to the calculation has increased. This has made it more difficult to identify and present the calculations of the Soviet leadership, and more difficult for the leadership to make them. Current trends suggest that in the future this calculation will in one sense become more complicated, but in another sense less so. It is likely to become more complex with the reemergence of challenges to regime authority, arising this time in Central Asia. These challenges undoubtedly will be based on primordial ties, but their exact nature cannot yet be specified. [29] Regardless of their precise nature, however, they will be perceived by the central Soviet leadership as threats to the authority of the regime. At the same time, the calculations of the Soviet leadership are likely to become less complex because of the declining importance of Jewish scientific and technical cadres for the achievement of policy goals. The emigration of large numbers of Jews has already had a significant sociodemographic impact on the Soviet Jewish minority. The number of Jews among students in Soviet higher educational institutions has been declining at an increasing rate, and this has meant a decline in the pool of future Jewish cadres. (For the decline in the number of Jewish students in Soviet higher educational institutions, see Tables 6.5A and 6.6A.) Thus, with time, the importance of Jewish cadres, and hence the negative utility of antisemitism, will decline.

The emergence in Central Asia of primordially based threats to the authority of the Soviet regime is likely to increase the probability of the emergence of similar threats elsewhere in the Soviet Union. Consequently, once the central leadership perceives a serious threat to regime authority in Central Asia, it will be compelled to move quickly to establish an alliance among the three Slavic peoples of the USSR. [30] In order to forge such an alliance, the Soviet leadership will have to defuse anti-Russian sentiments among Ukrainians and Belorussians, and to prevent the emergence of anti-Soviet sentiments among the Russians. Under these conditions, and in the absence of countervailing costs, the Soviet leadership is likely to perceive the use of antisemitism as providing extraordinary benefits.

TABLE 6.1A

Distribution of Soviet Scientific Workers,
by Nationality, 1950-73
(percent)

	1950	1955	1960	1965	1970	1973
Russians	60.9	64.4	64.8	66.4	66.0	66.7
Ukrainians	9.0	9.7	10.0	10.7	10.8	10.9
Belorussians	1.7	1.8	1.8	1.9	2.0	2.1
Uzbeks	.5	.7	1.1	1.0	1.3	1.3
Kazakhs	.5	.5	.7	.7	.9	.9
Georgians	2.6	2.4	2.4	1.9	2.0	1.9
Azerbaidzhanis	1.2	1.2	1.4	1.3	1.4	1.4
Lithuanians	.8	.8	.8	.9	.9	.9
Moldavians	.1	.1	.2	.2	.3	.3
Latvians	.9	.8	.8	.7	.6	.6
Kirghiz	.1	.1	.2	.2	.2	.2
Tadzhiks	.1	.2	.2	.2	.3	.3
Armenians	2.4	2.3	2.3	2.0	2.2	2.2
Turkmen	.1	.2	.2	.2	.2	.2
Estonians	.8	.7	.6	.5	.5	.5
Tatars	.8	1.0	1.0	1.2	1.3	1.3
Jews	15.5	11.0	9.5	8.0	6.9	6.1

Sources: 1950, Tsentral'noe Statisticheskoe Upravlenie
(TsSU), Narodnoe khoziaistvo (N. K.) SSSR v 1969 g. (Moscow:
Gosstatizdat, 1970), p. 696; 1955, TsSU, Kul'turnoe stroitel'stvo
SSSR (Moscow: Gosstatizdat, 1957), p. 254; 1960, TsSU, N. K.
SSSR v 1962 g. (Moscow: Gosstatizdat, 1963), p. 584; 1965, TsSU,
N. K. SSSR v 1965 g. (Moscow: Gosstatizdat, 1966), p. 711; 1970,
TsSU, N. K. SSSR 1922-1972 gg. (Moscow: Gosstatizdat, 1973),
p. 105; 1973, Vestnik statistiki (1974) no. 4: 92.

TABLE 6.2A

Rate of Change in Absolute Number of Scientific
Workers, by Nationality, 1950/55-1970/73
(percent)

	1950/55	1955/60	1960/65	1965/70	1970/73
Russians	45.8	59.1	92.1	38.8	20.9
Ukrainians	48.1	62.8	99.8	41.6	20.1
Belorussians	50.3	55.9	101.5	48.0	21.8
Uzbeks	86.6	137.7	79.7	80.3	18.0
Kazakhs	56.6	95.4	97.5	74.8	25.1
Georgians	23.6	57.6	55.2	43.0	15.4
Azerbaidzhanis	43.8	78.9	73.8	50.6	19.9
Lithuanians	43.5	70.0	96.6	43.3	19.9
Moldavians	142.1	93.4	135.9	78.5	17.5
Latvians	20.2	50.9	62.4	37.7	14.4
Kirghiz	207.4	102.8	75.1	85.4	24.8
Tadzhiks	113.7	141.2	60.5	69.6	22.4
Armenians	31.7	57.2	68.6	49.7	18.2
Turkmen	159.4	113.0	74.3	48.1	29.9
Estonians	27.0	30.6	68.4	36.1	14.1
Tatars	65.2	72.3	107.7	51.5	21.6
Jews	-2.0	36.2	58.6	21.1	5.3
Total	37.8	58.2	87.7	39.6	19.5

Sources: 1950, Tsentral'noe Statisticheskoe Upravlenie
(TsSU), Narodnoe khoziaistvo (N. K.) SSSR v 1969 g. (Moscow:
Gosstatizdat, 1970), p. 696; 1955, TsSU, Kul'turnoe stroitel'stvo
SSSR (Moscow: Gosstatizdat, 1957), p. 254; 1960, TsSU, N. K.
SSSR v 1962 g. (Moscow: Gosstatizdat, 1963), p. 584; 1965, TsSU,
N. K. SSSR v 1965 g. (Moscow: Gosstatizdat, 1966), p. 711; 1970,
TsSU, N. K. SSSR 1922-1972 gg. (Moscow: Gosstatizdat, 1973),
p. 105; 1973, Vestnik statistiki (1974) no. 4: 92.

TABLE 6.3A

National Composition of Scientific and Technical Cadres, Uzbek Republic, 1960-73

	1960	Per-cent	1961	Per-cent	1963	Per-cent	1966	Per-cent
Uzbeks	3,552	34.4	4,237	36.2	5,501	36.8	7,279	40.7
Tatars	566	5.5	635	5.4	813	5.4	984	5.5
Kazakhs	138	1.3	165	1.4	223	1.5	330	1.8
Karakalpaks	134	1.3	145	1.2	195	1.3	244	1.4
Tadzhiks	120	1.2	126	1.1	140	.9	193	1.1
Non-Europeans	4,510	43.7	5,308	45.3	6,881	45.9	9,030	50.4
Russians	3,971	38.5	4,409	37.6	5,478	36.6	5,936	33.2
Jews	857	8.3	962	8.2	1,231	8.2	1,348	7.5
Ukrainians	321	3.0	301	2.6	410	2.7	466	2.6
Armenians	207	2.0	232	2.0	297	2.0	319	1.8
Europeans	5,356	51.9	5,904	50.4	7,416	49.5	8,069	45.1
Total	10,329		11,722		14,987		17,903	

Note: Data for Jews, Tatars, and Armenians for 1961 and 1963 are estimates derived in the following manner: Both N. K. Uzbekskoi SSR v 1967 g. and N. K. Sredneii Azii v 1963 g. contain data for 1960 on the national composition of scientific workers in the Uzbek SSR. The groups shown in each case, however, differ. By combining these two sources, it is possible to determine the proportion of Jews, Tatars, and Armenians in the "other nationalities" category of the 1960 data shown in N. K. Sredneii Azii. These proportions were then applied to the "other nationalities" category shown in this source for 1961 and for 1963 to obtain the estimates.

1967	Per- cent	1968	Per- cent	1969	Per- cent	1971	Per- cent	1973	Per- cent
,261	41.5	9,670	43.4	10,493	43.6	11,963	45.4	13,217	46.9
,131	5.7	1,209	5.4	1,282	5.3	1,367	5.2		
372	1.9	421	1.9	481	2.0	508	1.9		
286	1.4	319	1.4	347	1.4	370	1.4		
212	1.1	238	1.1	277	1.2	320	1.2		
,262	51.5	11,857	53.2	12,880	53.2	14,528	55.2		
,494	32.6	6,957	31.2	7,473	31.0	7,885	29.9		
,391	7.0	1,488	6.7	1,611	6.7	1,685	6.4		
534	2.7	621	2.8	673	2.8	705	2.7		
365	1.8	384	1.7	408	1.7	441	1.7		
,784	44.1	9,450	42.4	10,165	42.2	10,716	40.7		
,923		22,274		24,079		26,335		28,191	

Sources: 1960, 1961, and 1963, Tsentral'noe Statisticheskoe Upravlenie bekskoi SSR (TsSUUzSSR), Narodnoe khoziaistvo (N. K.) Sredneii Azii v 3 g. (Tashkent: Uzbekistan, 1964), p. 331; 1960 and 1967, TsSUUzSSR, K. Uzbekskoi SSR v 1967 g. (Tashkent: Uzbekistan, 1968), p. 227; 1966, UUzSSR, N. K. Uzbekskoi SSR za 50 let (Tashkent: Uzbekistan, 1967), p. ; 1968, TsSUUzSSR, N. K. Uzbekskoi SSR v 1968 g. (Tashkent: Uzbekistan, 9), p. 299; 1969, TsSUUzSSR, N. K. Uzbekskoi SSR v 1969 g. (Tashkent: ekistan, 1970), p. 275; 1971, TsSUUzSSR, N. K. Uzbekskoi SSR v 1971 g. shkent: Uzbekistan, 1972), p. 303; 1973, Vestnik statistiki (1974), no. 4: 92.

TABLE 6.4A

Percentage Rate of Increase in Absolute Number of Scientific and
Technical Cadres, Uzbek Republic, 1960/61–1971/73

	1960/61	1961/63	1963/66	1966/67	1967/68	1968/69	1969/71	1971/73
Uzbeks	19.3	30.0	32.1	13.5	17.1	8.5	14.0	10.5
Tatars	12.2	28.0	21.0	14.9	6.9	6.0	6.6	
Kazakhs	19.6	35.2	48.0	12.7	13.2	14.3	5.6	
Karakalpaks	8.2	34.5	25.1	17.2	11.5	8.8	6.6	
Tadzhiks	5.0	11.1	37.9	9.8	12.3	16.4	15.5	
Non-Europeans	17.7	29.6	31.2	13.6	15.5	8.6	12.8	
Russians	11.0	24.2	8.4	9.4	7.1	7.4	5.5	
Jews	12.3	28.0	9.5	3.2	7.0	8.3	4.6	
Ukrainians	6.2	36.2	13.7	14.6	16.3	8.4	4.8	
Armenians	12.1	28.0	7.4	14.4	5.2	6.3	8.1	
Europeans	10.2	25.6	8.8	8.9	7.6	7.6	5.4	
Total	13.5	27.9	19.5	11.3	11.8	8.1	9.4	7.0

Source: Table 6.3A.

216

TABLE 6.5A

Percentage Distribution of Students in Higher Educational Institutions, by Nationality, 1960/61-1972/73

	1960/61	1962/63	1963/64	1965/66	1966/67	1967/68	1968/69	1969/70	1970/71	1972/73
Russians	61.8	61.3	61.0	61.2	60.5	60.3	59.9	59.7	59.6	59.9
Ukrainians	14.3	14.5	14.6	14.5	14.3	13.9	13.8	13.6	13.6	13.4
Belorussians	2.7	2.9	3.0	3.0	3.0	2.9	2.9	2.8	2.8	2.9
Uzbeks	2.2	2.4	2.4	2.5	2.7	2.9	3.2	3.2	3.3	3.2
Kazakhs	1.7	1.8	1.8	1.8	1.8	2.0	2.1	2.2	2.2	2.3
Georgians	2.0	2.0	1.9	1.8	1.9	1.9	1.9	1.9	1.9	1.9
Azerbaidzhanis	1.2	1.2	1.3	1.4	1.6	1.7	1.8	1.9	1.9	1.9
Lithuanians	1.1	1.1	1.1	1.1	1.1	1.1	1.1	1.1	1.1	1.1
Moldavians	.5	.5	.6	.6	.6	.7	.7	.7	.7	.7
Latvians	.7	.7	.6	.6	.6	.5	.5	.5	.5	.5
Kirghiz	.4	.4	.4	.4	.5	.5	.5	.5	.6	.6
Tadzhiks	.5	.5	.4	.5	.5	.5	.6	.6	.6	.6
Armenians	1.5	1.5	1.5	1.6	1.6	1.7	1.8	1.8	1.8	1.7
Turkmen	.4	.4	.4	.4	.4	.5	.5	.5	.5	.5
Estonians	.5	.5	.5	.5	.5	.5	.4	.4	.4	.4
Tatars	1.7	1.7	1.8	1.8	1.8	1.8	1.8	1.8	1.9	2.0
Jews	3.2	2.7	2.5	2.5	2.6	2.6	2.5	2.4	2.3	1.9

Note: Includes all categories (day, evening, corresponding).

Sources: 1960/61, Tsentral'noe Statisticheskoe Upravlenie (TsSU), Vysshee obrazovanie v SSSR (Moscow: Gosstatizdat, 1961), p. 85; 1962/63 and 1963/64, TsSU, Narodnoe khoziaistvo (N. K.) SSSR v 1964 g. (Moscow: Gosstatizdat, 1965), p. 691; 1965/66, TsSU, N. K. SSSR v 1965 g. (Moscow: Gosstatizdat, 1966), p. 701; 1966/67, TsSU, Strana sovetov za 50 let (Moscow: Statistika, 1967), pp. 280–81; 1967/68, TsSU, N. K. SSSR v 1967 g. (Moscow: Gosstatizdat, 1968), p. 803; 1968/69, TsSU, N. K. SSSR v 1968 g. (Moscow: Gosstatizdat, 1969), p. 694; 1969/70, TsSU, N. K. SSSR v 1969 g. (Moscow: Gosstatizdat, 1970), p. 690; 1970/71, TsSU, N. K. SSSR v 1970 g. (Moscow: Gosstatizdat, 1971), p. 446; 1972/73, TsSU, N. K. SSSR v 1972 g. (Moscow: Gosstatizdat, 1922–1972 gg. (Moscow: Gosstatizdat, 1973), p. 651.

TABLE 6.6A

Percentage Rate of Change in Absolute Number of Students in Higher Educational Institutions, by Nationality, 1960/63-1970/73

	1960/61-1962/63	1962/63-1963/64	1963/64-1965/66	1965/66-1966/67	1966/67-1967/68	1967/68-1968/69	1968/69-1969/70	1969/70-1970/71	1970/71-1972/73
Russians	21.9	10.2	18.8	5.6	4.2	2.9	1.5	.5	1.7
Ukrainians	24.2	11.6	17.3	5.7	1.7	2.8	.6	.1	-.4
Belorussians	33.4	15.2	17.1	7.0	2.4	1.9	.9	.8	2.7
Uzbeks	31.0	13.1	20.6	17.6	12.4	12.4	3.9	2.2	-.3
Kazakhs	27.0	12.0	20.5	8.6	12.4	9.7	4.9	2.1	4.0
Georgians	20.6	7.4	11.6	9.8	7.0	4.9	1.4	.2	-1.6
Azerbaidzhanis	28.4	18.0	25.0	18.3	13.5	11.9	5.7	.4	1.4
Lithuanians	23.3	13.8	18.2	7.5	3.0	.6	2.5	1.8	4.0
Moldavians	32.5	15.1	25.1	15.3	9.8	5.9	0	.3	-1.6
Latvians	20.0	5.1	2.9	6.1	-1.8	.9	-1.3	-1.8	.9
Kirghiz	20.2	11.8	21.8	15.4	7.0	10.0	10.9	8.2	3.4
Tadzhiks	13.4	7.4	20.7	13.7	15.1	10.5	7.9	2.9	5.3
Armenians	21.5	11.0	24.8	9.5	8.4	7.1	2.2	1.9	-1.8
Turkmen	24.2	7.6	22.8	14.1	7.9	10.4	7.1	-3.1	.9
Estonians	19.4	7.8	13.3	0	3.2	-1.5	-3.7	-2.7	-1.1
Tatars	28.1	14.5	15.7	8.1	4.6	5.4	3.7	3.9	4.0
Jews	2.7	4.2	14.5	12.4	3.5	1.7	-1.6	-3.9	-16.4
Total	22.9	10.8	18.4	6.8	4.6	3.7	1.8	.7	1.1

Sources: 1960/61, Tsentral'noe Statisticheskoe Upravlenie (TsSU), Vysshee obrazovanie v SSSR (Moscow: Gosstatizdat, 1961), p. 85; 1962/63 and 1963/64, TsSU, Narodnoe khoziaistvo (N. K.) SSSR v 1964 g. (Moscow: Gosstatizdat, 1965), p. 691; 1965/66, TsSU, N. K. SSSR v 1965 g. (Moscow: Gosstatizdat, 1966), p. 701; 1966/67, TsSU, Strana sovetov za 50 let (Moscow: Statistika, 1967), pp. 280-81; 1967/68, TsSU, N. K. SSSR v 1967 g. (Moscow: Gosstatizdat, 1968), p. 803; 1968/69, TsSU, N. K. SSSR v 1968 g. (Moscow: Gosstatizdat, 1969), p. 694; (Moscow: Gosstatizdat, 1970), p. 690; 1970/71, TsSU, N. K. SSSR 1922-

NOTES

1. For studies of the effects of the German occupation on the sentiments of the population of the occupied territories, especially with respect to the impact of Nazi propaganda about "Judeo-Bolshevism," see John A. Armstrong, Ukrainian Nationalism 1939-1945 (New York: Columbia University Press, 1955), passim; Alexander Dallin, German Rule in Russia 1941-1945 (New York: St. Martin's Press, 1957), passim, but esp. pp. 29, 73; Philip Friedman, "Ukrainian-Jewish Relations during the Nazi Occupation," YIVO Annual of Jewish Social Science 12 (1958/59): passim; Solomon Schwarz, The Jews in the Soviet Union (Syracuse, N.Y.: Syracuse University Press, 1951), passim, but esp. ch. V, pp. 309 ff.

2. The demographic impact of the war on the Soviet Jewish minority is discussed in Alec Nove and J. A. Newth, "The Jewish Population: Demographic Trends and Occupational Patterns," in Jews in Soviet Russia since 1917, ed. Lionel Kochan (New York: Oxford University Press, 1970), passim, but esp. pp. 139-42; Schwarz, op. cit., pp. 222-23, 227; and Shimon Redlich, "The Jews in the Soviet Annexed Territories 1939-1941," Soviet Jewish Affairs 1 (June 1971): 81-90.

3. Leon Leneman, La tragédie des juifs en U.R.S.S. (Paris: Desclée de Brouwer, 1959), p. 179. Leneman recounts the story of a Polish Jewess who had worked in the personal secretariat of Khrushchev, then first secretary in the Ukraine. This account is entitled "The Stalin of the Ukraine," and captures both the atmosphere of anti-Sovietism/antisemitism that pervaded the Ukraine in the period following the return of the Soviets, and the manipulative orientation of the Soviet leadership (Khrushchev) toward the role of the Jews with respect to the restoration of the authority of the Soviet regime.

4. For descriptions of the tone and content of the anti-cosmopolitan campaign, see W. W. Kulski, The Soviet Regime (Syracuse, N.Y.: Syracuse University Press, 1954), ch. 1, passim; and Y. A. Gilboa, The Black Years of Soviet Jewry (Boston: Little, Brown, 1971), passim.

5. See Shimon Redlich, "The Jewish Antifascist Committee in the Soviet Union," Jewish Social Studies 31, no. 1 (January 1969): 25-36; and Y. A. Gilboa, "The 1948 Zionist Wave in Moscow," Soviet Jewish Affairs no. 2 (November 1971): 35-39. See also Schwarz, op. cit., pp. 208-09.

6. According to Tsentral'noe Statisticheskoe Upravienie (TsSU), Narodnoe khoziaistvo SSSR v 1969 g. (Moscow: Gosstatizdat, 1970), in 1950, Jews constituted 83.5 percent of all scientific workers in the USSR (among the nationalities other than 15 republic-level nationalities). If we apply this proportion to the data for 1947--

shown in TsSU, Strana Sovetov za 50 let (Moscow: Gosstatizdat, 1967), p. 284--Jews can be estimated to have constituted 17.9 percent of the total.

7. Redlich, "The Jewish Antifascist Committee . . . ," pp. 29-31.

8. Gilboa, "The 1948 Zionist Wave . . ."; see also Benjamin Pinkus, "Soviet Campaigns against 'Jewish Nationalism' and 'Cosmopolitanism', 1946-1953," Soviet Jewish Affairs 4, no. 2 (1974): 53-72, esp. Table 1, pp. 56-57.

9. For a report on the content of the Soviet press campaign against "economic crimes," see Ronald I. Rubin, ed., The Unredeemed (New York: Quadrangle Press, 1966), pp. 115-26, which contains a report of the International Commission of Jurists on the treatment of Soviet Jews in this campaign.

10. See Jews in Eastern Europe 2, no. 4 (February 1964): 17-18, for data concerning the number of executions of Jews for "economic crimes."

11. See Donald A. Lowrie and William C. Fletcher, "Khrushchev's Religious Policy, 1959-1964," in Aspects of Religion in the Soviet Union 1917-1967, ed. Richard H. Marshall, Jr. et al. (Chicago: University of Chicago Press, 1971).

12. See Joshua Rothenberg, "Jewish Religion in the Soviet Union," in Kochan, op. cit., p. 178.

13. The Kichko affair is described in detail, including extensive excerpts from the text, in Jews in Eastern Europe 2, no. 5 (July 1964).

14. William Korey, The Soviet Cage (New York: Viking Press, 1973), p. 120.

15. Pravda, September 5, 1965, p. 1, as translated in Current Digest of the Soviet Press 17, no. 34 (September 15, 1965): 3-4.

16. The reemergence of Ukrainian nationalism as a serious concern for the central Soviet leadership is documented in Michael Browne, ed., Ferment in the Ukraine (New York: Crisis Press, 1973); and Vyacheslav Chornovil, ed., The Chornovil Papers (Toronto: McGraw-Hill, 1968).

17. See Ivan Dzyuba, "Speech at Babyn Yar," in Chornovil, op. cit., pp. 222-26; and Internationalism or Russification? (London: Widenfeld and Nicholson, 1968), passim, but esp. ch. 7.

18. The trials in which the central Soviet leadership prosecuted the exponents of Ukrainian nationalism are documented in Browne, op. cit.

19. Peter Reddaway, ed., Uncensored Russia (New York: American Heritage Press, 1972), pp. 312-14.

20. See Roman Rutman, "Jews and Dissenters: Connections and Convergences," Soviet Jewish Affairs 3, no. 2 (1973): 22-37;

Roy Medvedev, "Jews in the U.S.S.R.," Survey 17, no. 1 (Spring 1971): 192-99; and D. Pospielovsky, "The Samizdat Journal Veche: Russian Patriotic Thought Today," Radio Liberty Research Paper no. 45 (New York: Radio Liberty, 1971).

21. The emergence of the Zionist movement in the USSR in the wake of the 1967 Middle East war is documented in Reddaway, op. cit., pp. 298-318.

22. For a vivid presentation of the Soviet military's dependence on the productivity of scientific cadres, see the translation of N. A. Lomov, ed., Scientific-Technical Progress and the Revolution in Military Affairs (Moscow: Voenizdat, 1973) prepared by the U.S. Air Force (Washington, D.C.: U.S. Government Printing Office, 1974), esp. ch. 1.

23. For the change in content in the anti-Zionism campaign, see Jonathan Frankel, "The Anti-Zionist Press Campaigns in the U.S.S.R. 1969-1971: An Internal Dialogue?" Soviet Jewish Affairs no. 3 (May 1972): 3-26. Compare the campaign in this period with the earlier campaign, as described in Jews in Eastern Europe 3, no. 8 (March 1968); 4, no. 2 (July 1969): 7-46; 4, no. 5 (August 1970), passim; 5, no. 2 (November 1972), passim.

24. Frankel, op. cit., pp. 16-17.

25. Izvestiia, February 20, 1971, p. 3, as reported in Current Digest of the Soviet Press 23, no. 8 (March 23, 1971): 6. See also Izvestiia, December 14, 1969, p. 4, as reported in Current Digest of the Soviet Press 21, no. 50 (January 13, 1970): 21.

26. Pravda, July 31, 1970, p. 1, as translated in Current Digest of the Soviet Press 22, no. 31 (September 1, 1970): 15; and V. N. Turchenko, "The Scientific and Technical Revolution and Problems of Education," Voprosy filosofii, no. 2 (1973): 18-29, as abstracted in Current Digest of the Soviet Press 25, no. 23 (July 4, 1973).

27. Lomov, op. cit.

28. For a detailed description of the negotiations between the United States and the Soviet Union that involved the exchange of emigration for U.S. assistance, see Joseph Albright, "The Pact of the Two Henrys," New York Times Magazine, January 5, 1975, pp. 35-68.

29. For a Soviet sociological study that identifies the greater tendency toward internationality conflict among educated professionals than among the masses, see Iu. V. Arutiunian, "A Concrete Sociological Study of Ethnic Relations," Voprosy filosofii, no. 12 (1969): 129-39, as translated in Soviet Review 14, no. 2 (Summer 1977): 14-15. For a more recent work that indicates that this conflict has been increasing, see A. A. Susokolov, "The Influence on Interethnic Relations of Differences in the Educational Levels and

the Number of Ethnic Groups in Contact," Sovetskaia etnografiia
no. 1 (1976): 101-11, as translated in Soviet Review 18, no. 1
(Spring 1977): 31.

30. For references to the Slavic "brotherhood," see P.
Masherov, "On Certain Features of Nationality Relations in the
Conditions of Developed Socialism," Kommunist no. 15 (October
1972): 15-33, as translated in Current Digest of the Soviet Press 24,
no. 46 (December 13, 1972): 1-5; and Victor Perevedentsev, "Soviet
Nationalities: New Stage of Relations," Soviet Life no. 12 (1974):
6-7. Even Russian dissidents have picked up on this theme, as evidenced by Alexander Solzhenitsyn's lament: "No one has borne so
much of the suffering as the Russians, Ukrainians, and Byelorus-
sians." See his From under the Rubble (Boston: Little, Brown,
1975), p. 117. See also his Letter to the Soviet Leaders (London:
Harvill Press, 1973), passim.

SOVIET LANGUAGE PLANNING: GOALS, RESULTS, OPTIONS 7

Jonathan Pool

Whenever governments have tried to intervene in the everyday linguistic behavior of their peoples, the tendency of language to resist deliberate planning has been manifest. The Soviet Union is a superb case for the study of language policy, because the government has been extraordinarily ambitious in its attempts to reshape an extremely complex linguistic situation. In this study we shall see what makes the Soviet language situation a challenge to policy makers; how the Soviet leadership has tried to change mass linguistic behavior; where its principal language policies have succeeded and failed; and what policy options exist for the future.

THE SOVIET LANGUAGE SITUATION

The language situation of the Soviet Union is one of the most complex in the world. The 1970 census enumerated 104 nationalities, ranging in size from the 441 Aleuts to the 129 million Russians. It took 20 nationalities to account for 95 percent of the Soviet population. With a few exceptions, each listed nationality has a different characteristic language. Some of the members of each of these nationalities spoke its language as their mother tongue, according to the census, although the figure varied from a low of 13 percent among the Karaites (a Jewish minority of 4,571 persons originating in Persia, having a Turkic language, and inhabiting mainly Crimean and Lithuanian cities) to a high of 99.8 percent among the Russians. On the average, however, 94 percent of the Soviet population had a correspondence between declared nationality and mother tongue, thus making the languages of the USSR relatively "communalistic."[1]

Not only are there many mother tongues, each spoken by a substantial portion of the Soviet population, but they belong to a wide spectrum of language families. Besides Slavic and other Indo-European languages, the Soviet Union has at least a million people natively speaking languages in each of four unrelated families: Altaic (including the Turkic group), Uralic (including Estonian), South Caucasian (including Georgian), and North Caucasian (including Chechen).

The people of the Soviet Union have not learned each other's languages in large enough numbers to overcome this diversity of mother tongues. In the 1970 census 22 percent of the population claimed fluency in at least one Soviet language besides the native one.[2] Russian is by far the most widely known second language, but knowledge of it is far from universal. In 1970 it was called their mother tongue by 59 percent of the people, and those claiming second-language fluency in it brought the total to 76 percent. Thus there is still a major language barrier to overcome, particularly for a regime wanting to communicate intensively with every citizen.

The resolution of language problems in the USSR is made more difficult by the legacy of gross inequality among languages. During its last 45 years, both before and after the beginning of constitutional government in 1905, the Russian Empire pursued almost without interruption a policy of Russian colonization and land acquisition in non-Russian regions, cultural russianization of non-Russians, and government with even less representation of non-Russians than of Russians.[3] One result was the supremacy of the Russian language and its association with Russian domination. In this situation, while unity and efficiency both seem to demand the spread of Russian, any policy that gives supreme status to the traditionally dominant tongue and its already privileged speakers transgresses the norm of national equality.

The features of this situation can be found, individually, in other countries as well. The Indian census, for example, lists more than 1,000 "languages," about 18 of which are required to take in 95 percent of the population; and there are large numbers of speakers of languages in four unrelated families.[4] In Belgium, as in many other linguistically plural countries, two citizens with different mother tongues do not have a very great likelihood of possessing a means of communication. French-speaking people in Quebec want to learn English largely for economic gain, but with the language come memories of conquest and exploitation. The Soviet situation is composed of elements found elsewhere, but in a combination that would challenge even modest efforts at language planning.

THE POSSIBILITIES OF LANGUAGE PLANNING

"Language planning" refers to systematic policies designed to maintain or change existing language situations. Languages have

been created, revived, destroyed, reformed, and manipulated as far
back as the fifth century B.C.,[5] so the Soviet Union is certainly not
the first country in which this kind of planning has been practiced.
Language planners have attempted to control the statuses, roles,
and functions of languages in society (such as which language is made
official, which languages are taught in schools, or how the speakers
of minority languages are treated); they also have made plans for
preserving or reforming the vocabularies, sound systems, word
structures, sentence structures, writing systems, and stylistic rep-
ertoires of languages.

Language planning has various goals. Some of the most common are to bring about linguistic unity, to preserve or create linguistic distinctiveness or uniqueness, to make certain languages or
their speakers equal, to make one language or its speakers superior,
to develop a language so it can be used for new purposes, and to
make a language more efficient as a tool of communication or more
beautiful as a medium of expression. These goals have such consequences as national unity, educational progress, or a wider gap between elites and masses.

Even in fairly simple situations, language planning has limits.
Perhaps the chief one is the reluctance to engage in language planning, partly a product of the traditional belief that language is an or-
ganic entity with which people should not or cannot tamper. Where
an authoritative agency is intent on changing the language situation,
limits are still imposed by the rate at which people can learn new
language habits, the systematic and interrelated nature of each language, and the costs, as well as undesired by-products, of successfully implementing a policy whose outcome depends on changes in
mass, everyday, partly automatic behavior. Language planners
usually strive for several goals at once, but these often prove to be
incompatible. Because of these contradictions and the strong emo-
tions that language as a political issue generally arouses, and because the opposing sides in language controversies tend to be cut off
from each other by language differences, language planning is often
accompanied by fierce conflict and efforts at obstruction.

THE SOVIET EFFORT AT LANGUAGE DEVELOPMENT

In spite of the obstacles to comprehensive language policy making that history has revealed, the leaders of the Soviet Union have
attempted to do more than ignore or merely cope with their intricate
language situation. They have pursued a series of very ambitious
programs, making the USSR probably the best available case in which
to study the limits, other than lack of ambition, that language planners face.

Selecting from a multitude of possible goals, the Soviet leadership has made two major and overlapping thrusts.[6] The first began in the 1920s and was aimed at the development of languages other than Russian for mass use in education, the communications media, and public and professional life. The second thrust began in earnest about 1938, with the aim of universalizing the knowledge of Russian among the Soviet population. These two efforts have conflicted with each other and have often varied in intensity, but both continue today.

The first effort, which we might call the multilingual development effort, began while the Bolsheviks were still trying to put the pieces of the Russian Empire back together. The initial impetus was Lenin's struggle to stamp out the oppressive behavior of Russian settlers, soldiers, and administrators in the periphery and to bring the eastern peoples of Russia, as a model for eastern peoples everywhere, into full participation while reasserting firm central control. In this respect Lenin was opposed to most of the rest of the Bolshevik movement, which regarded Russian dominance as a natural and desirable concomitant of centralization.[7] Of the other two principal leaders, Leon Trotsky showed little concern for the importance of national rights, and Iosif Stalin believed that they had to be sacrificed to the inevitably incompatible aim of unitary government. Lenin almost singlehandedly insisted that both aims could, and must, be achieved.[8]

Besides intense political opposition, Lenin faced situational obstacles in most of the country that became clearer as the first, simplistic policies for implementing national equality began to fail. To accomplish the end result of full participation in public life by hitherto suppressed peoples, substantial numbers of those peoples had to be trained for administrative and technical roles, and their languages had to be used in the running of institutions where they lived. These goals in turn required that non-Russians learn to read and write, while Russian administrators, if Moscow were to maintain its governance over the outlying territories, had to learn the languages that were being made official. Thus each language had to be given a writing system or, if it had one that made mass literacy very difficult (such as the Arabic writing systems of the Turkic languages), a new writing system had to be devised. Hence, even when Lenin persuaded the Party and administration to undertake serious efforts at derussianizing the peripheral institutions, these efforts achieved little when there were broken links in the chain of preconditions.

In addition, the push from the center was not consistently strong. During the New Economic Policy the desire to avoid offending non-Russian nationalities implied that they should continue to be brought into the Party and government; but central funding and guidance for the educational and language-development prerequisites mostly disappeared, leaving much of the initiative in local hands. There was enough central coordination of experts in language planning, however, to produce a general pattern for the whole country. [9]

Within the resulting effort at multilingual development, we can distinguish four main components. First, about 40 speech varieties with no writing systems (except, in some cases, systems known only to missionaries or scholars) have been standardized and graphized. [10] This means that in each case the rules of the linguistic code of some group have been partly written down, a writing system has been devised for that code, and the code has been adopted as the language of formal speech and writing for those in the group and, often, those speaking a number of neighboring or related dialects as well. Most of these graphizations took place in the 1920s and early 1930s, and used the Roman alphabet, with modifications. It should be noted that this requires more than the mindless extension of some other language's writing system to the unwritten language. It requires investigating the latter's meaningful sound distinctions and its rules for combining meaningful elements into words, and then devising a set of symbols suitable for representing these. The complexity of the task undertaken by Soviet language planners becomes clearer when we consider that the Cyrillic alphabet, which is currently used for writing 60 of the 66 written Soviet languages, and which needs only 33 symbols for Russian, contains a total of 201 distinct symbols when the modified letters used to represent the non-Russian sounds in the other 59 languages are taken into account. [11]

Second, about 45 languages have had their writing systems thoroughly transformed. For about half of these, the authorities have carried out two such transformations, most commonly a change from an Arabic or Cyrillic alphabet to a Roman one, followed in 1938-40 by a change to (or back to) a Cyrillic writing system. "Transformation" here means a transition from one genetic type of alphabet to another, such as from Arabic to Roman or Roman to Cyrillic. In 1929 and 1930 there was serious discussion of converting Russian itself to a Roman alphabet, but this idea was abandoned. [12]

A third component of the multilingual development effort has been the eradication of illiteracy, pursued in the only practical manner: teaching people how to read and write in their native languages, once these have been furnished with writing systems. At the time of the October Revolution, only about half the population aged 9-49 was literate; and among some large categories, such as Central Asian rural Muslim females, literacy in this age group was between 0 and 5 percent. By 1959 the rate was no lower than 93 percent in any republic for any sex/urban-rural combination. [13] Literacy among rural females aged 9-49 in Uzbekistan and Azerbaidzhan, for example, has risen as shown below. [14]

Year	Uzbekistan	Azerbaidzhan
1897	0.2%	1.5%
1926	1.2	5.8
1939	70.2	70.6
1959	97.5	96.1
1970	99.6	99.3

The fourth major element in this effort has been to develop the terminologies of 14 Soviet languages other than Russian, to publish teaching materials in them, to employ them as media of instruction at all educational levels, and to use them for advanced professional communication and public affairs. In particular, these are the languages whose namesake territories have the status of union republics, and the primary locus for use of any such language is intended to be the corresponding republic.

This is the component most actively pursued at present and whose outcome is most in doubt. It appears that no one is planning to graphize any additional Soviet languages; only reforms, rather than basic transformations, of the writing systems of currently written languages are being discussed.[15] Literacy cannot rise appreciably, since it already stands at nearly 100 percent. The major question for multilingual development, then, boils down to this: In schools, workplaces, government, and media outside the RSFSR, how far and when will the use of the 14 major non-Russian languages expand and/or contract?

The two areas for which the most data on language selection are available are publishing and education. Rosemarie Rogers has analyzed the former and found that the quantity of publications in the 14 major languages, relative to the number of their native speakers, is substantial, but also substantially lower than it is in Russian.[16] Her statistical analysis shows that 18.0 percent of all copies of nonperiodical publications in Soviet languages were in non-Russian languages in 1970 (up from 16.1 percent in 1959) and that, theoretically, this gave a native Russian speaker about 3.2 times as many copies in his language as a non-Russian native speaker (down from 3.6 in 1959). The ratio of non-Russian to Russian publications varies considerably according to whether one measures it in copies or in titles, and with the category of publication. In general, however, the Russian preponderance is greater at higher levels of specialization. For example, while the Russian advantage is 1.8 to 1 in primary and secondary school textbooks, it is 10.3 to 1 in higher education texts. Even more striking are the differences among the non-Russian languages. The Baltic languages have the highest publication rates, followed by the transcaucasian languages. The advantages in access to copies in the native language, calculated from Rogers' figures, and using the rate for Russian as the unit value, were as follows in 1970:

Estonian	1.37
Latvian	1.21
Russian	1.00
Lithuanian	0.66
Georgian	0.55
Armenian	0.44
Kazakh	0.42
Uzbek	0.41
Ukrainian	0.39
Turkmen	0.37
Moldavian	0.36
Tadzhik	0.34
Kirghiz	0.34
Azerbaidzhani	0.32
Belorussian	0.19

In education, as suggested by the textbook publication figures above, the 14 major non-Russian languages have attained more use at lower than at higher levels. Over-time statistics permitting an accurate assessment of the language situation at all educational levels are not available, but there is enough evidence to conclude that a large majority of pupils outside the RSFSR who are native speakers of the nominal languages of the republics in which they live receive their primary and secondary instruction in those languages. Two published figures are that 68 percent of all Kazakh and 94.5 percent of all Azerbaidzhani pupils in their respective republics were taught in their national languages in the late 1960s (1966–67 and 1968–69, respectively).[17] These figures can be indirectly checked by comparing the number of pupils being taught in the republic language with the number of eligible children in the republic. In Table 7.1, a rough estimate of this comparison appears for each republic, except for Latvia and Armenia, for which data were not found.

The table shows that the number studying in the language of each republic is close to what we would expect if all eligible young people were in school and being taught in that language, except in Kazakhstan and Belorussia. Even in those two republics, at least two-thirds of the number of eligible children in the population were in native-language classes. In light of the table, the two figures for Kazakhstan and Azerbaidzhan cited above do not appear to be exaggerations. From the evidence available, we must conclude that the retreat of the major non-Russian languages as vehicles of instruction in the face of the relentless penetration of Russian, which seemed only a few years ago to be the dominant trend, did not last; instead, these languages have been largely consolidated as the teaching media for those who speak them as native tongues, and even, in some republics (or so it seems), for substantial numbers of others.[18]

TABLE 7.1

Use of Republic Language as Medium of Instruction in 12 Union Republics, 1967–68

A Republic	B Number of Pupils with Republic Language as Medium of Instruction, Grades 1–10, 1967–68	C Estimated Number of Members of Republic Nationality with Republic Language as Native Language, Ages 8–17, January 1968[e]	D Estimated Number of Members of Republic Nationality with Republic Language as Native Language, Grades 1–10, 1967–68[f]	E Column B as Percentage of C	F Column B as Percentage of D
Ukraine	4,605,883	5,343,277	4,936,404	86	93
Belorussia	906,702	1,240,439	1,264,676	73	72
Uzbekistan	1,805,279	1,765,018	1,746,370	102	103
Kazakhstan	630,128	941,001	863,070	67	73
Georgia[a]	262,892	250,776	264,960	105	99
Azerbaidzhan[b]	904,325	873,401	880,866	104	103
Lithuania	424,124	407,647	405,071	104	105
Moldavia[c]	228,383	214,674	221,352	106	103
Kirghizia[d]	279,756	295,551	294,486	95	95
Tadzhikistan	355,238	356,048	348,979	100	102
Turkmenistan	336,853	321,684	304,382	105	111
Estonia	122,075	123,976	113,927	98	107

[a]Figures are for grades 1–4 and ages 8–11. Column B is for whole USSR, less total number of pupils in grades 1–10 in Azerbaidzhan with Georgian as medium of instruction in 1968–69. Column D is based on a projection of total enrollments from 1966–67.

[b]Column B is, and column D is based on, a retrojection from 1968–69.

[c]Figures are for grades 1–4 and ages 8–11.

[d]Column D deflated and column F inflated by unknown amount because of exclusion from pupil base of pupils with Dungan as medium of instruction.

230

[e]Estimates for ages 8–17 in 1968 were computed by estimating ages 10–19 in 1970 by the following formulas:

$$N_{10-19(\text{est.})} = N_{11-15} + N_{16-19} + N_{10(\text{est.})}$$

$$N_{10(\text{est.})} = \frac{1}{2} \left(\frac{N_{0-10}}{P_{0-9} + P_{10(\text{est.})}} + \frac{N_{11-19}}{P_{10-19} - P_{10(\text{est.})}} \right) P_{10(\text{est.})}$$

$$P_{10(\text{est.})} = .08 \, P_{5-9} + .12 \, P_{10-14}$$

Estimates for ages 8–11 in 1968 were computed by estimating ages 10–13 in 1970 with the formula

$$N_{10-13(\text{est.})} = 2 \left(N_{10(\text{est.})} + \frac{1}{5} N_{11-15} \right)$$

In the above formulas, $N_{i(-j)}$ is the number of persons of the republic nationality with its language as their native language, aged i (to j years, inclusive) in the republic according to the 1970 census. $P_{i(-j)}$ is the number of persons aged i (to j, inclusive) in the republic according to the 1970 census. (Est.) indicates an estimate.
[f]Estimates for grades 1–10 were computed by the following formula:

$$\frac{\text{Figure in column C}}{P_{10-19}} \quad \text{(total enrollment in grades 1–10)}$$

Estimates for grades 1–4 were computed by the following formulas:

$$\frac{\text{Figure in column C}}{P_{10-13(\text{est.})}} \quad \text{(total enrollment in grades 1–4)}$$

$$P_{10-13(\text{est.})} = P_{10-14} - P_{14(\text{est.})}$$

$$P_{14(\text{est.})} = .11 \, P_{10-14} + .09 \, P_{15-19}$$

Hence $$P_{10-13(\text{est.})} = .89 \, P_{10-14} - .09 \, P_{15-19}$$

Sources: Iu. D. Desheriev, Zakonomernosti razvitia literaturnykh iazykov narodov SSSR v sovetskuiu epokhu: Razvitie obshchestvennykh funktsii literaturnykh iazykov (Moscow: Nauka, 1976), pp. 69–71, 94–95, 116–17, 143–45, 173–74, 214–15, 237, 285, 309–10, 359–60, 376–77; A. N. Baskakov, "Usloviia razvitiia azerbaidzhansko-russkogo dvuiazychiia," in Razvitie natsional'no-russkogo dvuiazychiia, ed. Iu. D. Desheriev (Moscow: Nauka, 1976), p. 39; Jonathan Pool and Jeremy R. Azrael, "Education" (part A), in Handbook of Soviet Social Science Data, ed. Ellen Mickiewicz (New York: Free Press, 1973), ch. 6, pp. 137–58, see p. 145; Itogi vsesoiuznoi perepisi naseleniia 1970 goda (Moscow: Statistika, 1973), 2: 20–73; 4: 377–82.

231

There is evidently far more to be done before the republic languages penetrate higher education to the same degree. Probably for this reason, comparative statistics are not available, other than those on textbook publishing mentioned above. Iu. D. Desheriev states that since 1940, all higher educational institutions in the Ukraine have conducted instruction in both Ukrainian and Russian, but says nothing about the number of enrollees in each language. He also claims that certain figures on the rising educational level of the Ukraine population "bear witness to the fact that higher education in the Ukrainian language has become the property of all sections of the Ukrainian population"--unfortunately a non sequitur doing nothing to refute the dissident claims of systematic official bias against the Ukrainian language.[19] Desheriev does, however, present a list of 27 specialized fields in the basic and applied natural and social sciences, as well as humanities, in which instruction in Ukrainian has been given.

More helpful are Desheriev's data on the situation in Uzbekistan. In 1968-69 about 70 percent of the 68,820 students there were studying in Uzbek. In 1969-70 about 9,000 out of the 15,000 students at Tashkent State University were doing the same, including unspecified numbers of Russian as well as Kazakh, Karakalpak, Tadzhik, and other students. Uzbek has been more widely used in the social than in the natural sciences, and in the latter more in the first years than the last years of study.[20]

Still more detailed data are available about the language situation at Azerbaidzhan State University, in Baku, the major institution of higher education in that republic.[21] A. N. Baskakov's figures imply the following distribution of students between the two sections of that university:

| | | Nationality of Student | | |
		Azerbaidzhani	Non-Azerbaidzhani	Total
Section of University	Azerbaidzhani	N = 7,260 Row % = 86.4 Col. % = 75.6	N = 1,140 Row % = 13.6 Col. % = 47.5	8,400 70.0
	Russian	N = 2,340 Row % = 65.0 Col. % = 24.4	N = 1,260 Row % = 35.0 Col. % = 52.5	3,600 30.0
	Total	9,600 80.0	2,400 20.0	12,000

It is impressive that three-fourths of the Azerbaidzhani students at
the university are receiving their training in Azerbaidzhani; but it is
astonishing that almost half of the non-Azerbaidzhani students are
doing the same, since Russians are almost never taught in any language but their own. To understand this figure we would need to
know the distribution across sections of each major non-Azerbaidzhani
group, including the students from 16 foreign countries reported to
be studying there.[22] Since 95 percent of the teaching faculty are
Azerbaidzhanis,[23] one can imagine the possibility that they attract
non-Azerbaidzhanis into the Azerbaidzhani section by teaching better
in their native language, or by providing a more complete program
of courses in that section. If the non-Azerbaidzhanis studying in
Azerbaidzhani include some native speakers of Slavic languages,
perhaps they elect to study in a second language for predominantly
"integrative" motives, such as those that typify English-speaking
Canadians wanting to learn French.[24] If they plan or expect to remain in Azerbaidzhan, their enrollment may also reflect a belief in
their future need for competence in the republic language. Information about the attitudes of students in the different language sections
of a university such as Azerbaidzhan State would help to interpret
the enrollment data and also would contribute to the comparative
study of language choice.

It remains to be seen how far the Soviet government will go in
giving a complete repertoire of modern roles to each of the 15 republic languages. According to Desheriev, those languages are already
the "main" media of higher education in Uzbekistan, Georgia, Azerbaidzhan, Lithuania, and Armenia.[25] In these and most of the other
republics, he says, work is being done or a trend is observable toward the increased use of the republic language, at the expense of
Russian, as the medium of instruction in higher education. Since
several capitals are becoming proportionally more populated with
members of the republic nationality,[26] the national compositions of
the student bodies in those republics presumably are changing in the
same direction. If so, the educational efficiency of using the republic language as the medium of higher instruction is increasing rather
than decreasing.

The amount that has already been accomplished is enormous,
compared with similar efforts elsewhere. New states attempting to
officialize even one language generally have stumbled for years
around a vicious circle: inadequate manpower to develop the language to train the manpower to ; . . .[27] Languages must be reduced
to writing if literacy is to be achieved. Textbooks must be published
and native teachers trained if a language is to be the medium of instruction in schools and universities. Before textbooks can be published, thousands of concepts must be incorporated into the terminology

of the language, a laborious process that, in the Soviet Union as elsewhere, has required innumerable hours of consensus building among linguists and subject specialists, while also leading to deep conflicts. The Soviet Union claims to be pushing this process ahead for 15 of its languages, and there is evidence to support this claim.

THE CAMPAIGN FOR MASS KNOWLEDGE OF RUSSIAN

The second thrust of language planning in the USSR has been an effort to make Russian a universally usable medium of domestic communication. (Parallel to this has been an effort to promote Russian abroad as well, but we need not consider this aspect here.) Essentially all Soviet leaders, including Lenin, have considered a knowledge of Russian by members of other nationalities to be a desideratum, either because they favored Russian hegemony or because they recognized that the spread of Russian would facilitate communication, control, and the dissemination of knowledge and cultural creations. Initially, however, Lenin apparently succeeded in persuading the rest of the leadership, in debates that had begun years before the October Revolution, that the voluntariness of the spread of Russian was much more important to the fate of the regime than the fact of the spread.[28] His sensitivity to the feelings of the non-Russians began to lose its impact on policy as soon as he became incapacitated by illness in 1922.[29]

By the late 1930s militant opposition to the regime had been disarmed; native-language literacy had reached a high level; and the Stalin administration's policy of cultural proletarianization had assumed the form of russianization, partly for the purpose of winning more support from the largest nationality. Linguistic manifestations of this policy included the cyrillicization of the writing systems of most Soviet languages, the promotion of direct borrowing from Russian as the way to develop the terminologies of other languages, and (as of 1938) the compulsory study of Russian in non-Russian schools.[30] As many Soviet commentators have pointed out, learning Russian is of course easier if one's first language is written with the same alphabet and if it has many Russian-derived words in its vocabulary.

The policy of cyrillicization was carried out fairly rapidly: it began in 1936 and was largely completed by 1941. It omitted those languages that had substantial literatures in, and popular loyalties to, other scripts (Latvian, Lithuanian, Estonian, Armenian, Georgian, and Yiddish). The resulting alphabets have caused considerable discontent. In their haste to complete the job, linguists made many decisions later viewed as obviously mistaken. Further, whether by design or because of uncoordinated work, they often created an unneces-

sary multitude of symbols for basically identical phonemes. Given
their desire to make alphabets correspond with the Russian one, in
some cases they omitted symbols for making distinctions fundamental
to speakers of the language in question--for instance, long versus
short vowels in Turkmen. On the other hand, the desire to make alphabets correspond to the sound systems of the target languages led
to the omission of some unneeded Russian letters, which distressed
those who favored the preservation of Russian spellings in words
borrowed from Russian. Disputation about these problems continues
today among Soviet linguists, and occasionally the alphabet of a language is reformed.[31]

The effort to achieve terminological uniformity through use of
Russian as the universal source of borrowed words has aroused considerable anxiety. One index of this is the tendency for Soviet linguists both to advocate and to oppose this policy whenever they discuss the problem.[32] In general there are three widely practiced
policies: (1) borrowing without alteration, (2) borrowing with phono-
logical modification to fit the patterns of the borrowing language,
and (3) translation of the concept with morphemes already present
in the language.

Alphabets seem easy to impose on users of a language, but imposed vocabularies can be evaded more easily. Soviet writers on
language policy never complain that someone is reverting to the
Roman, Arabic, or Mongolian alphabet. There are many complaints,
however, that "artificial" native words are being substituted for Russian borrowings, not only in private speech but even in published and
broadcast material. If the rates of publication in non-Russian languages continue to expand, vocabulary control will become more difficult, especially if the proportion of Russians knowing other Soviet
languages remains minute.

In the extreme case of Moldavian, it appears that vocabulary
policy is not working at all. Authoritative Soviet language planners
have strenuously emphasized the intimate historical contacts between
Moldavian and the Slavic languages, as part of the effort to deny that
Moldavian and Romanian are competing standards of the same language, thus deflating Romania's territorial and emotional claims on
the Moldavian SSR.[33] In spite of a clear policy of linguistic differ-
entiation, Nicholas Dima has found a dramatic exodus of Slavic-
origin words from Moldavian publications since the late 1940s. At
present, there are hardly any more Russian borrowings in literary
Moldavian than in literary Romanian, and new terms being coined in
Moldavia are Romance-based.[34] Developments like this may well
make the cognitive task of learning Russian more difficult. On the
other hand, language learning may depend more on attitudes than on
cognitions; and a perception of Russians as benevolent supporters of

authentic, independent, flourishing national languages might more
than compensate, in positive attitudes, for the barriers raised by
differences in vocabulary.

This brings us to the question of how well non-Russians learn
Russian in the USSR. In 1956 an experienced observer of Soviet life
wrote: "On the basis of available data it seems safe to predict that
within a relatively short time, perhaps ten years, almost all Soviet
citizens will have a good speaking and writing command of Russian."[35]
Today more data are available, and there is less basis for such confidence. The mammoth Soviet literature on this subject seems to add
up to the claim that everyone is learning Russian, combined with the
lament that few people are learning it well. Baskakov summarizes
the customarily cited reasons: "the limited amount of instructional
literature, the shortage of instructional and scientific manpower,
the unavailability of modern technology for language teaching, and
the inadequate development of the methodology of teaching Russian."
Sometimes, for example, a certain grammatical concept is taught in
the Russian courses before the pupils have reached the same concept
in their native-language curriculum.[36]

A four-year comparative study of Azerbaidzhan, Lithuania,
Estonia, and the Buriat ASSR has attempted to quantify the knowledge
of Russian in selected places in those republics and to describe in
detail the results of linguistic interference, that is, distortions in
second-language competence attributable to the first language.[37]
This study used ethnographic methods, questionnaire surveying,
written testing, and tape-recorded interrogation to supplement the
usual aggregate statistics. It paid some attention to the use of
Azerbaidzhani and other languages as second languages, as well as
Russian.

In Azerbaidzhan the study examined Zakatala raion (district),
where Azerbaidzhanis far outnumber all other nationalities and the
population is 83 percent rural. Of about 20,000 pupils in the raion,
5 percent are Russians and 0.6 percent are Armenians; they are
taught in Russian. The others (Azerbaidzhanis, Avars, Tsakhurs,
Georgians) study in Azerbaidzhani. The investigators intensively
surveyed two village schools and found that 16 of the 30 teachers in
one, and 23 of the 44 teachers in the other, knew only Azerbaidzhani.
No students were found in these schools who could speak errorless
Russian.[38] Rural pupils in the second, third, and fourth grades
were found to know only half the vocabulary required by the curriculum. Among fourth through eighth graders, it was found that only
14 percent of the rural pupils claimed to read books or listen to
radio programs in Russian.[39] When asked how well they knew Russian, pupils in the ninth and tenth grades of Azerbaidzhani schools
in the city all claimed to be fluent, but only a small minority made

this claim in the rural remainder of the raion.[40] Azerbaidzhanis' knowledge of Russian is considerably better by the time they begin their higher education, although the disadvantage among those whose schooling was in Azerbaidzhani and among those coming from rural homes remains considerable. In the survey of university and pedagogical institute students, half of those from rural areas claimed to have trouble speaking Russian. The study found many mistakes in the Russian even of upperclassmen.[41]

Students following the regular program of instruction in Russian, which begins halfway through the first grade in Azerbaidzhani schools, were found to have major deficiencies in the language. Tests of Russian competence in several schools revealed, however, that errors in Russian were reduced to insignificant numbers among pupils who had attended preschools conducted in Russian.[42] On the basis of these findings, Baskakov recommends Russian preschools, especially in rural areas without Russian-speaking populations.[43]

The Lithuanian part of the study concentrated on language knowledge and language choice among both Lithuanians and Russians. Each group tends to have a proportion knowing the other group's language that is positively associated with the proportion of the population in the area belonging to the other group.[44] The raion chosen for fieldwork has a Lithuanian preponderance (68 percent), with the only other large groups being Russians (20.3 percent) and Poles (10.2 percent); but the minorities are spread very unevenly across the raion. In one bilingual collective farm, when meetings are held each person speaks in Lithuanian or Russian, whichever he prefers. Another observed regularity was that the language of a ceremony or festive occasion is whichever language any monolinguals in the group speak.[45] But the language of interaction can also be determined by anticipated reactions, by following the lead of the person who speaks first, or by deferring to someone with "high social status."[46]

In the settlement of Deguchiai, with 62 percent Lithuanians, 250 residents were surveyed; all of them except 6 women over age 60 were orally bilingual. Competence in written Russian was widespread only among those Lithuanians aged 50 and younger. Almost all Lithuanians watched movies in Russian, fewer listened to Russian radio programs, and fewer still (22 percent) read Russian books-- the same percentage as that of Russians who read books in Lithuanian.[47]

The investigation of achievement in Russian showed substantial discrepancies between curriculum demands and pupil performance in Lithuania, but they were not as serious as in Azerbaidzhan. By the end of the third grade, most pupils knew 80 to 90 percent of the required vocabulary, but only 2 percent were able to pronounce Russian without a strong Lithuanian accent. Curriculum goals were met by about 50 percent of the pupils in oral Russian, by about 33 percent in reading, and by about 25 percent in writing.[48] Satisfaction of curriculum demands in vocabulary fell to about 75 percent of the required words by the eighth grade. In one translation test given to 50 pupils, 8 of the 12 worst scorers came from rural homes, while 80 percent of the perfect scorers came from urban homes.[49] As Lithuanians progress through the educational system their competence in, and use of, Russian grows. But the discrepancies between curriculum demands and achievement, between urban and rural achievement, and between the fluency derived from contact learning and the deficient knowledge derived from school learning remain. One-quarter of a tested group of students in higher education institutions could not say anything in Russian. Students from areas with small Russian populations made many mistakes in Russian and did not satisfy even secondary school requirements. Reading skills were superior to speaking skills, but still 16 percent of the students were not acquainted with even the most basic Russian terms in their own areas of study.[50]

The Estonian section of the comparative study furnished a wealth of ethnographic detail about language behavior in the Ryuge village soviet in Vyru raion, located in the southeastern corner of the republic. The national composition of the population is almost entirely Estonian, and the Estonian language prevails throughout. "In the store, the restaurant, and other establishments, strangers are usually addressed in Estonian (even if the speaker knows excellent Russian), on the assumption that everyone surely knows Estonian."[51]

In the raion capital of Vyru, the investigators studied the Russian school and industrial plant. Few Estonians attended the former, but most of the pupils knew Estonian as a second language. In the plant, the work force was 70 percent Estonian, with Russians making up most of the remainder; but knowledge of Russian among the Estonians was considerably more frequent than vice versa. It appears from the figures given in the analysis that non-Estonian workers in the plant who had lived in Estonia for 15 years or more were more likely to know the language than not; those who had lived there ten years or less were more likely not to know it than to know it. Russians ignorant of Estonian and Estonians ignorant of Russian both explained their monolingualism by the fact that they never needed the other tongue, since those with whom they dealt in service establishments were bilingual.[52]

The result of such bilateral linguistic self-sufficiency is the atrophy of the second language. This was vividly revealed by the study when higher education students were tested in Tartu and Talinn in 1968. Of the 1,065 students tested, faculty members in Russian

language, who did the initial grading, gave marks of "excellent" to
1.5 percent, "good" to 22.3 percent, "satisfactory" to 31.4 percent,
and "unsatisfactory" to 44.9 percent. The investigators reanalyzed
the graded test papers and found grammatical errors, however, in 5
of the 16 "excellent" papers. In 99.0 percent of the 1,065 cases,
therefore, "these students had not yet reached the first level of full
bilingualism, even though the Russian curriculum in Estonian schools
(2nd to 11th grades, exceeding 1300 hours of instruction) unconditionally anticipates the complete mastery of the Russian grammatical
system and active control over a vocabulary of several thousand
lexemes."

The students who were tested were also given questionnaires
about their knowledge and use of Russian. Of the 709 who returned
questionnaires, 53 (7.5 percent) claimed that they "freely command
the Russian language" (the same wording that appears in the USSR
census); but the investigators' analysis of their test papers allowed
them to grant this level of competence to only 10 of these 53 (18.9
percent).[53] Calculated the other way, only 20.1 percent as many as
rated themselves fluent were so rated by their professors. If this
same ratio applies to the whole Estonian population's ability to
assess its competence in Russian, then the percentage of Estonians
in Estonia who were fluent in Russian as a second language in 1970
was not 27.8 percent, as reported in the census, but about 5.5 percent. Others, too, have argued that the census overstates the number of bilinguals.[54]

Contrasting with the situations in Azerbaidzhan, Lithuania,
and Estonia, the Buriat ASSR emerges from the four-republic study
as a case of officially encouraged assimilation. Most education
takes place in Russian. A minority of rural elementary schools,
and one urban school, use Buriat as the medium of instruction; but
"taking into account multitudinous requests from parents," the
Buriat ASSR Supreme Soviet passed a resolution in 1973 urging that
Buriat as a language of instruction be limited to the first four grades
rather than five. In schools that teach in Buriat, pupils are expected
to know more than 2,000 Russian words by the end of the third grade,
while in schools with Azerbaidzhani (also an Altaic language) as a
medium of instruction, the envisioned vocabulary is only 925 words.[55]
Party and other organizations support the "initiative" of Buriat parents who choose to send their children to Russian schools from the
first grade on, and Russian is taught to Buriats in a "zeroth grade"
to prepare them for the Russian medium. The investigators studied
a state farm that ran its formal meetings in Russian even though
only 2 percent of the members were Russians. Buriats on the farm,
talking among themselves, used Buriat until they came to a technical
or sociopolitical subject, whereupon they would switch to Russian.[56]

Thus, there is a clear contrast between the limited spread of Russian where the alternative is one of the 15 republic languages, and the rampant penetration of Russian elsewhere. Both policies and results appear to make a sharp distinction between these two kinds of non-Russian languages.

PROSPECTS AND PROBLEMS

At the present time the two major thrusts of Soviet language policy appear to be moving toward success and failure in different arenas. The first effort--for multilingual development--has made remarkable strides toward completion or self-sustaining "takeoff" for 14 major languages in their respective union republics. It has faded, however, for other languages and in other territories. The second effort--to universalize competence in Russian--is moving quickly toward success among citizens who do not speak one of the 15 favored languages, and also among those whose native languages are closely related to Russian, or who are displaced from the home republic of their mother tongue. But gross gaps exist in the remaining republics between plans and performance--gaps that will not necessarily become easier to close as the republic languages expand their utility at the expense of Russian. If the observed trends and policies continue, the USSR will move in the direction of being a quindecanational and quindecalingual state. Russian will be the Russian national language and--for those who need it--the Soviet link language, but not the universal, unique language of the union. Fourteen other national languages will thrive under conscientious cultivation; but a hundred minor tongues will slowly shrivel, officially unlamented, into extinction.

No one can be sure, however, that the existing policies will stay in place. Language policy is a controversial issue with high stakes, possibly including the very survival of the USSR. Let us look, therefore, at three new policies that could possibly become predominant, and see whether they could change the current linguistic trends.

First, Soviet leaders may decide that they want to prevent the entrenchment of quindecanationalism and quindecalingualism, whether because of the victory of a russophilic faction, concern about the costs of linguistic multiplicity, or fear that secessionist movements would inevitably arise. They might thereupon decide to make an all-out effort to russianize the Soviet people completely. If the withering away of all languages but Russian became the official policy, would it succeed? One answer is that this will happen even if, or even because, no such policy is announced. If all non-Russians

were to succeed in learning Russian as a second language, the instrumental utility, or at least the essentiality, of their native languages would decline. They might then, if instrumentally motivated,
cultivate their Russian at the expense of their other languages. This
change would be assisted by the electronic and print media, which
would respond to the fact that everybody can be reached in Russian
by offering more and better material in Russian. This would further
increase the utility of Russian, inducing more parents to send their
children to Russian-medium schools, after which they would be likely to raise their children with Russian as the home language, especially if they married across native-language lines.

Two main forces, however, would act to retard the switch to
Russian. One is the existence of fairly homogeneous and expanding
non-Russian communities. Until the rural population is reduced to
a small fraction of its present size, this residential segregation can
be expected to persist, preserving enclaves of minority languages
that will not be changeable without coercion. Birth-rate projections
indicate that the non-Russian nationalities will increase their share
of the Soviet population for several more decades.[57] The second
force against russianization is the attitudes of the non-Russian
elites. This force is likely to grow, rather than shrink, as industrial development and urbanization proceed. The perceived importance of its language among the elite of a subordinate group tends to
be low when initial contact with a more advantaged language group is
made. Once those who wish to learn the latter group's language have
done so and some permanent assimilation to that language has begun,
it begins to be perceived as a threat to the survival of the native language. It is difficult to predict how far a movement of native-
language consciousness would go in a particular Soviet nationality,
but the movement probably would become strong as soon as virtually
all of the group's population had a moderate command of Russian
and a substantial trend toward the selection of Russian-medium education by parents had set in. Thus, when attitudes are taken into
account, assimilation may be a self-regulating mechanism.

We must also consider another scenario. The unique role of
Russian as the language of intergroup contact and individual mobility
may some day be seen as an unfair and un-Leninist privilege granted
to one nationality. The "voluntary" acceptance of assigning that role
to Russian may deteriorate. Soviet publications already recognize
that monolingualism among Russians obstructs the development of
favorable attitudes and relations between Russians and others.[58]
On the basis of these beliefs, a new policy might emerge: either
(1) bilingualism for all except RSFSR Russians or (2) universal bilingualism among the Soviet population (with RSFSR Russians learning the other Soviet language of their choice).

Could such a widespread bilingualism develop, even with complete government support? One can safely assume that the utility of a knowledge of Russian under all foreseeable conditions within a continued Soviet political order will remain much higher than the utility of a knowledge of any other Soviet language. Thus the serious question is whether any policy could succeed in making all Russians, or even all Russians outside their own republic, bilingual. There are hardly any cases of widespread reciprocal bilingualism in the world. Spanish-Guarani bilingualism in Paraguay and English-Afrikaans bilingualism among the white population of South Africa are both high, but neither is the result of a deliberate government policy imposed in a situation where such bilingualism was previously absent.

A recent attempt to turn asymmetrical bilingualism into reciprocal bilingualism has been made in Canada, preceded by millions of dollars worth of feasibility studies. There, although the main effort has been confined to federal civil servants, who have been given encouragement, help, and incentives to learn the other official language, and although this other language (French) has international prestige, recent studies indicate that the program of bilingualization has been a massive failure and that almost the only really bilingual officials remain those whose native language is French.[59] A comparison of the Soviet and Canadian censuses shows that Russians claim to know non-Russian languages considerably less than English Canadians claim to know French, if we control for the ethnic composition of the districts they live in. For example, a Russian surrounded by 98 percent non-Russians has a 5-10 percent likelihood of knowing their language, while an English Canadian living in an area that is 98 percent French-Canadian has a 70-80 percent likelihood of knowing French.[60]

On this basis it would seem less likely that a policy of reciprocal bilingualism could work in the USSR than in Canada. The facts that no major language in the USSR besides Russian has international status, and that many are linguistically very distant from Russian, add to the expected difference. The main force operating in the other direction is the greater capacity for rewarding, sanctioning, and controlling possessed by the Soviet authorities; but the policy in question would sorely test this capacity. To the extent that the policy (or the prevailing patterns of natality, migration, and manpower demands[61]) drove Russians from other republics back to the RSFSR, this migration would endanger the plan by depriving both Russians and non-Russians of the most crucial precondition for effective language learning: an environment in which the other language is common and useful.

Finally, there is yet a more extreme policy that has roots in Soviet tradition, and whose roots are not yet dead: a policy of letting--and helping--a hundred languages bloom. The mainstream of Soviet writings on the minor languages asserts that their preservation as living tongues is not per se a good thing. On the contrary, the most common view welcomes the tendency for speakers of these languages to become bilingual and then raise their children with Russian (or one of the other 14 union republic languages) as the native language. The belief in substantive cultural uniformity, expressed through different languages as mere alternative codes, negates the basis for valuing, as thinkers like J. G. von Herder, Benjamin Lee Whorf, and George Steiner have done, the multiplicity of languages major and minor. But the strenuous admonitions of Lenin against any kind of coercion and any degree of privilege among nations and languages provide a legitimate basis for criticism of the mainstream viewpoint.

V. A. Avrorin best exemplifies this criticism with his harsh attack on the works of F. P. Filin, Iu. D. Desheriev, and O. P. Sunik, who, he says, in both describing and praising the extermination of minor languages, have on the one hand falsified the facts and on the other hand advocated a policy of ethnic and linguistic inequality that is Kautskyite rather than Leninist. Avrorin argues that the state should help all speech communities make real use of their constitutional equal rights and should stop falsely assuming that their languages are in the process of dying out. [62] Even those in the mainstream who promote assimilation assert that it is voluntary, and that it actually strengthens rather than weakens the smaller languages, both internally and in terms of the roles they play. Although it may be hard to understand how "The observed transitions from monolingualism to bilingualism, and from there to monolingualism based on communication among nationalities, in no way imply the dying out of nationality languages,"[63] the fact that authorized publications on nationality policy say such things shows that the relevant public still attaches value to languages as entities. Avrorin implies such an evaluation when he says:

> Then Iu. D. Desheriev includes in this same group of
> hopeless, dying languages Andi and Didoi in Dagestan;
> Iazguliam and Ishkashim in the Pamirs; Udegei, Orok,
> Karaite, Chulym, Dolgan, etc., in other words, it
> seems, all the non-written languages of Soviet ethnic
> groups. Yet these are a little more numerous than the
> written ones--not in people, of course, but precisely
> in peoples. [64]

There is not enough experience anywhere to let us foresee the fate of a panlinguistic promotion movement in the Soviet Union if it were to obtain party and government support. As V. N. Durdenevskii remarked in 1927, Karl Kautsky's prediction that the Ossetians, the Kalmyks, and others were destined to go the way of the Bretons and the Basques was wrong on both counts: neither Soviet nor Western minorities disappeared.[65] Soviet writers on both sides of this fence agree that conscious intervention is assuming an increasing share of the ability to determine what happens to languages. There is some evidence that concern about the preservation of languages and cultures grows stronger again with the advent of the postindustrial syndrome, even in the Soviet Union.[66] If both these relationships hold, then the cultivation of minor languages could be both a popular and a successful policy.

In the meantime, under current conditions the politically most acceptable compromise seems to be slow progress toward stable, asymmetric bilingualism, with non-Russians increasingly learning Russian but not abandoning their original languages. This guarantees to each group what it cares most about: to the Russians a widespread and increasing ability to communicate with non-Russians without having to learn another Soviet language; to the non-Russians the continued and even growing vitality of their national languages; and to the political leadership the ability to avoid announcing alarming plans for the long-run linguistic future. As long as this progress is slow, the direction of movement can be a source of comfort to all; and the expectation that this movement will continue for many years can gratify the leaders. As soon as the movement stops or changes direction, new fears are likely. If the learning of Russian by each new generation of non-Russians retrogresses, there will be fears of separatism. If the intergenerational loss of the other 14 republic languages in favor of Russian begins to become substantial in comparison with the expansion caused by population increases, the fear will be one of absorption. But if the Soviet Union, by making good on its claim that Russian and the other republic languages are symbiotic rather than antithetical, can show that neither fear is warranted, it may provide a unique model for reconciling complete linguistic unity with a high degree of linguistic diversity.

NOTES

1. Ali A. Mazrui, The Political Sociology of the English Language: An African Perspective (The Hague: Mouton, 1975), p. 70.

2. Itogi vsesoiuznoi perepisi naseleniia 1970 goda (Moscow: Statistika, 1973), 4: 20-22.

3. Richard Pipes, The Formation of the Soviet Union (rev.
ed.; Cambridge, Mass.: Harvard University Press, 1964), chs.
1-2; Jaan Pennar, Ivan I. Bakalo, and George Z. F. Bereday,
Modernization and Diversity in Soviet Education, with Special Reference to Nationality Groups (New York: Praeger, 1971), pp. 23-35.

4. For a comparison of these two situations, see Ram Gopal,
Linguistic Affairs of India (Bombay: Asia Publishing House, 1966),
pp. 233-39.

5. Alfred Cooper Woolner, Language in History and Politics
(London: Oxford University Press, 1938), pp. 78-79; Winfred P.
Lehmann, ed., Language and Linguistics in the People's Republic
of China (Austin: University of Texas Press, 1975), p. 42.

6. Jacob Ornstein, "Soviet Language Policy: Continuity and
Change," ch. 3 in Ethnic Minorities in the Soviet Union, ed. Erich
Goldhagen (New York: Praeger, 1968), also divides Soviet language
policy into two stages but sees them as sequential periods. For a
four-stage periodization, see E. Glyn Lewis, Multilingualism in the
Soviet Union (The Hague: Mouton, 1972), pp. 66-80; for a five-stage
one, see M. I. Isaev, "Iazykovaia politika i iazykovoe stroitel'stvo
v kul'turnoi revoliutsii," in Razvitie iazykov i kul'tur narodov SSSR
v ikh vzaimosviazi i vzaimodeistvii, ed. N. A. Baskakov and R. G.
Kuzeev (Ufa: Bashkirskii Filial, Institut Iazykoznaniia, Akademiia
nauk SSSR, 1976), pp. 57-66, see 65-66.

7. Pipes, op. cit., p. 277.

8. Ibid., pp. 280-81.

9. Alexander G. Park, Bolshevism in Turkestan 1917-1927
(New York: Columbia University Press, 1957), pp. 178-89, 363-64.

10. K. M. Musaev, Alfavity iazykov narodov SSSR (Moscow:
Nauka, 1965); N. A. Baskakov, ed., Voprosy sovershenstvovaniia
alfavitov tiurkskikh iazykov SSSR (Moscow: Nauka, 1972); V. I.
Lytkin, "Osnovnye protsessy v formirovanii i razvitii finnougorskikh
i samodiiskikh iazykov v sovetskuiu epokhu," in Zakonomernosti
razvitiia literaturnykh iazykov narodov SSSR v sovetskuiu epokhu:
Osnovnye protsessy vnutristrukturnogo razvitiia tiurkskikh, finnougorskikh i mongol'skikh iazykov, ed. N. A. Baskakov (Moscow:
Nauka, 1969), pp. 239-67; K. M. Musaev, "Iz opyta sozdaniia
pis'mennostei dlia iazykov narodov Sovetskogo Soiuza," in Sotsiolin-
gvisticheskie problemy razvivaiushchikhsia stran, ed. Iu. D.
Desheriev et al. (Moscow: Nauka, 1975), pp. 243-59; A. Kalimov,
"Neskol'ko zamechanii o putiakh razvitiia dunganskogo iazyka," in
ibid., pp. 328-32.

11. Musaev, Alfavity, pp. 80-82 and passim. As Soviet
scholars themselves have since noted, not all these symbols were
necessary. But while they attribute the excess diversity of alphabets to poor organization, some others see it as a deliberate plot to
split the speakers of related dialects into relatively impotent groups:

Paul B. Henze, "Politics and Alphabets in Inner Asia," in Advances in the Creation and Revision of Writing Systems, ed. Joshua A. Fishman (The Hague: Mouton, 1977), pp. 371-420.

12. V. I. Lytkin, "Komi-Zyrianskii iazyk," in Baskakov, Zakonomernosti, pp. 302-51, see 328.

13. Jonathan Pool and Jeremy Azrael, "Education" (part A), in Handbook of Soviet Social Science Data, ed. Ellen Mickiewicz (New York: Free Press, 1973), ch. 6, pp. 137-58, see p. 139.

14. Iu. D. Desheriev, Zakonomernosti razvitiia literaturnykh iazykov narodov SSSR v sovetskuiu epokhu: Razvitie obshchestvennykh funktsii literaturnykh iazykov (Moscow: Nauka, 1976), p. 116; A. N. Baskakov, "Usloviia razvitiia azerbaidzhansko-russkogo dvuiazychiia," in Razvitie natsional'no-russkogo dvuiazychiia, ed. Iu. D. Desheriev (Moscow: Nauka, 1976), pp. 35-54, see p. 38; Pool and Azrael, loc. cit.

15. See Baskakov, Voprosy.

16. Rosemarie Rogers, "The Soviet Audience of Book and Other Publishing," paper presented at the Fifth National Convention of the American Association for the Advancement of Slavic Studies, Dallas, Texas, March 1972, pt. II. Cited with permission. Revised figures kindly furnished by Professor Rogers have been used here.

17. Desheriev, Zakonomernosti, p. 143; Baskakov, "Usloviia," p. 39. See also Brian Silver, "Bilingualism and Maintenance of the Mother Tongue in Soviet Central Asia," Slavic Review 35 (1976): 406-24, see 408.

18. See Pennar et al., op. cit., pp. 263, 293, 315, for evidence of the previous trend. I am indebted to Brian Silver for calling this contrast to my attention. Table 7.1 probably overestimates the ratios in general by assuming that the only eligible children are native speakers of the republic language who also belong to the republic nationality.

19. Desheriev, Zakonomernosti, p. 73; Ivan Dzyuba, Internationalism or Russification? (2nd ed.; London: Weidenfeld and Nicolson, 1970).

20. Desheriev, Zakonomernosti, pp. 121-22.

21. A. N. Baskakov, "Chetvertaia stupen' azerbaidzhansko-russkogo dvuiazychiia," in Desheriev, Razvitie, pp. 315-35, see 316. I have used the total figure of 12,000 students, although the author says "more than 12,000"; the ratios are not affected.

22. Faig Baġyrov, rector, Azerbaidzhan State University, personal communication, April 1975. Professor Baġyrov also stated that the university had 14,000 students, of whom 70 percent were in the Azerbaidzhani Section--both reasonably consistent with Baskakov's figures.

23. Baskakov, "Chetvertaia stupen'," loc. cit.

24. John C. Johnstone, Young People's Images of Canadian Society, Studies of the Royal Commission on Bilingualism and Bi-culturalism, 2 (Ottawa: Queen's Printer, 1969), pp. 86-87.

25. Desheriev, Zakonomernosti, pp. 121, 176, 198, 218, 340.

26. S. Bruk, "Natsional'nost' i iazyk v perepisi naseleniia 1970 g.," Vestnik statistiki 5 (1972): 42-53, see 47.

27. See, for instance, Richard Noss, Higher Education and Development in South-East Asia: Language Policy (Paris: UNESCO and International Association of Universities, 1967).

28. Park, op. cit., p. 178; Pipes, op. cit., pp. 45-46.

29. Pipes, op. cit., p. 282.

30. Robert Conquest, The Nation Killers (London: Sphere Books, 1972), pp. 133-34; Lewis, op. cit., p. 198.

31. Baskakov, Voprosy; Musaev, Alfavity; Henze, op. cit.

32. Jonathan Pool, "Developing the Soviet Turkic Tongues: The Language of the Politics of Language," Slavic Review 35 (1976): 425-42, see 435-39, 441-42.

33. N. G. Korlètianu, "Moldavskii literaturnii iazyk dosovetskogo perioda," in Zakonomernosti razvitiia literaturnykh iazykov narodov SSSR v sovetskuiu epokhu: Vnutristrukturnoe razvitie staropis'mennykh iazykov, ed. Iu. D. Desheriev (Moscow: Nauka, 1973), pp. 163-69, see 167-69.

34. Nicholas Dima, "Moldavians or Romanians?" ch. 3 in The Soviet West: Interplay between Nationality and Social Organiza-tion, ed. Ralph S. Clem (New York: Praeger, 1975), pp. 38-39, 42-43. See also Henze, op. cit., p. 405, on Uzbek.

35. Frederick C. Barghoorn, Soviet Russian Nationalism (New York: Oxford University Press, 1956), p. 92.

36. Baskakov, "Chetvertaia stupen'," pp. 316, 334. See also Lewis, op. cit., pp. 202-03; and M. Mobin Shorish, "The Pedagogi-cal, linguistic, and Logistical Problems of Teaching Russian to the Local Soviet Central Asians," Slavic Review 35 (1976): 443-62.

37. Desheriev, Razvitie.

38. Baskakov, "Usloviia," pp. 43-45.

39. A. N. Baskakov, "Vtoraia stupen' azerbaidzhansko-russkogo dvuiazychiia," in Desheriev, Razvitie, pp. 235-47, see 236.

40. A. N. Baskakov, "Tret'ia stupen' azerbaidzhansko-russkogo dvuiazychiia," in Desheriev, Razvitie, pp. 279-85, see 279.

41. Baskakov, "Chetvertaia stupen'," pp. 317-18.

42. A. N. Baskakov, "Pervaia stupen' azerbaidzhansko-russkogo dvuiazychiia," in Desheriev, Razvitie, pp. 184-201, see 185-87, 198.

43. Baskakov, "Chetvertaia stupen'," p. 335.

44. V. Iu. Mikhal'chenko, "Usloviia razvitiia litovsko-russkogo dvuiazychiia," in Desheriev, Razvitie, pp. 54-71, see 58.

45. Ibid., pp. 67-68.

46. Ibid., pp. 70-71.

47. Ibid., pp. 68-69.

48. V. Iu. Mikhal'chenko, "Pervaia stupen' litovsko-russkogo dvuiazychiia," in Desheriev, Razvitie, pp. 201-13, see 211-13.

49. V. Iu. Mikhal'chenko, "Vtoraia stupen' litovsko-russkogo dvuiazychiia," in Desheriev, Razvitie, pp. 248-57, see 250.

50. V. Iu. Mikhal'chenko, "Chetvertaia stupen' litovsko-russkogo dvuiazychiia," in Desheriev, Razvitie, pp. 335-51, see 337-39.

51. I. A. Selitskaia, "Usloviia razvitiia estonsko-russkogo dvuiazychiia," in Desheriev, Razvitie, pp. 72-85, see 80.

52. Ibid., pp. 82-85.

53. A. K. Reitsak, "Chetvertaia stupen' estonsko-russkogo dvuiazychiia," in Desheriev, Razvitie, pp. 351-65, see 351-53.

54. Murray Feshbach and Stephen Rapawy, "Soviet Population and Manpower Trends and Policies," in Soviet Economy in a New Perspective, ed. John P. Hardt (Washington, D.C.: U.S. Government Printing Office, 1976), pp. 113-61, see 148. But see also M. N. Guboglo, "Etnolingvisticheskie protsessy," in Sovremennye etnicheskie protsessy v SSSR, ed. Iu. V. Bromlei et al. (Moscow: Nauka, 1975), ch. 8, p. 306. Brian Silver has argued (personal communication) that the census question presumably refers to oral, not written, fluency, and that grammatical writing ability is an unfair criterion, since even many native speakers would fail to meet it.

55. A. A. Darbeeva, "Pervaia stupen' buriatsko-russkogo dvuiazychiia," in Desheriev, Razvitie, pp. 222-33, see 222; Baskakov, "Pervaia stupen'," p. 185.

56. A. A. Darbeeva, "Usloviia razvitiia buriatsko-russkogo dvuiazychiia," in Desheriev, Razvitie, pp. 85-102.

57. Feshbach and Rapawy, op. cit., pp. 122-23.

58. M. N. Guboglo, "Etnolingvisticheskie kontakty i dvuiazychie," in Sotsial'noe i natsional'noe, ed. Iu. V. Arutiunian (Moscow: Nauka, 1973), ch. 4, p. 268.

59. Paul Lamy, "Language Conflict and Language Planning in Canada," paper presented at the annual meeting of the Canadian Sociology and Anthropology Association, Quebec, May 1976.

60. Itogi vsesoiuznoi perepisi naseleniia 1970, IV; Stanley Lieberson, Language and Ethnic Relations in Canada (New York: Wiley, 1970), p. 135.

61. Feshbach and Rapawy, op. cit.

62. V. A. Avrorin, Problemy izucheniia funktsional'noi storony iazyka (Leningrad: Nauka, 1975), pp. 210-41.

63. F. K. Kocharli and A. F. Dashdamirov, eds., Sovetskii narod i dialektika natsional'nogo razvitiia (Baku: Elm, 1972), p. 320.

64. Avrorin, op. cit., p. 211.

65. V. N. Durdenevskii, Ravnopravie iazykov v sovetskom stroe (Moscow: Institut Sovetskogo Prava, 1927), p. 19.

66. Jeffrey A. Ross, "An Analysis of the Emergence of Ethnicity in the Politics of Post-Industrial Society," paper presented at the Seventeenth Annual Convention of the International Studies Association, Toronto, February 1976.

LANGUAGE POLICY AND THE LINGUISTIC RUSSIFICATION OF SOVIET NATIONALITIES

8

Brian D. Silver

The Soviet Union is a rich laboratory--in the words of a prominent Soviet sociologist, a "gigantic experiment"--for studying ethnic and linguistic relations.[1] Approximately 90 distinct nationalities are indigenous to the Soviet Union, representing a great variety of historical and cultural traditions, language groups, and interaction patterns. Moreover, the recent increase of published empirical research on ethnic relations by Soviet scholars, in addition to the enormous body of little-used census data, offers unprecedented opportunities to analyze Soviet ethnic processes.

This paper examines the language behavior of 45 non-Russian nationalities. It seeks to describe and to account for the extent to which non-Russians have adopted Russian as a native or a second language. Rather than identifying all factors affecting linguistic russification, the analysis will focus on a few key demographic, cultural, and political factors that account for a large majority of the variation in levels of linguistic russification among the 45 ethnic groups. Some of these factors will be shown to retard, and others to accelerate, the rates of linguistic russification.

Previous research has shown that, on balance, long-term trends favor the gradually increasing adoption of Russian as a native language among most non-Russian nationalities. Two broad classes of factors have been identified to explain these trends: _demographic_ factors, such as urbanization, geographic mobility, and interethnic group contact; and _political_ factors, such as the strong normative emphasis given by Soviet leaders to the learning of Russian and policies affecting the use of language in such spheres as schools, the mass media, and government operations.[2] But previous research on the linguistic russification of non-Russians has been limited in two important ways.

First, although this research has charted the relationships between demographic factors and the adoption of Russian, the distinctive impact of the political factors on language use has not been

250

demonstrated empirically. Although Western scholars generally argue that nationalities policy has been aimed at increasing the use of Russian in the USSR, they seldom acknowledge that official policies have not only encouraged the use of Russian but may have helped to sustain the non-Russian languages as well. The central thesis of this paper is that although the commitment of Soviet leaders to the spread of Russian as a second language has encouraged the use of Russian among all non-Russian nationalities, language policies that differentiate among nationalities help to account for differential rates of linguistic russification, as reflected in the extent of knowledge of Russian as both a second language and a mother tongue. In particular, variations in the provision of native-language schools and publications can be shown to slow the linguistic russification of some groups and to speed the russification of others. Moreover, as long as support for the national languages is provided by schools and mass communications media, the acquisition of Russian as a second language does not necessarily portend the loss of knowledge of the traditional national languages.

A second limitation of previous research on language shift among Soviet nationalities is that nearly all studies published in the West have used the 1959 Soviet census or earlier censuses as the primary source of information. These censuses provide information only on the professed native language (rodnoi iazyk) of the population. The 1970 census, on the other hand, permits a much more sensitive assessment of the patterns of language use because the questionnaire asked respondents to designate not only their native language but also any (though only one) other language of the peoples of the USSR in which they were fluent. As a result, one may now explore the possibility that the demographic and political factors that affect change of mother tongue may not affect the spread of second languages to the same degree or in the same way. In relying on the 1970 census as a principal data base, this study will focus on native-language use and second-language use as separate, though related, indicators of linguistic russification. Determining the varying roles of particular demographic and political factors in the growth of bilingualism and shift of mother tongue will be a major element of this study.

To reveal the distinctive impact of language policy on language change, one must take into account the effects of demographic and cultural factors on language use, since these factors have important independent effects on the rates of linguistic russification. Accordingly, the analysis will focus first on charting the effects of demographic and cultural factors on linguistic russification; it will then assess the relationship between political factors and the variation in linguistic russification that is not accounted for by the demographic and cultural factors. An important assumption in this research is that one can distinguish cultural and demographic factors (such as traditional religion, urbanization, and interethnic contact) that more or less autonomously affect language shift regardless of the goals or policies of political leaders, from political factors (such as the provision of native-language schools) that directly affect language use. However, since cultural and demographic characteristics of the nationalities are in turn affected by official policies, such as planned population movements and investment strategies, one cannot impose an absolute distinction between the two sets of factors. Nevertheless, one should not view all population or cultural change as if it were directed by regime policies. More important, even if one were to attribute differences in the demographic situations of non-Russians to official policies, it would still be useful to distinguish policies that affect patterns of language use indirectly, through demographic processes, from policies that are aimed at language use itself, such as control of language in the mass media and schools. Consequently, although the factors that are labeled here as cultural and demographic might ultimately be regarded as politically controlled or at least affected by regime policies, for analytic purposes I shall treat these factors as different from policies directed expressly toward language use.

SOME HYPOTHESES ABOUT LANGUAGE SHIFT

Demographic and Cultural Factors

One might assume initially that factors shown to be related to shift of native language from the traditional language of an ethnic group to Russian should also be related to the acquisition of Russian as a second language. Previous research on native-language shift among Soviet nationalities has supported the following five generalizations about the impact of demographic and cultural factors on the spread of Russian.

Proposition 1.   Urban non-Russians are substantially more russified linguistically than are rural non-Russians.

Proposition 2.   The level of linguistic russification of both urban and rural non-Russians is directly related to the extent of their contact with Russians.

Proposition 3.   Urban-rural residence and interethnic contact have a joint effect on linguistic russification. In particular, an increase in the extent of contact with Russians has a much greater impact on the learning of Russian among urban than among rural non-Russians;

and at any given level of interethnic contact, urbanites are more linguistically russified than are ruralites.

Proposition 4.   Muslims are far less susceptible to linguistic russification than are non-Muslims, regardless of either
the extent of their contact with Russians or whether
they reside in urban areas.

Proposition 5.   Traditional religion and demographic factors (urban-
rural residence, interethnic group contact) have
joint effects on linguistic russification. That is,
an increase in the extent of interethnic contact has
a much greater impact on non-Muslims than on Muslims; and urban-rural differences in linguistic russification are much larger among non-Muslims than
among Muslims, when the extent of contact with
Russians is held constant.

Exploring the rationales behind these generalizations will suggest
not only why the factors affect native-language shift in the ways they
do but also why they may affect second-language acquisition differently. After exploring these rationales and developing a full set of
propositions that encompass both demographic-cultural and political
explanations of native-language shift and second-language acquisition,
the propositions will be tested on the basis of 1970 Soviet census data.
      The first proposition is based on evidence from a number of
societies, including the Soviet Union, that urbanization tends to be
associated with a change in important values that affect ethnic loyalties. Because urban residents commonly have higher and more
flexible career aspirations than ruralites, they are likely to recognize and to accept the practical utility of learning Russian as an aid
to career advancement.[3] Furthermore, a change of residence from
a rural to an urban setting is often associated with a breakdown of
traditional ethnic group solidarities and allows the individual to
acquire new values that may support the adoption of a new language.[4]
Although urbanization also is frequently associated with a rekindling
of ethnic group consciousness or a transformation of earlier ethnic
sentiments into newer, urban-based ethnic ideologies, linguistic
evidence does not support this view with respect to the Soviet Union:
among all non-Russian nationalities, urbanites are more extensively
russified linguistically than are ruralites.[5] Finally, urban non-
Russians should be more russified linguistically than rural non-
Russians because urban populations are usually more ethnically
mixed. The urban areas of most non-Russian republics and provinces contain large and often predominant numbers of Russians and
other nonindigenous nationalities. To compete with Russians and

other outsiders for jobs, non-Russians may have to learn Russian. In addition, the opportunities to learn Russian should increase as the extent of contact between natives and Russians increases. In sum, a larger proportion of urbanites than of ruralites should be fluent in Russian because of the value changes associated with a shift from rural to urban residence, job competition from members of other ethnic groups, and opportunities to learn Russian where interethnic contact is higher.

Proposition 2 predicts a positive relationship between contact and the extent of linguistic russification of non-Russians in rural areas as well, since ruralites, too, should learn Russian more frequently as job competition from Russians and the opportunity to learn Russian increase. Because ruralites are likely to have lower career aspirations and a greater attachment to traditional ethnic values than do urbanites, however, proposition 3 predicts that at comparable levels of interethnic contact, ruralites will be less attracted to Russian than will urbanites.

Although previous research has shown that both urbanization and contact have substantial independent effects on the shift to Russian as a native language, one might not expect urbanization to have a strong impact on the adoption of Russian as a second language (except insofar as it increases the extent of interethnic contact between Russians and the indigenous nationalities).[6] Specifically, one might formulate an alternative hypothesis:

Proposition 3a. Urban-rural differences in the adoption of Russian as a second language are entirely due to the extent of interethnic group contact. That is, urbanites and ruralites are equally likely to acquire Russian as a second language, at any given level of interethnic contact.

The differences in values held by urban and rural residents may well be less important than the level of interethnic contact in accounting for the acquisition of Russian as a second language. Practical incentives to learn Russian may play a much more important role in the growth of bilingualism than in shift of mother tongue to Russian.

Proposition 4 asserts that Muslims are less susceptible to linguistic russification than are non-Muslims. Islamic culture differs much more markedly from the Russian than do the traditions of most Soviet ethnic groups that before the Revolution adhered to the Eastern Orthodox or some other Christian faith. Adherence to an "ethnic ideology" that helps Muslims individually to distinguish themselves from Russians and to identify with the Muslim community of believers may impede the influence of demographic factors on language change. [7] Therefore, whatever the place of residence or extent of their contact with Russians, Muslims should be less linguistically russified than non-Muslims would be. Furthermore, proposition 5 predicts that religion has not only a discernible independent effect on linguistic russification but also joint effects on linguistic russification with the demographic variables: the magnitude of the effect of religion on language shift should be contingent on the extent of urbanization and interethnic contact of the non-Russian group.

One should also consider, however, that although traditional religion impedes or accelerates the shift to Russian as a native language, it may have a small or negligible impact on the acquisition of Russian as a second language. Specifically:

Proposition 5a. The impact of traditional religion on the acquisition of Russian as a second language will approach zero, once the demographic factors of urbanization and interethnic contact are taken into consideration.

Like the value changes associated with urbanization, ethnic values associated with different traditional religions may help or hinder the adoption of Russian as a native language, but not as a second language. It is important to note, for example, that in a majority of cases where non-Russians have adopted Russian as a native language, they lose fluency in their traditional languages as second languages. [8] Thus, shift of mother tongue usually denotes a sharp break in linguistic (and, one might argue, cultural) affinity with the national group. Therefore, unlike the adoption of Russian as a native language, which typically involves eventual complete abandonment of the national language, learning Russian as a second language may reflect little more than a pragmatic consideration of the value of using Russian, and might not be regarded as an immediate threat to the solidarity of the national group.

Political Factors

According to the 1970 census report, 48.7 percent of the non-Russian population was fluent in Russian: 11.6 percent claimed Russian as a native language and 37.1 percent claimed it as a second language. Although we lack direct evidence to make longitudinal comparisons of second-language use, there undoubtedly has been a large increase in knowledge of Russian among non-Russians in the Soviet era. This conclusion is supported by evidence in the census report, for example, of the far more extensive knowledge of Russian among younger generations than among older ones. Much of this increase probably has occurred as a more or less natural outcome of increases in intergroup contact, urbanization, and geographical mobility of the non-Russian groups. The central thesis of this study, however, is that a significant proportion of the intergroup variation in levels of linguistic russification is attributable to Soviet language policy. This study will employ two measures of language policy: the use of languages in primary and secondary schools, and the availability of publications in the non-Russian languages.

School Policy

Primary and secondary schools in the Soviet Union employ more than 50 languages as the principal media of instruction. In such "national schools" the non-Russian pupil ordinarily studies Russian as a separate subject beginning in the first or second year, but the national language is the chief medium of instruction for most other courses. To be sure, even where national-language schools are available, not all non-Russians attend them. Non-Russian children who reside in rural areas are more likely to attend national schools than are urban children. Nominally, parents have the right to select the language of instruction for their children. [9] In most cases where non-Russian pupils attend schools conducted in a language other than their national language, Russian is the medium of instruction.

Unfortunately, few figures have been published on the proportion of pupils of each nationality who attend schools where Russian or their traditional national language is the medium of instruction (there are, moreover, some "mixed" schools, where two or more languages are employed). But there is systematic information on the maximum number of years in which native-language schools are available to non-Russian pupils residing in their official national areas. This information comes from two sources: reports by Soviet educators, and statistical compendia on books published in the USSR. [10] Especially noteworthy is the close correspondence between the maximum number of years in which native-language schools are available and the rank of a nationality's basic national area in the Soviet federal system. As far as we can judge from information published by Soviet educators, for example, for all nationalities whose official territories ranked as union republics in 1958, children could attend schools where their native language was the principal medium of instruction through complete secondary school (ten years). [11] At the same time, for nearly all groups whose territories ranked as autonomous republics, children could attend national-language schools through at most seven years (with two exceptions, the Tatars and Bashkirs, where the maximum was ten

years, and a few exceptions where it was less than seven years).
Groups with still lower official status generally had even less opportunity to send their children to schools conducted in their traditional
languages. A similar hierarchy of opportunities apparently has prevailed since the early 1930s, when most of the national school systems were established, though in the 1960s substantial reductions in
native-language schooling occurred for almost all nationalities whose
official territories ranked lower than union republic.

        To verify the reports by Soviet educators and to reveal the con-
tinuity in school language policy over time, data were gathered from
the Ezhegodnik knigi SSSR for several years. Table 8.1 reports the
highest class level in which textbooks in mathematics and natural
science were printed in the languages of 45 ethnic groups at seven
time points in the Soviet period. These are not all the languages in
which texts were published, but include only those examined in our
later analysis. In deriving this information from the Ezhegodnik,
only texts in mathematics and science were counted, for two reasons.
First, in some subjects, such as language, literature, and history,
texts are used by non-Russian pupils enrolled in Russian-language
schools either in the study of the national language as a subject in
school or as supplementary reading outside the classroom; whether
texts were published in mathematics and science in the national language is therefore a more reliable indication that the national language is in fact the principal medium of instruction in the schools.
Second, whether or not a language is employed as the medium of instruction in mathematics and science is a rigorous indicator of the
degree to which members of the nationality are encouraged to view
fluency in Russian as a prerequisite for obtaining advanced or specialized training and skilled jobs. School language policy thus structures the incentives and opportunities for upward social mobility for
members of a nationality or speakers of a particular language.

        Languages are grouped in Table 8.1 according to the current
status of the official republic or province of the national group in the
Soviet federal system. The figures reveal that union republic nationalities have consistently benefited from mathematics and science
courses in their traditional languages through complete secondary
education. Certain other groups, such as the Bashkirs, Karakalpaks,
and Volga Tatars, also have been consistently favored. Most striking about the long-term trends, however, is that whereas in the 1935
figures single-nationality autonomous republic groups fared just as
well as union republic nationalities, since the 1950s these groups
have suffered a serious decline in the availability of native-language
schooling. Over the 34-year span represented in the table, there
has been both a general decline in the average number of years of
native-language schooling and a growing disparity in treatment

TABLE 8.1

Highest Grade Level at Which Textbooks Were Reported
Printed in Mathematics and Natural Science,
by Language and Year of Printing, 1935-69

Current Status of National Region of Corresponding Nationality	Year of Printing						
	1935	1942–45	1950	1955	1960	1965	1969
Union republics							
Armenian	9	8	10	10	10	10	10
Azerbaidzhani	10	10	10	10	10	10	10
Belorussian	10	9	10	10	10	10	10
Estonian	[3][a]	11	10	11	10	10	10
Georgian	10	10	11	10	10	10	10
Kazakh	9	10	10	10	10	10	10
Kirghiz	8	8	10	10	10	10	10
Latvian	[8]	9	10	10	10	10	10
Lithuanian	[0]	1	10	10	10	10	10
Moldavian	9	8	10	10	10	10	10
Tadzhik	9	5	10	10	10	10	10
Turkmenian	9	8	10	10	10	10	10
Ukrainian	10	10	10	10	10	10	10
Uzbek	10	8	10	10	10	10	10
Single-nationality Autonomous republics							
Abkhazian	2	0	0	0	4	4	4
Bashkir	8	7	10	10	10	10	10
Buriat	5	10	9	8	6	6	6
Chuvash	10	10	7	9	7	4	4
Kalmyk	5	0	0	0	2	0	0
Karakalpak	8	5	10	10	10	8	9
Karelian	8	0	0	0	0	0	0
Komi (Zyrian)	8	6	7	6	4	0	1
Mari[b]	7	7	6	6	4	4	1
Mordvinian[b]	9	8	7	6	4	4	3
Ossetian[b]	8	7	7	4	4	0	0
Tatar (Kazan)	9	10	10	10	10	10	10
Tuvinian	[0]	[0]	9	7	7	7	8
Udmurt	9	5	7	6	4	0	2
Yakut	7	4	9	6	7	6	6
Other autonomous republics and autonomous provinces							
Adygei	4	4	0	3	4	0	2
Altai	0	0	6	4	6	0	4
Balkar	4	0	0	0	2	0	0

TABLE 8.1 (continued)

Current Status of National Region of Corresponding Nationality	Year of Printing						
	1935	1942-45	1950	1955	1960	1965	1969
Chechen	4	3	0	0	0	0	0
Cherkess (Kabardian)	3	4	9	4	4	0	0
Dagestani groups							
Nogai	4	4	3	2	4	0	0
Avar	5	4	4	3	4	0	0
Dargin	0	4	4	0	4	1	0
Kumyk	4	4	4	4	3	0	0
Lak	4	1	4	3	3	0	2
Lezghian	4	4	4	2	4	1	0
Ingush	4	3	0	0	1	0	0
Kabardins	3	4	9	4	4	0	0
Karachai	4	0	0	0	0	0	0
Khakas	4	7	9	2	4	0	2
National Okrugs							
Komi-Permiak	8	6	4	2	4	0	1
Average (with exclusions)[c]	6.5	5.6	6.6	5.8	6.1	4.6	4.8
Coefficient of variation	.450	.609	.575	.681	.563	1.002	.928

[a]Figures are given in brackets when no official territory of the nationality was included within the boundaries of the USSR at the time. Figures pertain only to books published within the Soviet Union and reported to the Ministry of Culture.

[b]Textbooks were printed in two major dialects for both the Mari and the Mordvinians. Figures given here for each language are the highest year for either dialect of that language. In the case of the Ossetians, one cannot distinguish whether Ossetians in the North Ossetian ASSR or the South Ossetian Autonomous Oblast (AO) benefited equally from texts published in Ossetian. There is similar uncertainty regarding the availability of texts to dispersed populations of the various nationalities.

[c]Averages are based on all languages except those whose figures are given in brackets for a particular year.

Source: Relevant annual volumes of Ministerstvo Kul'tury, Vsesoiuznaia Knizhnaia Palata, Ezhegodnik knigi SSSR (Moscow).

between the languages of union republic nationalities and the languages of most other groups. Even with these changes, however, the relative rankings of languages between and within the status categories show moderate to strong continuity over time. For example, the product-moment correlation between the maximum number of years of available native-language schooling for 1935 and 1960 is about .9 (for the 41 groups that had official territories in the USSR at both time points). If one excludes the groups having union republic status, the correlation between the 1935 and 1960 measures for the remaining national languages is about .5. The persistence of school policy variation over time, coupled with the fact that there is only a very weak correlation between school language policy in 1935 and the degree of linguistic russification that had been attained by the non-Russian groups at the time, allows us to treat school language policy as a potential independent contributor to the levels of linguistic russification registered in the 1970 census. *

Since non-Russian children who continue in school beyond the maximum number of available years of native-language schooling generally switch to schools or classes where Russian is the medium of instruction, one should expect to find an inverse relationship between the availability of native-language schools and spread of the Russian language. Accordingly, one might formulate the following hypothesis:

Proposition 6. The lower the maximum number of years in which national-language schools are available to non-Russian children, the greater will be the proportion of members of the national group who have learned Russian.

---

*That early school-language policy was not predicated on the degree of linguistic russification that had already been achieved among the non-Russian peoples can be supported by the fact that the product-moment correlation between the percent of the 1926 population that claimed Russian as a native language and the provision of native-language schools in 1935 is only about -.2. Instead, variation in the availability of native-language schools in the 1930s appears to have been determined to a considerable extent by the size of the population of the nationality: the larger the population, the greater the number of years of native-language schooling that were provided. The product-moment correlation between population size (transformed by log function) and 1935 school-language policy is about .8. In fact, population size has a stronger correlation with 1935 school policy than does the formal status of the group in the federal system.

It should be noted that since children attending national-language schools study Russian as a separate subject, the longer pupils remain in school, the greater will be their exposure to Russian, regardless of which language serves as the principal medium of instruction. At the same time, even where non-Russians attend Russian-language schools, they usually can study their traditional national languages as a separate subject. Except for members of nationalities residing outside their official national territories (or, in some cases, residing outside major regions of settlement of their ethnic group) or members of nationalities ranking lower than autonomous province in the federal structure, study of the national language as a separate subject was almost universally available in 1972 through at least the eighth year of formal schooling.[12] For all ethnic groups examined here, children residing within the boundaries of their national republics or provinces could study the national language as a separate subject through at least the eighth year. The average for the 45 groups was 9.3 years in 1972. For the same groups, however, the maximum number of years in which the national language could serve as the principal medium of instruction averaged 5.0 years in 1972. Therefore, these groups have simultaneously experienced an opportunity to gain literacy in their traditional national languages and a strong stimulus to learn Russian. This arrangement can be expected to be conducive in the long run to the development of widespread bilingualism.

One might therefore argue, contrary to Proposition 6, that as long as the traditional national language is maintained as a separate subject of study in the schools, little displacement of the national language by Russian as a mother tongue is likely to result from school language policy. But the considerable variation in the availability of national-language schools could well be strongly related to the spread of Russian as a second language, since the greater the number of years in which the child must study Russian or in Russian, the greater will be the opportunity and practical need to gain fluency in Russian.

Publications

A second measure of language policy that also is closely related to the official status of the nationality is policy regarding publications. The abundance or scarcity of publications in a given language reflects not only the degree of official recognition of the importance of the language but also the structuring of social opportunities for the speakers of the language. There is a great deal of variation in the production of books and periodicals in different languages-- much more variation than one would expect judging solely from the relative population sizes of the ethnic groups.[13]

Instead of attempting to link the number of publications in the national languages to levels of linguistic russification, this study will test whether there is a link between the variety of publications available in the national languages and the levels of linguistic russification of the non-Russian groups. Following up the efforts of Soviet linguists to create a theoretical framework for classifying languages by their social or functional development, Paul Hall has characterized the social-functional development of 67 Soviet languages by examining the variety of topic areas in which books and brochures were published during the 1960s.[14] Relying on information provided in Ezhegodnik knigi SSSR about the languages and topic areas of all books published in the Soviet Union in 1960, 1966, 1968, and 1969, Hall placed each language on a seven-point scale based on the number of different topic areas in which publications appeared. The 34 topic areas employed in the source books served as the basis of Hall's classification. The fewer the number of topics under which books appeared for a given language, the lower the functional development of the language. For example, for the year 1960 a language in which no books or brochures were published was classified at level 1 on Hall's scale of functional development; a language with books and brochures appearing under one to three topic headings was classified at level 2; and so on.

Languages at successively higher levels of functional development not only had books and brochures published in a larger number of topic areas but also had titles in a larger number of the more technical and scientific fields. For example, languages classified at level 4 had publications in from 9 to 14 categories, including government and law, education, health, history, and international relations, but not science and technology; while languages classified at level 5 had books in 15 to 20 topic areas, including not only most of the topics covered by level 4 languages but also the natural sciences, mathematics, and engineering. Languages at level 6 had publications in 22 to 33 topic areas and included (in addition to the topics covered by the level 5 languages) books on statistics, political economy, and finance. The criteria for locating languages on particular levels are more complex than can be described here, but one should note that the relative rankings of the languages were quite stable over the four years to which the classification scheme was applied--although there was a noticeable decline during the 1960s in the functional sophistication of the publications in a number of languages, a trend closely paralleling the decline in the availability of native-language schools during the same period for nationalities ranking lower than union republic in the federal system.

In 1960 only in Russian were books and brochures published in all 34 topic areas; Russian was therefore uniquely classified at

level 7. At the same time, the languages of all the other union republic nationalities were classified at level 6, and the languages of
all autonomous republic and autonomous province nationalities were
classified at level 5 and below (with the exception of Tatar, which
was located at level 6). Although there are a few conspicuous anomalies (for example, Karelian, which, despite the high official standing of the Karelian Autonomous Republic, was placed at level 1),
there is a strong overall correlation between the rank of a group's
basic national area in the federal hierarchy and the rank of its national language on Hall's scale of functional development.

Just as the availability of native-language schools may reflect
the hierarchy of opportunities and incentives for the maintenance of
the national language or the learning of Russian, so might the functional sophistication of the publications in non-Russian languages affect an individual's opportunities and incentives to learn Russian as
a vehicle for social advancement. A language's sociological completeness may structure the life choices of its speakers. Accordingly, the following hypothesis deserves examination:

Proposition 7.   The higher the level of functional development of a
                 language, the lower the proportion of the members
                 of the corresponding nationality who will be fluent
                 in Russian.

Although the ability to employ a language for varied social purposes
may thus shape the efforts of group members to learn Russian or the
national language, languages with low levels of functional development
(though not those at level 1) still have some publications, chiefly in
such areas as artistic literature, educational materials, public
health, and Marxism-Leninism. This minimal support for the national languages may provide a basis for maintenance of the traditional language as a mother tongue, even while the varied levels of
functional completeness of the publications in the language affect the
propensity to learn Russian as a second language.

One potential drawback to applying Hall's measure in the present
study is that a language's functional development may be just as much
a result as it is a cause of language maintenance or shift. Unlike
school policy, which appears (at least until the 1960s) not to have been
predicated on the level of linguistic russification already achieved by
the population, publications policy may have been continually adjusted
to reflect changes in the language behavior of the non-Russian population. * Those who set publications policy or are involved in everyday

---

*There is some evidence that as the availability of native-
language schools was being curtailed for several non-Russian

decisions about which books or brochures to publish would not print many books in a language if most members of the corresponding nationality lacked literacy in the language. Because we have not determined how much long-term continuity there has been in the hierarchy of functional development observed by Hall, we should be cautious about inferring from correlations between publications policy and linguistic russification that policy is the cause and russification the effect. On the other hand, the stratification of opportunities for instruction in the native language in schools suggests a conscious and enduring policy of restricting the opportunities for speakers of particular languages and of encouraging the development of fluency in Russian. In addition, it is of some interest at least to depict the relationship, if any, between the functional development of publications in the non-Russian languages and the spread of Russian among the non-Russian nationalities--although one must be cautious about imputing causality to this relationship and aware that the possibility of a reciprocal causal relationship means that the strength of the measured effect of functional development on linguistic russification may be exaggerated.

DATA AND MEASURES

The statistical analysis examines the impact of the demographic, cultural, and political factors on the linguistic russification of 45 non-Russian nationalities. These are the titular nationalities of all national territories in the Soviet federal system that have the rank of autonomous province, autonomous republic, and union republic.*

---

nationalities in the 1960s, the timing of the transfer to Russian as the medium of instruction was based in part on the prevailing level of bilingualism in the community. See Brian Silver, "The Status of National Minority Languages in Soviet Education," Soviet Studies 26 (January 1974): 35.

*Ossetians residing in the North Ossetian Autonomous Republic and Ossetians in the South Ossetian Autonomous Province are included as separate units or cases. Therefore, the study includes 45 nationalities but 46 "cases." Data for the Buriats employed here refer to the Buriats residing in the Buriat ASSR only. The Komi Permiaks, whose official territory has national okrug status, are included because of the close kinship between the Komi Permiaks and several neighboring groups that are included: Mari, Udmurts, Mordvinians, and (to a lesser degree) Chuvash.

Excluded from the analysis are the Jews, whose official Jewish Autonomous Province cannot be considered the homeland of Soviet Jews, and a few other groups (such as the Ajars and the numerous ethnic groups inhabiting the Pamir region of the Tadzhik Republic) that occupy officially autonomous territories but are not ethnically or linguistically distinguished in the 1970 census figures. In the few instances where two nationalities are recognized in the title of a province or republic (such as the Chechen-Ingush ASSR), both groups are considered. For the Dagestan Autonomous Republic, five nationalities are included. (A complete list of the nationalities examined is given in the appendix to this chapter.)

The statistical analysis centers only on that portion of each nationality that inhabits its official territory. Exclusion of dispersed populations allows one to distinguish the impact of the hypothesized factors from the impact of geographical dispersion. This procedure is especially important if we are to assess the effect of differential language policy on the spread of Russian, because the measures of language policy apply primarily to the members of a nationality who reside within their home territories. Although many non-Russians do receive native-language schools and publications outside their own republics (for example, Central Asian nationalities have native-language schools in more than one Central Asian republic), many do not--especially if they reside either in the Russian Republic or in areas not contiguous to their own republics or provinces. Discussion of the impact of geographic dispersion must be omitted in order to keep the present study to manageable size.[15]

Except for the measures of language policy, the data employed here come from the 1970 census report, which presents tabular breakdowns of the ethnic populations according to language use, territorial dispersion, urban-rural residence, age, and (for some nationalities) sex.[16] Because the population distributions on these variables are reported in multivariate contingency tables, we have direct cross-tabulations of such factors as nationality, language, and place of residence. Consequently, the problem of making inferences solely from the marginal distributions of these variables is avoided.* However, the data are aggregated into broad urban and

---

*However, estimates of the relative impact of the predictor variables on linguistic russification may still be distorted by the aggregation procedures employed in the census report. By relying almost exclusively on unstandardized regression coefficients rather than standardized regressors, one may mitigate distortion due to aggregation. Nevertheless, all of the predictors employed here are aggregate variables. Even if one avoids simply correlating "per-

rural population categories. With few exceptions, more detailed breakdowns of the ethnic populations by occupation, educational attainment, or units other than relatively gross, territorially defined aggregates are not available.*

The Language Measures

Three dependent variables are used in the analysis: the percentage of non-Russians who claim Russian as a native language, the percentage who claim Russian as a second language, and the sum of these two percentages (or the percentage who claim Russian as either a native or a second language). The census figures on language are derived through questions asking respondents to identify their native language (rodnoi iazyk) and any other language of the peoples of the USSR that they may "freely command" (svobodno vladet').

----

centage urbanized" with "percentage linguistically russified," our hypotheses concern the behavior of aggregates such as "urbanites" and "ruralites," relatively gross categories that necessarily obscure the variation within the urban and rural populations.

*For a few of the larger republics the census report provides breakdowns into smaller territorial units. I have not tried to incorporate these units into the present analysis. The census provides no information on the occupational structures of separate nationalities. One could, however, introduce the rather plentiful information on education as another explanatory factor. I did attempt to determine the possible effects of educational differences on linguistic russification in preliminary work with the data; but in part because differences in education are so closely correlated with urbanization, once the effects of the factors identified in propositions 1 through 5 are accounted for, educational differences had a decidedly small impact on rates of linguistic russification.

The method of transforming the data from tabular form to individual units of analysis suitable for electronic data processing is reported in Brian Silver, "Social Mobilization and the Russification of Soviet Nationalities," American Political Science Review 68 (March 1974): 45-66. The basic unit of analysis is not actually the nationality, but the urban or rural segment of each nationality. For each nationality the urban and rural populations become separate units of analysis or cases. Since data for 46 regions are employed, 92 such "cases" are created--46 urban and 46 rural.

Although the ambiguities of the census measures have been discussed frequently by Soviet scholars, there is little published research that attempts to test the validity and reliability of the measures.[17] Perhaps the most serious question of validity concerns the relationship between the census figures on language and actual language use. Especially ambiguous is the concept of "native language," which the census respondents might variously interpret to mean the language of their childhood, the language of their nationality, the language they know best, or the language they use most frequently. One Soviet scholar has suggested that the figures on native language may reflect language preference rather than actual language use.[18] In the present study I follow the practice of most Soviet scholars in treating the measure of native language as either the preferred language or the language the respondent knows best, but one cannot determine how extensively or in which social contexts the language may actually be employed. However, on the basis of independent survey evidence published by Soviet researchers, we should acknowledge that some non-Russians who claim a particular language as native no longer know or use it.[19]

At first glance, one might be surprised at how large a proportion of non-Russians claims fluency in Russian as a second language, and one might suspect that the test of fluency is weak. But since numerous independent surveys by Soviet social scientists attest to the rather high levels of knowledge of Russian as a second language among non-Russians, the census figures might not be far wrong.[20] Furthermore, it is important to observe that in recent discussions of the program of the 1979 census at an all-union conference of statisticians, a proposal was considered and rejected that the wording of the census question be changed from "freely command" to simply "command."[21] Hence, even though the 1970 census enumerators applied no formal tests of the linguistic abilities of the respondents, the wording of the census question may have constituted a strong test of fluency. In addition, one should bear in mind that the census-taking process itself may be an important constraint on reported language use. Since, with few exceptions, enumerators visited each household, respondents may well have been reluctant to claim free command of Russian or another language if in fact they could not speak it well. In this study I shall assume that reported free command of a second language indicates use of this language effectively in some important social activities, but I cannot directly validate this assumption.

The Explanatory Variables

A few features of the independent variables deserve special attention. First, the gross units of aggregation in the census report prevent precise measurement of interethnic contact. The Soviet census provides no breakdown of the population into census-tract units comparable with those of the United States census. Nor does it provide breakdowns of the ethnic populations for specific cities and towns (except for the capital cities of union republics). The operational measure of interethnic contact employed here is the "percentage of the population of a given administrative unit that is Russian." The Russian percentage of the population is calculated for the urban and rural areas separately, so that, for example, the "contact with Russians" experienced by rural Uzbeks is measured as the "percentage of the rural population of Uzbekistan that is Russian."

Questions have been raised elsewhere about the validity of such a measure of contact.[22] Given that we must rely upon aggregate census data, not field or survey research, we cannot actually determine the extent of contact among groups. The measure can be said only to approximate the probability of, or the opportunity for, contact among members of different groups. The obvious problem is that the gross units of aggregation preclude a true measure of contact among individuals of different ethnic groups; one can discern neither the extent of deliberate avoidance of contact nor the specific social contexts within which actual contact occurs. Nevertheless, this crude measure of contact will be shown to have a very strong ability to predict levels of linguistic russification.

In the later analysis, groups will be classified by traditional religion, not by their present religiosity. The measure of traditional religion is not meant to designate current religious practice, because no systematic data on such practice are available. Groups are labeled as "traditionally Orthodox," "traditionally Islamic," and so forth, according to the religious conviction held by most members of the given nationality in the nineteenth century. The concept of traditional religion can perhaps be most fruitfully interpreted as an indicator of the degree of cultural distance between Russians and non-Russians. Even where most group members no longer adhere to particular religious dogmas or religiously sanctioned customs, remnants of religious beliefs and practices may still survive, though perhaps lacking their strictly religious connotations. These remnants or survivals may well have a serious impact on intergroup relations. Thus, it has been observed that the Muslim intellectual of the Soviet Union today "may be indifferent to religious dogma and practice, but . . . remains attached to the whole body of customs and traditions which make up the special character of the Muslim way of life."[23] Attachment to the community of believers apparently still carries strong sanctions against intermarriage with non-Muslims.[24] One would expect such attitudes also to inhibit shift to

Russian as a native language because adoption of Russian could be viewed as a rejection of the community of believers.

On the other hand, groups that belonged to the Eastern Orthodox Church, especially those that converted to Orthodoxy as a result of the work of Russian missionaries in the centuries before the Revolution, should have fewer ideological barriers to close interpersonal relations with Russians. To be sure, some Orthodox groups might possess particular customs or historical experiences that inhibit russification. Moreover, the Armenians adhered to a distinct branch of the Orthodox Church, while many Ukrainians were affiliated with the Uniate Church. But for all groups that are close to Russians in traditional religion, at least one major barrier to assimilation by the Russians--one major source of cultural distance--should have been removed. In sum, the classification of Soviet ethnic groups as traditionally Muslim or traditionally Orthodox should be viewed not as a perfect indicator of cultural similarity to Russians, but as a surrogate measure that should reflect such similarity to a significant degree.

THE EFFECTS OF DEMOGRAPHIC AND CULTURAL FACTORS

Urban-Rural Differences in Linguistic Russification

The data in Table 8.2 illustrate that urbanites are more extensively russified linguistically than are ruralites. On the average, a 6.9 percentage point larger proportion of urban non-Russians than of rural non-Russians claimed Russian as a native language in 1970. For all 46 groups, urbanites displayed a stronger attraction to Russian as a native language than did ruralites. A similar relationship holds for the adoption of Russian as a second language: ruralites lagged an average of 19.7 percentage points behind urbanites in adopting Russian as a second language; and for all but two nationalities, urbanites showed a stronger attraction to Russian as a second language than did ruralites.* Summing the percentage of non-Russians

---

*The two exceptions are the Komi and the Udmurts, both of which display rather high percentages claiming Russian as a native language among urban populations, thereby limiting the percentage who could possibly claim Russian as a second language. For both of these nationalities, the total percentage that claimed fluency in Russian as either a native or a second language was larger among urban than among rural residents.

who claimed Russian as either a native or a second language, one finds an average difference of 26.5 percentage points between the proportions of urban and rural non-Russians who could speak Russian. Furthermore, within all 46 groups, urbanites were more russified linguistically than were ruralites. Thus the 1970 census data support proposition 1.

TABLE 8.2

Mean Percentages of Non-Russians Linguistically
Russified, by Urban-Rural Residence, 1970

Place of Residence	Percent Who Speak Russian as		
	Native Language	Second Language	Native or Second Language
Urban	8.3	63.7	72.0
Rural	1.4	44.0	45.5
Difference	6.9	19.7	26.5
Number of cases where urban exceeds rural	46	44	46
Total cases	46	46	46

Source: Compiled by the author.

Contact and Linguistic Russification

The figures in Table 8.2 can reveal nothing about the underlying causes of the urban-rural differences. However, we would expect from proposition 2 that for both urban and rural non-Russians, levels of linguistic russification will be directly correlated with the extent of contact between natives and Russians. Moreover, the urban-rural differences in language use could result simply from the greater contact between natives and Russians in urban areas, and not from any special susceptibility of urbanites to learning Russian. To test this hypothesis, we must determine whether at comparable levels of contact with Russians, urbanites display greater levels of linguistic russification than do ruralites. Evidence concerning this hypothesis is presented in Figures 8.1-8.3.

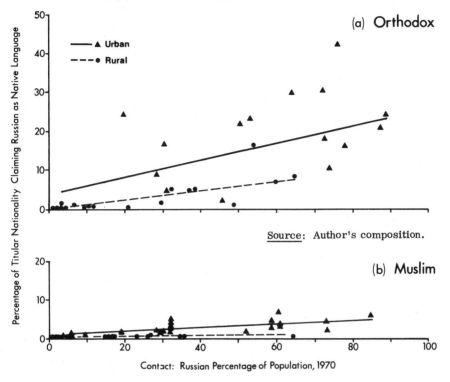

FIGURE 8.1

The Effect of Contact on Shift to Russian as a Native Language
among (a) Orthodox and (b) Muslim Nationalities

Source: Author's composition.

Contact: Russian Percentage of Population, 1970

Each figure displays the relationship between the Russian percentage of the (urban or rural) population of the republic or province
(on the horizontal axis) and the percentage of the titular nationality
who claimed knowledge of Russian in 1970 (on the vertical axis). A
different measure of linguistic russification is used in each figure.
The dots in the scattergrams in Figures 8.1 and 8.2 represent separate nationalities. The lines in each figure are the least-squares
regression lines, which may be interpreted as the estimated average
value of the dependent variable (linguistic russification) at each level
of the independent variable (Russian percentage of the population).*

---

*Each regression line represents the best-fitting form of the
relationship between the percentage of Russians and the extent of
linguistic russification. Using ordinary least-squares regression,
the best fit was determined by a series of steps. First, for each

FIGURE 8.2

The Effect of Contact on Acquisition of Russian as Second Language

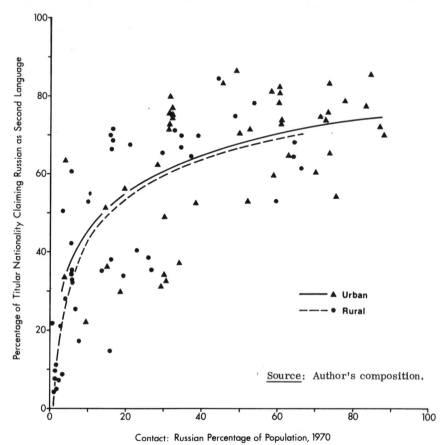

Contact: Russian Percentage of Population, 1970

dependent variable and setting, the relationship between contact and linguistic russification was plotted on a scattergram. Then, several plausible linear and nonlinear functions (log functions, second- and third-order polynomials) were estimated. The best fit in each case was determined by examining the size of the $\bar{R}^2$ (the proportion of the variance accounted for, adjusted for degrees of freedom) achieved by the alternative functional forms. Only if specification of a nonlinear function increased the $\bar{R}^2$ by at least 5 percentage points over the linear function was the nonlinear function given preference. This rule was adopted to simplify the analysis and presentation here, while producing a small reduction in the precision of the

FIGURE 8.3

The Effect of Contact on Percentage of Orthodox and Muslim
Nationalities Speaking Russian as either Native or Second Language

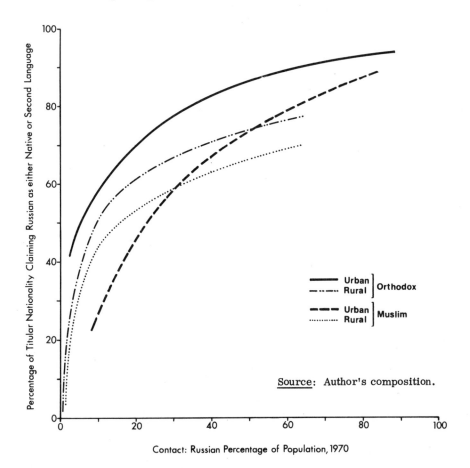

Source: Author's composition.

Contact: Russian Percentage of Population, 1970

estimates based on the regression lines. The equations used to generate the regression lines in Figures 8.1 through 8.3 are given below. In a few of the relationships a quadratic function had a margin-
ally better fit than did a log function. To facilitate comparison and
visual presentation here, however, whenever both a log and a quadratic nonlinear function provided a substantially better fit than a
linear one, a log function was chosen to represent the best-fitting
form of the relationship.

Rather than summarizing the link between the presence of Russians and the spread of Russian language in a single regression line for each figure, several lines are drawn. For example, in Figure 8.1,

---

Figure 8.1

Orthodox urban (N = 18)

$R_{nat} = 3.0 + .275C$ $\qquad\qquad \bar{R}^2 = .385$ (eq. 1)

(Sig.) (.512) (.004)

Orthodox rural (N = 18)

$R_{nat} = -0.6 + .153C$ $\qquad\qquad \bar{R}^2 = .541$ (eq. 2)

(Sig.) (.603) (<.001)

Muslim urban (N = 22)

$R_{nat} = 1.0 + .0368C$ $\qquad\qquad \bar{R}^2 = .257$ (eq. 3)

(Sig.) (.145) (.009)

Muslim rural (N = 22)

$R_{nat} = 0.6 + .00547C$ $\qquad\qquad \bar{R}^2 = .410$ (eq. 4)

(Sig.) (.039) (.001)

where

R_{nat} = Russian native language: percentage of the titular nationality of the republic or province that claimed Russian as a native language in 1970

C = contact: percentage of the (urban or rural) population of the region that was Russian in 1970.

Figure 8.2

Urban (N = 46)

$R_{sec} = 13.0 + 31.8(\lg_{10}C)$ $\qquad\qquad \bar{R}^2 = .319$ (eq. 5)

(Sig.) (.242) (<.001)

Rural (N = 46)

$R_{sec} = 10.4 + 33.0(\lg_{10}C)$ $\qquad\qquad \bar{R}^2 = .626$ (eq. 6)

(Sig.) (.023) (<.001)

lines are drawn summarizing the relationship between the presence of Russians and adoption of Russian as a native language among Muslims residing in urban areas, Muslims in rural areas, Orthodox in urban areas, and Orthodox in rural areas. Attempting to depict the relationship with a single line would be very misleading because the effect of contact on the adoption of Russian as a native language strongly depends on whether non-Russians are Muslims or non-Muslims, and on whether they reside in urban or rural areas. In

where

R_{sec} = Russian second language: percentage of the titular nationality of the republic or province that claimed Russian as a second language in 1970

$lg_{10}C$ = log of contact: common logarithm of percentage of of the (urban or rural) population of the region that was Russian in 1970.

Figure 8.3

Orthodox urban

$$R_{tot} = 21.0 + 37.8(lg_{10}C) \qquad \bar{R}^2 = .665 \quad (eq. 7)$$

(Sig.) (.060) (<.001)

Orthodox rural

$$R_{tot} = 15.1 + 34.6(lg_{10}C) \qquad \bar{R}^2 = .724 \quad (eq. 8)$$

(Sig.) (.032) (<.001)

Muslim urban

$$R_{tot} = -42.8 + 68.4(lg_{10}C) \qquad \bar{R}^2 = .503 \quad (eq. 9)$$

(Sig.) (.084) (<.001)

Muslim rural

$$R_{tot} = 8.5 + 34.5(lg_{10}C) \qquad \bar{R}^2 = .575 \quad (eq. 10)$$

(Sig.) (.219) (<.001)

where

R_{tot} = total Russian speakers: percentage of the titular nationality of the republic or province that claimed Russian either as a native or as a second language in 1970. The other term is as defined for Figure 8.2.

Figure 8.2, even though the differences between urban and rural populations are slight, two lines are drawn to illustrate the small size of the urban-rural differences. The extent and nature of the interdependencies between contact, urban-rural residence, and traditional religion will be explored later.

As predicted in proposition 2, contact has a positive impact on the linguistic russification of both urban and rural non-Russians, regardless of the measure of linguistic russification examined. Not only is the slope of the regression line positive for each language measure and subset of the non-Russian population (with the single exception of the relationship between adoption of Russian as a native language and interethnic contact among rural Muslims, as we shall discuss later), but the single measure of interethnic contact accounts for a substantial proportion of the variance in linguistic russification. That is, taking into consideration the degree of contact between the indigenous nationalities and Russians helps us to account for a large proportion of the intergroup differences in levels of linguistic russification.

But the graphs in Figure 8.1 reveal that the slopes of the regression lines are distinctively steeper for the urban than for the rural populations. Moreover, at each level of contact with Russians, urban non-Russians are much more likely to claim Russian as a native language than are rural non-Russians. Therefore, differences in contact alone do not account for the greater propensity of urbanites to claim Russian as a native language. However, data on second-language use suggest a different conclusion. As Figure 8.2 reveals, the relationship between the presence of Russians and the adoption of Russian as a second language differs very little between urban and rural non-Russians. Only at the tails of the contact dimension do the two populations differ much in second-language acquisition; but since there are few cases where the Russian proportion of the urban population is very low (less than 10 percent) and few cases where the Russian proportion of the rural population is very high (more than 60 percent), the urban-rural differences cannot be reliably compared at the extremes of the distributions. With regard to second language, then, the data in Figure 8.2 tend to contradict proposition 3, since urban-rural differences in second-language acquisition are almost negligible. The evidence tends, rather, to support the alternative, proposition 3a, which predicts that at comparable levels of contact between Russians and non-Russians, urban-rural differences in the acquisition of Russian as a second language should disappear.[25] Acquisition of Russian as a second language thus appears to be strongly determined by the incentives and opportunities to learn Russian associated with the presence of Russians in the national areas, but is not mediated by possible differences in the values of urban and rural non-Russians.

In sum, the impact of interethnic contact on the linguistic russification of non-Russians varies according to residence in an urban or
rural setting and to the measure of russification employed. Consistent with proposition 2, contact is positively related to the level of
linguistic russification for both residential settings and for all measures of russification. But proposition 3 receives mixed support:
when russification is measured by native-language preference, contact has a much greater impact on the shift to Russian among urbanites than among ruralites; but when russification is measured by
second-language preference, urban-rural differences in the impact
of contact on linguistic russification are negligible. To be sure,
urbanites in general are more likely than ruralites to adopt Russian
as a second language, because, on the average, urban populations
contain more than twice as large a percentage of Russians as do
rural populations (47 versus 20 percent). But where the proportions
of Russians in urban and rural areas are similar, urban and rural
non-Russians are almost equally likely to acquire Russian as a
second language.

Similarly, Figure 8.3, which depicts the relationship between
interethnic contact and the percentage of non-Russians who speak
Russian as either a native or a second language, shows small differences between the knowledge of Russian among urban and rural non-
Russians at comparable levels of interethnic contact. Of course,
because this measure of linguistic russification is composed of the
sum of the percentages who claim Russian as a native and as a second
language, one should expect to find these urban-rural differences.
But the foregoing analysis makes clear that the differences are almost
entirely due to the effect of urbanization on adoption of Russian as a
native language. *

----

*The effects of interethnic contact, urban-rural residence,
and traditional religion are best expressed by the following complex
equation.

$$R_{tot} = 10.7 + 31.6(\lg_{10}C) + 4.71(U*\lg_{10}C) + 7.09(\emptyset*\lg_{10}C) \quad (eq.\ 12)$$

(Sig.) (.015) (<.001)   (.069)   (.003)

$$\overline{R}^2 = .697$$

$$N = 80$$

where
  R_{tot} = total Russian speakers
  $\lg_{10}C$ = contact

Traditional Religion and Linguistic Russification

Previous research has shown that traditional religion mediates the impact of demographic change on the adoption of Russian as a mother tongue. Ethnic groups that traditionally adhered to Islam are much less susceptible to language shift than are non–Muslim groups.[26] Certain other groups having either marked cultural differences from Russians or histories of strong opposition to Russian control also are slow to adopt Russian as a native language, even under demographic conditions normally conducive to such language shift. In contrast, groups that belonged to the Orthodox Church prior to the Revolution tend to acquire the Russian language much more readily. As John A. Armstrong has noted, upon becoming socially mobilized, Orthodox groups are especially receptive to adopting Russian as a language.[27]

This section analyzes both the degree of impact of traditional religion on linguistic russification and the means by which religion works in combination with the demographic variables to affect rates of russification. For the sake of clarity, the analysis of the impact of religion will include only the traditionally Muslim and Orthodox nationalities. Thus, three Buddhist groups and three non–Orthodox Christian groups are excluded. * These exclusions reduce the number

---

U = urban–rural (1 if urban, 0 if rural)

$\emptyset$ = religion (1 if Orthodox, 0 if Muslim)

$\emptyset * \lg_{10} C$ and

$U * \lg_{10} C$ = multiplicative interaction terms expressing the combined or joint effects of pairs of variables. The $\emptyset * \lg_{10} C$ term takes a value of $\lg_{10} C$ if the group is traditionally Orthodox and a value of zero if the group is Muslum; the $U * \lg_{10} C$ term takes a value of $\lg_{10} C$ if the group is urban and a value of zero if it is rural.

Note that the "main effects" of the urban–rural (U) and traditional religion ($\emptyset$) terms drop out once the interaction effects are specified. This equation will be employed as the basic form of the combined effects of the demographic and cultural variables on the total percentage of the non–Russian group that claimed knowledge of Russian in 1970.

*Two of the Buddhist groups (Tuvinians, Kalmyks) behave linguistically more like Muslims than like Orthodox groups, showing comparatively little shift to Russian as a native language as a result of urbanization and contact with Russians; but the third (the Buriats)

of cases in this part of the analysis from 46 to 40. At a later stage
of the analysis, once the relationship between traditional religion and
linguistic russification has been explored, the six groups will again
be included with the others.

The Impact of Religion on
Native Language Shift

The impact of urbanization and contact on the shift to Russian
as a native language was established above. As Figure 8.1 reveals,
the two factors substantially affect rates of adoption of Russian as a
native language within the Orthodox and Muslim categories as well;
but the impact of the two factors differs greatly depending on the traditional religion of the group. Indeed, among rural Muslims the
slope of the regression line between the measure of contact and adoption of Russian as a native language is not significantly different from
zero: a 10 percentage point increase in the Russian percentage of the
population is associated with an infinitesimal .05 of a percentage
point increase in the adoption of Russian as a native language. The
data reveal that Muslims adopt Russian as a native language only if
two conditions are met simultaneously: urbanization and contact with
Russians. Among Muslims contact has a substantial impact on the
shift of mother tongue to Russian only among urban populations, and
urbanization produces a shift of native tongue to Russian only where
there is interethnic contact. *

---

behaves more like the Orthodox groups by being fairly susceptible to
native-language shift. The three Christian groups all behave more
like the Muslims than like the Orthodox groups. Estonians, Latvians,
and Lithuanians all resist shift to Russian as a native language.

*The equation expressing this relationship is as follows (calcu-
lated for Muslim cases only):

$$R_{nat} = 0.3 + .050C*U \qquad\qquad \bar{R}^2 = .716 \quad (\text{eq. 13})$$

(Sig.) (.135) (<.001)   N = 44

where

C*U = multiplicative interaction term expressing the joint ef-
       fects of contact (C) and urban-rural residence (U) on
       the adoption of Russian as a native language in 1970

Note that the regression coefficients for the main effects of contact
(C) and urban-rural (U) were not significantly different from zero.
Thus, neither contact alone nor urbanization alone produces shift
of mother tongue among Soviet Muslim nationalities.

In contrast, among Orthodox nationalities contact has a measurable impact on the shift to Russian as a native language among both urban and rural populations, though the effect is much greater among urbanites than among ruralites. As one can see in Figure 8.1, contact with Russians has a stronger impact on rural Orthodox nationalities than it does on either rural or urban Muslims. At the same time, for both Orthodox and Muslim groups, contact alone produces relatively little shift to Russian, since the major impact of interethnic contact is produced jointly with urbanization. * Thus propositions 4 and 5 receive considerable support: not only are Muslims less susceptible to shifting to Russian as a native language than are Orthodox groups, whatever the extent of their contact with Russians, but the size of the effect of religion on the adoption of Russian depends on the demographic factors of urbanization and contact with Russians.

That the demographic and cultural factors have combined effects on shift of mother tongue deserves emphasis. Treating the three variables as if they each affected the adoption of Russian independently would greatly weaken our ability to predict the extent of shift of mother tongue. Of course, by following such an approach (that is, by assuming simple additive effects of the three variables on adoption of Russian) one can account for just over half of the intergroup variance in the adoption of Russian ($\overline{R}^2 = .528$).† But this assumes that

----

*The joint effect of contact and urban residence on shift to Russian as a native language among Orthodox nationalities is expressed in the following regression equation:

$$R_{nat} = 0.7 + .123C + .188C*U \qquad \overline{R}^2 = .617 \text{ (eq. 14)}$$

(Sig.) (.718) (.085) (.004)   N = 36

Note that the main effect of urban-rural residence (U) is not significantly different from zero and hence is omitted from equation 14. Although the coefficient for contact (C) in the equation is significant at only the .085 level, the term is left in as a reminder that C can produce shift to Russian as a native language among rural Orthodox groups (that is, when U is zero and hence the C*U term is also zero).

†The simple additive model (based only on Orthodox and Muslim cases) is

$$R_{nat} = -4.6 + .142C + 3.40U + 7.56\emptyset \qquad \overline{R}^2 = .528 \text{ (eq. 15)}$$

(Sig.) (<.001) (<.001) (.037) (<.001)   N = 80

where all terms are defined as before.

it is meaningful to estimate the effects of each of the variables as if they were constant over all values of the other two variables--that is, as if the effects of each variable did not depend simultaneously on the values of the other variables. By this approach one would estimate, for example, that on the average each increase of 10 percentage points in the proportion of the rural population that is Russian is associated with an increase of about 1.4 percentage points in the proportion of the titular nationality that claims Russian as a native language (holding constant the effects of traditional religion and residence in an urban or rural area). But this estimate of the independent effect of contact with Russians is misleading, because the effect of contact depends on the values of the other variables. For example, in combination with urbanization, contact has a much greater impact on shift to Russian as a mother tongue than it does alone (that is, among rural populations). Similarly, the effects of the other variables acting in combination are far greater than the sum of their separate effects. Expressing the joint or combined effects of the demographic and cultural variables substantially improves our ability to predict shift of mother tongue: the accounted-for variance increases from .528 to .716. *

The form of these combined effects is important. The results make it clear that shift to Russian as a native language does not occur in the absence of contact. Hence contact is a necessary condition for shift of mother tongue to Russian. Although this finding makes intuitive sense, it was not wholly expected, because contact is not a necessary condition for the learning of Russian as a second language. As Figure 8.2 shows, substantial learning of Russian as a second language occurs among non-Russians even where Russians constitute a small percentage of the population. The results also

---

*Based on Orthodox and Muslim cases only, and dropping terms whose coefficients are not significantly different from zero and whose omission does not affect the magnitudes of the coefficients that remain, the equation is as follows:

$$R_{nat} = 0.4 + .047C*U + .131C*\emptyset + .138C*U*\emptyset \qquad \bar{R}^2 = .716 \text{ (eq. 16)}$$

(Sig.) (.590) (.054)   (.001)   (.005) $N = 80$

where $C*U*\emptyset$ is a second-order interaction term expressing the joint or combined effects of contact, urban-rural, and religion, and the other terms are defined as before.

show that, on the average, contact between Russians and non-Russians
is related to shift to Russian as a native language only if one or both
of two other conditions are present: either non-Russians are members of a traditionally Orthodox nationality or they are urbanites. Intergroup contact is thus a necessary but not a sufficient condition for
shift to Russian as a mother tongue. In combination with other conditions, contact has a very strong bearing on shift to Russian as a native language. Even rural non-Russians adopt Russian as a native
language if they belong to a traditionally Orthodox nationality and come
into contact with Russians; and even Muslims adopt Russian as a native language if they reside in urban areas and experience contact
with Russians. Furthermore, non-Russians who are both urbanites
and traditionally Orthodox experience a special impulse toward adopting Russian as a native language when Russians are present. *

The Impact of Religion on
Second-Language Acquisition

In contrast with the strong role of traditional religion in
mediating the effects of interethnic contact and urbanization on shift
of native language, religion neither accelerates nor impedes

---

*To determine the estimated R_{nat} for specific subpopulations,
and to illuminate the special impulse toward adoption of Russian felt
by urban Orthodox groups, one may disaggregate the terms in equation 16. First, restating equation 16 by substituting b for the numerical coefficients yields

$$R_{nat} = b_0 + b_1 C^*U + b_2 C^*\emptyset + b_3 C^*U^*\emptyset$$

One may derive estimates of R_{nat} for each urban-rural by religion
category as follows:

Category	R_{nat} Equals
Rural Muslim	b_0
Urban Muslims	$b_0 + b_1 C$
Rural Orthodox	$b_0 + b_2 C$
Urban Orthodox	$b_0 + b_1 C + b_2 C + b_3 C$

Thus, one can now see the special impulse ($b_3 C$) toward adoption of
Russian experienced by urban Orthodox groups over and above the
sum of the effects produced by urbanism ($b_1 C$) and Orthodoxy ($b_2 C$)
alone.

the acquisition of Russian as a second language. For the groups included in this study, the average percentage of the population who
claimed Russian as a second language in 1970 was 63.4 among members of Orthodox nationalities residing in urban areas, 64.7 among
Muslim groups residing in urban areas, 49.8 among Orthodox nationalities residing in rural areas, and 39.7 among Muslims residing
in rural areas. Thus, even before one takes into consideration the
differing levels of interethnic contact experienced by Muslim and
Orthodox groups, there is little difference in the average percentage
of Muslims and Orthodox who claim Russian as a second language.
Once the extent of intergroup contact is taken into consideration, the
Orthodox-Muslim differences are not significantly different from
zero. *

---

*The initial test for religion differences in second-language
acquisition was presented in equation 11. The estimated average
2.25 percentage point higher level of knowledge of Russian among
Orthodox than among Muslim groups (after adjusting for the effects
of interethnic contact and urban-rural residence) is not significantly
different from zero (p = .492). Attempts to specify interaction effects
between the predictors reveals a slightly different but surprising result, however:

$$\text{(eq. 17)}$$

$$R_{sec} = 5.0 + 37.6(\lg_{10}C) - 2.8U + 15.9\emptyset + 1.57(U*\lg_{10}C) - 10.6(\emptyset*\lg_{10}C)$$

(Sig.) (.389) (.001)   (.820) (.061) (.847)   (.079)

$$\bar{R}^2 = .619$$
$$N = 80$$

From equation 17 one can observe that specifying a nonadditive model
increases the explained variance by a minuscule .60 of a percentage
point over the additive model in equation 11. Moreover, the regression coefficient for the interaction term between religion and contact
$(\emptyset*\lg_{10}C)$ is not significant at the .05 level. However, if despite
these observations one were to maintain the interaction term and the
adjustment to the intercept $(\emptyset)$ in the equation strictly for theoretical
reasons, one would have to conclude that although at very low levels
of interethnic contact, Orthodox groups display substantially higher
levels of knowledge of Russian as a second language than do Muslim
groups (judging by the 15.9 percentage point adjustment to the intercept), the rate of increase in acquisition of Russian as a second
language in response to increases in the presence of Russians is
substantially lower among the Orthodox groups than among the Muslims (judging by the negative sign of the adjustment to the slope in
the final term in equation 17).

There is some evidence of a link between traditional religion and knowledge of Russian as a second language among urban non-Russians (once the level of interethnic contact is held constant). In particular, as Figure 8.4 reveals, among urban populations Orthodox nationalities appear to be more receptive to learning Russian as a second language than are Muslim nationalities, when the percentage of Russians in the area is quite low.* For example, estimates of the average levels of knowledge of Russian as a second language among the indigenous populations reveal that where Russians constitute 20 percent of the urban population, among Orthodox nationalities an average of 58.3 percent of the population claim knowledge of Russian as a second language, while among Muslim nationalities an average of 44.3 percent claim such knowledge.† But as the Russian percentage of the urban population increases, the gap between Muslim and Orthodox nationalities closes and Orthodox groups come to lag behind Muslims in claiming Russian as a second language. For example, when Russians are 30 percent of the urban population, an average of 61.8 percent of the indigenous Orthodox population and 56.0 percent of the indigenous Muslim populations claim Russian as a second language. When Russians constitute 40 percent of the urban population, the percentages of Orthodox and Muslim non-Russians who claim Russian as a second language are nearly identical: 64.2 and 64.0, respectively. When the Russian proportion of the urban population

------

*The regression lines in Figure 8.4 were derived from separate equations calculated for each category.

Urban Orthodox
$$R_{sec} = 32.7 + 19.6(\lg_{10} C) \qquad \bar{R}^2 = .335 \qquad \text{(eq. 18)}$$

(Sig.) (.006) (.007) $N = 18$

Urban Muslims
$$R_{sec} = -40.2 + 65.2(\lg_{10} C) \qquad \bar{R}^2 = .497 \qquad \text{(eq. 19)}$$

(Sig.) (.092) (< .001) $N = 22$

†The estimates in this paragraph are derived from the following regression equation. Only urban cases are included.

$$R_{sec} = -40.2 + 65.2(\lg_{10} C) + 73.0\emptyset - 45.5(\emptyset^* \lg_{10} C) \quad \bar{R}^2 = .439 \text{ (eq. 20)}$$

(Sig.) (.058) (< .001)   (.004)   (.004) $N = 40$

Note the large negative slope adjustment in the final (interaction) term.

rises to 50 percent, an average of 66.5 percent of the Orthodox and 70.5 percent of the Muslim indigenous populations claim knowledge of Russian as a second language. The lag of Orthodox groups behind Muslims increases further as the percentage of Russians in the population continues to rise.

FIGURE 8.4

The Effect of Contact on Acquisition of Russian as Second Language among Orthodox and Muslim Nationalities

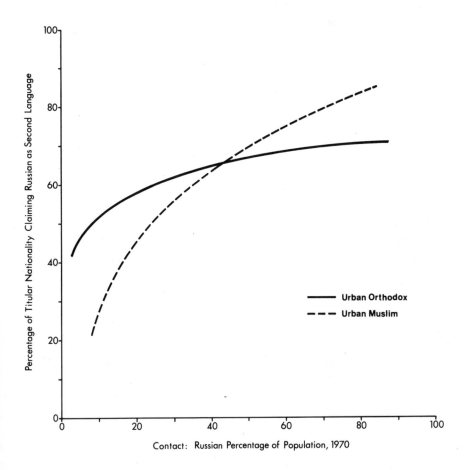

Source: Author's composition.

A hasty conclusion might be that Muslims are even more attracted to Russian than are Orthodox groups once the level of contact becomes very high. But on the contrary, previous evidence indicates that as the level of contact becomes very high, Orthodox groups shift to Russian as a native language in significant numbers, whereas Muslims do not. It is important here to recall the interdependence between the measures of native language and second language. If a non-Russian claims Russian as a native language, he cannot also claim it as a second language. Therefore, as the proportion of non-Russians who claim Russian as a native language increases, the proportion who could (at a maximum) claim Russian as a second language decreases. Consequently, because urban Orthodox non-Russians increasingly shift to Russian as a native language, the rate of increase in the percentage who claim Russian as a second language declines; in contrast, in similar demographic circumstances Muslims, who are not inclined to shift to Russian as a native language, increase their fluency in Russian as a second language at a faster rate than do Orthodox groups. The apparent effect of traditional religion on the acquisition of Russian as a second language among urban non-Russians probably is, therefore, largely attributable to the increasing adoption of Russian as a native language among Orthodox groups.*

In sum, there is very little difference in the propensity of urban Orthodox and Muslim groups to acquire Russian as a second language, in marked contrast with the strong impact of religion on native-language shift. This conclusion applies equally well to rural non-Russians. Hypothesis 5a therefore receives considerable support, since religion plays no direct role in either accelerating or retarding the acquisition of Russian as a second language.

---

*This explanation could be validated indirectly if, in place of the two terms ($\emptyset$ and $\emptyset*lg_{10}C$) expressing the effects of Orthodox religion, one substituted a term expressing the percentage of the population that claimed Russian as a native language. A further refinement might be to express this relationship only for cases where contact is relatively high and, hence, where shifting of mother tongue to Russian is likely to exert a downward constraint on the percentage of the population that could claim Russian as a second language. Using either procedure, one can account for virtually the same amount of variance in R_{sec} as one could in equation 20.

The Impact of Religion on
Linguistic Russification

We may now briefly consider how traditional religion affects the total percentage of non-Russians who claim Russian as a native or a second language. Because most acquisition of Russian is second-language acquisition rather than native-language shifting, one would expect religion to play a small but measurable role in the overall tendency to acquire Russian as either a second or a native language. Figure 8.3 presents the best-fitting regression lines for the relationship between interethnic contact and acquisition of Russian as either a second or a native language for four population groups.*

From the regression lines in Figure 8.3 and from the high proportion of the variance in the knowledge of Russian accounted for by the presence of Russians (the $\overline{R}^2$ ranges from .503 to .724 for the four subgroups), it is clear that the extent of contact with Russians has a strong bearing on the linguistic russification of non-Russian nationalities. Rural Muslims do appear to acquire Russian at a distinctively slower rate than the other three groups, while urban Orthodox nationalities appear to be especially receptive to learning Russian. Thus, with levels of interethnic contact held constant, Orthodox nationalities acquire Russian more readily than do Muslim nationalities. But the levels of linguistic russification among the four population categories are fairly close when Russians range between 20 and 60 percent of the population and where the greatest density of cases exists--and, hence, comparisons across categories are the most reliable. More important, as the evidence in Figures 8.1 and 8.2 makes clear, it is the special susceptibility of the Orthodox groups to shifting their native language to Russian, especially among urban residents, that appears to account for the religion-based differences in the knowledge of Russian.

THE EFFECTS OF LANGUAGE POLICY

The demographic and cultural factors account for a substantial proportion of the variation in levels of linguistic russification. Yet

---

*To facilitate comparisons, log transformations of the contact variable are used for all four categories even though in two categories quadratic functions produced slightly better fits.

to be determined is the extent to which variation in language policies can account for the remaining variation in russification. In the following analysis, I shall treat the demographic and cultural variables as a closed set. To assess the relation between language policy and linguistic russification, the effects of the demographic and cultural variables will be held constant (partialed out). No attempt will be made to test for joint or interaction effects between the demographic and cultural variables and the policy variables. All 46 cases are included in this part of the analysis. Restoring the six cases that were omitted from the examination of the effects of traditional religion introduces a very small amount of additional error in predicting linguistic russification from the demographic and cultural variables, but allows us to examine the effects of language policy on a larger number of groups.*

Native-Language Schools

Proposition 6 predicts that the lower the number of years in which primary and secondary schools with national language as the

---

*Employing all 46 cases (45 nationalities), the basic equations expressing the effects of the demographic and cultural variables on each measure of linguistic russification are as follows. Note that the dummy term for traditional religion here and in the remainder of the regression estimates takes a value of one if the group is traditionally Orthodox and zero if it is not. Thus the three Buddhist and the three Baltic groups are now categorized with the Muslim nationalities.

Native language Russian

$$R_{nat} = 0.3 + .0616C*U + .0132C*\emptyset + .0123C*U*\emptyset \quad \bar{R}^2 = .711 \quad \text{(eq. 21)}$$

(Sig.) (.614) (.003)   (<.001)   (.007) $N = 92$

Second language Russian

$$R_{sec} = 10.6 + 33.1(\lg_{10}C) \qquad\qquad\qquad \bar{R}^2 = .609 \quad \text{(eq. 22)}$$

(Sig.) (.009) (<.001) $N = 92$

Native or second language Russian

$$R_{tot} = 9.3 + 32.0(\lg_{10}C) + 7.59(\emptyset*\lg_{10}C) + 4.64(U*\lg_{10}C)$$

$$\bar{R}^2 = .697 \quad \text{(eq. 23)}$$

(Sig.) (.028) (<.001)   (.001)   (.055) $N = 92$

principal medium of instruction are available, the greater will be the proportion of the members of the national group who have learned Russian. The data on school language policy employed here refer to the 1958-59 school year. Both the information on the maximum number of years of available national schools (as of 1958) published by Soviet educators and the measure of science and mathematics textbook publications (as of 1959) were employed initially, since the two measures might have reflected slightly different aspects of native-language schooling. But since the results obtained with the two measures proved to be nearly identical, the estimates reported here will be based primarily on the 1958 school year information. On both measures, the maximum number of years of native-language primary and secondary education ranged from a high of 10 to a low of 0; the average number of years was 6.7 for the 1958 measure and 6.1 for the 1959 measure.

The simple product-moment correlations between the school measures and the three measures of linguistic russification are reported in Table 8.3. That the correlations are all in the expected direction lends support to the proposition that the existence of native-language schooling retards linguistic russification. But the simple correlation between school policy and native-language shift is so low that school policy does not account for a significant proportion of the variation in native-language shift (once the effects of the demographic and cultural variables are adjusted for). *

----

*Adding the 1958 school measure to the basic equation reduces the explained variance ($\overline{R}^2$) slightly, and the regression coefficient between adoption of Russian and school policy (S-1958) is not significantly different from zero.

$$R_{nat} = 0.7 + .0607C*U + .130C*\emptyset + .0125C*U*\emptyset - .0425(S-1958)$$

$$\text{(eq. 24)}$$

(Sig.) (.653) (.005)   (.001)   (.007)   (.804)

$$\overline{R}^2 = .708$$
$$N = 92$$

where
       S-1958 = school policy in 1958: maximum grade level in which schools were available where the national language served as the principal medium of instruction in 1958

A similar result occurs if one employs the 1959 measure of textbook publications in place of the 1958 measure.

TABLE 8.3

Correlations between Linguistic Russification and Maximum
Available Years of Native-Language Schooling, 1958 and 1959

| Year | Percent of Non-Russians Claiming Russian as | | |
	Native Language	Second Language	Native or Second Language
1958	-.211	-.600	-.571
1959	-.218	-.619	-.587

Source: Compiled by the author.

In marked contrast with its weak relationship to native-language shift, however, school policy not only has a moderate simple correlation with knowledge of Russian as a second language but also contributes a quite substantial 14 percentage points to the proportion of variance accounted for by the explanatory variables.* On the average, each additional year that national-language schooling was available is associated with a reduction of 3.2 percentage points in the proportion of the national group that claimed Russian as a second language in 1970 (with the effects of interethnic contact held constant).[†]

---

*Employing the same 1958 school measure, the result is as follows. (Compare with equation 22.)

$$R_{sec} = 38.9 + 28.0(\lg_{10}C) - 3.22(S{-}1958) \qquad \bar{R}^2 = .740 \qquad (eq.~25)$$

(Sig.) (<.001) (<.001)   (<.001)   N = 92

[†]The estimating equation is as follows:

$$R_{sec} = 28.1 + 27.2(\lg_{10}C) - 8.4(MD{-}S) - 22.0(HI{-}S) \quad \bar{R}^2 = .770 \quad (eq.~26)$$

(Sig.) (<.001) (<.001)   (.011)   (<.001)   N = 92

MD-S = moderate availability of national-language schooling
(MD-S = one if the maximum number of years is
seven to nine, and zero if not)

HI-S = high availability of national language schooling
(HI-S = one if the maximum number of years is ten,
and zero if not)

An alternative way to summarize the impact of school policy on the acquisition of Russian as a second language is to divide the nationalities into three broad categories of policy experience. The first category, which can be termed the high native-language school category, is composed of groups that had native-language schools in 1958 through complete secondary education (ten years). The second category benefited from a moderate number of years in which the national language could serve as the medium of instruction in schools: seven to nine years. The remaining nationalities can be considered as having a low availability of such schooling: six or fewer years of native-language schooling.

Employing these categories, further analysis of the data reveals that in comparison with the nationalities that had a maximum of six or fewer years of native-language schooling available in 1958 (the low category), groups that had a moderate number of years of such schooling had an 8.4 percentage point lower proportion of the population claiming Russian as a second language in 1970. Furthermore, in comparison with the same (low) category, among nationalities with a high availability of native-language schooling (ten years) a 22.0 percentage point lower proportion of the population claimed Russian as a second language in 1970.* Thus, with the effects of interethnic contact held constant, increases in the availability of national-language schooling are associated with large reductions in the proportion of non-Russians who claimed Russian as a second language.

From the foregoing analysis one would also expect to find a relationship between the availability of national-language schools and the total percentage of non-Russians who claim Russian as a native or a second language. Indeed, for each additional year of national-language schooling provided, there is an average decrease of 3.6 percentage points in the proportion of non-Russians who claimed a knowledge of Russian as a native or a second language

---

*The estimating equation is as follows:

$$(\text{eq. } 27)$$

$$R_{tot} = 41.9 + 24.0(\lg_{10}C) + 7.38(\emptyset^*\lg_{10}C) + 7.13(U^*\lg_{10}C) - 3.58(S-1958)$$

(Sig.) (<.001) (<.001)   (<.001)   (<.001)   (<.001)

$$\overline{R}^2 = .826$$

$$N = 92$$

in 1970. * Furthermore, it is important to note that the demographic, cultural, and school-language policy measures together can account for the overwhelming majority of the variation in knowledge of Russian: 83 percent of the variance in the percentage of non-Russians who in 1970 claimed knowledge of Russian as a native or a second language is accounted for by interethnic contact, urban-rural residence, traditional religion, and school-language policy. Thus the extent of linguistic russification is highly predictable once one takes into consideration a few important features of the demographic, cultural, and political settings of the nationalities.

That school policy has a moderately strong impact on knowledge of Russian as a second language, but no apparent impact on adoption of Russian as a native language, provides mixed support for the initial hypothesis that school policy would affect linguistic russification. In retrospect, however, these results make good sense. The results of the analysis of the effects of the demographic and cultural variables suggest that mother-tongue shift is strongly mediated by differences in ethnic values associated with traditional religion and urban-rural residence. In contrast, the fact that neither traditional religion nor urban-rural residence mediates the effect of interethnic contact on the spread of Russian as a second language suggests that second-language acquisition is essentially a pragmatic response to opportunities and incentives to learn Russian. Structuring of school curricula should therefore provide further incentives and opportunities for acquiring fluency in Russian as a

---

*The equation is as follows:

$$R_{nat} = 2.4 + .0557C*U + .0117C*\emptyset + .0137C*U*\emptyset - .441F \quad \text{(eq. 28)}$$

(Sig.) (.181) (.009)   (.003)   (.004)   (.215)

$$\bar{R}^2 = .713$$

$$N = 92$$

where

F = functional development of language: average level of functional development for 1960, 1966, 1968, 1969 on Hall's scale. Possible values range from 1 (lowest) to 6 (highest)

Note that attempts to define possible nonlinear functional relationships between native-language shift and publications policy, as well as attempts to relax the assumption of interval-level measurement of the policy variable, failed to provide evidence of an empirical link between publications policy and shift of mother tongue to Russian.

second language, but need not threaten to displace the traditional national language as the native language because mother-tongue shift is mediated by ethnic values. Especially since nearly all groups in this analysis are provided with ample opportunity to study their national languages as separate subjects in school, variations in the extent to which the national language may serve as the principal medium of instruction may not affect maintenance of the mother tongue.

Publications Policy

The relation of publications policy to the measures of linguistic russification closely resembles that between school policy and russification. Initially, let us assume that Hall's seven-point scale of functional development is an interval-level measure--that is, the distance between any two adjacent points on the scale (such as between level 2 and level 3) is identical to the distance between any other two adjacent points (such as between level 5 and level 6). This assumption that differences between adjacent scale positions represent equivalent differences in functional development is important if one is to interpret the scale ranks as numerical values. But the working assumption also can be relaxed or altered by treating the categories as ordinal or nominal measures; it turns out that changing the assumption about level of measurement has little bearing on the interpretation of the empirical relationships. Because there is some year-to-year instability in scores for particular languages, not all of which can be justifiably interpreted as over-time trends, rather than rely on the scores for any single year, the analysis is based on an average of the scores for the years 1960, 1966, 1968, and 1969. (Replication of the analysis using single-year scores made no meaningful difference in the empirical results.) For the 46 groups studied here, the mean score on this composite scale of functional development is 4.1. The standard deviation is 1.4, and the scores range from 1 to 6.

The simple correlations between a language's score on the scale of functional development and the percentage of the members of the corresponding nationality who claimed knowledge of Russian in 1970 accord with our expectation that the higher the level of functional development of a national language, the lower will be the extent of linguistic russification of the national group. Like the correlation between school policy and the different measures of linguistic russification, however, publications policy variation is more highly correlated with knowledge of Russian as a second language ($r = -.64$) than with adoption of Russian as a native language ($r = -.29$). Estimating the effects of publications policy on linguistic russification while adjusting for the effects of the demographic and cultural factors also produces results that are similar to those found with school policy.

Variation in publications policy is not related to variations in the percentage of non-Russians who claimed Russian as a native language in 1970. Of course, there may well be cases where publications policy has caused a shift of native language to Russian, but the evidence examined here suggests that on the average there is no such causal linkage. The relationship of publications policy to knowledge of Russian as a second language, on the other hand, is much stronger. Movement up the scale of functional development by one level is associated with an average decline of 6.5 percentage points in the proportion of non-Russians who claimed Russian as a second language in 1970 (adjusting for the effects of interethnic contact). Moreover, taking functional development of the language into account adds 13.1 percentage points to the variation in the knowledge of Russian as a second language that can be explained.*

To illustrate this link between knowledge of Russian as a second language and publications policy, let us follow a procedure employed in the analysis of school policy. By considering the substantive content of the books and brochures published in languages located at particular points on Hall's scale of functional development, one may place the languages into three broad categories. Languages whose average level of functional development was 6 are all characterized by an extremely large variety of publications, including publications in science, technology, political economy, finance, and philosophy. These groups may be placed in a high functional development category. Languages whose average level of functional development fell into the range 4.0 to 5.5 may be labeled as having a moderate variety of publications, including publications in the fields of international relations, public health, Marxism-Leninism, and (especially for languages at level 5) science and technology. Languages whose average scale score was below 4 had a very narrow range of publications, concentrated in the fields of popular literature, textbooks, government, and law. For purposes of analysis, this low category will serve as a standard of comparison with the more advanced languages.

---

*The relation between second-language acquisition and functional development of the national language is as follows:

$$R_{sec} = 46.0 + 26.5(\lg_{10}C) - 6.46F \qquad \bar{R}^2 = .740 \qquad (eq.\ 29)$$

(Sig.) (<.001) (<.001)   (<.001) $N = 92$

Using these new categories of functional development allows us to summarize the policy effects as follows. On the average, among ethnic groups whose languages had a moderate variety of books and brochures, an 8.2 percentage point smaller proportion of the population claimed Russian as a second language than among groups whose languages were low in functional development. And among nationalities whose languages had a high level of functional development, a 23.1 percentage point smaller proportion of the members claimed Russian as a second language than among groups whose languages had a low level of development. * These results reveal clearly, then, that whether the effects of functional development are measured in linear form or by grouping the languages into broad categories of functional development, the higher the level of functional development of the language, the lower the proportion of the members of the corresponding nationality who claim fluency in Russian as a second language. The same relationship could be shown between functional development and the percentage of the non-Russian population that claims Russian as either a native or a second language (that is, by adding the percentage that claims Russian as a native language to the percentage that claims Russian as a second language).

To summarize the examination of policy effects, variations in both publications policy and school policy correspond strongly to variations in the extent of knowledge of Russian as a second language, while variations in both measures of language policy have a very weak empirical connection with adoption of Russian as a native language. Whether one or the other of these two policies is the more important determinant of linguistic russification cannot be answered, however, because of the strong intercorrelation of the two policy variables

---

*Dividing the publications policy scale into categories yields the following results:

$$R_{sec} = 27.5 + 26.3(\lg_{10}C) - 8.19\,(MD\text{-}F) - 23.1(HI\text{-}F) \quad \overline{R}^2 = .752$$

$$\text{(eq. 30)}$$

(Sig.) (<.001) (<.001)   (.010)   (<.001)   N = 92

where

MD-F = moderate level of functional development of the language (MD-F = one if the average level of functional development is between 4.0 and 5.5, and zero if not)

HI-F = high level of functional development of the language (HI-F = one if the average level of development is 6, and zero if not) (r = about .9). Moreover, because of this redundancy between the two policy measures, inclusion of both in a single estimation equation does not increase the amount of variance accounted for above the amount accounted for by either of the two measures separately. Groups that have an ample number of native-language schools tend to be the same groups that benefit from the publication of a large variety of books and brochures in their native languages.

The Effects of Official Status

The intercorrelation of the policy measures is expected because of the high correlation between each of the two measures and the rank of the nationality's basic territory in the Soviet federal system. Given this correlation, one might be tempted to argue that status in the federal system is an independent factor accounting for linguistic russification (quite apart from the possible causal links between official status and language policy). Following procedures analogous to those employed earlier, one could estimate that ethnic groups whose official national areas rank as union republics in the federal system had an average 19.6 percent lower proportion of the population who claimed Russian as a second language in 1970 than did groups whose national areas rank as autonomous republics or autonomous provinces (with the effects of interethnic contact held constant). *
Furthermore, status of the nationality in the Soviet federal system is not independently related to the percentage of the group that claimed Russian as a native language, once one adjusts for the effects of interethnic contact, urbanization, and traditional religion.† But to give

---

*The effect on second-language acquisition of a nationality's having official status as a union republic (SSR) is estimated as follows:

$$R_{sec} = 24.9 + 26.7(\lg_{10}C) - 19.6SSR \qquad \overline{R}^2 = .737 \quad (eq.\ 31)$$

(Sig.) (<.001) (<.001)   (<.001)

where

        SSR = union republic status (SSR = one if the group's official territory has union republic status, and 0 if not)

    †The effect of union republic status on shift of native language to Russian is estimated as follows:

$$R_{nat} = 0.03 + .0642C*U + .0139C*\emptyset + .117C*U*\emptyset + .651SSR \quad \overline{R}^2 = .709$$

$$(eq.\ 32)$$

(Sig.) (.631) (.003)   (.001)   (.012)   (.547)   N = 92

a theoretical meaning to such status effects, one probably should view the status differences in terms of their direct implications for language policy: the hierarchy of groups in the federal system may closely determine the hierarchy of opportunities and incentives to learn Russian provided by language policy.

That differences in language policy are related to status differences of the nationalities in the federal system suggests the additional possibility, however, that the effects of language policies on levels of linguistic russification may be due primarily to the fact that different types of language policies are applied in union republics than in other national territories. Because of the evidence in Table 8.1 of the growing divergence between the availability of native-language schools among union republic groups, on the one hand, and the availability of such schools among all other groups, on the other, it is important to determine whether there are measurable effects of language policy on the spread of Russian within each of these two classes of nationalities. Unfortunately, due to the lack of measurable policy variation among the union republic (SSR) nationalities (for instance, on the evidence in Table 8.1, all SSR groups have had ten years of native-language schooling available in recent years), we cannot identify a distinctive relationship between school-language policy variation and levels of linguistic russification for the SSR groups taken separately. Similarly, the negligible variation in the publications policy measure among the SSR groups precludes an assessment of the effects of this policy on the linguistic russification of SSR groups. It is possible, however, to test whether school-language policy and publications policy have affected the linguistic russification of the lower-status (non-SSR) nationalities.

The evidence reveals that within the non-SSR nationalities, once the effects of interethnic contact, urbanization, and traditional religion are adjusted for, variation in school-language policy has no impact on the percentage of the population of the non-SSR groups that claims Russian as a native language, but a substantial impact on the percentage of the population that claims Russian as a second language (or on the combined total that claims Russian as a native or a second language).* On the average in 1970,

———————————————

*Estimating the effect of variation in school-language policy on native-language shift among the non-SSR nationalities results in the following equation:

among non-SSR groups, each additional school year in which native-language instruction was available is associated with an average decline of 2 percentage points in the proportion of the nationality that claimed Russian as a second language (or the combined total that claimed Russian as either a second or a native language). In short, the impact of school-language policy on the spread of Russian as a second language is not due solely to the different treatment of the SSR and non-SSR nationalities, but is partly due to differential treatment of the groups within the non-SSR category.

However, the measure of publications policy (Hall's index of functional development of languages) has an unexpected relationship with linguistic russification among non-SSR groups. As we found earlier when examining the relationship between publications policy and the linguistic russification of the entire set of non-Russian groups, the higher the functional development of the language, the lower the percentage of the corresponding non-SSR nationality that claims Russian as a second language. Each increase of one level on the scale of functional development is associated with an average

$$R_{nat} = 1.4 + .0712C*U + .0138C*\emptyset + .0103C*U*\emptyset - .261(S-1958) \quad \text{(eq. 33}$$

(Sig.) (.409) (.005)   (.001)   (.042)   (.334)

$$\overline{R}^2 = .731$$
$$N = 64$$

The estimated average effect of school-language policy on second-language shift among non-SSR groups is derived from the following equation:

$$R_{sec} = 34.2 + 27.8(\lg_{10}C) - 2.07(S-1958) \qquad \overline{R}^2 = .635 \quad \text{(eq. 34)}$$

(Sig.) (<.001) (<.001)   (.002) $N = 64$

The estimated effect of school policy on the total percentage of the non-SSR nationality that claims a knowledge of Russian either as a native or as a second language is expressed in the following equation:

(eq. 35)

$$R_{tot} = 35.5 + 26.0(\lg_{10}C) + 4.71(\lg_{10}C*\emptyset) + 7.27(\lg_{10}C*U) - 2.38(S-195$$

(Sig.) (<.001) (<.001)   (.007)   (<.001)   (<.001)

$$\overline{R}^2 = .785$$
$$N = 64$$

decrease of 3.5 percentage points in the proportion of typical non-SSR nationality that claimed Russian as a second language in 1970; and each increase of one level on the scale is associated with an average decrease of 4.5 percentage points in the total proportion who claimed Russian as either a second or a native language.* But in contrast with the negligible impact of publications policy on shift of native language among all SSR and non-SSR nationalities combined, there is a measurable, though small, impact of publications policy on native-language shift within the non-SSR groups taken separately. Each increase of one level on Hall's index is associated with an average decrease of 1.8 percentage points in the proportion of the non-SSR group that claims Russian as a native language.[†]

Thus, by one measure of language policy, the availability of native-language schools, the pattern of relationships between language policy and the different measures of linguistic russification is similar within the subset of non-SSR nationalities and the entire set of non-Russian nationalities: the availability of native-language schooling is inversely related to the spread of Russian as a second language and unrelated to the adoption of Russian as a native language. But by the other measure of language policy, the availability of books

---

*The effect of publications policy on the spread of Russian as a second language and as either a second or a native language among non-SSR groups is estimated below:

$$R_{sec} = 36.6 + 26.8(\lg_{10}C) - 3.50F \qquad \bar{R}^2 = .589 \quad \text{(eq. 36)}$$

(Sig.) $(<.001)$ $(<.001)$ $\qquad$ $(.037)$ $\qquad\qquad$ $N = 64$

$$R_{tot} = 45.6 + 23.7(\lg_{10}C) + 4.47C*\emptyset + 7.84C*U - 5.88F \qquad \text{(eq. 37)}$$

(Sig.) $(<.001)$ $(<.001)$ $\qquad$ $(.011)$ $\qquad$ $(<.001)$ $\qquad$ $(<.001)$

$$\bar{R}^2 = .785$$

$$N = 64$$

†The small effect of publications policy on the percent of the nationality that claimed Russian as a native language in 1970 among non-SSR groups is calculated below:

$$R_{nat} = 6.5 + .0653C*U + .0118C*\emptyset + .0122C*U*\emptyset - 1.84F \qquad \text{(eq. 38)}$$

(Sig.) $(.007)$ $(.006)$ $\qquad$ $(.003)$ $\qquad$ $(.012)$ $\qquad$ $(.004)$

$$\bar{R}^2 = .762$$

$$N = 64$$

and brochures in the language, the effects of policy differ between
the non-SSR subset and the entire non-Russian set of nationalities:
among the non-SSR nationalities, a greater variety of native-language
publications is inversely related to the adoption of Russian both as a
second language and as a native language, while among all non-
Russian ethnic groups, a greater variety of native-language publications is inversely related to the adoption of Russian as a second language but unrelated to the adoption of Russian as a native language.
One should bear in mind, of course, that publications policy may be
as much a result as it is a cause of linguistic russification (for reasons that were discussed earlier). Moreover, the measured effect
of this policy on the shift of native language among the non-SSR groups
is small. But other than these observations, it is difficult to account
for this anomalous empirical result.

CONCLUSION

The foregoing analysis reveals that particular demographic,
cultural, and political factors play very different roles in accounting
for bilingualism and shift of mother tongue in the USSR. The evidence strongly suggests that acquisition of Russian as a second language is essentially a pragmatic adjustment to incentives and opportunities to learn Russian. The level of contact between Russians
and the non-Russian populations has a great deal of bearing on the
spread of Russian as a second language, while traditional religion
and residence in an urban or rural area play no independent role in
mediating the acquisition of fluency in Russian as a second language.
That Soviet language policies have a strong independent bearing on
the levels of knowledge of Russian as a second language reinforces
the argument that second-language learning is a direct response to
demands and opportunities to learn Russian created by both social
circumstances and social policy.

The important role of traditional religion and residence in an
urban or rural area in mediating the adoption of Russian as a mother
tongue, on the other hand, suggests that the traditional national language is an important focus of ethnic group solidarity or identity.
Abandonment of the traditional national language for Russian as a
native language may well connote a serious weakening or shifting of
ethnic group loyalties. Perhaps as a result, change of mother tongue
is not an automatic extension of the pragmatic compromise involved
in second-language learning. Whether such native-language shift
occurs depends not simply on the incentives and opportunities to gain
fluency in Russian afforded by interethnic contact and language policies, but also on other values and ethnic loyalties. These other

values may intervene either to facilitate (for the Orthodox nationalities and for urban residents) or to retard (for Muslims and for rural residents) the shift of native language from the traditional national tongue to Russian.

In describing the role of ethnic values in mediating language change, it is important to emphasize the key role of interethnic contact. Contact between Russians and non-Russians strongly contributes to the acquisition of Russian as a second language but is not a necessary condition for such acquisition, since even where contact is very low, a large number of non-Russians acquire fluency in Russian--probably chiefly through the school system, mass media, and military service. In contrast, however, contact between Russians and non-Russians is a virtual precondition for switching to Russian as a native language. But it is not a sufficient condition, since even as contact increases to extremely high levels, Muslims and ruralites (especially Muslim ruralites) do not readily shift to Russian as a native language, but increasingly acquire Russian as a second language. Only if non-Russians are urban or Orthodox (or both) does contact have much effect on native-language switching.

The evidence presented here suggests that Soviet language policy has played a mixed role in expanding the use of Russian among the non-Russian nationalities. The extent of fluency in Russian as a second language is affected by two factors that play strong independent roles: contact between Russians and non-Russians, and the use of Russian and the non-Russian languages in schools and the mass media. But abandonment of the traditional national languages for Russian as a mother tongue has not been measurably affected by language policies (at least not, on the average, among the groups examined here). To explain this result, it is important to recall that even where the incentives to learn Russian are very strong-- that is, where the availability of native-language schooling and publications is highly restricted--these incentives are generally accompanied by measures of support for the non-Russian languages, such as teaching the language in school as a separate subject and publishing popular literature in the language. As long as such fundamental support for the non-Russian languages continues to be provided, policies designed to increase the knowledge of Russian as a second language need not lead to loss of the traditional national languages as mother tongues.

APPENDIX: LIST OF NATIONALITIES

Ethnic Group	1970 Population (entire USSR)	Dominant Traditional Religion
Abkhazian	83,240	Orthodox
Adygey	99,855	Islamic
Altai	55,812	Orthodox
Armenian	3,559,151	nr. to Orthodox
Avar	396,297	Islamic
Azerbaidzhani	4,397,937	Islamic
Balkar	59,501	Islamic
Bashkir	1,239,681	Islamic
Belorussian	9,051,755	Orthodox
Buriat	314,671	Buddhist
Chechen	612,674	Islamic
Cherkess	39,785	Islamic
Chuvash	1,694,351	Orthodox
Darginian	230,932	Islamic
Estonian	1,007,356	Lutheran
Georgian	3,245,300	Orthodox
Ingush	157,605	Islamic
Kabardin	279,928	Islamic
Kalmyk	137,194	Buddhist
Karachai	112,741	Islamic
Karakalpak	236,009	Islamic
Karelian	146,081	Orthodox
Kazakh	5,298,818	Islamic
Khakasy	66,725	Orthodox
Kirghiz	1,452,222	Islamic
Komi	321,894	Orthodox
Komi Permiak	153,451	Orthodox
Kumyk	188,792	Islamic
Lak	85,822	Islamic
Latvian	1,429,844	Lutheran
Lezghian	323,829	Islamic
Lithuanian	2,664,944	Roman Catholic
Mari	598,628	Orthodox
Moldavian	2,697,994	Orthodox
Mordvinian	1,262,670	Orthodox
Nogai	51,784	Islamic
North Ossetian } South Ossetian }	488,039	Orthodox
Tadzhik	2,135,883	Islamic
Tatar	5,930,670	Islamic
Turkmenian	1,525,284	Islamic
Tuvinian	139,388	Buddhist
Udmurt	704,328	Orthodox
Ukrainian	40,753,246	Orthodox
Uzbek	9,195,093	Islamic
Yakut	296,244	Orthodox

NOTES

1. Iu. V. Arutiunian, "O nekotorykh tendentsiiakh v izmenenii kul'turnogo oblika natsii," Sovetskaia etnografiia (1968), no. 4: 3.

2. On demographic factors, see M. N. Guboglo, "O vliianie rasseleniia na iazykovye protsessy," Sovetskaia etnografiia (1969), no. 5: 16-29; M. N. Guboglo, "Vzaimodeistvie iazykov i mezh-natsional'nye otnoshenii v sovetskom obshchestve," Istoriia SSSR (1970), no. 6: 22-41; E. Glyn Lewis, Multilingualism in the Soviet Union: Aspects of Language Policy and Its Implementation (The Hague: Mouton, 1972); Brian Silver, "The Impact of Urbanization and Geographical Dispersion on the Linguistic Russification of Soviet Nationalities," Demography 11 (February 1974): 89-103.

On political factors, see John A. Armstrong, "The Ethnic Scene in the Soviet Union," in Ethnic Minorities in the Soviet Union, ed. Erich Goldhagen (New York: Praeger, 1968), pp. 3-49; Vernon V. Aspaturian, "The Non-Russian Nationalities," in Prospects for Soviet Society, ed. Allen Kassof (New York: Praeger, 1968), pp. 143-98; Yaroslav Bilinsky, "Education of the Non-Russian Peoples in the USSR, 1917-1967: An Essay," Slavic Review 27 (September 1968): 411-37; Lewis, op. cit.

3. See Alex Inkeles, "Making Men Modern: On the Causes and Consequences of Individual Change in Six Developing Countries," American Journal of Sociology 75 (September 1969): 209-25; Murray Yanowitch and Norton T. Dodge, "The Social Evaluation of Occupa-tions in the Soviet Union," Slavic Review 28 (December 1969): 619-43; Ellen Mickiewicz, "Uses and Strategies in Data Analysis of the Soviet Union: Changes in Industrialized Society," in Handbook of Soviet Social Science Data, ed. Ellen Mickiewicz (New York: Free Press, 1973), pp. 1-47.

4. See Karl W. Deutsch, "Social Mobilization and Political Development," American Political Science Review 55 (September 1961): 493-514; Karl W. Deutsch, Nationalism and Social Communi-cation: An Inquiry into the Foundations of Nationality (2nd ed.; Cam-bridge, Mass.: MIT Press, 1966).

5. See Immanuel Wallerstein, "Ethnicity and National Integra-tion in West Africa," Cahiers d'études africaines 3 (October 1960): 129-39; Deutsch, Nationalism and Social Communication; Joshua A. Fishman, "Language Maintenance and Shift as a Field of Inquiry," Linguistics 9 (November 1964): 52-53; Abner Cohen, Custom and Politics in Urban Africa (Berkeley: University of California Press, 1969).

6. Brian Silver, "Social Mobilization and the Russification of Soviet Nationalities," American Political Science Review 68 (March 1974): 45-66.

7. On the notion of ethnic ideology, see Daniel Glaser, "Dynamics of Ethnic Identification," American Sociological Review 23 (February 1958): 32.

8. See the evidence presented in Brian Silver, "Methods of Deriving Data on Bilingualism from the 1970 Soviet Census," Soviet Studies 27 (October 1975): 574-97.

9. See Yaroslav Bilinsky, "The Soviet Education Laws of 1958-59 and Soviet Nationality Policy," Soviet Studies 14 (October 1962): 138-57; Bilinsky, "Education of the Non-Russian Peoples in the USSR."

10. Information for 1958 is available in F. F. Sovetkin, ed., Natsional'nye shkoly RSFSR za 40 let (Moscow: Izdatel'stvo Akademii Pedagogicheskikh Nauk, 1958), pp. 23-24. More recent information and changes in the availability of native-language schooling are discussed in Harry Lipset, "The Status of National Minority Languages in Soviet Education," Soviet Studies 19 (October 1967): 181-89; and Brian Silver, "The Status of National Minority Languages in Soviet Education: An Assessment of Recent Changes," Soviet Studies 26 (January 1974): 28-40.

11. Sovetkin, Natsional'nye.

12. Silver, "The Status of National Minority Languages."

13. Zev Katz et al., eds., Handbook of Major Soviet Nationalities (New York: Free Press, 1975), p. 459.

14. Paul R. Hall, "Language Contact in the USSR: Some Prospects for Language Maintenance among Soviet Minority Language Groups" (Ph.D. diss., Georgetown University, 1974).

15. But see Guboglo, "O vliianie rasseleniia" and "Vzaimodeistvie iazykov"; Lewis, op. cit.; and Silver, "The Impact of Urbanization and Geographical Dispersion."

16. The basic source is Tsentral'noe Statisticheskoe Upravlenie SSSR, Itogi vsesoiuznoi perepisi naseleniia 1970 goda (Moscow: Statistika, 1973), vol. IV. Page numbers are omitted from references to the census report in order to avoid unnecessary cumbersomeness. The impact of sex differences on linguistic russification is examined in Silver, "The Impact of Urbanization and Geographical Dispersion"; "Social Mobilization"; and "Bilingualism and Maintenance of the Mother Tongue in Soviet Central Asia," Slavic Review 35 (September 1976): 406-24. This factor is omitted from the present study because information on sex differences in language use in 1970 is not available for all 45 of the ethnic groups included in the analysis.

17. See S. I. Bruk and V. I. Kozlov, "Etnograficheskaia nauka i perepis' naseleniia 1970 goda," Sovetskaia etnografiia (1967), no. 6: 3-20; M. N. Guboglo, "Nekotorye voprosy metodiki pri sotsiologicheskom analize funktsional'nogo razvitiia iazykov," Sovetskaia etnografiia (1973), no. 2: 113-21; Silver, "Methods of Deriving Data on Bilingualism."

18. Guboglo, "Nekotorye voprosy metodiki."

19. For studies revealing the relationship between reported native language and the social contexts within which the language is actually employed, see M. N. Guboglo, "Sotsial'no-etnicheskie posledstviia dvuiazychiia," Sovetskaia etnografiia (1972), no. 2: 26-36; E. I. Klement'ev, "Razvitie iazykovykh protsessov v Karelii," Sovetskaia etnografiia (1974), no. 4: 26-36; E. I. Klement'ev, "Iazykovye protsessy v Karelii," Sovetskaia etnografiia (1971), no. 6: 38-44.

20. In addition to sources cited in note 19, see Iu. V. Strakach, "K metodike izucheniia sovremennykh etno-linguisticheskikh protsessov," Sovetskaia etnografiia (1969), no. 4: 3-13; A. I. Kholmogorov, Internatsional'nye cherty sovetskikh natsii (Moscow: Mysl', 1970); N. A. Tomilov, "Sovremennykh etnicheskie protsessy u tatar gorodov zapadnoi sibiri," Sovetskaia etnografiia (1972), no. 6: 87-97.

21. A. Isupov, "O metodologicheskikh i organizatsionnykh voprosakh vsesoiuznoi perepisi naseleniia 1979 goda," Vestnik statistiki (1977), no. 6: 29.

22. See Joshua A. Fishman, "Sociolinguistic Perspective on the Study of Bilingualism," Linguistics 39 (May 1968): 31-32.

23. Alexandre Bennigsen and Chantal Lemercier-Quelquejay, Islam in the Soviet Union, Geoffrey E. Wheeler and Hubert Evans, trans. (New York: Praeger, 1967), p. 213.

24. In evaluating the evidence on ethnic intermarriage among Soviet nationalities, Ethel Dunn and Stephen Dunn have characterized Islam as an organized manifestation of national consciousness. See Ethel Dunn and Stephen P. Dunn, "Ethnic Intermarriage as an Indicator of Cultural Convergence in Soviet Central Asia," in The Nationality Question in Soviet Central Asia, ed. Edward Allworth (New York: Praeger, 1973), pp. 54-55.

25. The initial test for the effects of the urban-rural and religion variables employed the two as dummy variables. On the use of dummy variables in regression analysis, see Jacob Cohen, "Multiple Regression as a General Data-Analytic System," Psychological Monographs 6 (1968): 426-43; Potluri Rao and Roger L. Miller, Applied Econometrics (Belmont, Calif.: Wadsworth, 1971), pp. 88-99. Only nationalities that have Islam or Orthodoxy as a traditional religion are included in the following calculation:

$$R_{sec} = 11.2 + 32.4(\lg_{10}C) + .589U + 2.25\emptyset \qquad \overline{R}^2 = .613 \qquad (eq.\ 11)$$

(Sig.) (.011) (<.001)   (.878)   (.492) $N = 80$

where

R_{sec} = Russian second language

C = contact

U   = urban–rural (1 if urban, 0 if rural)
Ø   = traditional religion: 1 if the group is traditionally
         Orthodox, 0 if it is traditionally Islamic

As the large significance level for the urban–rural coefficient shows, once the extent of contact is held constant, urban–rural residence has no independent impact on the acquisition of Russian as a second language. Further tests for interaction effects of the urban–rural and contact variables with R_{sec} failed to reveal a significant non-additive relationship between second-language learning, urban–rural residence, and contact.

26. See Silver, "Social Mobilization."
27. Armstrong, op. cit., p. 16.

PART IV

NATIONAL IDENTITY:
PERSISTENCE AND CHANGE

SOME FACTORS RELATED TO ETHNIC REIDENTIFICATION IN THE RUSSIAN REPUBLIC **9**

Barbara A. Anderson

The bulk of work on Soviet ethnic groups has stressed inter-ethnic friction and division. In contrast, this chapter presents evidence of extensive assimilation of members of some of the titular nationality groups for whom the nationality-based autonomous Soviet socialist republics (ASSRs) are designated. These ASSRs are territorially within and administratively subordinate to the Russian Soviet Federated Socialist Republic (RSFSR). Given the number of persons aged 0–19 in the 1959 Soviet census who were members of ASSR-level ethnic groups in the Russian Republic, there were far fewer persons recorded at ages 11–29 in the 1970 Soviet census than would be expected on the basis of known rates of mortality and migration between 1959 and 1970. These young persons, especially members of traditionally Orthodox groups in European Russia, seem to have changed their declaration of nationality from that of their group of birth in the 1959 census to (usually) Russian in the 1970 census. It is likely that citing Russian as one's mother tongue was an initial step in this assimilation process. An indicator of interethnic contact and other socioeconomic factors are found to be sensibly related to the extent to which members of particular nationality groups seem to have changed their nationality designation.

EVIDENCE OF ETHNIC REIDENTIFICATION

For the purposes of this research, ethnic reidentification among members of a given nationality group is detected by the deficiency in the number of individuals in a given birth cohort who declare themselves to be members of that nationality group in 1970 compared with the number in that cohort in 1959. * Age distribution

---

*A cohort is a group of persons all of whom begin something at the same time. In this case each cohort is a group of persons

data are available only for the 15 nationality groups that have their own union republics and for ASSR-level nationalities within the RSFSR. Thus, it is not possible to study the members of these ASSR-level groups outside the RSFSR. Nor is it possible to study ASSR-level groups from non-RSFSR ASSRs.[1] The change in the number of members in each cohort was examined by using the appropriate one of the following ratios:

$$(11-19)_{70}/(0-9)_{59}; \quad (20-29)_{70}/(10-19)_{59}; \quad (30-39)_{70}/20-29)_{59};$$

$$(40-49)_{70}/(30-39)_{59}; \quad (50+)_{70}/(40+)_{59}$$

These age groupings were dictated by the format of the census data. The ratios are not expected to equal one. Some persons will have died between the two dates. Moreover, the cohorts at the two dates do not exactly match because there were eleven years rather than ten between the censuses. Also, some age groupings, such as 11-19, are unusual for presentation of age data. Since, aside from the mismatching of age groups, the ratios do detect the proportion of those in a given age group in 1959 in the RSFSR who "survive" to be in that nationality and in the RSFSR in 1970, these ratios will be called survival ratios. In fact, they are the equivalent of demographic survival ratios.

This chapter is concerned with detecting the effect of nationality reidentification on the above survival ratios. However, the

---

born within a given span of years. This is called a birth cohort. Discovery of an unusual pattern in the age distributions of ASSR-level nationality groups in the RSFSR in the course of the author's joint research with Ansley Coale and Erna Härm at the Office of Population Research, Princeton University, led to this examination of ethnic reidentification. Fertility rates were computed for ASSR-level nationalities using a method that compares the number of persons under a certain age with the number over that age. If mortality is held constant, the higher the level of fertility in the recent past, the higher the ratio of younger to older persons. Using this method, the estimated Karelian crude birth rate was implausibly low. At 8 per 1,000, it was lower than the rate for urban Estonians or Latvians. See Ansley J. Coale, Barbara A. Anderson, and Erna Härm, Human Fertility in Russia: The Demographic Transition in a Unique Historical Setting (Princeton, N.J.: Princeton University Press, forthcoming).

observed survival ratios also will be affected by mortality between 1959 and 1970 and by migration into or out of the RSFSR between the two dates. The ASSR-level groups under consideration did not have unusual mortality experience (such as involvement in a war, which would affect some groups more than others, according to geographic location) between 1959 and 1970. The effect of normal mortality experience can be taken into account fairly easily, and will be discussed later in this chapter. However, several groups had high migration rates between the RSFSR and the rest of the Soviet Union between 1959 and 1970. The Ingush, for example, had 53 percent of their members in the RSFSR in 1959 and 87 percent of their members in the RSFSR in 1970. This change was due to extensive resettlement of the Ingush to their homeland in the RSFSR, from which they had been moved during World War II. To interpret the survival ratios for such groups as an indication of the extent of nationality reidentification would be unwarranted. Other groups had very low proportions in the RSFSR at both census dates. The Lezghians had less than 53 percent of their members in the RSFSR at each census date. The Lezghian territory (Dagestan ASSR) is near the border of the RSFSR, and the Lezghians have long been distributed between the RSFSR and Azerbaidzhan. When the proportion of a group in the RSFSR at both dates is small (even though the proportion may be similar at each date), there is a strong possibility that differential migration into and out of the RSFSR by age group may affect the relative size of a given cohort at the two dates. If this were the case, to interpret the survival ratios as an indication of the extent of nationality reidentification also would be unwarranted.

Because of these considerations, groups were excluded from the analysis if the ratio of the proportion of the group in the RSFSR in 1970 to the proportion of the group in the RSFSR in 1959 fell outside the range .95 to 1.05 (Balkars, Ingush, and Chechen). Groups also were excluded if the proportion of the group resident in the RSFSR at each census date was below .7 (Lezghians and Ossetians). After excluding those groups for which the proportion in the RSFSR either differed greatly at the two dates or was absolutely small at both dates, 16 ASSR-level nationality groups remain. Thirteen of these groups are traditionally either Orthodox or Muslim. Three are traditionally neither Orthodox nor Muslim (Buriats, Kalmyks, and Tuvinians). For this and other reasons, these groups were excluded from the analysis.* The remaining 13 Orthodox and Muslim

---

*The eastern Buriats differ substantially from the western Buriats in socioeconomic characteristics. This makes the interpretation of treatment of them as one group problematic. Also, the quality of the Kalmyk data is somewhat suspect.

groups that are titular nationalities of autonomous republics within
the RSFSR are the subject of analysis in this study.

The survival ratios for the two youngest birth cohorts of the
15 nationality groups of the union republics and the 13 selected ASSR-
level groups are shown in Table 9.1. These survival ratios are expressed as the number of individuals in the cohort declaring themselves to be members of the particular nationality in 1970 per 1,000
persons in the corresponding (or most closely corresponding) cohort
who made that declaration in 1959. The survival ratios (indicating
nationality identification) for those aged 20 or older in 1959 did not
differ markedly from what one would expect, based on reasonable
mortality assumptions, thereby indicating that no substantial changes
in the self-declared nationality identification of these individuals
occurred between 1959 and 1970.

However, for many ASSR-level groups the survival ratios for
the two youngest birth cohorts were extremely low.* Under reasonable mortality assumptions, the survival ratio for the youngest birth

---

*The range of reasonable survival ratios was obtained by using
female East model life tables, expectation of life at birth alternatively 55 and 70 years. These model life tables were based on the typical mortality experience of a set of countries where age-specific
mortality data were known to be accurately recorded. (Germany,
Austria, Poland, and Czechoslovakia were among the countries included for periods of time in the late nineteenth and twentieth centuries.) Earlier work has shown that this set of tables closely
matches the pattern of mortality for the Soviet Union. See Ansley
J. Coale, Barbara A. Anderson, and Erna Härm, Human Fertility
in Russia (Princeton, N.J.: Princeton University Press, forthcoming). In these tables mortality data are given by five-year age groups
except for the youngest age group, where values are presented separately for those aged zero years and those aged one through four
years. Within the age intervals, the 1959 single-year age distribution estimated by J.-N. Biraben for the Soviet Union as a whole was
used. This single-year age distribution was used to make the birth
cohorts correspond in the 1959 and 1970 Soviet censuses. This procedure took some account of the effect of war on the age distribution.
For the single-year age distribution, see Jean-Noël Biraben,
"Naissances et répartition par âge dans l'Empire russe et en Union
soviétique," Population 31, no. 2 (March-April 1976): 441-78. For
the life tables used, see Ansley J. Coale and Paul Demeny, Regional
Model Life Tables and Stable Populations (Princeton, N.J.: Princeton University Press, 1966).

cohort in a given nationality, expressed as the number aged 11-19 in 1970 per 1,000 persons aged 0-9 who declared themselves members of the nationality group in 1959, normally should fall in the range 872-901 if no reidentification occurred between 1959 and 1970. In Table 9.1 this first survival ratio has been labeled S_1. Similarly, the survival ratio for the second birth cohort, expressed as the number aged 20-29 in 1970 per 1,000 persons in the group aged 10-19 in 1959, normally should fall in the range 946-970. This second survival ratio has been labeled S_2. One may summarize the behavior of the two youngest birth cohorts by averaging S_1 and S_2. This averaged survival ratio should fall in the range 909-936. This averaged indicator of the extent of nationality identification has been labeled S.

For none of the republic-level groups do both S_1 and S_2 fall below the reasonable range of values. Among the ASSR-level nationalities, the values of both S_1 and S_2 are above the range only for the Kumyks. For seven ASSR-level groups, however, the values of both S_1 and S_2 fall below the reasonable range (Bashkir, Chuvash, Darginian, Karelian, Mari, Mordvinian, and Udmurt). It is practically certain that substantial nationality reidentification took place within these seven groups between 1959 and 1970, while there is no such conclusive evidence for any republic-level group. *

Whether some Dagestani groups were shifting identification to that of other Dagestani groups is difficult to determine. It is possible that Avars and Darginians were reidentifying as Kumyks. In 1970, 30 percent of those Avars and Darginians who did not declare the language of their group as their mother tongue declared the language of another Dagestani group (usually Kumyk), although the proportions not declaring the language of their group as their mother tongue were quite small.

Among the republic-level nationalities, the Russians and the Kazakhs exhibit both S_1 and S_2 values above the range of reasonable

---

*The high values of S_1 for the republic-level groups (those above 901) can be explained by the high fertility of those groups in all cases except the Russians and Georgians. When fertility in the recent past has been very high, the age distribution even within the young ages (such as ages 0-9) is skewed more toward the youngest ages than would otherwise be the case. At the mortality levels that are plausible for Soviet subpopulations, a heavy skewing toward the young ages means that the actual survival ratio will be higher than it would be otherwise. Among ASSR-level groups, high fertility in the recent past might be the explanation for high S_1 values for the Avars and the Kumyks, although it is difficult to be certain.

TABLE 9.1

Number Surviving per Thousand Population, and Socioeconomic Variables, for Selected Soviet Ethnic Groups

Group	S_1 $\frac{(11-19)_{70}}{(0-9)_{59}}$	S_2 $\frac{(20-29)_{70}}{(10-19)_{59}}$	S Average of S_1 and S_2	Number per Thousand Claiming Russian as Mother Tongue	Number per Thousand not in Designated Area	Number per Thousand in Urban Places	Population Aged 0-19 (thousands)
Christian republic-level groups							
Russian	904	994	949				
Latvian	889	918	904	46	73	475	367
Estonian	875	944	910	47	95	470	254
Ukrainian	885	936	911	122	137	392	12,468
Lithuanian	896	941	919	12	75	351	798
Moldavian	896	941	919	36	148	129	902
Belorussian	893	946	920	153	175	324	2,839
Georgian	954	928	941	13	34	361	972
Armenian	950	959	955	83	443	565	1,101
Muslim republic-level groups							
Kirghiz	906	931	919	3	136	108	461
Azerbaidzhani	943	896	920	12	152	348	1,350
Tadzhik	907	941	943	5	248	206	679
Uzbek	944	946	945	5	162	218	2,927
Turkmen	933	962	948	7	78	253	455
Kazakh	925	986	956	12	230	241	1,735

Orthodox ASSR-level groups

Karellan	701	694	698	279	479	300	45
Mordvinian	761	690	726	200	704	266	424
Mari	823	747	785	42	439	110	197
Chuvash	836	797	817	83	464	185	547
Udmurt	862	826	844	102	227	217	220
Komi	871	886	879	99	133	289	102
Yakut	891	895	893	23	43	169	105

Muslim ASSR-level groups

Bashkir	850	766	808	22	227	181	420
Darginian	844	784	814	7	29	141	66
Tatar	877	904	891	62	670	421	1,686
Avar	921	903	912	7	41	104	102
Kabardin	930	904	917	16	52	139	90
Kumyk	965	988	977	12	91	325	57

Note: All values for republic-level groups refer to the group within the entire Soviet Union. All values for ASSR-level groups refer to the group within the Russian Republic. Thus the designated area variable for republic-level groups is the number per 1,000 members of the group living in the Soviet Union but not in the group's union republic. The designated area variable for ASSR-level groups is the number per 1,000 members of the group living in the Russian Republic but not in the group's ASSR.

Source: See note 1.

values. It is possible that Karakalpaks may have been reidentifying as Kazakhs. Unfortunately, it is impossible to determine this from the information available in the censuses.

EXTENT OF REIDENTIFICATION

If one considers only those ASSR-level groups for which the survival ratios of both of the two youngest birth cohorts were below the estimated reasonable range of values and uses the lower bounds of the estimated ranges as a basis for comparison, one finds that at least 6 percent of those aged 0-9 in 1959 who declared themselves to be members of one of the seven ASSR-level groups were not declaring themselves to be members of their respective groups in 1970, and at least 20 percent of those aged 10-19 in 1959 were not declaring themselves as members of their respective groups in 1970. This means a "loss" of at least 189,715 persons from these seven groups alone. Other groups, such as the Komi, probably were also losing members through reidentification, although this is not as certain as for the seven groups cited above. At the same time, using the upper values of the estimated reasonable ranges of values of the survival ratios as bases for comparison, in 1970 there were at least 75,139 too many Russians aged 11-19 compared with the number of Russians aged 0-9 in 1959 and at least 395,179 too many Russians aged 20-29 in 1970 compared with the number aged 10-19 in 1959. This means that there were at least 2.5 times as many excess Russians aged 11-29 in 1970 as could be accounted for by reidentification of the seven ASSR-level groups who were most likely to have experienced substantial reidentification. Thus it is quite likely that the phenomenon of nationality reidentification took place between 1959 and 1970 not only among the seven ASSR-level groups considered here, but among other nationality groups as well.

Except for the Darginians and the Bashkirs, it is likely that the bulk of those among the seven ASSR-level nationality groups who reidentified declared themselves to be Russians. As mentioned earlier, Darginians may have been declaring themselves to be Kumyks. Also it is likely that Bashkirs were reidentifying as Tatars. It is unlikely one could convincingly claim to be a member of a nationality group if one were not fluent in the language of that group. Except for the Kumyks and the Bashkirs, choosing a language other than the language of one's group as mother tongue meant choosing Russian. For Bashkirs, the overwhelming choice was Tatar. Of 344,977 Bashkirs not choosing Bashkir as their mother tongue in 1959, 344,566 chose Tatar. This is plausible, since the Bashkir ASSR and the Tatar ASSR are contiguous. The importance of mother tongue will be discussed in greater detail later.

FACTORS RELATED TO REIDENTIFICATION

Two alternative explanations of why reidentification between 1959 and 1970 occurred primarily among the members of the two youngest cohorts are possible. The first explanation would suggest that such reidentification is a phenomenon specific to a given stage of life. According to this explanation, reidentification has been occurring among young persons for quite some time and will continue to occur in the future. This explanation suggests that if additional census data were available showing the age distribution of members of each nationality group, the survival ratios for the two youngest birth cohorts (the youngest two birth cohorts at the first census date compared with the second and third cohorts at the later census date) should be low for each pair of censuses, indicating substantial reidentification by young persons during each intercensal period. On the other hand, according to this explanation, the survival ratios of the cohorts older than age 20 at the first of a pair of census dates should appear unexceptional, indicating that once persons reached their twenties or thirties, they reidentified to a minor extent at most. The second explanation would suggest that something happened to the generation aged 29 and younger in 1970 that caused members of at least some ASSR-level nationality groups to reidentify to a substantial extent. This "something" may have happened during the period 1959-70 or even earlier. From this line of reasoning, those aged 10-19 in 1959 may have begun the process of reidentification in the period 1949-59. Such an explanation suggests that the 1979 census would reveal evidence of continued reidentification during the period 1970-79 by persons who were aged 20-29 in 1970.

It is not possible to determine from the available data which of these explanations is true. However, in the absence of data from additional censuses, the explanation suggesting a stage-of-life phenomenon seems more plausible. The ages in 1970 of the young persons under study (ages 11-29) encompass those ages at which persons become adults and start their own lives. If a person wanted to reidentify because of some perceived advantage to be gained, the late teens or early twenties would be an optimum time to do so, before one was firmly established in a job where others knew one's nationality. It is important to recall that the census was taken orally, without a check of identity cards.[2] Thus a person could have declared himself to be Russian, regardless of the nationality recorded on his identity card.

Many persons marry in their early twenties. Ethnically mixed marriages provide opportunities for nationality reidentification. A non-Russian married to a Russian, for example, might be likely to declare Russian nationality to the census taker. Also, children of mixed marriages choose their permanent passport nationality at age 16. Soviet sociological research on the determinants of passport identification of children of mixed marriages indicates that when one parent is a member of an ASSR-level nationality and the other is a member of a republic-level nationality, children tend to assume the republic-level nationality.[3] This is especially likely when the republic-level nationality is Russian or when the child does not live in the ASSR of the ASSR-nationality parent. Thus mixed marriages provide opportunities for nationality reidentification both for the parent and for the child in the teens or early twenties.

What factors differentiate the seven ASSR-level nationality groups that most surely experienced substantial reidentification (Bashkir, Chuvash, Darginian, Karelian, Mordvinian, and Udmurt) from the other six ASSR-level nationalities? Using a discriminant analysis, the most important distinguishing factor was found to be the number of persons in the group who chose Russian as mother tongue in 1959 per 1,000 population in the RSFSR. The second most important factor was the number of persons in the group who lived in urban places in the RSFSR per 1,000 persons in the group living in the RSFSR in 1959. These factors most effectively differentiate the seven groups in which substantial reidentification had almost certainly occurred from the six other groups in which it was less certain. Other factors considered included the traditional religion of the group (Orthodox or Muslim), measures of population size, and educational level measures.*

The Russian-language variable behaved as expected. The higher the proportion of persons in a group declaring Russian as their

---

*In the discriminant analysis, a stepwise procedure was used that picked the best differentiating variables. The same two variables, the Russian-language variable and the urban variable, were picked whether the entry criterion was the increase in Rao's V or the value of Wilk's lambda. The level of significance of the F statistic for the discriminant function with both variables included was .054. The Russian-language variable was the first variable picked whichever entry criterion was used. With only the Russian-language variable included, the value of the F for the discriminant function was not statistically significant. When the urban variable was added, the significance of the change in Rao's V was .013. Thus the urban variable was individually significant. Although the discriminant function as a whole misses differentiating significantly between the two groups at the 5 percent level, the results of the discriminant analysis are suggestive and are supported by the regression analysis performed later in this chapter.

mother tongue, the more likely the group was to experience substantial reidentification. It is likely that declaring Russian one's mother tongue is a first step in the process of reidentifying as Russian, regardless of one's nationality at birth. Soviet sociological research has indicated that fluency in Russian is related to attitudes that would tend to increase an individual's willingness to reidentify; fluency in Russian has been related to a positive attitude toward multinational work collectives and to the ascription of little importance to the nationality of supervisors.[4]

The relationship of the urban residence variable to reidentification, on the other hand, was somewhat surprising. Given equal proportions of Russian-language speakers in 1959, the higher the proportion urban, the less likely the group was to experience substantial reidentification. This is true even though urban members of ASSR-level nationalities are more likely to declare Russian as their mother tongue than are rural members of the same groups. For example, in 1959, 38 percent of urban Karelians living in the Karelian ASSR declared Russian as their mother tongue, while only 10 percent of rural Karelians in the Karelian ASSR did so. The urban sociologist Basil Zimmer has suggested that if a member of an ASSR-level nationality group lives in an urban area and does not claim Russian as his mother tongue, this may mean he lives in an ethnic enclave or at least is a member of a culturally and linguistically cohesive group in which the chances for reidentification are less and in which there may be substantial social pressure against reidentification.[5]

Fluency in Russian is more important in urban than in rural areas, especially for occupational success. A person in an urban area may have assumed Russian as his mother tongue simply because of the practical advantages of being able to use it as a language of daily conversation. Such language acquisition would not necessarily indicate a favorable attitude toward Russians or an inclination to reidentify as Russian. In rural areas, however, where the practical advantages of Russian fluency are less clear, declaring Russian as one's mother tongue may be more indicative of positive attitudes toward Russians and of a person's inclination to reidentify as Russian.

It is also possible that fluency in Russian may be less indicative of positive attitudes toward Russians and toward reidentification for persons in higher-status than in lower-status occupations. In his study of the Tatar ASSR, Iu. V. Arutiunian found that although fluency in Russian was generally related to a more positive attitude toward members of other nationalities, the relationship was weaker among professionals than among farm laborers, even though knowledge of Russian was much more widespread among professionals than among farm laborers. When knowledge of Russian is held constant, farm laborers tend to have a more favorable view of members of other nationalities than do professionals.[6]

Although the differences between the seven ASSR-level nationalities and the others are interesting, we require a more refined measure of the extent of reidentification than simply whether a group does or does not conclusively experience substantial reidentification. The average of the survival ratios for the first two birth cohorts, S, was used as such a measure. This takes into account the reidentification experience of all persons in the group under age 20 in 1959. Table 9.1 includes the values of S for all 13 ASSR-level groups and for the 15 union republic-level groups. The values of various socioeconomic variables for each of the groups also are shown in Table 9.1. Values of socioeconomic variables for Russians are not shown, since no explanation is sought of why Russians identify as Russian. The correlations among the three survival ratios and various socioeconomic variables and among the socioeconomic variables are displayed in Table 9.2. The variable "Orthodox" is a dummy variable which has the value one if the group is traditionally Orthodox and the value zero if the group is traditionally Muslim. The correlations of any given socioeconomic variable with each of the survival ratios are quite similar. This is not surprising, since the correlations among the survival ratios are above .92. The correlations that are stronger than what would occur by chance less than 5 percent of the time are indicated by an asterisk.

As was found in the discriminant analysis, traditional Orthodoxy is not highly related to the propensity to reidentify. (The correlation between the Orthodoxy variable and S_1 is statistically significant, but the correlations between the Orthodoxy variable and S_2 and S are not statistically significant.) However, the correlation between traditional Orthodoxy and the proportion of a group that declares Russian as the mother tongue is quite strong and statistically significant, indicating that members of traditionally Orthodox groups are more likely to declare Russian as the mother tongue than are members of traditionally non-Orthodox groups. The proportion of members of a group who declared Russian as their mother tongue is quite strongly related to the proportion of younger members of the group who reidentify. Thus a single explanation of the reidentification process that does not directly involve traditional religious identification may be adequate for both Orthodox and Muslim groups. That is, it is possible that declaring Russian as one's mother tongue is a first step in the process by which an individual reidentifies as Russian (it is not possible to know whether this is true without data for individuals), and that a member of a traditionally Muslim group who declares Russian as the mother tongue may be just as likely to reidentify as a member of a traditionally Orthodox group who declares

Russian as the mother tongue. Were this the case, traditional Orthodoxy would affect the likelihood of reidentification to Russian only indirectly, by increasing the likelihood of declaring Russian as the mother tongue.

TABLE 9.2

Pearson Correlations among Survival Ratios and Socioeconomic Variables for ASSR-Level Nationality Groups

	Russ	ASSR	Orthodox	Urban	ln Pop(0-19)
Russ	1.000	.631*	.611*	.430	-.005
ASSR	.631*	1.000	.361	.501	.674*
Orthodox	.611*	.361	1.000	.005	.011
Urban	.240	.310	-.083	1.000	.302
ln Pop(0-19)	-.005	.674*	-.011	.302	1.000
S_1	-.849*	-.646*	-.574*	-.125	-.088
S_2	-.644*	-.554*	-.476	.159	-.138
S	-.745*	-.603*	-.528	.040	-.118

n = 13.   *$p < .05$, two-tailed test.

   Russ = number citing Russian as mother tongue, per 1,000 population of those living in the RSFSR in 1959.

   ASSR = number not living in the group's designated ASSR but still living in the RSFSR, per 1,000 members of the group living in the RSFSR in 1959.

   Orthodox = a dummy variable with value one if the group is traditionally Orthodox and value zero if the group is traditionally Muslim.

   Urban = number in the RSFSR living in urban places in 1959, per 1,000 living in the RSFSR in 1959.

   ln Pop (0-19) = natural logarithm of the number of persons aged 0-19 (in thousands) living in the RSFSR in 1959.

   S_1 = number aged 11-19 in the RSFSR in 1970, per 1,000 in the group aged 0-9 in the RSFSR in 1959.

   S_2 = number aged 20-29 in the RSFSR in 1970, per 1,000 in the group aged 10-19 in the RSFSR in 1959.

   S = average of S_1 and S_2.

   Source: See note 1.

The two variables that correlate most strongly with each of the survival ratios are the Russian-language variable, "Russ," and the variable labeled ASSR. It may be easier for someone in the RSFSR who is by origin a member of an ASSR-level nationality group to convince a census taker that he is a member of some other nationality group (in most cases, Russian) if he does not live in the autonomous republic of the group of his origin. ASSR also can be interpreted, however, as an indicator of interethnic contact. If a person does not live in his group's ASSR, he is more likely to interact with members of other ethnic groups, such as Russians. A substantial amount of Soviet research, for example, indicates that a person living outside his group's designated area (an ASSR in the case of ASSR-level groups and a republic in the case of republic-level groups) is much more likely to enter into a mixed marriage than is a person living in his group's designated area. [7] As was suggested earlier, for many persons entering a mixed marriage may be a first step in the process of ethnic reidentification.

The relationship between the averaged survival ratio, S (which is the indicator of the extent of nationality identification of those less than age 20 in 1959), and the Russian-language variable is shown in Figure 9.1. Traditionally Orthodox groups are indicated by circles and traditionally Muslim groups by squares. The extent of reidentification increases (indicated by a decreasing value of S) as the number of individuals who declare Russian as their mother tongue increases. The one-variable regression line is shown to indicate the trend of the relationship. In Figure 9.1 much of the relationship between the two variables is due to the values for the Karelians and Mordvinians. However, the strong correlation (-.745) is not due to a simple difference in the relationship between Russian language and the survival ratio between Orthodox and Muslim groups. Considering the Orthodox groups alone, the correlation between the survival ratio and the Russian-language variable is -.817, which is quite strong and is still statistically significantly different from zero at the 5 percent level. Figure 9.2 shows the relationship between the number per 1,000 who live in the RSFSR but not in the group's ASSR and the survival ratio. Also in Figure 9.2, the one-variable regression line is shown. Higher values of the ASSR variable are related to lower values of S, indicating that there was a tendency for a group to experience more reidentification the higher the proportion of the group that did not live in its designated ASSR. The relationship between ASSR and S clearly is not due to the values for a few groups. Even within the Orthodox groups, the correlation between ASSR and S is -.878, which is significantly different from zero at the 5 percent level. The maintenance of the strength of the correlations even when the Orthodox groups are considered alone further supports

the contention that a common explanation may suffice for traditionally Orthodox and traditionally Muslim groups considered together.

FIGURE 9.1

Relationship between Average Survival Ratio and Number
Citing Russian as Mother Tongue in 1959

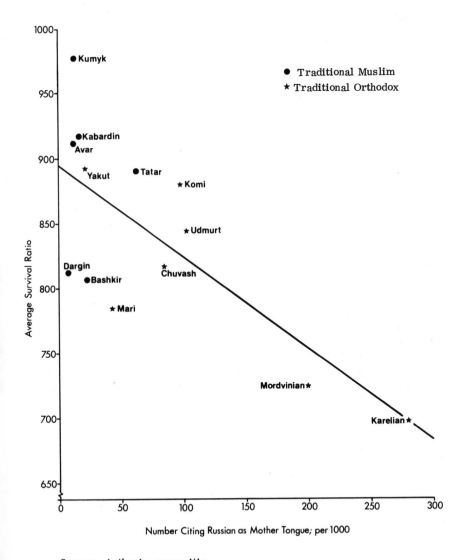

Source: Author's composition.

FIGURE 9.2

Relationship between Average Survival Ratio and Number
not Living in Their Designated ASSR in 1959

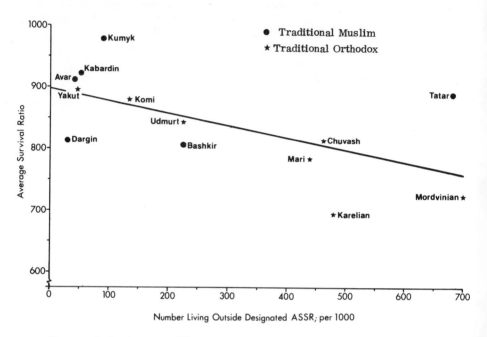

Source: Author's composition.

The joint effect of the Russian-language variable and the variable indicating the proportion of the group that lives in the RSFSR
but not in the group's ASSR on the averaged survival ratio also can
be examined. The two-variable regression equation yielded by these
variables is

$$S = 905 - .579\text{Russ}^* - .071\text{ASSR} \quad R^2 = .58 \quad F = 7.04^* \quad (\text{eq. 1})$$
$$\quad\quad\quad (2.31) \quad\quad\quad (.84)$$

The t values of the individual coefficients appear below the coefficients. For an equation with this number of variables (2 variables)
and this number of units of analysis (13 groups), a coefficient of an
individual variable is significantly different from zero at the 5 percent level if the t value of the coefficient is greater than 2.2. The
entire equation explains a significant amount of the variability in the
dependent variable if the F value of the equation is greater than 4.1.

By these standards, the overall equation explains a significant amount
of the variability in the averaged survival ratio. Fifty-eight percent
of the variability in S is explained by the equation. Also, the coefficient for the Russian-language variable is individually statistically
significant. One interpretation of the coefficient of the Russian-
language variable is that if each of two groups has equal proportions
of its group not living in its respective ASSRs, then if one group has
a greater proportion of its members claiming Russian as mother
tongue of 100 per 1,000 more than the other group, the group with a
greater proportion claiming Russian will have 58 out of 1,000 more
persons who were below age 20 in 1959 reidentifying by 1970 than
will the group with a smaller proportion claiming Russian as its
mother tongue.

The coefficient of the variable ASSR is not individually statistically significant due to the strong relationship between ASSR and
the Russian-language variable. (The correlation between Russ and
ASSR is .631.) Research on the determinants of linguistic russification has indicated that interethnic contact within an official nationality area (SSR, ASSR, AO, or NO), as measured by the proportion of
the area's population that is Russian, is positively related to the linguistic russification of the members of the titular nationality within
the area. (See chapter 8.) This is consistent with the strong positive correlation between the Russian-language variable and ASSR.

In combination with the Russian-language variable, the second
variable that best accounts for the variation in the averaged survival
ratio is the urban residence variable, which was also found to be important in the discriminant analysis. This variable indicates the
number of group members who lived in urban areas within the RSFSR
in 1959 per 1,000 group members who lived anywhere in the RSFSR
in 1959. The two-variable regression equation yielded by the Russian-
language and urban variables is

$$S = 828 - .895 \text{Russ}^* + .368 \text{Urban}^* \quad R^2 = .71 \quad F = 12.51^* \quad \text{(eq. 2)}$$
$$(5.00) \phantom{\text{Russ}^* + .}(2.36)$$

In this equation both the Russian-language variable and the urban variable make significant independent contributions. Also, the equation as
a whole explains a significant amount of the variability in S (71 percent).
As was found in the discriminant analysis, if groups do not differ in the
proportion declaring Russian as mother tongue, then the group with the
higher proportion living in urban areas will tend to have less reidentification by its members who were aged less than 20 in 1959. This
supports the earlier suggestion that speaking Russian may have a quite
different meaning for urban than for rural residents. The equation
implies that if groups do not differ in the proportion living in urban

areas, then a difference of 100 per 1,000 in the proportion of the group claiming Russian as mother tongue will be associated with a difference of 90 per 1,000 in the number of those under age 20 in 1959 who reidentify by 1970, with the group having a larger proportion declaring Russian as mother tongue experiencing more reidentification.

PREDICTIONS FOR REPUBLIC-LEVEL
NATIONALITY GROUPS

One may ask whether the same factors that seem to relate to reidentification by members of ASSR-level nationality groups in the RSFSR also operate for republic-level nationality group members in the Soviet Union as a whole. Can the finding that none of the republic-level nationality groups seem to have experienced substantial reidentification be explained by the values that the republic-level nationalities have on variables related to reidentification by members of ASSR-level nationality groups?

The survival ratios (indicating nationality identification) and values of socioeconomic variables for the republic-level nationality groups appear in Table 9.1. These values all refer to the group within the Soviet Union as a whole. The analysis that provided the best explanation for ASSR-level groups within the RSFSR was based on the number of persons per 1,000 declaring Russian as their mother tongue in 1959 and the proportion of the population living in urban areas in 1959. This was shown in equation 2. Using equation 2 as a prediction equation with the values for republic-level groups shown in Table 9.1, the lowest predicted values of the averaged survival ratio, S, were for Ukrainians, Belorussians, Moldavians, and Kirghiz.* The predicted values were 863, 810, 843, and 865, respectively. However, the actual S values for these four groups, shown in Table 9.1, were higher and were within the accepted range for S: Ukrainian 911, Belorussian 920, Moldavian 919, Kirghiz 919. Thus, members of the republic-level groups seem not to reidentify even when factors associated with reidentification among ASSR-level

---

*Some other republic-level groups had predicted S values slightly below the cut-off value of 909: Kazakhs 902, Uzbeks 904, Tadzhiks 899. The actual values for these groups were 956, 945, and 943, respectively. Given the imprecision of such prediction equations, such small differences from 909 as were found for the Kazakhs, Uzbeks, and Tadzhiks were not taken seriously.

groups are present. The actual values of S are low. However, they are not low enough to say unambiguously that any of these republic-level groups were experiencing substantial reidentification. In each case the relatively low actual S value was the result of a survival ratio for the youngest birth cohort within the accepted range (slightly above the accepted range for Kirghiz) and a survival ratio for the second birth cohort slightly below the range.

One possible explanation for the failure of republic-level groups to reidentify may be the size difference between the ASSR-level nationality groups and the republic-level nationality groups. The Ukrainians and the Belorussians were the largest republic-level nationality groups (excluding the Russians), and even the Moldavians were more numerous than any ASSR-level nationality group except the Tatars. There was some suggestive evidence even within the analysis of ASSR-level nationality groups that size may have affected the tendency for a group to experience reidentification. If one examines Figures 9.1 and 9.2, it is clear that the value of the averaged survival ratio for Tatars was higher (indicating less reidentification) than would be expected if one considers either the proportion of Tatars declaring Russian as their mother tongue or the proportion of Tatars not living in the Tatar ASSR. Although the relatively high value of S for Tatars may be partially due to Bashkirs reidentifying as Tatars, the large size of the Tatar group may also have inhibited reidentification.

Thus it was decided to obtain as good a prediction equation as possible that included a measure of population size based on the 13 ASSR-level groups under consideration. In this analysis the natural logarithm of population size relates more strongly to the tendency of a group to reidentify than does the untransformed measure of population size. The natural logarithm increases less rapidly than population size itself. This means that an increase from 5 million to 6 million has less impact on the size of the natural logarithm than does an increase from 1 million to 2 million. Of course, if one group is larger than another, the larger group will have a larger natural logarithm of its population size. After some preliminary analysis, it also was clear that the size of the younger part of the population is more important than the size of the total population. This is reasonable, since evidence of reidentification among the young was the motivation for this study.

The size of the population of each group aged 0-19 years in 1959, in thousands, appears in Table 9.1. This was converted to the natural logarithm of the number of persons under age 20, in thousands, through a computer transformation. Using the 13 ASSR-level nationality groups to obtain such a prediction equation, the variable that in combination with the natural logarithm of the population under age 20 in thousands, resulted in the best equation was the variable indicating the proportion of the ASSR-level group that lived in the RSFSR but outside of the group's ASSR.* The resulting prediction equation was

$$S = 725 - .310ASSR* + 39.699\ln \text{Pop}(0\text{-}19) \quad R^2 = .517 \quad F = 5.36* \\ \quad\quad (3.23) \quad\quad\quad (1.78) \quad\quad\quad\quad\quad\quad\quad\quad (\text{eq. } 3)$$

The overall equation explains a significant amount of the variability in S at the 5 percent level. Also, the coefficient of the variable indicating the extent to which group members in the RSFSR did not live in the group's ASSR (ASSR) is significantly different from zero. The coefficient of the population variable is not individually statistically significant.

---

*The "best" equation was chosen through a combination of a high R^2 value and a reasonably high, even if nonsignificant, value of the t statistic for the population variable. The highest R^2 value for an equation including the natural logarithm of the number of persons under age 20 in 1959 and one other variable included the Russian-language variable rather than the variable ASSR. The R^2 value for the equation with the language variable and the population variable was .57, which is slightly higher than the R^2 value of .52 obtained for the population variable combined with the variable ASSR. In the equation with the language variable and the population variable, the coefficient of the language variable was quite significant (the t statistic was 3.6). However, the population variable was essentially inconsequential. Its t statistic was .58. It has been observed that even if a variable has a statistically insignificant coefficient at some reasonable probability level, such as 5 percent, the variable can still substantially affect a prediction equation if the t statistic for the coefficient is at least 1.00. In the equation including ASSR, the population variable clearly is meaningful in this sense (the t statistic for the population variable was 1.78), while this condition was not met in the equation including the population variable and the language variable. It seemed ridiculous to try to obtain an equation including a population variable and then to accept one where the population variable's coefficient was statistically insignificant and the t statistic was so low that the entire effect of the population variable on the prediction variable was questionable. Thus the equation including ASSR was accepted, even though the R^2 value was somewhat lower than for the equation including the language variable.

When this equation was applied to republic-level nationality groups, the variable measuring the proportion of the group not living in the territory of its own ASSR was replaced by a variable measuring the proportion of the group not living in the territory of its own republic. When this is done, the lowest predicted value of the averaged survival ratio for a republic-level nationality is for the Armenians (a predicted value of 866, compared with an actual value of 955). This low predicted Armenian survival ratio (predicting substantial reidentification) is due to the large proportion of Armenians not living in Armenia (44 percent). Most Armenians who did not live in Armenia were in Georgia or Azerbaidzhan. Only 13 percent of Armenians in the Soviet Union in 1959 lived in a republic other than Armenia, Georgia, or Azerbaidzhan. Azerbaidzhan and Georgia have long been areas of Armenian settlement. Armenians in these areas generally live in compact communities and enjoy a relatively well-developed cultural infrastructure of their own. At least in Georgia and Azerbaidzhan, therefore, settlement outside the borders of the Armenian Republic cannot reasonably be interpreted as exposing Armenians to contact and interaction with members of other nationalities in a manner that would predispose such Armenians to reidentify. When one replaces the ASSR value for Armenians of 443 per 1,000 (the number per 1,000 not living in Armenia) by a value of 126 per 1,000 (the number per 1,000 not living in Armenia, Georgia, or Azerbaidzhan), the predicted averaged survival ratio for Armenians becomes 964, which is well above the minimal acceptable value for the averaged survival ratio. *

The findings for the Armenians suggest that where members of a nationality group (especially a republic-level nationality group) settle when they move outside the borders of their own republic may be an important factor in determining the extent of nationality reidentification. Exact criteria for when a movement might be expected to increase the chance of reidentification are unclear, but

---

*Using equation 3 as a prediction equation, the only group other than the Armenians with a predicted value of S below 909 was the Tadzhiks, with a predicted value of 905. Tadzhiks have long settled in the Uzbek Republic. Twenty-five percent of Tadzhiks in the Soviet Union in 1959 did not live in the Tadzhik Republic, but only 3 percent of Tadzhiks in the Soviet Union in 1959 lived neither in the Tadzhik nor in the Uzbek Republic. When the proportion of Tadzhiks living in neither Tadzhikstan nor Uzbekistan is used for the value of the ASSR variable for Tadzhiks, the predicted value of S for Tadzhiks is well above 909.

they might include the length of settlement by members of the nationality of the migrants in the destination area and the relative size of
the migrants' nationality group at the destination.

Thus, not only is there no strong evidence of reidentification
among republic-level nationalities of the Soviet Union, but the use
of predictors drawn from the analysis of ASSR-level groups suggests that there ought not to be any evidence. It may be the large
size of the republic-level nationality groups that accounts for their
apparent lack of reidentification.

PREDICTIONS FOR 1979

All of the explanatory variables used in this analysis were
from the 1959 Soviet census. It is sensible for possible explanatory
variables to predate the phenomenon they are attempting to explain.
The next Soviet census is scheduled for 1979. It is possible to use
the values of the variables in the 1970 Soviet census (the variables
that were important on the basis of 1959 explanatory variables and
1970 survival) to predict what survival ratios may look like on the
basis of the comparison of the 1979 and 1970 Soviet censuses.

If equation 2 is used with the values of the Russian-language
variable and the urban residence variable from the 1970 census,
then the tendency of ASSR-level groups to reidentify by 1979 can be
predicted, under the assumption that the Russian-language variable
and the urban residence variable capture those characteristics that
are related to reidentification by members of ASSR-level groups.
The rate of reidentification in 1970-79, based on equation 2, is predicted to be approximately the same as the rate in 1959-70. Between
1959 and 1970, an average increase of 40 percent in the proportion
citing Russian as their mother tongue was almost exactly offset by an
increase of 47 percent in the proportion living in urban places. Using
equation 2, the average predicted value of the averaged survival
ratio, S, for 1970 (using explanatory variables from 1959) was 843
for the 13 ASSR-level groups, while that based on 1970 explanatory
variables was 849.

There were 11 years between the 1959 and 1970 censuses,
while there are only nine years between the 1970 and 1979 censuses.
One can convert the predicted values of the averaged survival ratio
into a yearly rate of reidentification out of the group of birth. In
this manner, one can estimate the number of persons who will have
reidentified by 1979. In order to convert the value of S into a yearly
rate, one estimates the number of persons who would remain in
their group of birth if the next census were in 1981, 11 years after
the 1970 census, taking into account expected mortality under the

assumption that mortality conditions will not change appreciably for young persons in that period. This is done by applying the transformation

$$\frac{x}{1000} = \frac{\text{predicted value of S from 1970 values}}{909} \qquad \text{(eq. 4)}$$

The predicted value of S is compared with 909, the lower bound of the range of S estimated to appear if there is not substantial reidentification by members of the group. The number of persons remaining in the group of birth 11 years after 1970, per 1,000 persons who would be in the group if no one had reidentified, is represented by x. Using the fact that there were 11 years between 1959 and 1970, one can employ the values of x to estimate an annual rate of reidentification out of the group of birth by assuming that persons leave the group of origin in a negative exponential manner.* The rate of reidentification may then be found by using the following transformation:

$$r = \frac{-(\ln \frac{x}{1000})}{11} \qquad \text{(eq. 5)}$$

Then r is the number of persons under age 20 in 1970 who leave their nationality group of birth per year, per 1,000 persons under age 20 in 1970 who remain in that group of birth. Using equations 4 and 5, about 5 out of every 1,000 persons aged 0–19 in 1970 are predicted to reidentify each year out of the 13 ASSR-level groups considered. Karelians have the highest predicted rate of reidentification, 28 per 1,000 persons per year. Among those seven ASSR-level groups that seem to have experienced substantial reidentification between 1959 and 1970, approximately 172 per 1,000 of those under age 20 in 1970 (more than 7 percent of their total populations under age 20 in 1970) should have reidentified by 1979, assuming that the correlates of reidentification remain unchanged between 1970 and 1979.

----

*When persons leave a population at a constant rate based on the number of persons remaining in a population at a given time, they leave the population in a negative-exponential pattern. This is similar to compound interest. The equation for r was obtained by solving the equation

$$1000e^{-r11} = x$$

where x persons remain after reidentification has occurred for 11 years.

One also can consider the republic-level groups. Using equation 3, none of the groups are predicted to have experienced substantial reidentification by 1979. The only predicted S value below 909 was for the Armenians (899). This value was well above the predicted S value for Armenians based on the 1959 census explanatory variables (866). Even in 1970 a substantial proportion of Armenians did not live in the Armenian Republic (38 percent). However, as in 1959, the majority of those not living in Armenia lived in the other two transcaucasian republics, Georgia and Azerbaidzhan. Only 12 percent of Armenians in the Soviet Union in 1970 did not live in a transcaucasian republic. When the proportion not living in Armenia, Georgia, or Azerbaidzhan is substituted for the proportion not living in Armenia as the ASSR variable, the predicted value of the averaged survival ratio (S) is well above 909. All of the republic-level groups grew in size between 1959 and 1970, and this increase somewhat inhibits reidentification, in the sense implied by equation 3. Moreover, the proportion of republic-level groups not living in their republics somewhat decreased, on average, between 1959 and 1970.

CONCLUSIONS

In many ways the finding of high levels of ethnic reidentification among members of ASSR-level nationalities within the Russian Republic and very little reidentification among republic-level nationalities is consistent with the Soviet policy of respecting the integrity of republic-level nationalities while encouraging nationality groups with lower political status to become assimilated into a republic-level group. This is reflected, for example, in Soviet school policy, which has served to encourage the linguistic russification of many of the groups found here to be reidentifying. (See Chapter 8.)

The 1979 census should allow one to determine which of the two alternative explanations for such reidentification cited earlier is more powerful. If the age-specific explanation is correct, the survival ratios (indicating the extent of reidentification) between 1970 and 1979 should look normal for those birth cohorts aged 20 or older in 1970. However, if the alternative based on a generational argument is correct, then the group aged 30-39 in 1979 should show a low survival ratio, indicating continuing reidentification after the persons reached age 20. The determination of whether the reidentification process discussed in this chapter continues in the future and specification of the nature of the reidentification process itself await the results of the 1979 Soviet census.

NOTES

1. The sources of data used in this paper are USSR, Tsentral-noe Statisticheskoe Upravlenie, Itogi vsesoiuznoi perepisi naseleniia, 1959 goda (Moscow: Gosstatizdat, 1962-63), RSFSR vol., tables 53, 54a, and 54d, USSR vol., tables 53, 54a, and 54d; and USSR, Tsentralnoe Statisticheskoe Upravlenie, Itogi vsesoiuznoi perepisi naseleniia, 1970 goda (Moscow: Statistika, 1972-73), 4: tables 4, 5, 32, 33.

2. Murray Feshbach, Chief, Russia and Eastern Europe Branch, Foreign Demographic Analysis Division, Department of Commerce, pointed this out to me.

3. Brian D. Silver, "Inventory of Propositions Drawn from Soviet Empirical Research on the Attitudes of Soviet Nationalities," paper presented at the AAASS Nationalities Project Workshop, Banff, Canada, September 2-4, 1974.

4. On the attitude toward work collectives, see L. M. Drobizheva, "Sotsial'no-kul'turnye osobennosti lichnosti i national'nye ustanovki (po materialan issledovanii v Tatarskoi ASSR)," Sovetskaia etnografiia (1971), no. 3: 3-15; and M. N. Guboglo, "Sotsial'no-etnicheskie posledstviia dvuiazychiia," Sovetskaia etnografiia (1972), no. 2: 26-36; on nationality of supervisors, see Iu. V. Arutiunian, "Opyt sotsial'no-etnicheskogo issledovaniia (po materialam Tatarskoi ASSR)," Sovetskaia etnografiia (1968), no. 4: 3-13; and Guboglo, op. cit.

5. Personal conversation with Basil Zimmer.

6. Iu. V. Arutiunian, "Konkretno-sotsiologischeskoe issledovanie natsional'nykh otnoshenii," Voprosy filosofii (1969), no. 12: 129-39.

7. Silver, op. cit. See also M. V. Kurman and I. V. Lebedinskii, Naseleniia bol'shogo sotsialosticheskogo goroda (Moscow: Statistika, 1968); N. A. Tomilov, "Sovremennye etnicheskie protsessy u Tatar gorodov zapadnoi sibiri," Sovetskaia etnografiia (1972), no. 6: 87-97.

MUSLIM CONSERVATIVE OPPOSITION TO THE SOVIET REGIME: THE SUFI BROTHERHOODS IN THE NORTH CAUCASUS

10

Alexandre Bennigsen

Today the Muslim regions of the USSR are quiet; but in the past the North Caucasus and Central Asia have been the site of violent anti-Russian and anti-Soviet movements, including most notably the Daghestani-Chechen revolt of 1920-21 and the Basmachi uprising between 1919 and 1928. These movements were inspired and led by the Sufi brotherhoods of Islam, extremely conservative and traditionalist groups that apparently passed from the Soviet scene in the late 1920s. Now, however, we have evidence that these brotherhoods have reappeared and that their influence among Soviet Muslims is growing, especially in the North Caucasus. Given their significant role in the past, we must be attentive to these developments and carefully examine their possible role in Muslim movements in the dramatically changed conditions of today. Here I will examine briefly the relationship of the Sufi brotherhoods to official Islam, their history and current state, and their possible roles in future anti-Russian and anti-Soviet movements among Soviet Muslims.

THE TWO FACES OF ISLAM

In the Soviet Union today, Islam has two faces: an official, public one and a nonofficial, underground one. Until recently only the first was visible to the West, and today it presents a sad picture. No more than 300 mosques remain in official operation, compared

---

This chapter is dedicated to the memory of Haidar and Zeinab Bammate, who honored me with their friendship.

with some 25,000 in 1917;* and there are fewer than 2,000 "registered" clerics. Only two religious schools are "working,"† and
there are few publications. More important, Soviet Islam has been
reduced by the regime to a private affair for individual believers
and to a thoroughly domesticated and intellectually backward bureaucratic ecclesiastical establishment.[1] These aspects of the public
face of Islam in the Soviet Union suggest that it is--as Soviet spokesmen usually put it--an unimportant survival of another age now rapidly disappearing in the conditions of developed socialist society.
Soviet Islam is divided into four spiritual directorates (three Sunni
and one mixed Shi'a-Sunni) headed by muftis: Tashkent, which is
responsible for Central Asia and Kazakhstan, and which uses Uzbek
as its administrative language; Ufa, which is responsible for European Russia and Siberia, and which uses Kazan Tatar as its administrative language; Buinakst in Daghestan, which is responsible for
the North Caucasus and uses Arabic as its administrative language;
and Baku. The chairman of this last directorate is the Shi'a Sheikh
ul-Islam, who is responsible for all Shi'a communities of the USSR;
the vice-chairman is the Sunni mufti, who is responsible for the
Sunnis of Transcaucasia. The language of this directorate is Azeri

---

*Prior to 1914 there were some 12,000 mosques in Central
Asia and Kazakhstan; according to an official Soviet count, there
were only 250 left in 1964, but even this number seems to be an exaggeration. A recent traveler in the Soviet Union reported to the
author that a representative of the Spiritual Directorate in Tashkent
stated that there were 12 working mosques in Tashkent oblast, 65 in
Azerbaidzhan, and 146 in Central Asia and Kazakhstan as a whole.
These figures seem closer to the truth. In Daghestan before the
Revolution there were some 2,060 mosques, including 360 cathedral
mosques and 800 Koranic schools. See M. Z. Magomedov, "Iz
istorii reshenii natsional'nogo i religioznogo voprosov na severnom
Kavkaze," Voprosy nauchnogo ateizma 14 (1973): 45. By 1967 in
Daghestan and the Chechen-Ingush ASSR the number of "working"
mosques had been reduced to 27 and the number of Koranic schools
to zero. I. A. Makatov, "Kul't sviatykh v Islame," Voprosy
nauchnogo ateizma 3 (1967): 176. In the Tatar ASSR the number of
mosques probably is less than 20 and there are no religious schools.
In 1927 there were 2,200 mosques, 4,000 mullahs, and 800 religious
schools with 30,000 students in this same territory. See L. I.
Klimovich, "Bor'ba ortodoksov is modernistov v Islame," Voprosy
nauchnogo ateizma 2 (1966): 78.

†The medressehs of Mir-i Arab in Bukhara and Baraq Khan in
Tashkent together graduate fewer than 50 students each year.

Turkic. These four directorates control the working mosques and the two medressehs, and they appoint and pay the "registered" clerics. The religious publications of the directorates consist of a religious calendar (some 10,000 copies per year) and a quarterly journal, Musul'mane sovetskogo vostoka, in Uzbek, Arabic, English, and French. This Islamic equivalent of the Zhurnal moskovskoi patriarkhii has a strong propagandistic character. Since World War II the directorates have been able to publish only two editions of the Quran (in 1947 and 1964).

That Islam has another, unofficial, and more important face in the Soviet Union is suggested by the vociferous anti-religious campaigns directed against Muslim believers, campaigns that would hardly be necessary were Islam as weak as its official face suggests, and by the increasing number of serious monographs on Islam.[2] From these two sources we learn much of what we know about the real situation of Muslims in the USSR: from the first, because of what is attacked, and from the second, because of what is investigated.

Soviet anti-Islamic campaigns generally are directed at "survivals of the past" (perezhitki proshlogo), including such "harmful socioreligious traditions" as kalym (bride price), polygamy, Ramadan fasting, circumcision, "feudal-reactionary" attitudes toward women, "primitive superstitions," and the cult of holy places. The campaigns typically condemn the traditional Muslim way of life as "anti-social" and "parasitic," and its customs as "disgusting" and "unhygienic." At the same time, and in sharp contrast with those conducted in the Stalin era, Soviet anti-Islam campaigns today seldom attack Islam's foreign origins, "class character," "unscientific" theology, and "anti-progressive" legal apparatus. They never attack the official hierarchy of Soviet Islam. This selectivity suggests that the popular, cultural, and unofficial aspects of Islam are increasingly powerful and dangerous to the regime, and that the Soviet leadership is not attacking "official" Islam lest it drive even more Muslims from under its direct supervision and into clandestineness.

Soviet scholars have provided additional information on the dangers of this previously hidden face of Islam in the Soviet Union. First, they have suggested that there is an increasing confusion in the popular mind between Islam and nationalistic ideas, and that this confusion has complicated the problem of fighting "survivals" of the past.[3] And, second, they have presented evidence that shows underground Islam to be a vital and aggressive force in present-day Soviet society. L. I. Klimovich, the senior, and perhaps most qualified, anti-Islamic specialist, has written:

In Islam--both Sunni and Shia--there exist two opposite trends: the official "mosque" trend led by the

muftis, the Sheikh ul-Islam and other representatives
of the four official Muslim Spiritual Directorates, and
the non-official, "non-mosque" trend. The latter is a
communitarian trend, sufi-dervish, murid trend, led
by ishans, pirs, sheikhs, and ustads. . . . Everywhere the clerics of the "non-mosque" trend are many
times more numerous than the clerics of the official
Islam. In some important areas--for instance in the
North Caucasus and in particular in the Chechen-
Ingush ASSR--almost all clerics belong to a murid-
dervish brotherhood.[4]

The rise of this nonofficial Muslim clergy has been possible because
Islam does not have a clergy as such, and because there is no canoni-
cal difference between official, registered clerics and unofficial, unregistered ones. Now we must investigate the Sufi brotherhoods, to
which most of the unofficial clerics are attached. They form the
most powerful core of underground Islam in the Soviet Union.

SUFISM PAST AND PRESENT

Contemporary underground Islam in the USSR has its roots in
a very old religious-political movement--Sufism--that appeared in
Islam during its earliest period.[5] Sufism began as a method of
moral psychology for the practical guidance of individuals, and continued to be based on the premise that behind the official exoteric
faith there is an esoteric knowledge available only to the initiated
adept. By the twelfth century, Sufism began to lose its individualistic character and to become a collective, militant movement. At the
root of this transformation was the idea that it is impossible for an
individual to proceed to a higher level of spiritual knowledge without
the help of a master (sheikh, ustad, pir, murshid). These masters
were to be obeyed blindly, for only with their assistance could individual mystics succeed in their journeys to God. This same discipline and hierarchy also was applied to such mundane duties as the
waging of holy war (jihad, gazavat) for the purity of Islam against
infidels or "bad Muslims."

In the course of this transformation, Sufism gave birth to
numerous brotherhoods, the tariqas (which meant "paths" or "ways"
to God). The tariqas were communities of initiated adepts grouped
around a master, a man of forceful personality often reputed to be
blessed with near-miraculous powers. Each tariqa had its own system of rules and rites for spiritual training, systems whose general
features have continued to the present day. To become an adept, the
novice (murid) was initiated according to a secret ritual and given

oral instructions concerning the rules of the brotherhood. Once admitted, the initiated adept typically lived in close association with his master, either permanently in a special monastery or on a temporary retreat. He was obliged to perform certain vigils, offices, invocations, and litanies. The litanies consist of fixed phrases that are repeated aloud ("loud zikr") or in the mind ("silent zikr"); these repetitions are accompanied by special breathing and physical movements that are to prepare the adept for a state of intense mental concentration and to develop a sense of iron discipline.

Membership in the Sufi orders always has been of two kinds: a higher class of initiates engages in mystic duties while a larger body of "lay" members meet on special occasions for the ceremony of zikr but otherwise follow their individual secular occupations. This double character of Sufism has given the brotherhoods a genuinely popular aspect. As H. A. R. Gibb has written, "The strength of Sufism lay in the satisfaction it gave to the religious instinct of the people. "[6]

The role played by the Sufi brotherhoods in the expansion, strengthening, and later defense of Islam in Central Asia, India, black Africa, and Southeast Asia was immense. One brotherhood in particular--the great Naqshebandi tariqa, founded in Bukhara by Baha ud-Din Naqsheband (d. 1388)--has dominated the history of Muslim Asia since the fifteenth century. Almost all Muslim resistance movements against the conquering "infidel"--the British in the Punjab, the Chinese in Sinkiang, the Dutch in Indonesia, and the Russians in Turkestan and in the Caucasus--were inspired or led by the Naqshebandi sheikhs. [7] However, by the end of the nineteenth century, the military strength and political influence of most tariqas had declined almost to the vanishing point; and in many areas of the Muslim world, the brotherhoods came to be looked on almost as heretics by the official Islamic establishment. The Sufis were accused of various theological transgressions, of conducting dangerous supererogatory exercises, of the abuse of stimulants, and of blind submission to the will of their respective masters. Their invocation of saints--one of the bases of Sufism--was attacked as polytheistic by Orthodox Muslims. [8] "In many places," notes Louis Massignon, "the acrobatics and the juggling practiced by certain adepts of the lower classes and the moral corruption of too many of their leaders aroused against almost all of them the hostility and the contempt of the modern Muslim world. "[9] But at the same time, in spite of its moral and organizational decline, Sufism remained until the twentieth century an "aristocratic" creed, opposing personal experience of the select few to the rational, but secondhand, knowledge of official Islam.

In Russia the history of the Sufi tariqas was different. Because of the unrelenting threat posed by the conquering Christian world, Sufism in Russia did not go into decline; and no antagonism emerged between official Islam and the mystical brotherhoods, a unique case in the history of Islam. A complete symbiosis existed between the orthodox Islamic establishment and the tariqas, largely because the latter represented the strongest bastions of Muslim resistance to Russian conquest. In some areas of the Russian Empire-- particularly in the North Caucasus--the Sufi orders nearly absorbed official Islam.

In Central Asia the Naqshebandi tariqa dominated the political affairs of the emirate of Bukhara throughout the nineteenth century, and it was the vanguard of the Andizhan uprising against the Russians in 1898. Naqshebandi influence spread to the Middle Volga region, where some of its leaders played a major role in the Tatar intellectual, cultural, and religious revival of that time. [10] But it was in the North Caucasus that the Sufi brotherhoods assumed their most spectacular historical role. The Naqshebandis penetrated into Shirvan from eastern Anatolia in the second half of the eighteenth century; and from 1785 to 1791 a Naqshebandi Chechen murshid, the imam Mansur, led the mountaineers into their first holy war against Russian encroachment. [11] In the nineteenth century this resistance was continued by the Naqshebandi murshids Ghazi Mohammed, Hamzat Beg, and the legendary Shamil. Despite its ultimate defeat, this tariqa gained immense prestige throughout Asia as a result of this heroic, almost century-long resistance.

In the late 1850s another brotherhood appeared in the North Caucasus, the tariqa of Kunta Haji, founded by a Daghestani, Kunta Haji Kishiev. This group was a branch of the old Qadiriya. * Rising after the defeat of Shamil, at a time when infidel domination had to be accepted, this tariqa was very different from the militant Naqshebandi. Its outlook developed in an apocalyptic atmosphere and was marked more by mustic asceticism than by the appeal to holy war. Adepts of this tariqa practiced the "loud zikr" and their rites included dances, songs, and ecstasies. However, like all other tariqas in Russia, the Kunta Haji order blended mystical detachment from the world with what it perceived to be the necessity of resisting Russian pressure. Such resistance often assumed violent forms. In 1863, Kunta Haji was arrested and sent to Siberia, where he died. This incited his followers to attack Russian troops in Chechenia the following year; and although this revolt was crushed by the 1870s, the

---

*The Qadiriya was founded by Abd al-Qadir Gilani (1077-1166) of Baghdad. The leadership is hereditary. The tariqa has many regional suborders loosely connected to the central institution in Baghdad.

brotherhood was already solidly rooted in the region and remained strong. Later it split into four groups, the most important of which was the Bammat Hoja tariqa, founded by another Daghestani, Bammat Giray Mitaev. [12]

During the Bolshevik revolution and the Russian Civil War, the Sufi tariqas again played an important role. The two most important popular uprisings against Russian domination in Muslim lands were heavily influenced by the Naqshebandis. The Daghestani-Chechen revolt of 1920 was led by the brotherhood;* and the Central Asian Basmachi movement, which began in 1918 and lasted until 1928 (and in some places even to 1936), included a large number of Naqshebandi adepts in its leadership and ranks.† Both movements were eventually defeated by the Red Army after prolonged and bitter fighting; but this fierce resistance by these ultraconservatives seeking to preserve the purity and glory of their faith stands in stark contrast with the rather halfhearted and inefficient efforts by Muslim liberal and right-wing socialist groups to ward off Soviet power. To the Muslim conservatives, Soviet power was simply another variant of Russian encroachment, and would be met in the same way as its tsarist predecessors had been.

After 1928 the tariqas disappeared from public view. Outlawed and persecuted, their leaders were hunted down, arrested, and liquidated as "parasites," "anti-social elements," and--in the 1930s-- spies and traitors. The number of adepts fell dramatically, and the surviving brotherhoods moved underground to continue their activities clandestinely.‡ Consequently, it is difficult to determine the extent

---

*The Naqshebandi sheikh, Uzun Haji, dominated the political scene of Daghestan-Chechenia between February 1917 and March 1921. He fought on all fronts--against the Russian Whites of Denikin, against the Bolsheviks, and against his own liberal countrymen. He used to proclaim: "I am weaving a rope to hang the students, the engineers, the intellectuals, and more generally all those who write from left to right" (meaning those who wrote Russian). The imam Najmuddin of Gotzo, who led the 1920-21 uprising, was also a Naqshebandi murshid.

†No serious work has yet been published on the Basmachi movement, and our knowledge of its social and political structure is limited. We do know that the names of many of the leaders were followed by the title ishan, sheikh, or pir, which suggests a strong Sufi background. Also, one of the leading Kurbashis, Khal Hoja, was a Naqshebandi murshid.

‡In 1926 the tariqas were still powerful in the North Caucasus. In the Chechen Republic, with a population of some 400,000, there were some 60,000 murids, 806 mosques, 126 mektebs, and 427 medressehs with 3,567 students, as opposed to 31 Soviet schools with 3,746 students. At the same time in Daghestan, there were 61,200 murids, 19 sheikhs, and 60 vakifs. See M. Z. Magomedov,

of anti-Soviet activity of Sufi brotherhoods in the North Caucasus
during World War II. Given the tradition of holy war, however, it
is not unlikely that the still-powerful brotherhoods actively participated in the 1942 anti-Russian and anti-Soviet upheavals in the
Chechen-Ingush ASSR. These actions resulted in the exile of thousands to Siberia and the wastes of Central Asia. Significantly, this
deportation did not destroy the tariqas but actually led to their expansion, as Klimovich acknowledges in his writings. [13] For the deported Muslims the Sufi orders not only became a symbol of their
nationhood in the lands to which they were deported, but also proved
to be efficient organizers for community survival. Alexander
Solzhenitsyn notes one example of this superior organization among
the Chechen deportees to Kazakhstan; and, not without a touch of
envy, he reports that this iron discipline and cohesion enabled these
Caucasian Muslims to survive and to live almost completely outside
the Soviet order. [14]

Since the war Sufism has survived in much the same mode it
adopted after the defeat of Shamil and the liquidation of the Daghestani-
Chechen revolt of 1920: it concentrates its energies on mystical and
spiritual pursuits, the appropriate posture for periods when Islam is
recouping its forces for another round against the infidels. The
more mystical Qadiriya and its branches seem better adapted to
these conditions and more popular than the more militant Naqshebandiya. Soviet anti-religious periodicals, the daily press, and
special monographs report that the tariqas remain active in their
traditional stronghold of the North Caucasus, where they appear to
be more numerous and influential than before World War II. [15] Elsewhere, too, Sufism appears to have undergone a substantial and significant revival. In Central Asia, the North Caucasian Sufi groups
who were deported there during the war have taken root and thereby
reinforced the existing tariqas native to the region. [16]

The organization of today's brotherhoods is a curious blend of
the traditional and the new. The latter serves to give the brotherhoods greater protection against the Soviet authorities and to root
them more deeply in the popular masses. Among the most important
innovations are the following. First, in some areas, and especially
in the North Caucasus, certain Sufi orders are limiting their recruitment of adepts to specific clans. Such is the case of the Naqshebandi
of the Chechen-Ingush territory. This practice provides the tariqa
with greater secrecy than it formerly possessed, for adepts are subject to the dual loyalties of brotherhood and clan. [17] Second, the Sufi

---

"Iz istorii reshenii natsional'nogo i religioznogo voprosov na
severnom Kavkaze," Voprosy nauchnogo ateizma 14 (1973): 47.

orders have begun to accept women adepts in large numbers.[18] Indeed, certain official sources lament the fact that the tariqas seem to be more effective at mobilizing Muslim women than the Soviet anti-religious organizations are.[19] And third, the membership of the tariqas has become much younger than before and is increasingly drawn from the Soviet intelligentsia.

Soviet sources provide abundant information concerning the intense activities of the Sufi brotherhoods and suggest that the tariqas are one of the main reasons why Islamic beliefs, traditions, and customs continue in the USSR. Indeed, they report that in some areas the Sufi brotherhoods constitute a parallel "church" without which the Muslim faith could not have survived the onslaught of scientific materialism. In the Chechen-Ingush ASSR, according to one source, more than half of all Muslim believers are members of a brotherhood.[20] The activities of the Sufis usually are centered on various "holy places," which often are the tombs of mythical or real men—frequently those who died fighting the Russians—and serve as substitutes for the mosques the Soviet regime has closed.

According to Soviet sources, there were 27 "working" official mosques, "one hundred prominent holy places," and "many times that number of less important local places of pilgrimage" in Daghestan and the Chechen-Ingush ASSR in 1967. Among the most famous holy places mentioned are the tomb of Haji Murat, the companion of Shamil killed by the Russians in the village of Qypchaq; the tomb of Tasho Haji, another naib of Shamil in the village of Saiasian; the village of Akhulgo, former residence of Shamil, where many of his murids were killed by the Russians; the tombs of the victims of the 1877 uprising; the tomb of Kunta Haji's mother in the village of Haji Otrar (Kunta Haji died in Siberia); and the most popular of all, the mazar of Uzun Haji. In 1961 Soviet authorities closed the last two holy places, "but masses of pilgrims are still coming from everywhere, from the Chechen republic, from all other republics and regions of the North Caucasus and even from the mountains of Northern Georgia by car and on foot."[21] These holy places serve as meeting places for adepts, where the latter perform the zikr and are taught prayer, the Koran, the Arabic language, and the rudiments of Islamic theology. They are the subject of pilgrimages for simple believers as well: surrogates for the impossible hajj to Mecca. These tombs, therefore, provide an excellent forum for the brotherhoods to influence the Muslim masses during religious festivals and other holy events. Considering the constant barrage of criticism directed at such events by the Soviet press, it is evident that the Soviet authorities are very concerned about the potential successes of the proselytizing Sufis.

The most revealing of recent Soviet sources on the subject of holy places and the "cult of the saints" in Islam is the monograph by V. N. Basilov.[22] He lists a large number of holy places and explains the essence of pilgrimage. According to him, the veneration of holy men is based on three different traditions: pre-Islamic cults, the cult of clan ancestors, and respect for the Sufi masters. In this way veneration combines two sets of powerful loyalties: clan-tribal solidarity and the prestige enjoyed by the Sufi orders.[23] Such a combination is clearly a potent one for Muslim believers.

The veneration of holy places has some tangible effects as well. Most Muslim cemeteries are located near them, often near the tomb of a Sufi sheikh; and as a rule the guardians of the cemetery are also adepts of a tariqa.[24] Generally, Muslims--including Communist Party officials--are buried in Muslim cemeteries, from which all non-Muslims are excluded. Sometimes the guards can go to extremes in making their point, as the following incident demonstrates. In 1961 the Russian wife of a Daghestani Communist Party member died, and the local Muslim community refused to allow her body to be buried in the Muslim cemetery. When, under pressure from higher authorities, the burial was performed, local Muslims, with the agreement of the husband, posthumously "converted" her to Islam.[25] In addition, it is not uncommon to discover a clandestine mosque or prayer house run by unofficial mullahs in these cemeteries.

Another area of Sufi activity in which adepts can exercise their missionary zeal is the still-active traditional Muslim guilds. Since the late 1940s these guilds have been infiltrated by Sufi adepts, and many of these organizations are now directed by them.[26] There are active Muslim guilds among the copper workers of the city of Khanki, the barbers of Khiva, and the taxi drivers of Uzbekistan. Muslim guilds maintain the traditional ritual of initiation, have their own special patron saints (the Prophet David in the case of the taxi drivers), and their own religious festivals. In the North Caucasus, tariqa adepts are attempting, sometimes successfully, to gain control over another traditional institution, the jema'at, which are popu-assemblies of the aul, or mountain settlements. According to Soviet sources, these assemblies are still very much alive, and often enjoy greater prestige and authority than do the local soviets. They are authoritarian organizations, strictly limited to the natives; Russians and other aliens living in the aul are excluded. Indeed, they may completely neutralize the authority of the local soviet and even of the Soviet courts. One Soviet source reports, "It is not infrequent that the illegal clanic court (Jema'at) reverses the decisions of our Soviet people's Court."[27]

From all that has been said, it is clear that the high incidence of religious observance in Muslim areas of the USSR is due in large part to the intense, daily propaganda efforts of the Sufi brotherhoods. Their activities are not limited to the mere observance of the cult, however, as Soviet sources readily admit. The brotherhoods dominate many sectors of the private and collective life of the Muslim populations that are still run according to the traditional pattern of Islam. In doing so, they also have an important impact on public opinion. [28] Statistics reveal part of their success. In 1974, 46 percent of Daghestani rural dwellers[29] and 53 percent of all Chechens declared themselves to be believers. (This compares with a figure of 12 percent among Russians.) Only 21 percent of the Chechens identified themselves as atheists (among Russians, 69 percent). [30] But statistics mask what is perhaps an even stronger indication of the importance of Islam in the daily life of Muslim areas. As one Soviet social scientist remarked: "Under the influence of a 'collective conservative public opinion,' non-believers are obliged to hide their atheistic ideas from their relatives and friends. "[31]

Curiously, the official Soviet Islamic establishment has not been pressed into service by the Soviet regime to condemn the unofficial Sufi brotherhoods; and its rare criticisms of Sufism are generally very mild. [32] Members of the tariqas, even when they are fanatically anti-Soviet, reciprocate in this and never attack the representatives of official Islam, even those who are thoroughly compromised with the regime. Sufi adepts have all but replaced the regular clergy in the lives of millions of Muslim believers. In the majority of cases, religious rites are not performed by the few official clerics who are registered at the muftiate, but by unregistered mullahs, who usually are adepts of a Sufi order, or by former regular mullahs whose mosques have been closed by the authorities. [33] Sometimes they are performed by self-designated dervishes who possess some knowledge of Arabic and can recite the necessary prayers. [34] These unregistered clerics also maintain the large underground network of religious schools where Arabic and the rudiments of the Muslim catechism are taught and the thousands of unofficial mosques--both breaches of the Soviet criminal statutes.

SUFISM AND NATIONALISM AMONG SOVIET MUSLIMS

Soviet writers now rank the Sufi brotherhoods among the most intractable and dangerous adversaries of the Soviet regime because the tariqas are the only authentic anti-Soviet mass organizations in the USSR. V. G. Pivovarov estimates that more than half of the believers in the Chechen-Ingush ASSR are members of various Sufi orders. The total number of the Chechens and Ingushes being 770,000 in 1970, the tariqa adepts thus would number some 220,000 persons.[35] Just how significant a threat these groups are viewed as presenting in both religious and national terms can be seen from the following quotations, taken from recent Soviet sources:

> Recent sociological investigations in the Chechen-Ingush Republic reveal the close interconnection between religious and nationalistic survivals . . . and the active role played in their preservation by the various murid brotherhoods. . . . These groups do not limit their activity to the observance of the religious cult. . . . they favor inter-ethnic antagonism. . . . they support obnoxious customs [that are] presented as sacred national traditions. . . .[36]

> The leaders of murid communities, the heads of the families and clans . . . teach the believers--including the younger generation--that the respect due to the memory of the former Sufi leaders and the observance of religious rites and customs are symbols and conditions of the preservation of familial and clanic honor and of national existence.[37]

> Islam is presented as the guardian of national-cultural values and a negative attitude toward religion--the "faith of the ancestors"--is deemed a national treason.[38]

> The clerics pretend that religious feasts . . . are in reality national rather than religious. They prey on the national feelings of the people, especially of the younger generation who cannot distinguish the national from the religious.[39]

> In the cult of the saints, religious superstitions are tightly intertwined with the national feelings of the Daghestanis and the Chechen-Ingush. . . . In order to develop religious feelings in the population, clerics play on the clanic-familial system of relationships, especially in recent years.[40]

This linkage of religion and nationality tells us a great deal about the perceptions of the Soviet leadership, but it should also make us attentive to the possibility that the tariqas may again serve as the nucleus for communal and even national movements in the Muslim regions of the USSR. As we have seen, the Sufi brotherhoods in the North Caucasus and Central Asia are tightly knit religious organizations with a strong leadership and disciplined apparatus. They enjoy increasing support not only from the Muslim masses but also

from members of the educated Muslim elite. They are well suited
to clandestine activity and have survived all efforts by the Soviet
regime to destroy them. And although the brotherhoods remain extremely conservative, closed societies for which religion alone is
the proper basis of unity for the Muslim Umma--the "community of
believers"--it is not impossible that these religious forms will be
infused with nationalist content. In any case, the increasing strength
of the Sufi brotherhoods suggests that any national movements that
may emerge among Soviet Muslims are likely to be strongly influenced by the conservative and traditionalist ideas of the tariqas and
to depend on them to provide the mass base necessary for success.

NOTES

1. See Nugman Ashirov, Evoliutsiia Islama v SSSR (Moscow:
Znanie, 1973); and Islam i natsii (Moscow: Znanie, 1975).

2. Ibid.

3. Nauka i religiia, April 1967, p. 51.

4. L. I. Klimovich, "Bor'ba ortodoksov is modernistov v
Islame," Voprosy nauchnogo ateizma 2 (1966): 66-67.

5. For a survey, see John Spencer Trimingham, The Sufi Orders in Islam (Oxford: Clarendon, 1971); Arthur John Arberry,
Sufism (London, 1950); Louis Massignon, Essai sur les origines du
lexique technique de la mystique musulmane (Paris, 1968); O. Depont
and X. Coppolani, Les confréries religieuses musulmanes (Algiers,
1897); Alfred LeChatelier, Les confréries musulmanes in Hedjaz
(Paris, 1887); R. A. Nicholson, The Mystics of Islam (New York:
Schocken, 1975).

6. H. A. R. Gibb, Mohammedanism (London: Oxford University Press, 1950), p. 139.

7. The history of the Great Naqshebandi order is yet to be
written, but two specialists are actively working on this problem:
Professor Hamid Algar of Berkeley and Professor Joseph Fletcher
of Harvard. Algar has published "The Naqshebandi Order: A Preliminary Survey of Its History and Significance," Studia Islamica 44
(1977): 123-52, and is currently working on the early history of the
order. The history of the Naqshebandiya in China is the subject of
a forthcoming publication by Fletcher.

8. Gibb, op. cit., p. 138.

9. Louis Massignon, "Tariqa," in Shorter Encyclopedia of
Islam (Leiden, 1953), p. 574.

10. See V. V. Bartold, "Sheikh Zeinulla Rasulev, 1833-1917--
Nekrolog," Musul'manskii mir (Petrograd) 1 (1917): 73-74; and

Chantal Quelquejay, "La Vaisisme à Kazan. Contribution à l'étude des confréries musulmanes chez les Tatars de la Volga," Die Welt des Islams 6, no. 1/2 (1959): 95-113.

11. See Alexandre Bennigsen, "Un mouvement populaire au Caucase au XVIIIme siècle. La guerre sainte du Sheikh Mansur 1785-1791, page mal connue et controverse des relations russo-turques," Cahiers du monde russe et soviétique 5, no. 2 (1964): 159-205.

12. A Soviet work on the Qadiriya order in the North Caucasus is A. D. Iandarov, Sufizm i ideologiia natsional'nogo osvoboditel'nogo dvizheniia. Iz istorii razvitiia obshchestvennykh idei v Checheno-Ingushetii v 20-70 godakh XIX veka (Alma Ata: Nauka, 1975).

13. Klimovich, op. cit., p. 85.

14. Arkhipelag Gulag, III (V-VI-VII) (Paris: YMCA Press, 1975), pp. 420-24.

15. On the increasing numbers of tariqas, see V. G. Pivovarov, Na etapakh sotsiologicheskogo issledovaniia (Groznyi: Chechen-Ingush. Kn. Iz-Vo., 1974), pp. 129, 201; and Partiinaia organizatsiia i ateisticheskoe vospitanie (Moscow: Znanie, 1975), p. 184.

16. According to Partiinaia, in 1972 there were 22 different tariqas active in the Chechen-Ingush Republic, compared with only four or five before the Revolution. Among the most active were the Qadiriya branches: Bammat Gizay, Ali Mitaev, Chim Mizzoev, and Battal Hoja.

17. See A. Hakimdzhanov, "Religioznaia sushchnost' Islama," Kazakhstanskaia pravda, September 17, 1954, which mentions the foundation "in many areas of Kazakhstan" of "new Muslim sects" including the Caucasian Kunta Haji tariqa.

18. Iandarov, op. cit., pp. 139, 147; Iu. V. Krianev, "Typologiia religioznykh ob'edinenii i differentsiatsia ateisticheskogo vospitaniia," Voprosy nauchnogo ateizma 3 (1967): 55. Qadiriya orders have no clan limitations.

19. I. A. Makatov, "Kul't sviatykh v Islame," Voprosy nauchnogo ateizma 3 (1967): 177, mentions female murshids leading groups of Naqshebandi and Qadiri adepts.

20. V. G. Pivovarov, "Sotsiologicheskie issledovaniia problem byta kul'tury natsional'nykh traditsii i verovanii v Checheno-Ingushetskoi ASSR," Voprosy nauchnogo ateizma 17 (1975): 316.

21. See Makatov, op. cit., pp. 164, 175, 180; and Groznenskii rabochii, December 23, 1964.

22. V. N. Basilov, Kul't sviatykh v Islame (Moscow: Znanie, 1970).

23. Ibid., pp. 74-76.

24. Ibid., pp. 82, 90-91.

25. A. Kadyrev, Prichiny suschestvovaniia i puti preodoleniia perezhitkov Islama (Leninabad: Gosizdat, 1966), p. 61.

26. Ibid., p. 33; Basilov, op. cit., p. 23.

27. Pivovarov, "Sotsiologicheskie . . .," pp. 314-15; Makatov, op. cit., pp. 176-79; M. A. Mamakaev, Chechenskii taip (rod) v period ego razlozheniia (Groznyi: Chechen-Ingush. Kn. Iz-Vo., 1973), p. 78.

28. E. G. Filimovov, "Sotsiologicheskie issledovaniia protsessa preodoleniia religii v sel'skoi mestnosti. Itogi, problemy, perspektivy," Voprosy nauchnogo ateizma 16 (1974): 80.

29. Ibid., p. 74.

30. Pivovarov, Na etapakh . . ., pp. 158-59.

31. Pivovarov, "Sotsiologicheskie . . .," p. 318.

32. Makatov, op. cit., pp. 173-74, reproduces the text of a fetwa of the mufti of Buinakst concerning certain activities of the Sufi brotherhoods:

Question: Does the Shari'yat law authorize prayers at a
    mazar ?
Answer: No, such prayers are unlawful.
Question: Is it lawful to ask Saints to help us ?
Answer: No, such demands are sinful.
Question: Is it permitted for men and women to meet
    at a mazar ?
Answer: No, this is contrary to Islam.

33. Klimovich, op. cit., p. 67.

34. M. M. Saltanov and F. G. Kocharli, "Razvitie ateizma v sovetskom Azerbaidzhane," Voprosy nauchnogo ateizma 5 (1968): 56.

35. Pivovarov, Na etapakh . . ., pp. 158-59.

36. Klimovich, op. cit., p. 85.

37. Pivovarov, "Sotsiologicheskie . . .," p. 318.

38. L. Ostorushko, "Boevye zadachi partiinykh organizatsii," Nauka i religiia (1976), no. 12: 87.

39. Makatov, op. cit., pp. 168, 177.

40. Sovetskaia iustitsiia 8 (1962): 23-24, and 10 (1964): 12-13.

THE GREAT RUSSIANS AND THE SOVIET STATE: THE DILEMMAS OF ETHNIC DOMINANCE

11

S. Enders Wimbush

Today a new national self-consciousness and even a new nationalism have appeared among the Great Russians of the Soviet Union. This new mood is the result of important changes in Russian corporate and personal life. It has found expression in official actions, in the public press, in samizdat (privately circulated, unpublished writings), and in personal and social behavior. At the present time, Russian nationalism--and by this I mean both the programs of those who explicitly identify themselves as Russian nationalists and the programs of those so identified by others--includes a great variety of themes, frequently combined in unexpected ways. The degree of support for specific sets of ideas and even for all expressions of Russian nationalism taken together remains unclear. What is clear is that Russian nationalism has taken on a momentum of its own, changing the traditional relationship between Russian nationalism and the Soviet state. Prior to 1953 the leaders of the USSR viewed Russian nationalism as an instrument of policy, a useful mobilizing tool to be brought out in times of crisis and then to be put away. Now, Russian national consciousness and Russian nationalism have a quasi-autonomous existence, and it is by no means clear that the regime can use them in a strictly instrumental fashion. In this essay I examine the origins and themes of this new Russian nationalism and the responses to it by the Soviet state.

CAUSES AND CATALYSTS

Russian nationalism today is in large measure the product of changes in Soviet political and social life since the death of Stalin in 1953. Although Stalin had never permitted the independent expression of Russian national ideas or the complete displacement of the official ideology's international elements by Russian national ones,

he had incorporated many Russian national elements into this ideology
during the war and afterward. In consequence, many Russians considered him a truly Russian leader whose leadership had restored
Russia to its proper place as a world power and an imperial center.
His death raised the specter of a decline of Russian prestige and
status at home and abroad. Anxiety on this score was compounded
when Nikita Khrushchev denounced Stalin's crimes and blunders.
While only Georgians rioted over this initial attack, many Russians
were profoundly shaken and suspicious of the precise intentions of
the new leadership. To make matters worse, this denunciation was
associated with a new stress both on the need to equalize development and opportunities among Soviet nations and on the importance
of proletarian internationalism as a basis for legitimacy and as a
mobilizing tool. The former aspect of this policy suggested to many
non-Russians that they had a right to a greater share of the scarce
resources of the state; to many Russians it suggested that once again
they would be required to make sacrifices for others. The latter
aspect, which Khrushchev elaborated to include the idea of the biological merger (sliianie) of all Soviet nations into a higher community,
provoked in the minds of many Russians distasteful images of mixed
marriages and national degeneration.

At the same time, Khrushchev's attacks on Stalin enabled many
Russians to ask previously impermissible questions about their own
past, about the horrors of Stalinism and the Stalinist tradition, about
the reasons for their sacrifices on the battlefield as the main defenders of the Soviet state, and about the future of the Russian nation
itself. It became possible to explore these questions more fully when
Khrushchev declared a "thaw" in literature and culture, thereby increasing the number of public forums in which many kinds of ideas
could be expressed and discussed. Among the potentially most explosive of these questions were those concerning national cultures
and national pasts--both Russian and non-Russian. Many Russians
took advantage of these opportunities to resurrect previously re-
pressed aspects of their own national culture, national past, and
national present, although many of the participants were not yet self-
consciously nationalistic. [1]

Among those who entered the discussion of Russian culture was
Andrei Amalrik, whose attacks on Russian culture from his vantage
point within the Russian nation itself helped to push many Russians
even further in the direction of specifically nationalist ideas. In his
two best-known works, Will the Soviet Union Survive Until 1984? and
Involuntary Journey to Siberia, Amalrik fired a broadside at the
Russian people by implying that they deserved the kind of regime with
which they had been forced to live. Like Piotr Yakovlevich Chaadaev
a century earlier, Amalrik argued that the Russians are a people

without a culture, without a past, and without a future. He suggested that Russians have suffered from a lack of exposure to the humanistic traditions of Europe, and that they lack all moral criteria.[2] Instead, he wrote, Russians are "motivated by a hatred of everything outstanding, which we make no effort to imitate but, on the contrary, try to bring down to our level by hatred of any sense of initiative, of any higher or more dynamic way of life than the life we live ourselves."[3]

In addition to these challenges from the regime and from within the ranks of their own intelligentsia, Russians began to hear new sounds of unrest from the non-Russians. As it had among Russians, the "thaw" provided many non-Russians with an opportunity to question the condition of their own national cultures, their current relationship to the Soviet state, and their future relationship to the Russian nation. In the rewriting of their national histories--which Khrushchev encouraged--non-Russian scholars became more nationally self-assertive. Many of these authors for the first time implicitly, and occasionally openly, questioned the previously prescribed doctrinaire interpretation of the Russian conquest of the non-Russian lands and peoples as a "progressive phenomenon" or as the "greater good." Moreover, they questioned the impact on and place of Russian culture in their own local cultures, and suggested that Russian culture had done little, if anything, to enhance their already rich cultural heritages. One bold Soviet non-Russian of Turkic origin even claimed that this equation should be reversed: benefits had flowed the other way. In his estimation, Russians had profited from the Tatar yoke. Russian culture generally--including the Russian national epic, The Lay of Igor--he argued, had drawn heavily on Asian models.[4]

In a more direct challenge to Russian dominance, a number of non-Russians have punctuated their new-found national self-assertiveness with open protest. Jews have demanded to emigrate. Crimean Tatars, Meskhetian Turks, and Volga Germans have engaged in open national protest. Caucasians and Balts have staged violent local demonstrations, including some bombings in Georgia. Irredentist movements among Moldavians have gathered momentum. Nationalist dissent of various shades has intensified in the Ukraine. In Central Asia, national elites have self-consciously glorified and attempted to consolidate the nations that the Russians "created" decades earlier in hopes of impeding pan-Turkic and pan-Islamic tendencies. Social discrimination and even violence against Russians have increased in the national republics, including the more and more frequently and openly expressed sentiment "Russians go home." All of these activities have evoked Russian anger at the "ingratitude" of those for whom most Russians feel they have done so much, as well as real fear of rising insubordination among the non-Russians.

This fear was exacerbated when the results of the 1970 Soviet census were published. This census revealed that Russians rapidly are approaching zero population growth, thus raising the possibility that within several decades they will begin to suffer a decline in their absolute numbers. On the other hand, the census pointed to a population explosion among Turkic and Muslim peoples of the USSR. This new demographic dimension has had a profound impact on the way most Russians are inclined to view the future of the largely Russian state, for it became apparent with the 1970 census that Russians ultimately are destined to be reduced to a minority population within their own country. Moreover, these reported increases surprised many Soviet policy makers in Gosplan and elsewhere, and lent a new immediacy to the intensifying debate over the regional allocation of scarce resources. These census data stimulated the public discussion of Soviet society in national terms. Such discussion was encouraged by the regime, which was concerned about the possible loss of Russian control of the borderlands, about the increasing competition between Russians and non-Russians for elite positions, about dwindling Russian labor resources and the possibility that non-Russian labor would have to be imported to the RSFSR from Central Asia, and about rates of regional development.

THE THEMES OF RUSSIAN NATIONALISM TODAY

The developments outlined above have raised the national consciousness of many Russians. They also have led some of them to advance a variety of more or less explicitly nationalist ideas and platforms. Here I will survey the most important themes developed by these new Russian nationalists. One of these themes stresses the need to purge Russia of alien influences, including Marxism-Leninism. These alien, usually Western, influences have led Russians into a condition of moral degeneration symptomized by drunkenness, crime, selfishness, debauchery of motherhood, the loss of elemental notions of beauty, caddishness, and banality.[5] Russians have lost their spiritual attachment to one another, to their nation. Marxism-Leninism has encouraged this disintegration, these Russian nationalists claim, because it is inconsonant with Russian national traditions and conventions and because it rejects the nation as the fundamental and lasting unit of human organization. Marxism-Leninism, the more "liberal" nationalist Igor Shafarevich concludes, is "the enemy of every nation. . . . its fundamental trend is toward the maximum destruction of all nations."[6]

Another related, but distinctly alien, influence is Soviet internationalism: the demand that at some level there be an interpenetration of all cultures of the USSR. To counter this demand, some Russians have asserted the purity of Russian culture by such acts as purging their writings of words of recent Soviet or Western derivation and by employing only traditional Russian vocabulary and syntax.[7] On another level, some Russians have questioned openly the doctrinally required confluence of international and national in art. "How is it," asks the popular Russian writer Vladimir Soloukhin, "that I, a Russian man of letters, sitting at my writing desk should consciously create for all peoples. I simply am not up to the task. Better that I should write of my own Russian nature, my own Russian countryside, and of my own Russian people."[8]

Soloukhin's concern with the Russian countryside, a theme that runs through most of his work, is echoed by many popular Russian writers who have been dubbed "ruralists" (derevenshchiki) by critics in the official press because they strongly insinuate in their works that one must go "back to the land" to find the real Russia and real Russians. The true Russian national character, the ruralists argue, is molded by the basic rural values of the Russian peasant and not by mechanical, urban-industrial values of the big-city proletariat.[9] Moreover, the ruralists imply that the peasant's religious faith, especially in the face of the regime's repeated anti-religious offensives, is the cornerstone of these basic values and virtues; Russia's fate, therefore, is inextricably linked to Orthodoxy and to the Orthodox Church. The writings of the ruralists have given strong support to, and have themselves been influenced by, the interest in Orthodoxy among the wider Russian population, especially the youth. This interest is demonstrated by increased church attendance, the wearing of crosses in public, the collection and restoration of icons, and the enthusiastic participation by many Russians in the activities of voluntary societies for the preservation of monuments of history and culture--often churches.[10] To ignore or repress these basic aspects of the Russian national character, the writers argue, would mean the destruction of an important sense of Russian community, and would be tantamount to "destroying the genetic nucleus of the nation."[11]

As this quotation indicates, a number of Russian nationalists have gone beyond expressions of concern for Russia's spiritual and moral purity to suggest that Russia's genetic purity is in danger as well. Thus, there is an unmistakable racial dimension to some Russian nationalist protests. Nationalists claim that mixed marriages, which the regime encourages, will increase "random hybridization," which will speed the "biological degeneration [that] threatens both the Russian nation and the entire white race."[12] A similar racial theme has found an outlet in the official press. One Russian scholar has argued that because ethnos--the inherited essence that distin-

guishes members of different ethnic groups--is biologically determined, the union of members of different ethnic groups leads inevitably to the genetic decline of the progeny and, ultimately, of the
political states and social institutions that these progeny will constitute. National assimilation, he concludes, is nationally self-
destructive.[13] The 1970 Soviet census made the specter of "yellowing" even more ominous to most Russians. Many have concluded,
like those writing above, that if Russian society is to be rescued and
purified, efforts must begin at the cradle.

Not only do many Russians object to mixing with non-Russians;
they also object to supporting them economically. The USSR, some
Russian nationalists argue, should be an empire much like the one
that preceded it, in which the Russians extract from other peoples
what they require for their national welfare. After all, they contend, it is the material wealth of Russia and the human sacrifices of
Russians that have made the Soviet empire economically and politically viable. Furthermore, Russian sacrifices have made the existence of many minority nationalities possible. Hence, these nationalists continue, the Marxist-Leninist doctrine of national equality dis-
criminates first and foremost against Russians because it calls on
them to take the initiative in reducing the economic disparity between
nations, at great human and material cost to the Russian nation.
"The Russians no less than others are its victims," notes one concerned Russian nationalist; "indeed, they are the first to come under
its fire."[14]

Not surprisingly, many Russians have begun to question the
wisdom of allocating massive amounts of Russian resources for the
development of non-Russians. Indeed, many Russians, including
Alexander Solzhenitsyn, have concluded that Russia's material and
human resources should be allocated first to develop such Russian
territories as Siberia and the Russian North. Such presently underdeveloped regions, these Russian nationalists believe, could provide
a margin of safety for Russians in the future. Solzhenitsyn's warn-
ing--originally Piotr Arkadevich Stolypin's--strikes a poignant note
among them: "If we remain plunged in our lethargic sleep, these
lands will be running with foreign sap, and when we wake up they
will perhaps be Russian in name only."[15]

If Russian nationalists vary in their ideas on culture, race,
and economics, they differ even more in their political beliefs. One
of the most important disagreements is that between the Russians
who advocate a "little Russia" and those who advocate an empire.
Those who support the first position--and they appear to be a distinct
minority--believe that Russia should be reconstituted on those territories that are inhabited almost entirely by Russians or that are historically Russian, such as the Russian North and Siberia, and that

the non-Russians should be allowed to go their own ways. They argue that Russian resources should be used only for Russia's welfare. Those who support the idea of an empire or "greater Russia" are far more numerous, but they are divided over how the non-Russians should be treated. Many in this group are classical imperialists, and would repress any self-assertiveness by minorities and strengthen Russian dominance over them in every possible way. But others--who might be called "liberal" nationalists--advocate some accommodation of the non-Russian minorities in a loose federal system. They would grant the non-Russians such real rights as those now promised by the Soviet Constitution but largely nonexistent in practice, including the right to secede from the federation. Such rights, these Russian nationalists maintain, would carry with them the responsibility for paying one's fair share for development and defense. Thus, the "liberalism" of these Russians is really a function of their nationalism: the political arrangements they espouse would free Russians of many of the expensive obligations they now bear for other peoples.

Another issue over which Russian nationalists divide concerns the proper organization of political power in a future Russian state. There are a few "liberal" nationalists who seek a vaguely defined representative or quasi-representative system in which many voices would be heard, including those of the minorities; however, most Russian nationalists opt for more authoritarian solutions. Some who might be called neo-Slavophile advocate rule by a few, particularly by those individuals who have an intuitive understanding of the material and spiritual needs of the Russian people. In their scheme of things, the Russian Orthodox Church once again would become a dominant influence in the state. Other authoritarian Russian nationalists--often called neo-Stalinists because of their propensity for unequivocal dictatorial decision making backed by force--seek to install a strong man or a strong regime at the head of the Russian state. Some of these look to men like General Mikhail Dmitreievich Skobelev, the conqueror of southern Turkestan, as a model Russian leader.[16] Others look to Stalin. And still others point to Ermak, the conqueror of Siberia; Dezhnev, one of the explorers of Kamchatka; and Erofei Khabarov, one of the first Russians to fight the Chinese, who is remembered for terrorizing his victims and burning them alive.[17] This is the strong, militarist, and centralist kind of authority that many Russians would like to see reinstated.

THE RESPONSES OF THE SOVIET STATE

The Soviet regime clearly has no intention of acceding to these extreme Russian nationalist demands. Marxism-Leninism has not been cast aside. There have been no basic changes in the political realm, no reorganization of the Soviet polity. The new Soviet Constitution failed to redraw republic boundaries; and it did not provide the RSFSR with its own Communist Party organization, as many Russians had hoped it would. Instead, the new constitution reaffirmed the federal status of minorities. Furthermore, the Politburo now contains three Turkic members; and the Russian nationalists in the top leadership, notably A. N. Shelepin, have been purged. While there has been considerable talk about developing Russia's northern territories, actual development there has been slow; and the development of non-Russian territories remains a relatively high priority of the regime. No clear-cut policies have emerged to regulate the runaway birthrate among Soviet Muslims or to provide satisfactory incentives to Russians to have more children.[18] Jews have been allowed to emigrate without expressing their thanks to the Russian nation for the educational and cultural benefits it has bestowed upon them. Other minorities continue to receive the regime's favor, including cultural resources--like academies of science--to sustain what most Russians believe to be ersatz nationhood. And the regime has imposed unwelcome internationalist themes on the movement for the preservation of cultural and historical monuments. Moreover, those Russians who have spoken out forcefully in favor of Russian nationalist policies have been arrested and sent to work camps or, like Solzhenitsyn, into exile.

If the regime has rejected and moved against the extreme demands of the Russian nationalists, it has not been altogether insensitive to the rise of Russian national self-consciousness. Indeed, the regime has used Russian national symbols and images in order to heighten Russian self-awareness or to provide an outlet for the awareness that already exists. It has permitted a public, albeit limited, rehabilitation of Stalin and a lively discussion of his positive qualities as the leader of the Russian nation in wartime.[19] It has encouraged more Russians to tour places of especially strong historical importance to the Russian nation. The regime has reemphasized its tolerance of the Orthodox Church,[20] on occasion even citing Lenin as justification for the preservation of church buildings and religious shrines. It has underwritten patriotic extravaganzas, such as the thirtieth anniversary of the victory over fascist Germany, in which the special contributions of Russians as the primary defenders of the Soviet state are extolled. It has licensed some journals and books to convey Russian nationalist messages to the Russian masses. It has rereleased the brilliant film "Andrei Rublev," albeit with significant cuts. And it has accepted and moved to co-opt certain especially spontaneous expressions of Russian national self-assertiveness. For example, it has attempted to co-opt the voluntary societies for the preservation of cultural and historical monuments by endorsing them, supplying them with key leadership personnel, and then creating or reviving parallel state-run organizations to assume some of the tasks of the voluntary ones.

In part through these concessions, the rise in Russian national self-consciousness and self-assertiveness has not yet taken the form of militant national protest it has among other nationalities, the kind of protest that might force the regime to make still further and more significant concessions. Instead, the picture is one of relative quietude, nearly free from violent and threatening outbursts. However, it is not clear that the regime has solved the problem of Russian nationalism. In the first place, there is enough evidence to suggest that more violent protest is possible, especially by Russian colons living in the non-Russian borderlands, who are feeling increasingly isolated and who are affected most by militance among minorities. In the second, the regime once again may be forced to engage in an all-out mobilization of Russians to accomplish domestic objectives or to defend the state from foreign aggressors.

THE FUTURE

It is possible that events outside Russia will convince the regime that the Russians must be mobilized. War with China is a real possibility, as are new confrontations in Eastern Europe. If Leonid Brezhnev's successor were to find himself in the situation in which Stalin found himself in 1941, he, too, would be forced to mobilize Russians through an intensification of Russian national symbols and by appeals to save Mother Russia. Russian boys will not fight "because the sacred truth is written on page 533 of Lenin and not on page 335 as our adversary claims," Solzhenitsyn reminds Soviet leaders, but it is doubtful that these leaders have so soon forgotten such an elemental truth.[21]

The regime may be persuaded to mobilize Russians to counter internal threats as well. Non-Russians will continue to grow more nationally self-assertive as non-Russian populations grow, thereby increasing the probability of more intense ethnic conflict between Russians and non-Russians over jobs, training, education, and resource allocation. It is not unlikely that in the face of such challenges, the regime will seek to mobilize the Russians through the use of nationalist symbols and themes in order to secure the identification of Russians with the Soviet state. The regime also may be increasingly tempted to use Russian nationalism as a mobilizing tool to achieve its developmental goals. The "logic" of Marxism-Leninism and propaganda extolling the heroic struggle to build the Communist utopia have failed to inspire many Russians. Yet the Russians remain the largest and best-educated national group in the USSR, and the one on which the regime is most dependent. Hence, Soviet leaders are likely to use Russian nationalism for these reasons as well.

The use of Russian nationalism in any or all of these situations of course, would encourage Russian nationalist groups and other nationally self-conscious Russians to become more militant and to make greater demands. In such a situation it is by no means certain that the regime, having turned to Russian nationalism for help, will be able to turn against it or even to bring it under control. This is because Russian nationalism now has the potential to become an autonomous or quasi-autonomous movement. Such a development no doubt would be quickened by the reaction of other Soviet nationalities, who know firsthand the real dangers of unleashed Russian nationalism and who are unlikely to stand idly by while it engulfs them.

NOTES

1. The symposium from Slavic Review 32 (March 1973) is an especially good portrait of this revival: Jack V. Haney, "The Revival of Interest in the Russian Past in the Soviet Union," pp. 1-16; Thomas E. Bird, "New Interest in Old Russian Things: Literary Ferment, Religious Perspectives, and National Self-Assertion," pp. 17-28; George L. Kline, "Religion, National Character, and the 'Rediscovery of Russian Roots'," pp. 29-40.

2. Andrei Amalrik, Will the Soviet Union Survive Until 1984? (New York: Harper and Row, 1970), pp. 36-37.

3. Ibid.

4. "Discussion of a Book by Olzhas Suleimenov," Voprosy istorii (1976), no. 9: 147-54, as abstracted in Current Digest of the Soviet Press (hereafter CDSP) 28, no. 5 (January 1977): 15-16.

5. "Veche," Arkhiv samizdata 21, no. 1013.

6. Igor Shafarevich, "Separation or Reconciliation? The Nationalities Question in the USSR," in Alexander Solzhenitsyn et al., From Under the Rubble (New York: Bantam Books, 1975), pp. 92-96.

7. See Evgenii Yevtushenko, "Stikhi o starukhakh," Moskva (1967), no. 3: 155; K. Iakovlev, "Tvagolenie ili oliagoshchenie?" Molodaia gvardiia (1968), no. 9: 290-99; P. Antokolskii, "V rel'su," Iunost' (1972), no. 8: 68-72. Solzhenitsyn has argued strongly for purifying the Russian language. In his The First Circle (New York: Harper and Row, 1968), pp. 211-12, his character Sologdin gives himself penalty marks for using words of foreign origin. Solzhenitsyn takes up this note again in "For the Good of the Cause," in his Short Stories and Prose Poems (New York: Bantam Books, 1970), p. 90,

when his character Grachikov inveighs against the use of military
terminology in nonmilitary life.

8. Vladimir Soloukhin, S liricheskhikh pozitsii (Moscow:
Khudozhestvennaia literatura, 1965), pp. 104-05.

9. Writers of rural prose include: F. Abramov, V. Belov,
Vladimir Soloukhin, V. Potanin, V. Shukshin, V. Astafayev, S.
Melishin, V. Afonin, Iu. Galkin, D. Granin, Ye. Nosov, B.
Mozhayev, V. Rasputin, A. Romanov, M. Alekseyev, A. Ivanov,
P. Proskurin, and V. Likhonosov. See Gleb Zekulin, "The Contem-
porary Countryside in Soviet Literature: A Search for New Values,"
in The Soviet Rural Community, ed. James R. Millar (Urbana: Uni-
versity of Illinois Press, 1971), pp. 376-404.

10. Bird, op. cit., pp. 23-27; "Preservation of Historical and
Cultural Monuments," Soviet Union (1972), no. 10: 4; S. T. Palmer,
"Restoration of Ancient Monuments in the USSR," Survey no. 74-75
(Winter-Spring 1970): 163-74; Vladimir Desyatnikov, "Preserving
the Past," Soviet Life, March 1978, pp. 33-36.

11. See review of remarks by M. Lobanov in Georgy Radov,
"Whose Heirs Are We?" Literaturnoye obozreniye (1973), no. 3: 52-
54; CDSP 25, no. 44 (1973): 10-11.

12. Arkhiv samizdata 11, no. 590.

13. V. I. Kozlov, "On the Biological-Geographical Conception
of Ethnic History," Voprosy istorii (1974), no. 12: 72-85; CDSP 27,
no. 20 (1975): 1-5.

14. Shafarevich, op. cit., pp. 92-96.

15. Alexander Solzhenitsyn, Letter to the Leaders of the
Soviet Union (New York: Harper and Row, 1974), p. 27.

16. Arkhiv samizdata 21, no. 1013.

17. Viktor Chalmaev, "Neizbeznost'," Molodaia gvardiia
(1968), no. 9: 259-89.

18. See B. Urlanis, "Demographic Policy in the Modern World,"
Mirovaia ekonomika i meshdunarodnye otnosheniia (1975), no. 5,
translated in Soviet Review 17, no. 2 (Summer 1976): 86-102; R.
Galetskaya, "The Areas of Demographic Policy," Voprosy ekonomiki
(1975), no. 8: 149-52; CDSP 27, no. 45 (1975): 15-16. The latter
article notes that the desire of Central Asian women to have large
families could be controlled by enrolling more of them in the work
force to perform "socially useful labor."

19. Anatoly Yolkin, "My Love and My Pain," Moskva (1974),
no. 11: 214-18, in CDSP 27, no. 11 (1975): 6; V. P. Morozov, "Some
Questions of the Organization of Strategic Leadership in the Great
Patriotic War," Istoriia SSSR (1975), no. 3: 12-29, in CDSP 27, no.
49 (1975): 19-21; Anatoly Mednikov, "Many Are Indebted to Them,"
Literaturnoye obozreniye (1975), no. 3: 22-24, in CDSP 27, no. 34
(1975): 13-14.

20. See Izvestiia, January 26, 1974, p. 6; and October 2, 1975, p. 6.

21. Solzhenitsyn, Letter to the Leaders of the Soviet Union, p. 17.

PART V
EMERGENT PROBLEMS

EMERGENT NATIONALITY PROBLEMS IN THE USSR 12

Jeremy R. Azrael

This essay examines some of the policy problems that will confront the Soviet leadership in the 1980s and 1990s as a result of the rapidly changing ethnodemographic composition and ethnopolitical orientation of the Soviet population. Unlike some recent commentaries, the essay does not contend that these problems foreshadow a breakdown of the Soviet system, or even that they are likely to reach crisis proportions.[1] Contrary to the view that still prevails in many quarters, however, it <u>does</u> contend that these problems are neither adventitious nor recessive, and could significantly influence the future development of the Soviet system.[2]

ETHNODEMOGRAPHIC TRENDS

The most elemental of the ethnodemographic problems confronting the regime is the large and persistent disparity in the growth rates of the country's "European" (Slavic and Baltic) nationalities and its "non-European" (Caucasian and Central Asian) nationalities.* As

---

*The reader will, of course, recognize that the categories "European" and "non-European" are synthetic and that each includes nationalities that differ from one another in important respects. In the case of the "non-Europeans," the crucial internal distinction is probably between Christians (Georgians and Armenians) and Muslims (Azeri, Uzbeks, Turkmen, Tadzhiks, Kirghiz, and Kazakhs). Except for the Tadzhiks, all of the Muslim nationalities speak mutually comprehensible languages and share a common Turkic background that may be more important to them than their Soviet-sponsored national identities. A striking bit of evidence to this effect is the

can be seen in Figure 12.1, of the major "European" nationalities, which constitute about 80 percent of the country's total population and therefore dominate its overall demographic performance, only the Moldavians have increased by more than 1.2 percent per annum in recent years, and some of them have scarcely increased at all. (See appendix for fuller detail.) Of the major "non-European" nationalities, on the other hand, only the Georgians and Tatars have fallen below a 2 percent increase per annum; and the Central Asian nationalities have achieved annual increases of close to 4 percent. As a result, "non-Europeans" have increased their share in the country's total population from 11.5 percent in 1959 to a conservatively estimated 17 percent in 1977.[3]

FIGURE 12.1

Average Annual Population Growth Rates of Major "European" and "Non-European" Nationalities, 1959-1970

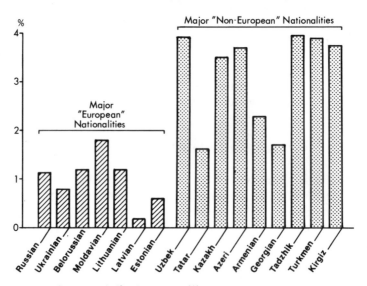

Source: Author's composition.

statement by the Kirghiz novelist Chingiz Aitmatov that recent literary output in Central Asia filled him with "Turkic national pride." Quoted in N. Khudaiberganov, "Vdokhnovennaia ispoved'," Pravda vostoka, December 10, 1976, p. 3. That such a statement presently could be made about "Slavic" or "Baltic" national pride seems doubtful. On the mutual comprehensibility of Soviet Turkic languages, see G. K. Dulling's review of a major Soviet study of Turkic languages in Central Asian Review 15, no. 2 (1967): 160.

This disparity (the size and persistence of which the regime apparently had underestimated prior to the 1970 census) has become a source of mounting official concern. There is little doubt, for example, that it was instrumental in the regime's decision to create a special high-level Scientific Council on Nationality Problems under the Presidium of the Academy of Sciences.* In addition, it almost certainly was a factor in Brezhnev's recent call for the formulation of an official demographic policy that would take account of "a number of population problems which have lately become exacerbated."[4] For the immediate future, however, there is little that the regime can do to stimulate the growth rate among "European" nationalities; and no conceivable combination of pro- and anti-natalist policies can avoid a lengthy continuation of the overall trends displayed in Table 12.1. In consequence, by the end of the century, between 20 and 25 percent of the country's total population and almost 40 percent of its teen-agers and young adults will be "non-Europeans," of whom the vast majority will be Central Asians.†

That this prospect has aroused deep-seated psychological and political anxieties among members of the ruling elite is indicated, among other things, by the epithet "yellowing" (ozheltenie) that is applied to it in the private conversations of many Soviet officials. These anxieties in turn are strongly reinforced by the "jokes," which have gained currency in certain Central Asian circles, about the impending restoration of the Tatar yoke, the forthcoming confirmation of the proposition that "when you scratch a Russian you find a Tatar," and the fate that will befall the Russians when the Chinese "liberate" Turkestan.[5] Nonetheless, the current ruling elite is not discernibly racist in its outlook or composition, and it is doubtful that it feels

---

*This council was created in late 1969 or early 1970, but apparently was moribund until 1974-75, when it went into high-gear operation. For an account of its work, see M. N. Guboglo, "V sektsii obshchestvennykh nauk Prezidiuma AN SSSR--v nauchnom sovete po natsional'nym problemam," Voprosy istorii (1976), no. 4: 148-50.

†See appendix. The lowest U.S. government projections, which are based on assumptions that almost certainly understate probabilities on the Muslim side and probably overstate them on the European side, envision a 21.3 percent Muslim component (65 million) in a 307 million population. Compare J. F. Besemeres, "Population Politics in the U.S.S.R.," Soviet Union/Union soviétique (1975), no. 2, pt. 1: 69, who, after citing these figures, concludes that they "are so cautious [as regards Muslim growth rates] as to be almost foolhardy."

TABLE 12.1

Changing Composition of USSR Population, 1959-70

Nationality	Percent of Total Population		Percent Change
	1959	1970	
Major "European"	79.6	77.2	−2.4
Russian	54.6	53.4	−1.2
Ukrainian	17.8	16.9	−0.9
Belorussian	3.8	3.7	−0.1
Moldavian	1.1	1.1	0.0
Latvian	0.7	0.6	−0.1
Lithuanian	1.1	1.1	0.0
Estonian	0.4	0.4	0.0
Major "non-European"	12.6	15.2	+2.6
Uzbek	2.9	3.8	+0.9
Tatar	2.4	2.4	0.0
Kazakh	1.7	2.2	+0.5
Azeri	1.4	1.8	+0.4
Armenian	1.3	1.5	+0.2
Georgian	1.3	1.3	0.0
Tadzhik	0.7	0.9	+0.2
Turkmen	0.5	0.6	+0.1
Kirghiz	0.5	0.6	+0.1
Others	7.8	7.6	−0.2
Selected national groups			
Slavs[a]	76.3	74.0	−2.3
Non-Slavic "Europeans"[b]	3.3	3.2	−0.1
"Non-European" Christians[c]	2.6	2.8	+0.2
"Non-European" Muslims[d]	10.0	12.4	+2.4
All other	7.8	7.6	−0.2

[a]Slavs are defined as the total of the Russian, Ukrainian, and Belorussian populations.

[b]Non-Slavic "Europeans" are defined as the total of the Moldavian, Lithuanian, Latvian, and Estonian populations.

[c]"Non-European" Christians are defined as the total of the Georgian and Armenian populations.

[d]"Non-European" Muslims are defined as the total of the Uzbek, Tatar, Kazakh, Azeri, Tadzhik, Turkmen, and Kirghiz populations.

immediately threatened by an erosion of "white supremacy" or the emergence of a Chinese "fifth column." The fact that it has chosen to treble the number of Turkic representatives on the Politburo (from one to three, with the addition of an Azeri, G. A. Aliev, and a Kazakh or Uighur, K. A. Kunaev, to the Uzbek incumbent, Sh. R. Rashidov) on the eve of a potential succession crisis suggests a relative indifference on the first count; and there is no evidence to suggest that the Central Asians, who are, of course, not yellow but brown, have any real (as against rhetorical) sympathy for the Chinese. Although Chinese propaganda against the domination of Central Asia by "new tsars" undoubtedly strikes responsive chords, its pro-Chinese content is filtered through an almost primordial Sinophobia and a widespread awareness (cultivated by the Soviet regime) of the unhappy fate of the Turkic minorities in the People's Republic of China.[6]

At a minimum the Kremlin's concern on both these counts is almost certainly less urgent than its concern over the implications of the "yellowing" process for the national economy. In this connection, moreover, what is most troubling is not the shift in the ethnic balance per se but the low "European" (and, hence, all-union) growth rates and the fact that the Central Asian nationalities have remained outside the mainstream of the country's economic development and contain a heavy preponderance of undereducated peasants with a weak-to-nonexistent knowledge of Russian and a tenacious aversion to interregional or even intraregional migration.[7]

ECONOMIC DILEMMAS

What the shortfall in the country's "European" population means for the economy is that the latter will no longer be able to provide large-scale reinforcements for the industrial work force. By the late 1980s the number of "Europeans" reaching working age will decline from the present average of about 4 million per annum to only slightly over 2 million per annum, and the regime will be extremely hard pressed to find enough "European" workers to replace those whose retirement (even if extended beyond the current norms of 60 for men and 55 for women) can no longer be delayed.[8] What makes this prospect particularly unsettling is the fact that the vast bulk of the increase in industrial output that has occurred in the postwar Soviet Union is attributable to increases in the "European" work force rather than to increases in per capita labor productivity, which has grown only modestly despite the regime's frantic efforts to raise it.[9] Even if it manages to replenish its "European" work force--by reducing draft terms and/or draft quotas, curtailing full-time secondary education, or accelerating the already rapid flight of young "Europeans" from the countryside--the only way the regime can hope to staff the many new enterprises on which it has staked so much of its prestige and credibility is either to locate the bulk of them in Central Asia or to mobilize large numbers of Central Asians for work in other regions.* Unfortunately for the regime, however, these policies could exact a very heavy price.

Whatever its ultimate benefits, a rapid buildup of Central Asia's industrial capacity obviously would require the diversion of a great deal of scarce capital and equipment both from the already in-dustrialized regions of the country and from underdeveloped regions such as Siberia and the Far North, which are far richer than Central Asia in essential (and hard-currency-convertible) natural resources. In addition to capital and equipment, moreover, such a buildup could easily have the ironic but historically familiar effect of drawing scarce manpower away from other regions into Central Asia. De-spite rising educational levels and urbanization rates, the number of native engineers, technicians, and skilled workers is still extremely limited; and local plant and factory directors have good reason to favor the long-distance recruitment of experienced "European" work-ers over the employment of ready-to-hand but inexperienced Central Asians, who are perceived as undependable and are actually far more likely to miss work and change jobs than their "European" counter-parts.[10] Finally, resources (including human resources) that are transferred to Central Asia (or are retained there when they could be productively relocated) and that do not directly contribute to Soviet area-defense capabilities could be exposed to Chinese weapons when they might otherwise be largely out of range.

Moreover, in contrast with the situation that may have existed in the 1950s or 1960s, it can no longer be assumed that the mere fact

---

*It is also possible, of course, that the Soviet Union could re-cruit large numbers of foreign workers, thereby emulating not only the labor-deficit countries of Western Europe but also some of its East European neighbors. See Malcolm W. Browne, "Czechoslo-vakia Is Importing Vietnamese Workers," New York Times, April 25, 1976, p. 10. That such a policy is thinkable for the Soviet Union is indicated by the extensive importation of Chinese workers during the mid-1950s and by the current employment of some East European and Scandinavian workers on special projects. Nevertheless, a sys-tematic mass recruitment policy would be almost impossible to sus-tain without drastically changing current economic and political premises and practices.

of their location in Central Asia will make strategic objectives significantly less accessible or less vulnerable to U.S. forces. In consequence, those who advocate the rapid industrialization of the one
region of the country with a large natural surplus of otherwise scarce
labor are likely to encounter strong resistance from military planners, as well as from those Party and managerial cadres and foreign-
trade officials who are eager to increase Soviet exports and prevent
a sharp deterioration in the country's balance of hard-currency payments. * As these advocates undoubtedly will point out, however, it
may be no less difficult and risky to move the industrial mountain to
Mohammed than to attempt the process in reverse.

The chances that large numbers of Central Asians will spon-
taneously migrate into the labor-deficit regions of the country are
virtually nil. To be sure, in the absence of accelerated industrialization of their own region, hundreds of thousands, if not millions,
of natives will be unable to find full-time employment in the public
sector (industrial or agricultural) of the local economy. [11] In addition, thanks to the tenacity of early marriage and prolific childbear-
ing practices, many of those concerned undoubtedly will have a large
number of dependents to support. As is the case today, however,
the very existence of large families will serve as a constraint on
migration to cities in general and to overcrowded "European" cities
in particular; and these constraints will be further reinforced by the
nexus of tradition of which early marriage and high fertility are a
part. [12] Moreover, in the absence of strong counteractions by the
regime, many natives who cannot find jobs in the public sector will
still be able not only to survive but also to prosper on the proceeds
of the individual or familial cottage industries and private household
plots that already account for a sizable share of Central Asian personal income. [13]

These earnings undoubtedly could be curtailed if the regime
were willing to pursue the necessary restrictive policies. Such
policies, however, would be not only intrinsically difficult and costly
to enforce but also potentially dangerous. At a minimum, they would
create serious local shortages of at least temporarily irreplaceable
foodstuffs, consumer goods, and personal services. In addition,
they might well lead to a slowdown in centrally planned cotton and
silk production by the disgruntled native collective farmers who
would be the principal victims. Furthermore, they could touch off

---

*The military undoubtedly will continue to favor a transporta-
tion buildup in Central Asia to facilitate its logistical operations on
the Sino-Soviet "front."

violent protests and terrorist outbursts similar to those that accompanied a recent official crackdown on private entrepreneurship in Georgia.[14] Even if these policies accomplished their immediate purpose, moreover, both the time-tested welfare practices of the still-prevalent extended family system and the legally mandatory income-sharing procedures of the collective farms system would significantly reduce their efficacy as spurs to out-migration. *

A search for other, potentially more effective policies that the regime might use to increase the supply of Central Asian gastarbeiter yields two basic alternatives: administrative mobilization and economic stimulation. In administrative mobilization, the already existing requirement that graduates of institutions of higher and specialized secondary education work for two to three years at state-assigned jobs could be focused to generate a steady westward flow of younger Central Asian cadres. In addition, the regime could make more extensive use of the already common practice of conscripting militarily "superfluous" or "marginal" Central Asians into the armed forces and posting them to units that perform essentially civilian economic tasks.† Going further in the same direction, it could reintroduce a compulsory labor draft of the sort that existed under Stalin, with the sole difference that Central Asian draftees could no longer expect job assignments in their home regions. This last measure would almost certainly have to be accompanied by the reimposition of a large number of highly counterproductive Stalinist controls, however, and even the more moderate variants seem likely to entail political and social costs that would be hard to "recapture" from the output of transient and disgruntled Central Asian workers who accurately viewed themselves as victims of a system of involuntary and discriminatory servitude.

----

*Although collective farms can legally expel members, superfluity or redundancy is not an authorized ground for doing so.

†Representative Les Aspin has calculated that the Soviet armed forces include some 250,000 men who are kept in uniform to do civilian construction work. The Defense Intelligence Agency allegedly has confirmed the basic accuracy of this figure. See John W. Finney, "U.S. Statistics on Soviet Question Extent of Threat," New York Times, April 24, 1976. Representative Aspin also contends that 75,000 troops are permanently assigned to "military farms," a claim that the DIA denies, while acknowledging that large numbers of Soviet soldiers are assigned to farm details on an intermittent basis. Soviet refugees uniformly report that construction units contain a highly disproportionate number of Central Asians.

The problems associated with reliance on "Eurocentric" relocation bonuses or pay incentives to attract Central Asian gastarbeiter are substantially different from those just mentioned, but are in no way less problematical. At the very least, such incentives would be extremely difficult to design and administer, and would powerfully reinforce the already strong inflationary pressures within the all-union economy. In addition, it is likely that the native respondents would include a disproportionate number of skilled workers and technical cadres whose contribution to the all-union economy would be equally great (or greater) on their home ground, and whose enticement away from home would be strongly resented by local Party and government leaders with an interest in the economic performance and progress of Central Asia. Finally, a "Eurocentric" wage or bonus policy could easily precipitate a mass exodus of Central Asia's "European" settlers, whose departure would not only leave key sectors of the regional economy (including the agricultural economy) at least temporarily crippled but would also deprive the regime of some of its most reliable agents of central control.[15] Over the long run, the regime may lose most of these agents anyway, since the combined demands of Central Asian workers for local jobs and of "European" employers for "European" employees will generate strong pressure for their "repatriation." Even if the regime had no reason to resist this pressure, it undoubtedly would prefer to accommodate it incrementally, in order to prevent repatriation from becoming an unregulated and headlong process.

The prospect of choosing among such unpalatable alternatives would give any leader pause, and it would not be surprising if Brezhnev continued to substitute further study for decisive action. Moreover, it is not unlikely that his successors also will try to "muddle through." Over the longer run, however, the only way in which they can reasonably hope to maintain anything like current growth rates without recourse to measures of the kind discussed above is to secure substantial technology transfers from the West and to implement administrative and managerial reforms that will curb their own day-to-day power and weaken the overall framework of central control. Given the resistance that these prospective outcomes are certain to engender and the difficulties in acquiring and using Western technology, the chances for a successful nullification of the ethnodemographic constraints on the Soviet economy of the 1980s and 1990s seem rather dim. In consequence, it would not be surprising if industrial growth rates declined substantially and if the regime found it increasingly difficult to satisfy both its own appetite for international power and the rising economic expectations of its citizens.

MILITARY CONSEQUENCES

Unless there is a rise in international tensions or wider reliance on military conscription as a form of de facto labor draft, the size of the Soviet armed forces is likely to decrease in the 1980s (it is now estimated to be 4 to 5 million men).[16] Even if the reduction in the draft term from three to two years were rescinded, it would be exceedingly difficult and costly to secure the requisite number of conscripts (currently estimated to number about 1.5 to 1.6 million per year) from a country in which the entire cohort of 18-year-old males will be only slightly over 2 million (as against 2.6 million today) and in which, because of the age structure of the general population and the virtually complete (except in Central Asia) "emancipation" of women, there cannot possibly be an increase in the size of the overall civilian work force except at the military's expense.[17] In addition to facing a prospective cutback, moreover, the armed forces seem almost certain to undergo a very extensive "yellowing." This outcome is foreshadowed, if not foreordained, by the fact that the proportion of "non-Europeans" among prime draft-age males will rise from a low of 20 to 25 percent in the late 1980s to almost 40 percent by the turn of the century.

Indeed, if the regime were to follow the dictates of economic rationality alone, the military would become an almost entirely "non-European" institution. In this way it would be possible not only to avoid the inordinately high civilian opportunity costs of "European" soldiers but also to realize disproportionately high civilian returns on its investments in in-service training programs. Although these programs are often redundant for European trainees, they frequently provide Central Asians with new and readily transferable skills, as well as with a career orientation that could make them somewhat less averse to postservice out-migration. For reasons that by now are familiar, however, an economically rational conscription policy would significantly exacerbate the already serious military and military-political problems that the natural "yellowing" of the armed forces is sure to pose.

Even if the regime were to flout economic logic and overconscript "Europeans," it would have to abandon what seems, by nearly all refugee accounts, to be its current practice of assigning only a few atypical Central Asians to high-priority military units, including not only units of the strategic rocket forces and antiaircraft defense but also of the air force, the armored corps, the artillery, and even the front-line motorized infantry. Although these units could be kept preponderantly "European," their ranks would still have to be filled with typical Central Asians, who now are assigned mostly to construction, supply, and rear service functions. By the late 1980s and 1990s, it is true, typical Central Asian conscripts probably will be somewhat better-educated than their contemporary counterparts, who average less than ten years of formal schooling. * Barring a massive educational breakthrough, however, the vast majority of them will almost certainly still be graduates of second- and third-rate rural schools, which will continue to offer rudimentary versions of the military training courses that are becoming standard features of the senior high school curriculum.[18] In consequence, there is little prospect that any impending decline in the quantity of Soviet military manpower could be counterbalanced by a significant increase in its quality, let alone by an increase that would keep pace with the accelerating "scientific-technological revolution in military affairs."

The difficulties created by the low educational attainments and technical skills of typical Central Asian conscripts will be exacerbated and compounded by their rudimentary command of Russian, which is the only authorized medium of communication within the armed forces, and will almost certainly remain the only language spoken by the majority of senior officers.[19] If there is a significant increase in the percentage of Central Asians who are urbanized, the proportion of Central Asians who speak Russian with some fluency may rise above the current 16 percent.† However, there is little prospect that it will rise sharply, and present trends suggest that it actually may decline as the proportion of "Europeans" in Central Asia becomes progressively smaller.[20] In any event, the language-related command, control, and communication problems that have heretofore been largely confined to relatively low-priority units are likely to become prevalent in other units as well, with corresponding degrading effects on the country's military capabilities.[21] Judging

---

*Although ten years of education is compulsory in the Soviet Union and the numbers of rural residents who have completed the tenth grade are higher in Central Asia than in the USSR as a whole, Soviet sources leave no doubt that the quality of rural education is far lower than its urban counterpart; and the vast majority of Central Asians live in rural areas, whereas most "Europeans" are city dwellers. Furthermore, there is reason to believe that official data on Soviet educational attainments in general and Central Asian educational attainments in particular are substantially inflated. See Jeremy Azrael, "Bringing up the Soviet Man: Dilemmas and Progress," Problems of Communism 17, no. 3 (May/June 1968): 23-31.

†On the other hand, the very fact that the cities in question will be undergoing substantial "indigenization" may reduce their role as centers of russianization.

by what is reported to have occurred in various enterprises and offices in Central Asia, there is good reason to believe that units in which Central Asian natives become a substantial minority will be particularly prone to demoralizing ethnic tensions and open ethnic conflicts.[22]

Many of these difficulties could be at least partially alleviated by the reinstitution of national military formations of the sort that were the norm until 1936 and were selectively rehabilitated during World War II.[23] Assuming that this was not accompanied by a politically provocative and militarily counterproductive injunction against "home-basing," such a measure could yield a number of other benefits. For one, it would chasten critics of the spurious character of the "sovereignty" of the Soviet Union's constituent republics, including several outspoken dissidents who have placed the absence of national military formations high on their list of grievances.[24] In addition, it could foster a closer identity between national pride and Soviet patriotism, two sentiments that the regime has long sought to reconcile and fuse and that in fact can both coexist and be mutually reinforcing. Finally, the existence of national military formations could lead to more efficient and effective civil-military cooperation at the local level in the event of an all-out mobilization, civil defense emergency, or resort to martial rule.

In view of these considerable advantages of a return to "military federalism," it would not be surprising if the possibility of such a return has been deliberated in official circles. That it has in fact been done is at least indirectly suggested by the expanded treatment of the interrelationship between national policy and military policy that differentiates the otherwise only slightly modified first (1974) and second (1975) editions of the late Marshal A. A. Grechko's highly authoritative The Armed Forces of the Soviet State.[25] Furthermore, an extremely reliable and unusually well-informed refugee source has reported that in the early 1970s the Kazakh and Estonian Party leaderships both submitted official requests that conscripts from their republics be assigned predominantly to local garrisons rather than intentionally dispersed, and that the Kazakh request was granted.[26]

Whatever discussions or experiments may be occurring, however, the regime is unlikely to sanction a return to full-fledged military federalism or to permit the "indigenization" of local bases and garrisons to become a general policy. Rather, the fact that the constitution ratified in 1978, to replace the so-called Stalin Constitution of 1936, drops both of the latter's references (in Articles 14-g and 18-b) to republic-level military formations suggests that the regime is eager to stifle all hopes and expectations to the contrary. * Like the late Marshal Grechko, official commentators probably will continue to dwell on "the difficulty of preparing training manuals in different national languages" and the importance of reinforcing internationalist sentiments. [27] The underlying motive, though, will almost certainly be a fear that indigenous units might provide tacit or open military support for nationalist challenges to central authority.

That such fear can be a significant factor in official thinking is indicated, for example, by Nikita Khrushchev's conduct during the riot opposing de-Stalinization that broke out in Tbilisi, Georgia, in March 1956. Although this riot clearly was beyond the control of the civil authorities, Khrushchev canceled the marching orders of a nearby military unit that happened (by a rare anomaly) to be predominantly Georgian, and allowed the rioters to rampage for 12 hours while more typical, ethnically heterogeneous troops were dispatched from outlying bases. [28] Some years later, it is true, Khrushchev proposed creation of a territorial militia to compensate for the troop reductions that he was introducing, partially in response to mounting demographic pressures. [29] Moreover, there is no doubt these pressures (which stemmed from a sharp but temporary drop in the country's supply of teen-agers) were mild compared with those that are now emerging.† Before drawing any hasty inferences from these facts, however, it is worth recalling that Khrushchev's militia proposal was never implemented and that any future analogues, let alone cognate proposals affecting the regular army, will be evaluated in the light of recent ethnopolitical developments that make it clear (as it was not clear in 1960) that the Tbilisi riot was not the last such event and that even greater disturbances may be in the offing.

---

*Article 14-g of the 1936 Constitution grants the central government the right to establish "guiding principles" for "the organization of the military formation of the union republics." Article 18-b affirms that "each union republic has its own military formations." The draft of the new constitution makes no mention of republic formations and states that the central government is responsible for "the organization of defense and leadership of the armed forces." Izvestiia, June 4, 1977, p. 3.

†The scarcity of teen-agers in the late 1950s and early 1960s was, of course, a consequence of sharply falling wartime birth rates.

POLITICAL CURRENTS

When Brezhnev alleged in 1972 that the past 50 years had witnessed the formation of a new "Soviet nation" or "Soviet people" (sovetskii narod) that was now sufficiently robust to survive any ethnopolitical crisis, and eventually would encompass the entire population of the USSR, he may or may not have been engaged in wishful thinking.[30] At a minimum, he could point to indisputable and massive demonstrations of all-union loyalty during World War II and to a steady, albeit slow and by no means universal, postwar growth in bilingualism, ethnic intermarriage, and interregional mobility. However, when he went on to assure his audience that the Soviet Union definitely had solved its "historic nationality problem"-- the problem of national deviationism and centrifugal nationalism--he was clearly and knowingly overstating what was at best a dubious, if not a completely indefensible, case.[31] Indeed, the countervailing evidence is so well known that a detailed exposition seems gratuitous. A summary rundown will serve to remind the reader.

1. Many members of the country's major diaspora nationalities, including not only the Jews but also the Volga Germans, the Greeks, and the Meskhetian Turks, have become so embittered at the continued denial of their communal rights that they have renounced their Soviet citizenship and have demanded to be "repatriated" to their quite foreign "homelands."[32]
2. Nearly all of the country's "European" and Caucasian nationalities and at least one Turkic nationality (the Crimean Tatars) have produced outspoken critics of official nationality policies and practices. These critics have managed not only to replenish their own ranks in the face of hundreds, if not thousands, of arrests, but also to establish dynamic and resilient dissident organizations, ranging from clandestine parties, through editorial boards for the preparation of regular samizdat or underground journals, to networks for the public circulation of programs, petitions, and letters of protest, including one 1972 petition (to U.N. Secretary-General Kurt Waldheim) that was signed by more than 17,000 Lithuanians.[33]
3. A number of nationalistically inspired acts of violence have included a two-day riot in Kaunas, Lithuania, in 1972 and several recent protest bombings and reported assassination attempts in Georgia.[34]
4. There have been numerous organized protest demonstrations against centrally imposed curbs on national self-expression, including several mass gatherings by Crimean Tatars and a 1965 street vigil in Erevan that reportedly was attended by 100,000 Armenians.[35]

5. There has been an extremely rapid increase in the membership
    of republic and local ethnographic societies and so-called so-
    cieties for the preservation of architectural and historical monu-
    ments that were established in the 1960s to provide outlets for
    environmentalist and conservationist concerns. There is no
    doubt that the mushroom growth of these societies and their ex-
    ceptional popularity reflect a more than merely antiquarian or
    folkloristic interest in national history and culture. In fact,
    there is every reason to suspect--as some Soviet security offi-
    cials clearly do--that many of their members are no less nation-
    alistic than the members of the not-so-remotely analogous
    Matica Hrvatska and Matica Srpska organizations that provided
    key recruitment bases for the massive national protest move-
    ments that have rocked Yugoslavia. [36]

6. There have been numerous cases in which native Party and state
    officials, including two republic Party first secretaries with
    seats on the Politburo (a Georgian, V. P. Mzhavandze, and a
    Ukrainian, P. Ye. Shelest), have shown a certain laxity in com-
    bating the forces of "local nationalism" and have pursued the
    "parochial" interests of their fellow nationals at the expense of
    their all-union responsibilities. * These cases have been widely
    publicized in the Soviet press, and there is no reason to doubt
    that most of the officials concerned are at least partially "guilty"
    as charged, and have in fact encouraged (or failed to discourage)
    the retention of local resources for local use, the curtailment of
    immigration by ethnic "aliens," the preferential treatment of
    native cadres, the publication of "nationally pretentious" books
    and articles, the "tendentious" designation of historical monu-
    ments, the perpetuation of "archaic" traditions and retrograde
    survivals of the past, and even the lenient treatment of dissident
    nationalist intellectuals. [37]

Although these manifestations of national self-affirmation and
self-assertiveness are a far cry from the explosive international or
center-periphery confrontations that took place in earlier periods of
Soviet history (during the Revolution and Civil War, and the early
wartime and postwar years) or that have recently occurred in a number of other multinational polities (Yugoslavia, Canada, Belgium,
the United Kingdom), they are more than sufficient to demonstrate

---

*In addition to the Ukraine and Georgia, Armenia has suffered
a particularly extensive "renewal" of leading cadres as a result of
the regime's vigilance campaign against "local nationalism."

that the USSR has neither transcended its own history nor become immune to worldwide trends.[38] Unless the regime undergoes an improbable re-Stalinization or an even more improbable liberal-democratic transformation, such manifestations are likely to become more frequent and more insistent over time.[39] Although piecemeal reforms and partial crackdowns undoubtedly could have a tranquilizing effect, they would at best produce a temporary and deceptive calm; and there is a strong possibility that they would merely further agitate an already turbulent situation. Summarily stated, this seems to be the "lesson" of both the Khrushchev and Brezhnev-Kosygin eras; and it is a lesson that is likely to retain its validity for the foreseeable future.[40]

One reason for anticipating an escalation in national self-affirmation and self-assertiveness is the accelerating "modernization" of the Central Asian nationalities, who have been conspicuously passive since their great uprising in the early 1920s, but who are almost certain to become more militant as, in one way or another, they are drawn into the mainstream of the country's economic development.[41] At the same time, moreover, the "European" nationalities are likely to become increasingly restive as they are subjected either to an "onslaught" of Central Asian gastarbeiter or to an "expropriation" of "their" resources to speed the industrialization of distant Central Asia. In this connection, a particularly strong reaction probably can be expected from the Russians, among whom are numerous spokesmen who contend that the regime has sacrificed Russia's economic welfare and cultural integrity for the sake of an illegitimate "internationalism," and who will soon undergo the psychological distress of losing their majority status within the country's total population.[42] Also, increasing education and urbanization and improved communications will make it much harder for the regime to isolate the masses from dissident nationalist spokesmen or from the demonstration effects of nationalist protests within the Soviet Union or in the outside world. Finally, an increasing number of actual and potential nationalist protesters are likely to possess weapons and explosives, as a result of the diffusion of scientific and technical know-how, the multiplication of laboratories and workshops (including those in homes), and the proliferation of local civil defense and preinduction training arsenals.[43]

Barring a breakdown of central control that might accompany a major war or the political degeneration that might accompany a prolonged and unfettered succession struggle, there is little likelihood that national protest will rise to unmanageable levels.[44] Under more normal circumstances, centrally manipulated sanctions and incentives will almost certainly suffice to prevent large communal uprisings or national insurgencies. This seems all the more certain because, as the examples of the United States during the Cold War and of China today suggest, even the most hostile foreign powers are unlikely to risk the retaliation that might follow efforts to provide would-be insurrectionaries with significant external support. The most that can be readily conceived, therefore, is "merely" more of the same--that is, more numerous acts of individual and small-group terrorism, more frequent episodes of collective violence, more massive protest demonstrations, and more extensive public or semi-public dissent. Even such manageable outcomes, however, would impose serious constraints on the regime.

At a minimum, the regime would be forced to increase its police budget and to introduce security procedures that not only would be economically counterproductive but also would demoralize and even disaffect citizens on whose loyalty and commitment it otherwise could rely. In the second place, the regime would find it increasingly difficult to persuade even strongly détente-oriented Western governments to sponsor or authorize the volume of technology transfers, grain sales, and development credits that could significantly brighten its somewhat gloomy economic prospects. Try as they may, such governments will be harder put to ignore Soviet violations of communal rights as the victims of these violations escalate their protests, especially if the latter come, as they almost certainly will, from groups such as the Jews, Germans, Lithuanians, and Ukrainians whose foreign conationals (in the United States, West Germany, Canada, and Australia) constitute important domestic political constituencies. In the same vein, moreover, the regime could find it difficult to maintain or consolidate profitable political and economic relations with a range of non-Western countries whose native populations have strong ethnic affinities with restive nationalities in the USSR--a category of countries that includes Romania (Moldavians), Iran (Tadzhiks and Azeri), Afghanistan (Azeri and Turkmen), and Turkey (Meskhetian Turks and the entire Soviet Turkic population), and that could, by extension, include all of the countries of the Muslim world. Finally--at least for present purposes--escalating national protest would further discredit the Soviet "model" of international integration everywhere in the Third World and would undermine the regime's credibility as a spokesman for the oppressed nationalities in non-Communist countries.

IMPLICATIONS FOR THE WEST

Despite the ethnodemographic and ethnopolitical pressures that it faces, the Soviet regime probably will remain an imperialistic and potentially expansionistic dictatorship. As already indicated, these pressures are more likely to lead to increased domestic coercion and repression than to a liberal–democratic transformation of the regime. In addition, they are likely to strengthen the regime's determination to retain its East European empire. If these pressures became sufficiently intense, the regime may be tempted to try to dissipate them by initiating political-military confrontations of a sort that could activate an otherwise recessive or inoperative "Soviet patriotism." Unless they happen to be "gratuitously" relieved by Western actions, however, these pressures also seem likely to offer some favorable opportunities for the containment and redirection of Soviet power.

For one thing, the Soviet Union could become more amenable to balanced force reduction agreements of the sort it has hitherto refused seriously to entertain. In addition, it might become more sensitive to the danger that its continued support of "national liberation movements" in other countries could lead to a retaliatory campaign on behalf of the oppressed nationalities of the USSR. At the moment the People's Republic of China is the only major power pursuing such a campaign in earnest, but the West's relative forbearance (as illustrated by U.S. actions to downplay Captive Nations Week, to semi-recognize Soviet incorporation of the Baltic states, to modulate the tone of official propaganda broadcasts, and to stress individual rather than communal rights in its diplomatic exertions) is at least a potentially reversible decision that the Soviet Union may be more than ordinarily eager to keep in force. Finally, the Soviet Union is likely to become substantially more dependent on Western economic cooperation and assistance, which will thereby acquire greater potential as negotiating instruments and sources of diplomatic leverage.

Whether these opportunities can be utilized to the West's advantage will depend importantly on the ability of the United States to act in concert with its allies in a purposeful and timely fashion. Unfortunately, this capability is far easier to invoke than to attain, and by no means all currently observable signs are auspicious. Furthermore, policies designed to capitalize on these opportunities are likely to provoke strong normative, strategic, and tactical disagreements within the United States. Although some of these disagreements probably could be avoided by a more systematic assessment of past experiences and a more rigorous formulation of analytical guidelines, others seem certain to persist. How these disagreements will be resolved is intrinsically unpredictable, and this paper is not the place for even a preliminary consideration of the potentially contentious issues. Given the continuing competition between the Soviet Union and the West, however, it seems appropriate to suggest that opportunities to induce a less expansive Soviet "globalism" and a lower Soviet profile in international affairs should not be rejected a priori or dismissed as chimerical before they have been prudently but seriously tested in practice.

APPENDIX

	National Population (thousands)		Annual Growth Rate[a] (percent)	Straight-Line Projection of Population[b]				"Eurocentric" Projection of Population[c]	
				(thousands)		(percent of total)		(thousands)	(percent of total)
	1959	1970		1985	2000	1985	2000	2000	2000
"European"									
Russian	114,114	129,015	1.12	153,427	180,305	51.2	47.9	183,483	50.2
Ukrainian	37,253	40,753	0.82	46,061	52,062	15.4	13.8	55,084	15.1
Belorussian	7,913	9,052	1.23	10,874	13,063	3.6	3.5	13,063	3.6
Moldavian	2,214	2,698	1.81	3,533	4,626	1.2	1.2	4,626	1.3
Lithuanian	2,326	2,665	1.24	3,208	3,862	1.1	1.0	3,862	1.1
Latvian	1,400	1,430	0.19	1,472	1,515	0.5	0.4	1,760	0.5
Estonian	939	1,007	0.63	1,118	1,219	0.4	0.3	1,337	0.4
Total "European"	166,159	186,620	1.06	219,693	256,652	73.2	68.1	263,215	71.9
"Non-European"									
Uzbek	6,015	9,159	3.90	16,250	28,832	5.4	7.7	21,871	6.0
Tatar	4,968	5,931	1.62	7,552	9,616	2.5	2.6	9,442	2.6
Kazakh	3,622	5,299	3.52	8,904	14,958	3.0	4.0	11,984	3.3
Azeri	2,940	4,380	3.69	7,543	12,991	2.5	3.5	10,152	2.8
Armenian	2,787	3,559	2.25	4,967	6,933	1.7	1.8	6,567	1.8
Georgian	2,692	3,245	1.71	4,187	5,401	1.4	1.4	5,235	1.4
Tadzhik	1,397	2,136	3.94	3,811	6,800	1.3	1.8	5,129	1.4
Turkmen	1,002	1,525	3.89	2,704	4,794	0.9	1.3	3,639	1.0
Kirghiz	969	1,452	3.75	2,520	4,375	0.8	1.2	3,392	0.9
Total "non-European"	26,392	36,686	3.03	58,438	94,700	19.5	25.1	77,411	21.2
All other	16,135	18,334	1.16	21,823	25,411	7.3	6.7	25,411	6.9
Total population	208,686	241,640	1.34	299,954	376,763	100.0	100.0	366,037	100.0

[a]Annual growth rates were obtained by solving the following equation: $(1 + r)^t = P_{70}/P_{59}$ for r, where $t = 11$.

[b]Straight-line projections for 1985 and 2000 were obtained by using the formula $P_{70}(1 + r)^t$, where $t = 15$ for 1985 and $t = 30$ for 2000.

[c]"Eurocentric" projections for 2000 were obtained by using the formula $P_{85}(1 + r)^t$, where P_{85} is the straight-line projection of population in 1985, and altering the annual rates of growth (r) in the following manner:

For Russians, Ukrainians, Latvians, and Estonians, the annual growth rate was increased to 1.20 percent.

For Moldavians, Belorussians, and Lithuanians, the annual rate of growth for 1959–70 was continued.

For Armenians, Georgians, and Tatars, the annual rate of growth was decreased to 1.50 percent.

For Uzbeks, Kazakhs, Azeri, Tadzhiks, Turkmen, and Kirghiz, the annual rate of growth was decreased to 2.0 percent.

381

NOTES

1. See the remarks of Richard Pipes in "Reflections of a Nationality Expert," in Nationalities and Nationalism in the USSR: A Soviet Dilemma, ed. Carl A. Linden and Dimitri K. Simes (Washington, D.C.: Center for Strategic and International Studies, Georgetown University, 1977), pp. 9-11, esp. 10. For a somewhat more qualified statement by Pipes, see his "Reflections on the Nationality Problem in the Soviet Union," in Ethnicity, ed. Nathan Glazer and Daniel P. Moynihan (Cambridge, Mass.: Harvard University Press, 1975), pp. 453-65, esp. 464-65. Compare also the prediction of President Mu'amaar al-Qadhaffi, of Libya, in his political treatise The Third Theory, that, as a result of "the nationalist movement," "a day will come when it [the Soviet Union] will split." Mu'ammar al-Qadhaffi, Fi-al-nazerayah al-thalithah (Benghazi, 1974), p. 28. According to Zbigniew Brzezinski, "the national question . . . creates a major block to gradual evolution" in the USSR and "could prove itself to be the fatal contradiction of Soviet political evolution." Brzezinski, Soviet Politics: From the Future to the Past? (New York: Research Institute on International Change, Columbia University, 1975), p. 31.

2. For a sophisticated and well-informed defense of the proposition that the Soviet Union has become essentially "denationalized" and that the evidence to the contrary derives from a brief and anomalous flare-up of interethnic tensions in the period 1965-70, see David Zil'berman, "Ethnography in Soviet Russia," Dialectic Anthropology (1976), no. 1: 135-53, esp. 149.

3. S. I. Bruk and M. N. Guboglo, "Development and Interaction of Ethnodemographic and Ethnolinguistic Processes in Soviet Society," Istoriia SSSR (July/August 1974), no. 4: 26-45, in Translations on USSR Political and Sociological Affairs no. 556, JPRS 62984 (September 17, 1974): 90-123, esp. 93.

4. Translated in Current Digest of the Soviet Press 28, no. 8 (March 24, 1976): 27. Even prior to Brezhnev's statement, the legal implications of possible official demographic policy were discussed at a "roundtable" convened by the editors of the journal Soviet State and Law and attended not only by jurists but also by representatives of the Central Statistical Administration and the Lenin Military-Political Academy. See "Legal Aspects of Demographic Policy," Sovetskoe gosudarstvo i pravo (January 1975), no. 1: 25-28, in Translations on USSR Political and Sociological Affairs no. 621, JPRS 64573 (April 18, 1975): 1-14, esp. 5.

5. As reported by numerous Soviet émigrés and Western visitors to the USSR. See Igor Shafarevich, "Separation or Reconciliation, in Alexander Solzhenitsyn, Michael Agursky, et al., From Under the

Rubble (New York: Bantam Books, 1976), p. 87, where the author affirms that "In our Central Asian cities I and many others have often heard the cry, 'Just wait til the Chinese come, they'll show you what's what!'"

6. For representative Chinese attacks on Soviet nationality policy, see Hung Chuan-yu, "The New Tsars--Common Enemy of the People of All Nationalities in the Soviet Union," Peking Review (July 4, 1969), no. 27: 25-27; and an unsigned article, "Soviet Social-Imperialism Pursues a Policy of National Oppression," Peking Review (May 28, 1976), no. 22: 19-23. Although these and other Chinese statements deal with the "plight" of all non-Russian nationalities, the focus is on the nationalities of Central Asia and on the Ukrainians, who constitute a significant proportion of the "European" population in Kirghizia and Kazakhstan. For a typical Soviet commentary on China's maltreatment of its Turkic minorities, see V. A. Bogoslovskii, A. M. Kuz'mina, et al., Velikoderzhavnaia politika maoistov v natsion-al'nykh raionakh KNR (Moscow: Isdatel'stvo Politicheskoi Literatury, 1975). See also the speech of the Kazakh Party first secretary, D. A. Kunaev, to the Twenty-Fifth Party Congress, Current Digest of the Soviet Press 28, no. 9 (March 31, 1976): 42; the speech of the Kirghiz Party first secretary, T. U. Usubaliyev, to the Twenty-Fifth Party Congress, Current Digest of the Soviet Press 28, no. 11 (April 14, 1976): 15-16; and the review of a new Uighur-language book by M. K. Khamraev in Kazakhstanskaia pravda, August 23, 1973, p. 3, which is synopsized in ABSEES, January 1974, p. 31. For a description of a Soviet newspaper published for the tens of thousands of Turkic refu-gees from China, see Christopher S. Wren, "Kazakhstan Beckons Refugees from China," New York Times, April 24, 1976, p. 8. See also Rasma Silde-Karklins, "The Uighurs between China and the USSR," Canadian Slavonic Papers 17, nos. 2 and 3 (1975): 341-65.

7. On the extremely low rates of interregional mobility among Central Asians, see V. N. Korovaeva, "Population Migration in the USSR," in Vsesoiuznaia perepis' naseleniia 1970 goda, ed. G. M. Maksimov (Moscow: Statistika, 1976), esp. p. 259. The proportion of Central Asian natives who claim fluency in Russian is under 20 percent among all nationalities except the Kazakhs, where it is al-most 42 percent. See Sovetskaia pedogogika (November 1971), no. 11: 65.

8. Derived from Murray Feshbach and Stephen Repaway, "Soviet Population and Manpower Trends and Policies," in Congress of the United States, Joint Economic Committee, Soviet Economy in a New Perspective, 94th Cong., 2nd Sess. (Washington, D.C.: U.S. Government Printing Office, 1976), p. 150, Table 16.

9. See TsSU SSSR, Narodnoe khoziaistvo SSSR v 1974 godu (Moscow: Statistika, 1975), p. 85. According to this official Soviet

source, the annual percentage growth of labor productivity in Soviet industry rose from 3.7 in 1964 to 6.3 in 1974. 1974 was a peak year, however; and the annual growth rate figures during the intervening decade were substantially lower. In the 1976-80 Five-Year Plan, the planned average annual growth in industrial labor productivity is 5.7 percent. See Izvestiia, March 7, 1969, p. 5.

10. According to Narodnoe khoziaistvo Kazakhstana (1971), no. 10: 76-80, translated in ABSEES, April 1972, p. 12, the "deficit" of Central Asian engineers and technicians is indicated by the fact that Kazakhs make up only 17 percent of the specialists in their re-public's nonferrous metallurgy, 13 percent in light industry, and only 10-24 percent of the students in technical institutes. In Tadzhikistan, Tadzhiks constituted less than one-third of all specialists with second-ary education in 1966. See L. M. Drobizheve, "O sblizhenii urovnei kul'turnogo razvitiia soiuznykh respublik," Istoriia SSSR (1969), no. 3: 61-79. On the preferences of local factory directors and the rea-sons for them, see V. Perevedentsev, "Shagni za okolitsu," Komsomol'skaia pravda, January 28, 1976, p. 2; and L. Chizhova, "Regional'nye aspeckty izpol'zovaniia trudovykh resursov," in Naselenie ekonomika, ed. D. Valenti (Moscow, 1973), p. 25, where the author reports that "practice has shown that some of them [i.e., Central Asians] still adapt badly to industrial labor."

11. Agricultural underemployment, as measured by the aver-age number of "labor days" worked by individual collective farmers, is already high in parts of Central Asia and can be expected to grow rapidly as a result of ongoing and accelerating mechanization. See V. Litvinov in Pravda vostoka, November 3, 1974, p. 2, summarized in ABSEES, July 1974, p. 55.

12. The average size of rural Uzbek families grew from 4.8 to 5.8 persons between 1959 and 1970, and the "ideal" family envi-sioned by younger Central Asian women is larger than the current average Central Asian family. See E. K. Vasil'eva, Sem'ia i ee funktsii (Moscow: Statistika, 1975), p. 42; T. N. Roganova, 'Num-ber and Composition of Families in the USSR," in Vsesoiuznaia perepis' naseleniia 1970 goda, sbornik stat'ei, ed. G. M. Maksimov (Moscow: Statistika, 1976), pp. 260-75; Izaslaw Frenkel, "Attitudes toward Family Size in Some Eastern European Countries," Population Studies 30, no. 1 (March 1976): 56.

13. The earned income of Central Asian collective farm fam-ilies, as of 1970, was significantly higher than that of their European counterparts; and the Central Asian cost of living index is lower than that in central Russia. See Gertrude Schroeder, "Soviet Wage and Income Policies in Regional Perspectives," ACES Bulletin, Fall 1974, pp. 3-19, and Ekonomicheskie nauki (January 1972), no. 1: 52. See also O. Latifi, "Problems of the Rational Utilization of Labor

Resources in Tadzhikhistan," Pravda, June 1, 1975, p. 2, translated
in Current Digest of the Soviet Press 27, no. 12 (June 25, 1975): 1:
"If we place a house and a personal plot of ground on one side . . .
and a city apartment on the other . . . there is no doubt that for the
time being the scales will tip toward the first alternative--out of economic advisability and from the standpoint of social psychology."
(Emphasis added.)

14. According to informed reports, a great deal of the recent
unrest in Georgia stems from the regime's pressure on the republic's flourishing "second economy" rather than from directly political sources. See Soviet Analyst 2, no. 12 (June 7, 1973): 3.

15. "European" out-migration from the Caucasus, Kazakhstan,
and Kirghizia has been increasing (see Bruk and Guboglo, op. cit.,
p. 106), and the regime has raised wages in Central Asia in a clear
effort to stem the tide. See Izvestiia, December 28, 1976, p. 1.
One source of this out-migration has been the repatriation (to the
RSFSR) of Volga German collective farmers in Kazakhstan. The
number of German repatriates has reached 10,000 per annum and is
likely to remain at this level for some time to come. J. A. Newth,
"The 1970 Soviet Census," Soviet Studies 24, no. 2 (October 1972):
204.

16. Some informed Western analysts estimate Soviet military
manpower to be only slightly more than 4 million, whereas others
consider 5 million a likely figure. 4.5 million is the low estimate of
General Daniel Graham, head of the DIA, for 1975. See Congress of
the United States, Joint Economic Committee, Allocation of Resources in the Soviet Union and China--1975, 94th Cong., 1st Sess.
(Washington, D.C.: U.S. Government Printing Office, 1975), pp.
73, 121.

17. See Feshback and Repaway, op. cit., p. 147, for current
conscription estimates, and p. 150, Table 16, for supply of 18-year-
old males in the 1980s and 1990s. This supply, which is currently
more than 2.6 million, will fall to 2.01 million during the 1980s and
will not begin to rise until 1989, at which point it will rise only slowly and remain below current levels throughout the 1990s. See also,
and more generally, Z. Perevedentsev, "Each of Us and All of Us,"
Literaturnaia gazeta (August 13, 1975), no. 33: 22; and "The Family:
Yesterday, Today, and Tomorrow,"Nash sovremennik (June 1975),
no. 6: 118-31, in Translations on USSR Political and Sociological
Affairs no. 682, JPRS 65850 (October 6, 1975) and no. 645, JPRS
65142 (July 3, 1975), respectively.

18. On the introduction and spread of military training programs in the schools, see H. Goldhamer, The Soviet Soldier (New
York: Crane, Russak, 1975), pp. 47-67.

19. Ibid., pp. 188-89.

20. Thus, according to a verbal communication from Murray Feshbach, the results of the 1970 census suggest a slight decline in the proportion of younger Central Asians who claim fluency in Russian. See also Radio Liberty Research, RL 287/76 (June 2, 1976): 1, for the report of a Soviet demographic conference--described in Voprosy ekonomiki (1975), no. 8: 149-52--at which one speaker contended that "the number of people of non-Russian nationality who do not speak Russian is increasing." Also see S. I. Bruk and M. N. Guboglo, "Bilingualism and the Drawing Together of Nations in the U. S. S. R. (from 1970 Census Data)," Sovetskaia etnografiia (July/August 1975), no. 4: 18-32, in Translations on USSR Political and Sociological Affairs no. 693, JPRS 66078 (November 5, 1975): 10-29, esp. 26, for the lower percentage of Russian-speaking bilinguals among 11-to-19-year-old Georgians, Azeris, Armenians, Lithuanians, and Estonians than among 30-to-49-year-olds in these national groups. For a report on a recent official meeting on the problems of teaching Russian to non-Russians, see Narodnoe obrazovanie (March 1974), no. 3: 7-10, in Translations on USSR Political and Sociological Affairs no. 517, JPRS 61706 (April 9, 1974): 37-47. According to this report, there is a serious shortage of Russian-language teachers in the Central Asian and Caucasus republics "as a result [of which] the question about teaching the Russian language in the elementary grades of many schools, particularly the rural schools, has become a very acute one" (p. 39). See also O. Chelpanov and S. Matevosyan, "Time for Examinations, and Still . . .," Uchitel'skaia gazeta, June 28, 1973, p. 3, in Translations on USSR Political and Sociological Affairs no. 457, JPRS 60524 (November 1973): 23-28, esp. 23-24, where it is reported that in an Armenian senior high school in Erevan, "senior grade pupils cannot answer in Russian the most simple questions . . ." and that the best high school graduates in rural Armenian high schools "do not even satisfy the requirements [in Russian] stipulated in the elementary program"; and the recent article by Uzbek SSR Minister of Education S. Shermukhamedov, who reports:

> The Russian language was not taught at all in some
> schools and in other schools was only partially taught
> in individual classes . . . because of the lack of Rus-
> sian language teachers. . . . the subject was not
> taught in 191 schools during the 1971-72 school year.
> Russian language instruction in the elementary grades
> has been conducted and is still being conducted [not]
> only by non-specialists but by teachers who have a poor
> command of the Russian language.

Translations on USSR Political and Sociological Affairs no. 689, JPRS 65986 (October 22, 1975): 2, from "Unremitting Attention to

Russian Language Study," Narodnoe obrazovanie (September 1975), no. 9: 6-10.

21. The nature of these problems is indicated by the materials cited in Goldhamer, op. cit., pp. 188-89. Refugee reports are far more eloquent.

22. These reports come from both Western observers and Soviet refugees. In this connection, the Soviet shipboard mutiny in the Baltic is rumored to have been at least partially sparked by ethnic frictions. See John K. Cooley, "Mutinied Soviet Destroyer Dispatched on Long Voyage," Christian Science Monitor, June 29, 1976, p. 6. It is worth noting the report of Soviet ethnographers that 9.3 percent of a 1970 sample of Tatar workers who did not know Russian resented being directed by persons "of another nationality" (overwhelmingly Russian), while only 2.8 percent of those who know Russian expressed such resentment. See I. V. Arutiunian, Sotsialnaia struktura sel'skogo naseleniia SSSR (Moscow: Izdatel'stvo Mysl', 1971), p. 195, Table 2. Concern on these accounts may well have been one of the factors responsible for the inauguration in the late 1960s of a major Soviet research program in military sociology and the sociology of the armed forces. See Ilya Zemtsov, IKSI: The Moscow Institute of Applied Social Research (in Russian), Soviet Institution series, no. 6 (Jerusalem: Soviet and East European Research Center, Hebrew University, 1976), pp. 26-29.

23. For a brief but authoritative outline of the history of national military formations, see A. A. Grechko, Vooruzhennye sily sovetskogo gosudarstva (2nd ed.; Moscow: Voennoe Izdatel'stvo, 1975), pp. 133-57. See also M. I. Kulichenko, Natsional'nye otnosheniia v SSSR (Moscow: Izdatel'stvo Mysl', 1972), pp. 324-25.

24. See, for example, the protest letter of 17 Soviet political prisoners, first published in Sweden in August 1974 and translated from the Swedish in USSR National Affairs--Political and Social Developments 3 (August 16, 1974): R12.

25. See Grechko, loc. cit.; and Grechko, Vooruzhennye sily sovetskogo gosudarstva (1st ed.; Moscow: Voennoe Izdatel'stvo, 1974), pp. 125-43.

26. Personal communication to the author and to Murray Feshbach.

27. Grechko, op. cit., 2nd ed., p. 150.

28. See Paul K. Cook, "The Soviet Union in the Year 2000" (unpublished seminar notes, Russian Research Center, Harvard University, December 19, 1974), p. 15. The Tbilisi riot took place on March 9, 1956, and, according to an untitled and unsigned Georgian samizdat report in the present author's possession, resulted in the death of around 500 rioters, some of whom were machine-gunned by tank units.

29. See N. S. Khrushchev, "Disarmament Is the Path towards Strengthening Peace and Ensuring Friendship among Peoples," report to a session of the USSR Supreme Soviet, Pravda and Izvestiia, January 15, 1960, pp. 1-5, translated in Current Digest of the Soviet Press 12, no. 2 (February 10, 1960): 3-16, 23.

30. L. I. Brezhnev, O piatidesiatiletti SSSR (Moscow, 1973), p. 19.

31. Ibid., p. 24.

32. The Jewish exodus movement is too well-known to require any further commentary. The Greek exodus, which has been reported in various sources, apparently has not been seriously impeded by the regime, and therefore has not been accompanied by any overt protest. For the German exodus movement, see Robert C. Toth, "Germans in Russia," Los Angeles Times, April 24, 1976, pp. 1, 25; David K. Shipler, "Soviet Germans Rally in Red Square," New York Times, March 9, 1977, p. A12. On the Meskhetian Turks, see S. Enders Wimbush and Ronald Wixman, "The Meskhetian Turks: A New Voice in Soviet Central Asia," Canadian Slavonic Papers 17, nos. 2-3 (1975): 320-40; Ann Sheehy, The Crimean Tartars, Volga Germans, and Meskhetians, Minority Rights Group, no. 6 (London, 1973).

33. For a good survey of Soviet national dissidence and national protest up to 1972, see Conflict Studies no. 30 (December 1972): 1-27. For the Ukraine, see Michael Browne, ed., Ferment in the Ukraine (New York: Macmillan, 1971). For the trial of members of a separatist party in Armenia, see Christopher S. Wren, "Separatist Group Tried in Armenia," New York Times, November 17, 1974, p. 9. For the Baltic states, see V. S. Vardys, "Modernization and Baltic Nationalism," Problems of Communism, September/ October 1975, p. 47. On samizdat especially, and dissident activity more generally, see Gayle Durham Hollander, "Political Communication and Dissent in the Soviet Union," in Dissent in the USSR, ed. Rudolf L. Tokes (Baltimore and London: Johns Hopkins University Press, 1976), pp. 233-75.

34. See Theodore Shabad, "Lithuanian Trial of Eight Starts," New York Times, September 26, 1972, p. 15; Soviet Analyst 2, no. 12 (June 7, 1973): 3.

35. On the Crimean demonstrations in Tashkent and Chirchick, Uzbekistan, see Sheehy, op. cit., p. 17. In 1966 the Tatars also presented the Kremlin a protest letter, demanding repatriation to their Crimean homeland, with over 130,000 signatures--the greater part of the adult Crimean Tatar population. See Roy Medvedev, On Socialist Democracy (New York: W. W. Norton, 1975), p. 35, n. 4. On the Erevan demonstration, see Wren, "Separatist Group Tried in Armenia," p. 9.

36. For secret policy concern about these societies, see Soviet Analyst 3, no. 19 (September 19, 1974): 1-2. More generally, see "Preservation of Historical and Cultural Monuments," Soviet Union (1972), no. 10, and S. T. Palmer, "The Restoration of Ancient Monuments in the USSR," Survey no. 74/75 (Spring/Summer 1970): 163-74. The first of these articles quotes a Soviet source (p. 4) that claims these societies have more than 7 million individual and 41,000 collective members.

37. For charges to these effects, see the articles translated in Current Digest of the Soviet Press 25, no. 11 (April 11, 1973): 12-16, and 25, no. 16 (1973): 5-10, 36. See also the article by Armenian Party first secretary Shevarnadze translated in Current Digest of the Soviet Press 24, no. 14 (November 29, 1972): 15, and in Translations on USSR Political and Sociological Affairs no. 386, JPRS 59134 (May 25, 1973): 25 ff., esp. 29-30. See also I. I. Groshev, Bor'ba partii protiv natsionalizma (Moscow: Politizdat, 1974), esp. pp. 113-14.

38. For a good treatment of nationality conflicts during the Revolution and Civil War, see Richard Pipes, The Formation of the Soviet Union (Cambridge, Mass.: Harvard University Press, 1954). For the war and immediate postwar periods, see John Armstrong, The Politics of Totalitarianism (New York: Random House, 1961), esp. pp. 144-57.

39. See Zbigniew Brzezinski, ed., Dilemmas of Change in Soviet Politics (New York: Columbia University Press, 1969).

40. See Jeremy R. Azrael, "Communal Protests and Communal Rights in the USSR," paper delivered to the Council on Foreign Relations, New York, 1976.

41. There were, however, reports of a riot in Tashkent in 1969, during which many demonstrators shouted "Russians out of Uzbekhistan"; see Chronicle of Current Events no. 8 (June 30, 1969); Soviet Uzbekistoni, June 10, 1969. In addition there apparently was some sort of nationality-related disturbance in the Narab region of Tadzhikistan in September 1970. See Barbara Wolfe Jancar, "Religious Dissent in the Soviet Union," in Tokes, op. cit., p. 219.

42. On the "revival" of Russian nationalism, see the following articles in Slavic Review 32, no. 1 (March 1973): Jack V. Haney, "The Revival of Interest in the Russian Past," pp. 1-16; Thomas E. Bird, "New Interest in Old Russian Things," pp. 17-28; and George L. Kline, "Religion, National Character, and the 'Rediscovery of Russian Roots'," pp. 29-40. Also see Sergei Vikulov, ed., Nash sovremennik: Izbrannaia proza zhurnala, 1964-74 (Moscow: Sovremennik, 1975). For an officially published, though publicly criticized, pseudoscientific genetic "theory" of Russian racial superiority, see the articles of L. N. Gumilev, cited in V. I. Kozlov, "On the Biological-

Geographical Conception of Ethnic History," Voprosy istorii (December 1974), no. 12: 72-85, abstracted in Current Digest of the Soviet Press 27, no. 20 (June 11, 1975): 1-5. According to Kozlov, Gumilev's ideas lead to the conclusion that virtually all of the non-Slavic peoples of the USSR are "illegitimate," and could not survive without the aid of the genetically better-endowed Slavs, who are able to preserve this superior endowment only by resisting intermarriage. On dissent manifestations of Russian integral nationalism and xenophobia, see Dmitri Pospielovsky, "The Samizdat Journal Veche: Russian Patriotic Thought Today," Radio Liberty Research Papers no. 45 (1971). For an interesting Ukrainian émigré criticism of the views of Russian dissidents on the nationality problem, see the editorial in Ukrainian Quarterly 31, no. 4 (Winter 1975): 350-57.

43. For a very unusual Soviet article on the need for stricter gun control and on legislation to implement such control, see Yu. Feofanov, "Reflections on a Well-Known Truth," Izvestiia, June 12, 1976, p. 5, translated in Current Digest of the Soviet Press 28, no. 24 (July 14, 1976): 13. See also the even more interesting article by Colonel General D. Molashvili, chief of staff of the Georgian Republic Ministry of Internal Affairs, "Who Has Explosives?" Zaria vostoka, April 1, 1976, p. 4, translated in Current Digest of the Soviet Press 28, no. 19 (June 9, 1976): 13. This article, which clearly was inspired by the contemporaneous outbreak of terrorist bombings in Tbilisi, calls for the creation of "a single organization to conduct all work with explosives in the republic," since the control exercised by the 23 ministries that "do a significant amount of work with explosives" is often lax and "the evidence indicates that it isn't very difficult" to steal explosives from their stockpiles, storage facilities, work sites, and other places.

44. As is well known, several prominent Soviet dissidents have predicted that the outbreak of a major war, especially a war with China, would lead to violent national uprisings and international pogroms. See John P. Dunlop, "Solzhenitsyn in Exile," Survey 21, no. 96 (Summer 1975): 136; Peter Dornan, "Andrei Sakharov," in Tokes, op. cit., pp. 360-71; Andrei Amalrik, Will the Soviet Union Survive Until 1984? (New York: Harper and Row, 1970), pp. 62-64.

ABOUT THE EDITOR
AND CONTRIBUTORS

JEREMY R. AZRAEL, editor of this volume, is professor of political science and chairman of the Committee on Slavic Area Studies at the University of Chicago. He is the author of Managerial Power and Soviet Politics and Communal Conflicts and Communal Rights, and of numerous journal articles.

BARBARA A. ANDERSON is associate professor of sociology at Brown University. She is coauthor of a forthcoming volume in a series on decline in fertility rates in Europe, Human Fertility in Russia Since the Nineteenth Century, and of several papers on this general topic.

JOHN A. ARMSTRONG is professor of political science at the University of Wisconsin-Madison. He is the author of Ukrainian Nationalism; The European Bureaucratic Elite; The Politics of Totalitarianism; and Ideology, Politics and Government in the Soviet Union; and editor of Soviet Partisans in World War II. In addition, he has published numerous journal articles.

ALEXANDRE BENNIGSEN is professor of history at the University of Paris and professor of Russian-Turkic history at the University of Chicago. He is the author of Les mouvements nationaux chez les musulmans de Russie--le Sultan-galievisme au Tatarstan (with Chantal Lemercier-Quelquejay); La presse et les mouvements nationaux chez les musulmans de Russie avant 1920 (with Chantal Lemercier-Quelquejay); Islam in the Soviet Union (with Chantal Lemercier-Quelquejay); Russes et Chinois avant 1917; and A Revolutionary Strategy for the Colonial World (with S. Enders Wimbush); and of numerous articles in various encyclopedias, journals, and collections.

YAROSLAV BILINSKY is professor of political science at the University of Delaware. He is the author of The Second Soviet Republic: The Ukraine after World War II and of many other monographs and articles on Soviet politics, Soviet nationality policy, and Ukrainian nationalism.

STEVEN L. BURG is a lecturer in the Division of the Social Sciences at the University of Chicago, where he is completing a dissertation entitled "Conflict Regulation, Decision-Making, and Institutional Change in Multinational Polity: The Case of Yugoslavia, 1966-1976." He is the author of several articles on Yugoslav and Soviet politics.

HÉLÈNE CARRÈRE D'ENCAUSSE is maître de recherche at the Fondation Nationale des Sciences Politiques (Paris). She is the author of Reforme et révolution chez les musulmanes de l'Empire russe; L'Union soviétique de Lenine à Staline; and La politique soviétique au Moyen-Orient; and editor (with Stuart Schram) of Marxism and Asia. In addition, she has written numerous articles on Marxism and Soviet politics.

CHARLES H. FAIRBANKS, JR., is assistant professor of political science at Yale. He is the author of a forthcoming volume on arms races, to be published under the auspices of the Twentieth Century Fund, and of several articles and chapters in books.

JONATHAN POOL is assistant professor of political science at the University of Washington, and is the author of numerous journal articles.

BRIAN D. SILVER is associate professor of political science at Michigan State University. He is the author of numerous articles in leading professional journals, including American Political Science Review, Slavic Review, and Soviet Studies. He is on the editorial board of Slavic Review and is a member of the Research and Development Committee of the AAASS.

S. FREDERICK STARR is secretary of the Kennan Institute for Advanced Russian Studies. He is the author of Decentralization and Self-Government in Russia, 1830-1870, and author and editor of numerous other books and articles.

S. ENDERS WIMBUSH is a Soviet affairs analyst in the Social Science Division of the Rand Corporation and is currently completing a dissertation entitled "Great-Russians and the Soviet State: The Dilemmas of Ethnic Dominance." He is coauthor (with Alexandre Bennigsen) of A Revolutionary Strategy for the Colonial World, and has published several articles and chapters on Soviet nationality politics.